Lecture Notes in Computer Science　　11599

More information about this series at http://www.springer.com/series/7410

Andrea Bracciali · Jeremy Clark ·
Federico Pintore · Peter B. Rønne ·
Massimiliano Sala (Eds.)

Financial Cryptography and Data Security

FC 2019 International Workshops, VOTING and WTSC
St. Kitts, St. Kitts and Nevis, February 18–22, 2019
Revised Selected Papers

 Springer

Editors
Andrea Bracciali ⓘD
Stirling University
Stirling, UK

Jeremy Clark ⓘD
Concordia University
Montréal, QC, Canada

Federico Pintore ⓘD
University of Oxford
Oxford, UK

Peter B. Rønne
University of Luxembourg
Esch-sur-Alzette, Luxembourg

Massimiliano Sala ⓘD
University of Trento
Trento, Italy

ISSN 0302-9743   ISSN 1611-3349   (electronic)
Lecture Notes in Computer Science
ISBN 978-3-030-43724-4   ISBN 978-3-030-43725-1   (eBook)
https://doi.org/10.1007/978-3-030-43725-1

LNCS Sublibrary: SL4 – Security and Cryptology

This Springer imprint is published by the registered company Springer Nature Switzerland AG
The registered company address is: Gewerbestrasse 11, 6330 Cham, Switzerland

WTSC 2019 Preface

These proceedings collect the papers accepted at the Third Workshop on Trusted Smart Contracts (WTSC 2019, http://fc19.ifca.ai/wtsc/) associated with the Financial Cryptography and Data Security 2019 (FC 2019) conference held in St. Kitts on February 22, 2019.

The WTSC series focuses on smart contracts, i.e., self-enforcing agreements in the form of executable programs and other decentralized applications that are deployed to and run on top of (specialized) blockchains. These technologies introduce a novel programming framework and execution environment, which, together with the supporting blockchain technologies, carry unanswered and challenging research questions. Multidisciplinary and multifactorial aspects affect correctness, safety, privacy, authentication, efficiency, sustainability, resilience, and trust in smart contracts and decentralized applications. WTSC aims to address the scientific foundations of trusted smart contract engineering, i.e., the development of contracts that enjoy some verifiable "correctness" properties and to discuss open problems, proposed solutions, and the vision on future developments among a research community that is growing around these themes and brings together users, practitioners, industry, institutions, and academia.

This was reflected in the multidisciplinary Program Committee of this third edition of WTSC, comprising members from companies, universities, and research institutions from several countries worldwide, who kindly accepted to support the event. The association with FC 2019 provided an ideal context for our workshop to be run in. WTSC 2019 was partially supported by the University of Stirling, UK, the University of Trento, Italy, and Quadrans (https://quadrans.io/). This third edition of WTSC 2019 received 17 submissions by about 40 authors, of which, after peer review, 9 were accepted as full papers, 3 as short papers, and 2 as SoK (systematisaztion of knowledge) papers. The accepted papers are collected in the present volume. These works analyzed state and side channels, incentives, and payment schemes, as well as addressed aspects of verification, security, and privacy.

WTSC 2019 enjoyed Ian Grigg (https://iang.org/) and Igor Artamonov (ETCDEV Founder) as keynote speakers. Ian gave a talk on trust and its implication within blockchain and smart contracts applications, while Igor discussed models for smart contracts and their present and future perspectives.

The WTSC 2019 chairs would like to thank all those who supported the workshop for their valuable contributions: authors, Program Committee members and reviewers, and participants. WTSC 2019 also enjoyed the support of IFCA, FC 2019, and Ray Hirschfeld in the organization of the event.

June 2019

Andrea Bracciali
Federico Pintore
Massimiliano Sala

WTSC 2019 Organization

General Chairs

Andrea Bracciali	University of Stirling, UK
Federico Pintore	University of Oxford, UK
Massimiliano Sala	University of Trento, Italy

Keynote Speakers

Igor Artamonov	Ethereum Classic Dev
Ian Grigg	https://iang.org/

Program Committee

Igor Artamonov	Ethereum Classic Dev
Bob Atkey	Strathclyde University, UK
Marcella Atzori	UCL, UK, and IFIN, Italy
Daniel Augot	Inria, France
Massimo Bartoletti	University of Cagliari, Italy
Devraj Basu	Strathclyde University, UK
Stefano Bistarelli	University of Perugia, Italy
Christina Boura	Versailles SQT University, France
Andrea Bracciali	University of Stirling, UK
Daniel Broby	Strathclyde University, UK
Bill Buchanan	Napier University, UK
James Chapman	IOHK, Hong Kong
Martin Chapman	King's College London, UK
Tiziana Cimoli	University of Cagliari, Italy
Nicola Dimitri	University of Siena, Italy
Nadia Fabrizio	Cefriel, Italy
Jamie Gabbay	Heriot-Watt University, UK
Laetitia Gauvin	ISI Foundation, Italy
Neil Ghani	Strathclyde University, UK
Oliver Giudice	Banca d'Italia, Italy
Davide Grossi	University of Groningen, The Netherlands
Yoichi Hirai	Brainbot Technologies AG, Germany
Lars R. Knudsen	Technical University of Denmark, Denmark
Ioannis Kounelis	Joint Research Centre, European Commission, Italy
Victoria Lemieux	The University of British Columbia, Canada
Loi Luu	National University of Singapore, Singapore
Carsten Maple	Warwick University, UK
Michele Marchesi	University of Cagliari, Italy

Fabio Martinelli	IIT-CNR, Italy
Patrick McCorry	King's College London, UK
Neil McLaren	ConsenSys, UK
Sihem Mesnager	University of Paris VIII, France
Philippe Meyer	Avaloq, Switzerland
Bud Mishra	NYU, USA
Carlos Molina-Jimenez	University of Cambridge, UK
Massimo Morini	Banca IMI, Italy
Immaculate Motsi	University of Warwick, UK
Alex Norta	Tallin University of Technology, Estonia
Federico Pintore	University of Oxford, UK
Massimiliano Sala	University of Trento, Italy
Jason Teutsch	Truebit, USA
Roberto Tonelli	University of Cagliari, Italy
Luca Vigano'	University of Verona, Italy
Philip Wadler	University of Edinburgh, UK
Yilei Wang	Hong Kong Polytechnic University, Hong Kong
Ales Zamuda	University of Maribor, Slovenia
Santiago Zanella-Beguelin	Microsoft, UK

WTSC 2019 Sponsors

http://www.cs.stir.ac.uk/

https://www.unitn.it/

https://quadrans.io/it/

This conference was organized with the support of EasyChair conference system.

VOTING 2019 Preface

These proceedings collect the papers accepted at the 4th Workshop on Advances in Secure Electronic Voting (VOTING 2019) associated with the Financial Cryptography and Data Security 2019 (FC 2019) conference held in St. Kitts on February 22, 2019.

This year's workshop covered a variety of different themes, all related to election integrity, security, and privacy. In particular, papers covered election auditing, voting system efficiency, voting system usability, and new technical designs for cryptographic protocols for voting systems.

An important discussion was held with our panel titled "Real World Verifiable Elections: Future or Fata Morgana?" The premise of the panel was that verifiable voting systems have crossed over from research into real world pilots, and yet we also seem stuck in the pilot stage with no wide commercial deployment of this technology on the horizon. To help discuss this, we recruited researchers with experience deploying systems like Scantegrity, Helios, vVote, Pret a Voter, and Remotegrity in real world elections. The panelists were Olivier Pereira, Peter Y. A. Ryan, Vanessa Teague, and Filip Zagórski.

We received 17 papers and accepted 9 for publication. While increasing the popularity of our workshop is an important future challenge, each accepted paper received a lot of attention from our expert reviewers and improvements were discussed in-depth within the Program Committee (PC). In the spirit of a workshop, we felt the peer-review process was not merely a gatekeeping exercise but resulted in improved and polished final papers.

As chairs, we are grateful to our PC for their time and effort, the authors of all submitted papers, Ray Hirschfield and IFCA for organizing all the logistics of the event, and the FC 2019 workshop chairs for their continued support of VOTING. VOTING 2020 will be held in Malaysia, with Matt Bernhard and Peter B. Rønne serving as Program Chairs.

June 2019

Jeremy Clark
Peter B. Rønne

VOTING 2019 Organization

Program Chairs

Jeremy Clark   Concordia University, Canada
Peter B. Rønne   University of Luxembourg, Luxembourg

Program Committee

Roberto Araujo   Universidade Federal do Pará, Brazil
Chris Culnane   The University of Melbourne, Australia
Jeremy Clark   Concordia University, Canada
Jeremy Epstein   SRI
Aleksander Essex   Western University, Canada
David Galindo   University of Birmingham, UK
Kristian Gjøsteen   Norwegian University of Science and Technology,
                               Norway
Rajeev Gore   The Australian National University, Australia
Rolf Haenni   Bern University of Applied Sciences, Switzerland
Oksana Kulyk   Karlsruhe Institute of Technology, Germany
Steve Kremer   Inria Nancy, France
Robert Krimmer   Tallinn University of Technology, Estonia
Olivier Pereira   Université catholique de Louvain, Belgium
Peter B. Rønne   University of Luxembourg, Luxembourg
Peter Ryan   University of Luxembourg, Luxembourg
Steve Schneider   University of Surrey, UK
Carsten Schuermann   IT University of Copenhagen, Denmark
Philip Stark   University of California, Berkeley, USA
Vanessa Teague   The University of Melbourne, Australia

Contents

Advances in Secure Electronic Voting Schemes

Trusted Smart Contracts

Two-Party State Channels
with Assertions

Chris Buckland[✉] and Patrick McCorry

Kings College London, London, UK
cpbuckland88@gmail.com, patrick.mccorry@kcl.ac.uk

Abstract. An empirical case study to evaluate state channels as a scaling solution for cryptocurrencies demonstrated that providing an application's full state during the dispute process for a state channel is financially costly (i.e. \$0.24 to \$8.83 for a battleship game) which can hamper their real-world use. To overcome this issue, we present *State Assertion Channels*, the first state channel to guarantee an honest party is always refunded the cost if it becomes necessary to send an application's full state during the dispute process. Furthermore it ensures an honest party will pay an approximate fixed cost to continue an application's execution via the dispute process. We provide a proof of concept implementation in Ethereum which demonstrates it costs approximately \$0.02 to submit evidence regardless of the smart contract's application.

1 Introduction

Blockchain-based cryptocurrencies do not scale. The community is pursing three approaches to alleviate the scalability issue. These are: new blockchain protocols [2,8,19], sharding transactions into distinct processing areas [1,12,13] and off-chain protocols [5,10,11,15,17,18,20]. While the first two approaches can strictly increase the network's throughput, they harm the network's public verifiability as they reduce the diversity of peers with the computational, bandwidth or storage requirements to validate all transactions on the network and ultimately hold the miners accountable. [4,9] This paper focuses on the off-chain (or so-called Layer 2) approach that simply aims to reduce the network's load.

One prominent off-chain approach are state channels that lets a group of parties process transactions (and execute a smart contract) locally amongst themselves instead of on the global network. In the best case, the application is no longer restricted by the underlying blockchain's latency and all execution is free as it remains local between the parties. If there is a disagreement about the latest state of the smart contact, then any party can trigger a dispute and rely on the underlying blockchain to arbitrate the dispute's outcome. To arbitrate, the blockchain provides a fixed time period to collect evidence from all online parties before using this evidence to decide the off-chain smart contract's new state. So far, there are two types of dispute processes for a state channel. The first is called *closure dispute* [6,15,20] as the dispute process is responsible for closing the channel, re-deploying the smart contract with the new state and letting

© International Financial Cryptography Association 2020
A. Bracciali et al. (Eds.): FC 2019 Workshops, LNCS 11599, pp. 3–11, 2020.
https://doi.org/10.1007/978-3-030-43725-1_1

parties continue its execution via the blockchain. The second is called *command-issuance dispute* [3, 10, 14, 16] as the dispute process collects commands from each party and then executes the command to compute the new state.

A recent case study empirically evaluated state channels as a scaling solution by building the two player game battleship [15]. It highlights that sending the application's full state during the dispute process can be financially expensive which may deter real-world use of state channels. For example, the case study claimed that sending the full game state approximately costs \$0.24 when the blockchain is not congested, but it can potentially sky-rocket to \$8.83 if the blockchain is congested. The above can clearly hamper real-world use of state channels as an honest party will not use the dispute process if it is too costly (and thus they cannot self-enforce the application's correct execution). The case study also highlights the need to preserve liveness of an application. If one party is no longer co-operating off-chain, then a state channel should ensure the application's progress can continue via the blockchain. Again, this can be costly if progressing the application is computationally expensive or if it requires a significant number of transactions.

To alleivate the above issues, we propose *State Assertion Channels*. It builds upon state channels with command-issuance disputes and relies on the concept of an optimistic Combined, honest parties can always assert the hash of a new state (and thus progress an application's execution) without the blockchain computing the state transition directly. Our contributions:

- We propose the first state channel that ensures an honest party never pays the cost to send the application's full state during the dispute process.
- Our state channel is also the first to ensure the cost of progressing an application is based only on the number of transactions required to reach a terminal state, thus it is independent of the application's computational cost.
- We provide a proof of concept implementation and experimentally demonstrate that it is cost-effective to deploy.

2   Background

Optimistic Smart Contracts. An optimistic smart contract trades the cost of computation for time. This lets a smart contract accept an application's new state if no one has proved it is invalid within a fixed challenge period. Briefly, one party submits to the optimistic smart contract the application's $state_i$, a command cmd, its inputs, the next $state_{i+1}$ and a financial bond. This asserts that $state_{i+1}$ is the next state if the smart contract were to compute $state_{i+1} = \text{Transition}(state_i, cmd, inputs)$. Other interested parties can compute the transition locally to verify its validity. If the asserted state is invalid, then anyone can issue a challenge by notifying the smart contract to compute the transition. If the challenge is successful, then a bond is used to refund the challenger. Eigenmann, Moore and Johnson provided the first demo implementation of an optimistic contract for the Ethereum Name Service [7], but so far this technique has alluded real-world use.

Command Issuance State Channels. Sprites proposed the concept of a command-issuance state channel, and since then it has been extended by PISA [14], Counterfactual [10] and Magmo [3]. At a high level, one party can submit the latest state$_i$ agreed by all parties before triggering the dispute process. The smart contract provides a fixed time period for all parties to submit commands and the contract is responsible for computing every command (i.e. state transition). In Sprites (and PISA), all commands are executed after the dispute process has expired. Whereas in Counterfactual and Magmo, the command is executed when it is submited and the dispute period's expiry time is reset (i.e. it dispute period is extended for every command). The dispute process can be cancelled if one party submits a later state agreed by all parties, or after the expiry time.

3   State Assertion Channels

The state assertion contract **SC** and the application contract **AC** must be deployed on the blockchain. Each party must lock coins into the state assertion contract before the state channel is activated. Both parties can co-operatively execute the application off-chain amongst themselves by executing every state transition for **AC** locally and exchanging signatures for every new state. If there is a disagreement off-chain, then both parties can continue its progression via the dispute process.

Our contribution involves changing the dispute process to avoid sending the full application's state, and to avoid computing the next states on-chain. Instead parties will assert an application's new state by submitting a hash of the previous state hstate$_i$, the command cmd, its inputs, a hash of the next state hstate$_{i+1}$ and a financial bond. The dispute process provides a fixed time period for the counterparty to verify the assertion by computing the state transition locally. To challenge an assertion, the party submits the previous state$_{i-1}$ which lets **SC** verify the assertion was indeed correct by executing the transition via **AC**. If the honest party successfully challenges an assertion and proves it is invalid, then they are sent the bond as a refund.

Thus an honest party can always continue an application's execution via the blockchain's dispute process by asserting a hash of the next state. As well, they are always refunded the cost of sending the application's full state in order to challenge an invalid state assertion.

3.1   Application Contract Assumptions

Turn-Based Application. We assume that the parties execute a turn-based application where each party performs their state transition in turn until a terminal state is reached. As well, **AC** must be instantiated on the blockchain to ensure its address is provided to the state assertion contract **SC**.

Single Transition Function. The application contract implements a transition function which accepts the full state, a command and a list of inputs. The application contract is responsible for computing a state transition and returning a hash of the new state via $\mathsf{hstate}_{i+1} := \texttt{Transition}(\mathsf{state}_i, \mathsf{cmd}, \mathsf{inputs});$. The application contract is stateless consequently the state must be supplied to compute a state transition.

No Exceptions or Out-of-Gas Errors. In Ethereum, an entire transaction's execution can be reverted if a smart contract throws an exception (i.e. out of gas). If the application **AC** can throw an exception, then it can be used to revert the execution of an honest party's challenge. Thus the application's transition function should not permit exceptions. We propose the transition function should return hstate and if the command doesn't exist or its execution simply fails, then it should return $\mathsf{hstate} = 0$. This ensures an honest party can always issue a challenge via **SC.challenge**() as the state transition (and the verification) will always complete its execution.

3.2 Assertion Channel Overview

Figure 1 presents the state channel assertion contract. We'll use it to aid the following overview on how to instantiate the contract, authorise states off-chain, how to trigger a dispute, how to submit and challenge assertions, and finally how to close the channel.

Channel Status. The channel has three flags $\texttt{Status} = \{\texttt{DEPOSIT}, \texttt{ON}, \texttt{DISPUTE}\}$. Both parties must deposit coins in **SC** before it will transition from $\texttt{DEPOSIT} \rightarrow \texttt{ON}$. While the channel's status is set as $\texttt{ON}$ both parties can co-operatively continue the application's progression off-chain by exchanging signatures for new states. If there is a disagreement about a state transition, then one party can trigger a dispute which changes the status from $\texttt{ON} \rightarrow \texttt{DISPUTE}$.

Instantiating Contract. One party must deploy **SC** to the blockchain and initalise it with the address of both parties $\mathcal{P}_1, \mathcal{P}_2$, the application's address **AC**, the fixed dispute period Δ and the required security bond bond. Both parties must review the contracts **SC, AC** and the intialisation values before sending their deposit via **SC.deposit**(). After **SC** has received both deposits (and before turning on the channel), it will compute the initial state $\mathsf{state}_{\mathsf{initial}} = (\perp, \mathsf{balance1}, \mathsf{balance2})$ and declare the first turn will be taken by $\mathcal{P}_1$.[1]

Progressing Application Off-Chain. Both parties can begin exchanging signatures to execute the application off-chain when the channel is $\texttt{ON}$. In each round, one party is responsible for proposing a state transition, and the other party is responsible for verifying the state transition before co-operatively authorising it. To propose, the party computes $\mathsf{state}_{i+1} = \texttt{Transition}(\mathsf{state}_i, \mathsf{inputs}, \mathsf{cmd})$, they hash the state $\mathsf{hstate}_{i+1} = \mathsf{hash}(\mathsf{state}_{i+1})$ and they sign its hash $\sigma_{\mathcal{P}_1} = \mathsf{Sign}(\mathsf{hstate}_{i+1}, i+1, \mathbf{SC}, \mathcal{P}_{\mathsf{turn}})$, where $\mathcal{P}_{\mathsf{turn}}$ specifies the next party's turn. The proposer must send $\mathsf{hstate}_{i+1}, i+1, \sigma_{\mathcal{P}}$ to the counterparty. To verify, the counterparty computes state transition and the state hash hstate'_{i+1} before checking

---

[1] We highlight a subtle difference between the initial state $(\perp, \mathsf{balance1}, \mathsf{balance2})$ and the terminal state $(\mathsf{balance1}, \mathsf{balance2})$.

```
contract StateAssertionChannel {
  enum Status {DEPOSIT, ON, DISPUTE}, address[] plist;
  Status status; uint deadline; hash hstate_i; uint i; address turn;
  address asserter; hash hstate_{i+1}; bytes input; uint cmd; bool assertion;

  function setstate(bytes[] _sigs, uint _i, address _turn, hash _hstate_i) {
    require(_i > i)); // Largest counter so far
    hash hmsg = hash(_i, _hstate_i,_turn, address(this));
    require(verifySigs(hmsg, sigs, plist)); // Everyone signed new hstate
    delete(input,cmd,hstate_{i+1},asserter, assertion); // Delete assertion
    status = Status.ON; i = _i; hstate_i = _hstate_i; turn = _turn; // Agreed state
  }

  function triggerDispute() {
    require(status == Status.ON & onlyParties()); // Only parties trigger
    status = Status.DISPUTE; deadline = now + disputePeriod;
  }

  function assertState(hash _hstate_i, hash _hstate_{i+1}, bytes _input, uint _cmd) {
    require(status == Status.DISPUTE AND checkCallerTurn());
    if(!assertion) {
      assertion = true; require(hstate_i == _hstate_i) // First assertion
    } else { require(hstate_{i+1} == _hstate_i); } // Extending existing assertion
    asserter = msg.sender; input = _input; cmd = _cmd; // Store assertion
    hstate_i = hstate_{i+1}; hstate_{i+1} = _hstate_{i+1}; // i accepted. i+1 assertion
    deadline = now + disputePeriod; // Reset deadline after an assertion
    progressTurn()); // Increment the turn counter
  }

  function challengeAssertion(bytes _oldstate) {
    require(status == Status.DISPUTE AND checkCallerTurn());
    require(hstate_i == hash(_oldstate) AND assertion); // Assertion exists
    hash check = AC.transition(asserter, _oldstate, input, cmd); // Compute
    if(hstate_{i+1} != checkh) { // Send all coins and bond to non-cheater. }
  }

  function timeOut() {
    require(now >= deadline && status == Status.dispute);
    // Send all coins/bonds to asserter (i.e. last party to respond).
  }

  function resolve(uint balance1, uint balance2) {
    if(status == Status.Dispute) {
      require(checkCallerTurn()); // Non-asserter must resolve b4 timeout.
    } else { require(status == Status.ON); } // No on-going dispute.
    require(hstate == hash(balance1, balance2)); // Terminal state?
    // Send each party their final balance and bond.
  }

  function deposit(); // Not implemented due to space - INCLUDES BOND
  function onlyParties() returns(bool); // Check if tx signer is whitelisted
  function refundAllBonds() internal; // Refunds all bonds
  function checkCallerTurn() returns(bool); Enforce turn based disputes
  function progressTurn() returns(bool); Update the turn counter
  function verifySigs(bytes hmsg, bytes[] sigs, address[] signers) returns(bool);
}
```

Fig. 1. Example of the state assertion contract

if $\mathsf{hstate}'_{i+1} == \mathsf{hstate}_{i+1}$. If this condition is satisified (and $i+1$ is the largest counter so far), then the counterparty signs $\sigma_{\mathcal{P}_2} = \mathsf{Sign}(\mathsf{hstate}_{i+1}, i+1, \mathbf{SC}, \mathcal{P}_{\mathsf{turn}})$ and sends their signature $\sigma_{\mathcal{P}_1}$ to the proposer.

Triggering a Dispute. In general, a dispute must be triggered if the counterparty stops responding in the state channel (i.e. they do not agree with the state update and they refuse to sign it). There are two cases to consider. Either the proposer is waiting on a signature from the verifier to authorise the new state, or the verifier is waiting on the proposer to propose a new state transition. In both cases, each party waits for a local time-out before submiting the most recently hstate_i via **SC.setstate()** and triggering a dispute via **SC.triggerDispute()**. The signed state hash includes $\mathcal{P}_{\mathsf{turn}}$ and thus **SC** waits for a new state assertion from the named party before $\mathtt{deadline} = \mathtt{now} + \Delta$. To continue off-chain and cancel the dispute, one party must submit a co-operatively signed hstate (with a larger counter i) via **SC.setstate.**

Submitting a State Assertion. The named party $\mathcal{P}_{\mathsf{turn}}$ must send an asserted hstate_{i+1}, the command cmd and its inputs inputs using **SC.assertState()** before the dispute process expiry time $\mathtt{deadline}$. Every time a state assertion hstate_{i+1} is submitted, the contract resets the deadline $\mathtt{deadline} = \mathtt{now} + \Delta$ and stores the previous state assertion hstate_i as accepted. Furthermore the contract records that it is the counterparty's turn to respond. In terms of the financial bond, the contract only needs to store a single **bond** per party which can be collected when the party asserts a new state or when the parties send their initial deposit.

Responding to a State Assertion. The counterparty is responsible for verifying if a state assertion is correct by computing $\mathsf{state}_{i+1} = \mathtt{Transition}(\mathsf{state}_i, \mathsf{cmd}, \mathsf{inputs})$ locally and checking if the asserted hstate_{i+1} represents state_{i+1}. If the state assertion is valid, then the counterparty can continue the application's execution by responding with a new state assertion using **SC.assertState()**. By continuing the application's execution, the counterparty is agreeing that the previous state assertion is valid. If the state assertion is invalid, then the counterparty can challenge it by supplying the plaintext state state_i to the contract using **SC.challenge()**. The contract will compute the transition and confirm if hstate_{i+1} represents the new state state_{i+1}. If the challenger is successful and proves the state assertion as invalid, they are sent all coins in the channel (including the counterparty's **bond** to refund the cost of this transaction).

Reaching the Terminal State. In Sect. 3.1, we assumed an application's execution will always reach a terminal state which is simply the final balance of both parties $\mathsf{state}_{\mathsf{final}} = (\mathtt{balance1}, \mathtt{balance2})$. The final $\mathsf{hstate}_{\mathsf{final}}$ must be accepted by the assertion contract **SC** before both parties are sent their final balance by supplying $\mathsf{state}_{\mathsf{final}}$ to **SC.resolve()**. It is clear if both parties continue the application's execution co-operatively off-chain, then they can simply send the terminal state hash via **SC.setstate()** before resolving the channel. On the other hand, the dispute process enforces turn-based state assertions to ensure that one party will eventually propose the terminal state hash via **SC.assertState()**.

When the terminal state hash is reached, the counterparty's only option is to submit state$_{final}$ before the deadline using **SC.resolve**().

4   Discussion and Future Work

Proof of Concept Implementation. We developed a proof of concept for the Ethereum blockchain. Our smart contract is written in Solidity[2], and gas costs were measured using a private network. The assertions contract costs 2,943,664 gas to deploy, approximately \$0.97 using the gas price of 2.6 Gwei and the conversion rate of 1 ether = \$127 which was the real world rate in January 2019. The cost to make a state assertion is only $59,774 + 39.5n$ gas (\$0.02 at 2.6 Gwei and \$0.77 on a congested network at 96 Gwei) where n corresponds to the number of bytes supplied as inputs to the assertion. Compared to the 725,508 gas (\$0.24 at 2.6 Gwei and \$8.83 at 96 Gwei) required to send the full battleship state.

Honest Party Can Always Verify State Assertions. To issue a challenge or continue the application's execution, an honest party must have the state$_i$ which corresponding to the contract's accepted hstate$_i$. There are only two situations when a new hstate$_i$ can be accepted by **SC**. In the first situation, hstate$_i$ will be accepted by **SC** if it is submitted using **SC.setstate**(), but this requires both parties to have already signed it (and thus acknowledge they know state$_i$). In the second situation, a new hstate$_i$ will be accepted by **SC** if the counterparty has asserted it using **SC.assertState**() and if the honest party continues the application's execution by asserting the next hstate$_{i+1}$ via **SC.assertState**(). We highlight the contract accepts hstate$_i$ as the honest party has countinued its execution instead of challenging it. As the above demonstrates, an honest party will always have a copy of state$_i$ if the corresponding hstate$_i$ is accepted by the contract. Thus they can always verify state transitions and issue challenges.

Motivation for Turn-Based Commands. There are two motivations for the turn-based channel. First each party can submit a state assertion and the counterparty is always provided an opportunity to accept or challenge it. Second, each state assertion must strictly build upon a previously accepted state hash. If there are two or more state assertions that reference the same previous state hash, then **SC** can only accept one state assertion. Because of the requirement to strictly order state assertions and the need to 'accept the first received state assertion', this lets an attacker simply pay a higher fee and front-run an honest party to ensure their state assertion is always accepted first (i.e. front-running ensures an honest party's state assertion is never accepted by **SC**). Thus the turn-based nature of this state channel prevents the above front-running attack.

Enforcing Time-Based Events. The assertion channel is responsible for enforcing time-based events with the dispute period Δ. When the application is cooperatively progressing off-chain, an honest party will wait for a local timeout

---

[2] Our PoC is an optimised for Solidity https://pastebin.com/UBVvZ0FU.

before triggering a dispute via the blockchain. For every new state assertion, the dispute process is reset to ensure each party has a time period of Δ to take their next move. If a party doesn't assert a new state before the deadline, then the honest party will notify the contract via **SC.timeout**(). This terminates the application and sends all coins (including the bonds) to the honest party.

Bond Requirement. Each party must deposit a bond to cover the cost of a successful challenge to their assertion. A bond's value must consider the worst-case when a transaction fee spikes due to network congestion. For example, in the battleship empirical case study it was highlighted that submitting the game's state can sky rocket from $0.24 to approximately $8.83 during network congestion. If the security bond isn't sufficient to challenge a state assertion, then the counterparty may not challenge it.

Offline Parties and PISA. If the honest party is offline, then the counterparty can trigger a dispute with the latest agreed hash and then assert an invalid state hash (i.e. sends the counterparty all the coins in the channel). If the offline party relies on a watching service, like PISA [14], then the watching service must have a copy of the latest state in plaintext to verify the invalid state transition and issue a challenge. This hinders state privacy as the watching service can view the channel's internal state. As well, a watching service cannot perform a valid state transition on the offline party's behalf, so the offline party must ensure the only valid state transition for the counterparty is the application's terminal state.

Extending to N-parties. Future work should investigate how the state assertion paradigm could be extended to n-party state channels. Channels could progress in a round-robin fashion and store the last **n** state assertions. This is so that a party can be sure that a state assertion will not be accepted unless they explicitly apply their own state assertion after it.

Acknowledgements. Chris Buckland and Patrick McCorry are supported by an Ethereum Foundation scaling grant, Ethereum Community Fund grant and a Research Institute grant.

References

1. Al-Bassam, M., Sonnino, A., Bano, S., Hrycyszyn, D., Danezis, G.: Chainspace: a sharded smart contracts platform. arXiv preprint arXiv:1708.03778 (2017)
2. Bano, S., et al.: Consensus in the age of blockchains. arXiv preprint arXiv:1711.03936 (2017)
3. Close, T., Stewart, A.: Force-move games (2018). https://magmo.com/force-move-games.pdf
4. Croman, K., et al.: On scaling decentralized blockchains. In: Clark, J., Meiklejohn, S., Ryan, P.Y.A., Wallach, D., Brenner, M., Rohloff, K. (eds.) FC 2016. LNCS, vol. 9604, pp. 106–125. Springer, Heidelberg (2016). https://doi.org/10.1007/978-3-662-53357-4_8

5. Decker, C., Wattenhofer, R.: A fast and scalable payment network with Bitcoin duplex micropayment channels. In: Pelc, A., Schwarzmann, A.A. (eds.) SSS 2015. LNCS, vol. 9212, pp. 3–18. Springer, Cham (2015). https://doi.org/10.1007/978-3-319-21741-3_1

6. Dziembowski, S., Faust, S., Hostáková, K.: General state channel networks. Cryptology ePrint Archive, Report 2018/320 (2018). https://eprint.iacr.org/2018/320

7. Eigenmann, D.: Optimistic contracts. https://medium.com/@decanus/optimistic-contracts-fb75efa7ca84. Accessed 10 Jan 2019

8. Eyal, I., Gencer, A.E., Sirer, E.G., Van Renesse, R.: Bitcoin-NG: a scalable blockchain protocol. In: NSDI, pp. 45–59 (2016)

9. Gervais, A., Karame, G.O., Wüst, K., Glykantzis, V., Ritzdorf, H., Capkun, S.: On the security and performance of proof of work blockchains. In: Proceedings of the 2016 ACM SIGSAC Conference on Computer and Communications Security, pp. 3–16. ACM (2016)

10. Horne, L., Coleman, J., Xuanji, L.: Counterfactual: generalized state channels (2018). https://l4.ventures/papers/statechannels.pdf

11. Khalil, R., Gervais, A., Felley, G.: NOCUST-A non-custodial 2 nd-layer financial intermediary. Technical report, Cryptology ePrint Archive, Report 2018/642. https://eprint.iacr.org/2018/642 (2018)

12. Kokoris-Kogias, E., Jovanovic, P., Gasser, L., Gailly, N., Syta, E., Ford, B.: OmniLedger: a secure, scale-out, decentralized ledger via sharding. In: 2018 IEEE Symposium on Security and Privacy (SP), pp. 583–598. IEEE (2018)

13. Luu, L., Narayanan, V., Zheng, C., Baweja, K., Gilbert, S., Saxena, P.: A secure sharding protocol for open blockchains. In: Proceedings of the 2016 ACM SIGSAC Conference on Computer and Communications Security, pp. 17–30. ACM (2016)

14. McCorry, P., Bakshi, S., Bentov, I., Miller, A., Meiklejohn, S.: Pisa: arbitration outsourcing for state channels. IACR Cryptology ePrint Archive (2018)

15. McCorry, P., Buckland, C., Bakshi, S., Wüst, K., Miller, A.: You sank my battleship! a case study to evaluate state channels as a scaling solution for cryptocurrencies

16. Miller, A., Bentov, I., Kumaresan, R., Bakshi, S., McCorry, P.: Sprites: payment channels that go faster than lightning. CoRR abs/1702.05812 (2017)

17. Poon, J., Buterin, V.: Plasma: scalable autonomous smart contracts. White paper (2017)

18. Poon, J., Dryja, T.: The bitcoin lightning network: scalable off-chain instant payments. Draft version 0.5, 9:14 (2016)

19. Sompolinsky, Y., Lewenberg, Y., Zohar, A.: Spectre: a fast and scalable cryptocurrency protocol. IACR Cryptology ePrint Archive, 2016:1159 (2016)

20. ScaleSphere Foundation Ltd. ("Foundation"): Celer network: bring internet scale to every blockchain. Technical report. https://www.celer.network/doc/CelerNetwork-Whitepaper.pdf. Accessed 10 Jan 2019

Short Paper: Secure Offline Payments in Bitcoin

Taisei Takahashi[✉] and Akira Otsuka

Institute of Information Security, Yokohama, Japan
{mgs174503,otsuka}@iisec.ac.jp

Abstract. Double-spending attacks on fast payments are one of the fatal architectural problems in Cryptocurrencies. Dmitrienko et al. proposed an offline fast payment scheme that relies on tamper-proof wallets produced by trustworthy manufacturers. With the wallets, the payee can immediately trust the transactions generated by the wallets without waiting for their registration to the blockchain. Secure coin-preloading to the wallet is important, while illegal coin-preloading can cause over/double-spending by the trusted wallets. For this, they proposed an interesting protocol that makes use of a fragment of the main blockchain to prove to the wallets the legitimacy of preloaded coins. One drawback is that, in proving that the fragment are from honest miners, their protocol requires a trusted online time-stamp server so that the wallets can verify the timestamps to see if the blocks in the fragment is mined with sufficiently large amount of computing resources. Otherwise, it sacrifices usability. In order to eliminate such an online trustee, in this paper we took the opposite approach that the payee (not the wallets) verifies the legitimacy of preloaded coins at the time of offline payment. As a consequence, our result shows that, with light-weight tamper-proof wallets, completely decentralized offline payment is possible without any modification to the existing Bitcoin network.

Keywords: Blockchain · Offline payment · Tamper-proof wallet

1 Introduction

Double-spending attacks on fast payments [4] are the one of the fatal architectural problems in Cryptocurrencies. Double spending refers to the payment where the same coin is spent twice in a way that the receiving party cannot notice the invalidity of the payment. We study an offline immediate payment scheme based on blockchain secure against the double-spending attacks on fast payment assuming the security of tamper-proof wallet. Dmitrienko et al. [1] pointed out that Bitcoin requires clients to be online to perform transactions and a certain amount of time to verify them, and also offline payments raise non-trivial challenges, as the payee has no means to verify transactions. Even online, fast payments are shown to be vulnerable to double-spending attacks [4].

© International Financial Cryptography Association 2020
A. Bracciali et al. (Eds.): FC 2019 Workshops, LNCS 11599, pp. 12–20, 2020.
https://doi.org/10.1007/978-3-030-43725-1_2

Offline immediate payments is long demanding in cryptocurrencies. In practice, without changing the ongoing systems, "fast payment" is widely used such that the payee could accept the transaction immediately by checking the signature, and the payer's balance for confirming that the payer has enough money to spend. Karame et al. [4] pointed out that, for such a fast payment scheme, double-spending attack is possible if a malicious payer makes use of the race condition of the double-spending transactions that reach the payees with different timing in the peer-to-peer network. Dmitrienko proposed a solution for immediate payment and offline payments that relies on tamper-proof wallets manufactured by trustworthy manufacturer and deploys time-based transaction confirmation verification mechanism. They make use of a fragment of the main blockchain to prove the legitimacy of preloaded coins to the wallets. Their scheme solved the double-spending problem as Karame et al. suggested. The wallet loses their credibility if a malicious user succeeds to pre-load illegal coins by intention. Thus, it is enormously important to establish secure coin preloading to the wallet. In order to achieve this, Dmitrienko propose an interesting protocol that proves the fact that a pre-loading payment to the wallet existed using a subchain, a fragment of the main blockchain. They considered that a subchain is a part of the mainchain if and only if the total PoW to mine the blocks in the subchain is greater than some predetermined lower-bound and the average time to produce the subchain is less than some constant time period. Thus, to verify the proof inside the tamper-proof wallet, it is necessary to measure the total computation time consumed to generate the subchain objectively. (A) A trivial solution to this is to assume a trusted time-stamp server, which supplies a time-stamp to a block everytime the corresponding block is created. (B) Another solution proposed in [1] is to set the expiration time of the pre-loading coins. This also convinces the wallet that the subchain is produced within some bounded time period. Apparently, the construction (A) with the trusted time-stamp server requires the additional trusted third party. The construction (B) is decentralized, but it sacrifices the usability to the great extent.

Other studies of interest include Teechan, an offline payment channel, proposed by Lind et al. [5]. It assumes tamper-proof wallets in both side and achieves offline payments. However, it has to deposit some fund, which corresponds to our preloading, into the 2-of-2 multisig address between the payee and the payer sufficiently before the offline payment occurs. Thus, the setting differs from ours. In the theoretical aspect, Garay et al. [3] formulated the basic properties of the blockchain in Bitcoin [6] such as "common prefix" and "chain quality", assuming that the hashing power of an adversary controlling a fraction of the parties is strictly less than $1/2$. Further extensions are made for variable difficulty [2], a security analysis in the "semi-synchronous" network model [7].

We propose a novel offline payment scheme alternative to the Dmitrienko's protocol. The advantage of our scheme is its fully decentralization, that is, it does not assume any external trusted time-stamp server. Further, we do not need to set any expiration time to the pre-loaded coins.

2   Preliminaries

- $\mathbb{C}$: a blockchain.
- B_i: i-th block in $\mathbb{C}$ is a triple $\langle \mathsf{hash}(B_{i-1}), \boldsymbol{x}_i, nonce \rangle$.
- τ: a transaction of a form $\mathsf{Sign}(sk_A; A \to B, value)$.
- $\boldsymbol{x}_i$: a root of Merkle Tree for a set of transactions $\{\tau_1, \tau_2, \ldots\}$ in B_i.
- $\mathcal{U}$: a set of users.
- $\mathcal{H}$: a set of honest users, $\mathcal{H} \subseteq \mathcal{U}$.
- $X, Y \in \mathcal{U}$: (typically, X as a payer, Y as a payee).

To analyze the security of our scheme, we follow the notions introduced by Garay et al. [3]. All players are bounded interactive Turing machines and are all synchronized and message are exchanged in a discrete time frame called round. $\{EXEC_{\Pi,\mathcal{A},\mathcal{Z}}^{t,n}(z)\}_{z\in\{0,1\}^*}$ denotes the random variable ensemble that determines the output of the environment $\mathcal{Z}$ on input z for a protocol Π with adversary $\mathcal{A}$. $VIEW_{\Pi,\mathcal{A},\mathcal{Z}}^{t,n}(z)$ denotes the concatenated view of all parties after the completion of an execution $EXEC_{\Pi,\mathcal{A},\mathcal{Z}}^{t,n}(z)$. A "flat" model is assumed where all parties executes exactly q mining trials (hash queries) per round. Then, each mining trials by various players are modeled as a Bernoulli distribution with different parameters and the deviation from the expected probability is estimated. We denoted by κ the length of hash function output, by η parameter determining block to round translation and by f probability at least one honest party succeeds in finding a POW in a round. Garay et al. [3] showed that any consecutive rounds S of length $|S| > \eta\kappa$ in the blockchain protocol is a "typical execution" with probability $1 - e^{-\Omega(\kappa)}$ where honest and adversarial mining trials succeed as expected within a bounded probability fluctuation of at most ϵ. Then, we have the followings.

Lemma 1 *(Common-Prefix Lemma [3]). Assume a typical execution and consider two chains $\mathbb{C}_1$ and $\mathbb{C}_2$ such that $\mathrm{len}(\mathbb{C}_2) \geq \mathrm{len}(\mathbb{C}_1)$. If $\mathbb{C}_1$ is adopted by an honest party at round r, and $\mathbb{C}_2$ is either adopted by an honest party or diffused at round r, then $\mathbb{C}_1^{\lceil k} \preceq \mathbb{C}_2$ and $\mathbb{C}_2^{\lceil k} \preceq \mathbb{C}_1$, for $k \geq 2\eta\kappa f$.*

3   Secure Offline Bitcoin Payments

Our immediate payment protocol construction basically follows the Dmitrienko's protocol [1] but without the existence of the time-stamp server. The main difference of the protocol is that the correctness of the coin-preloading to the tamper-proof wallet is verified by the payee in our construction, not the payer as in the Dmitrienko's protocol. Similarly to their scheme [1], our construction also assumes the tamper-resistant wallet to incorporate overspending prevention. Tamper-resistant wallet has a secret key sk_T which was created by the wallet manufacturer T. The wallet also has a variable *balance* (≥ 0). It increases in coin preloading phase and decreases in offline payment phase. Our construction has 3 phases: (i) online coin preloading, (ii) offline payment, and (iii) coin redemption and wallet revocation. The details are as follows (Fig. 1).

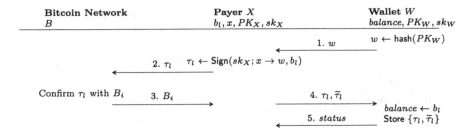

Fig. 1. Coin Pre-loading protocol

Coin Preloading. In the coin-preloading phase, the payer X requests a new account w from the wallet (Step 1), then create the preloading transaction τ_l transferring b_l bitcoins from her account x to w and commit it to the networks (Step 2). As soon as τ_l is verified and integrated into the Bitcoin network in a block, say B_i, X takes B_i (Step 3), and provides τ_l and the witness of the membership proof $\widetilde{\tau}_l$[1] to W (Step 4). W sets its *balance* to b_l and stores τ_l, $\widetilde{\tau}_l$, and replies status (Step 5)[2]. For simplicity, we assume one-time coin preloading for every account w such that once an amount b_l is preloaded to w, the wallet W never accepts preloading transaction to w any more and only makes payments while *balance* ≥ 0. It is not hard to extend it to multiple coin preloading.

Secure Offline Transaction. In the offline transaction phase, the payee Y sends the public key PK_Y and the requested amount b_o to the payer X which are immediately forwarded to W (Step 1). W checks the balance and if *balance* $\geq b_o$, it decreases *balance* by b_o and generates a transaction $\tau_o = \mathsf{Sign}(sk_w; w \to y, b_o)$. Further, W generates a *proof* $= \mathsf{Sign}(sk_T; \tau_o, \tau_l, \widetilde{\tau}_l)$ that shows τ_o was created within the tamper-proof wallet by signing with sk_T. The resulting τ_o, *proof* and $cert_T$, a trustworthy vendor certificate, are sent to Y (Step 3). Y accepts the transaction if τ_l is confirmed and τ_o is valid and issued by a tamper-proof wallet. More formally, Y accepts τ_o and *proof* if and only if

$$\begin{cases} cert_T \text{ is trustworthy} \\ \mathsf{Verify}(PK_T; proof) = 1 \\ \tau_o \in (\mathcal{V}_{\mathbb{C}_Y} \cap \mathsf{Sign}(sk_W; w \to \cdot, b_o)) \\ \tau_l \in \left(\mathbb{C}_Y^{\lceil k} \cap \mathsf{Sign}(\cdot; \cdot \to w, b_l)\right) \end{cases}$$

If all checks succeed, Y stores τ_o, *proof* and replies to W with status (Step 4) (Figs. 2 and 3) .

---

[1] $\widetilde{\tau}_l$ is a set of hash values such that $\mathsf{member}(B, \tau, \widetilde{\tau}) = 1$.

[2] The wallet does not check the validity of coin preloading transaction τ_l. Payments made from unconfirmed τ_l will be rejected by payees.

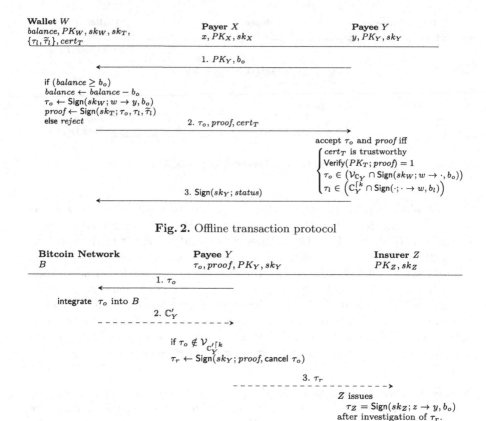

Fig. 2. Offline transaction protocol

Fig. 3. Coin redemption and double-spending wallet revocation protocol

Coin Redemption and Wallet Revocation. When Y gets online, Y proceeds to the coin redemption and wallet revocation phase. Y broadcasts τ_o to the Bitcoin network in order to redeem the coins received from W (Step 1). Next, the Bitcoin network verifies τ_o and integrates it to the blockchain. The payee Y observes the Bitcoin network and periodically updates its local chain $\mathbb{C}'_Y$ reflecting the newly mined blocks (Step 2). Y waits until τ_o is confirmed or τ_o becomes invalid, $\tau_o \notin \mathcal{V}_{\mathbb{C}'_Y}$. If τ_o is invalid, Y initiates revocation by creating a revocation transaction $\tau_r = \mathsf{Sign}(sk_Y; proof, \mathsf{cancel}\ \tau_o)$ and send it to Insurer Z (Step 3). Z investigate τ_r and in order to compensate Y for the damage of b_o, issues τ_Z then committed to the Bitcoin network (Step 4).

4   Security Model

Definition 1. τ *is said to be* valid *with respect to a blockchain $\mathbb{C}$ if and only if τ satisfies[3] all the pre-agreed requirements[4] with respect to the blockchain $\mathbb{C}$. Further, we denote by $\mathcal{V}_\mathbb{C}$ a set of all possible* valid *transactions with respect to $\mathbb{C}$ such that*

$$\mathcal{V}_\mathbb{C} = \{\tau \mid \tau \text{ is valid with respect to } \mathbb{C}\}.$$

valid transactions are correctly formed and not over-spent more than the balance of the payer's account as far as regarding the given blockchain $\mathbb{C}$ as the mainchain. Once valid transactions are broadcasted to Bitcoin network by peers, they may be integrated into the mainchain if the given chain $\mathbb{C}$ is shared by honest miners, and thus the transaction is valid for those honest miners. Note that this is not guaranteed. Because the given chain $\mathbb{C}$ may contradicts with the localchains of other honest miners. Furthermore, the set of valid transactions will change as chains evolve.

Definition 2. *A transaction τ is said to be* confirmed[5] *if and only if for every honest player $X \in \mathcal{H}$ the transaction τ can be found on his localchain $\mathbb{C}_X$, that is, $\tau \in \mathbb{C}_X$ for all $X \in \mathcal{H}$.*

Once a transaction τ is confirmed, the transaction must be in the mainchain $\mathbb{C}$ where $\mathbb{C}$ is the longest prefix of all localchains held by honest players such that $\mathbb{C} \preceq \mathbb{C}_X$ for all $X \in \mathcal{H}$. Where $\preceq$ is a prefix relation [3]. We consider confirmed transactions are valid. That is, τ is confirmed $\implies \tau \in \mathcal{V}_{\mathbb{C}_X}$ for all $X \in \mathcal{H}$.

Definition 3. *Given a security parameter k, τ_o is said to be* verified *by a proof of a form* Sign$(sk_T; \tau_o, \tau_l)$ *with respect to a localchain $\mathbb{C}$ if and only if*

$$\begin{cases} cert_T \text{ is issued by a trustworthy provider} \\ \text{Verify}(PK_T; proof) = 1 \\ \tau_o \text{ is a transaction of a form } \text{Sign}(sk_W; w \rightarrow \cdot, b_o) \\ \tau_l \text{ is a transaction of a form } \text{Sign}(\cdot; \cdot \rightarrow w, b_l) \\ \tau_o \in \mathcal{V}_\mathbb{C} \\ \tau_l \in \mathbb{C}^{\lceil k} \end{cases} \quad (1)$$

---

[3] Dmitrienko [1] have introduced a slightly different term CheckSyntaxT for transaction validation. CheckSyntaxT refers to the syntactical conformance of transactions to the requirements in the blockchain. On the other hand, valid refers to all the requirements for integrating into the blockchain. Those are the syntactical conformance of transactions, correctness of payer's signature and further requirements such as "the payer's account must exist", "balance after the transaction must not be negative".

[4] In Bitcoin, the requirements (e.g., Bitcoin Improvement Proposals) are subject to change. New proposals will be incorporated in the requirements after agreed among majority of miners through voting process in the blockchain.

[5] In practice, a transaction is *confirmed* after the block that contains the transaction has at least 6 blocks built on top. This is the situation where our notion of confirmed is satisfied with high probability.

where $cert_T$ is a certificate issued to a public key PK_T which is generated within a tamper-proof wallet W at the production time. (PK_W, sk_W) is a key pair generated by W, and w is an account related to PK_W.

In the offline payment, a payee Y verifies the received transaction τ_o by a proof $\mathsf{Sign}(sk_T; \tau_o, \tau_l)$ with his localchain $\mathbb{C}_Y$. If all of the above conditions are satisfied, Y is convinced that the coin-preloading transaction to the payer's wallet τ_l is confirmed by all honest players with overwhelming probability in k. As far as the tamper-proof wallet honestly produces the payment transaction τ_o, Y can believe that τ_o is not an overspending transaction and will be confirmed later on. To see whether τ_l satisfies the last condition $\tau_l \in \mathbb{C}^{\lceil k}$, in a naive construction, the payee must keep the whole set of transactions previously registered in the blockchain $\mathbb{C}$. For efficiency purposes, we assume that all transactions in a block B are kept in a form of a Merkle Tree and B only keeps the root hash value of the tree. Let $\widetilde{\tau}_l$ be a witness of the membership proof, or a set of all sibling hash values in every branch in the path from the root to the leaf τ_l. Using the witness $\widetilde{\tau}_l$, the membership proof can be efficiently proved since there exists a function $\mathsf{member}(\cdot)$ such that

$$\mathsf{member}(B, \tau, \widetilde{\tau}) = \begin{cases} 1 & \text{if } \tau \in B \\ 0 & \text{otherwise} \end{cases}$$

We replace the *proof* with $\mathsf{Sign}(sk_T; \tau_o, \tau_l, \widetilde{\tau}_l)$ where offline payee needs efficiency.

Theorem 1. *We assume there exists a tamper-proof wallet W. Given a security parameter k and an offline transaction τ_o accepted by a payee Y such that τ_o is verified by a proof $= \mathsf{Sign}(sk_w; \tau_o, \tau_l)$ with respect to the payee's localchain $\mathbb{C}_Y$, the probability that the transaction τ_o, later on, changes its state to invalid is negligible in k. That is, with $\mathbb{C}_Y^{\lceil k} \preceq \mathbb{C}_Y'$, we have*

$$\Pr[\tau_o \notin \mathcal{V}_{\mathbb{C}_Y'}^{\lceil k} \mid \tau_o \text{ is verified by proof with respect to } \mathbb{C}_Y] < \mathsf{negl}(k).$$

Proof. Given τ_o is verified by *proof* with respect to $\mathbb{C}_Y$, Eq. (1) holds. Under the tamper-proof assumption, the tamper-proof wallet W never overspends exceeding the preloaded balance b_l. Therefore, if the preloading transaction τ_l is confirmed, that is, $\tau_l \in \mathbb{C}_X$ for all $X \in \mathcal{H}$, then the offline transaction τ_o cannot become invalid with respect to $\mathbb{C}_Y'$.

Since τ_l is already in a localchain of Y, that is, $\tau_l \in \mathbb{C}_Y^{\lceil k}$, for τ_l not to be confirmed, there must exist an honest player Z with a localchain $\mathbb{C}_Z$ such that $\tau_l \notin \mathbb{C}_Z$. The common-prefix property states that all localchain $\mathbb{C}$ held by honest players must satisfy $\mathbb{C}^{\lceil k} \preceq \mathbb{C}_Z$ with negligible error probability in k. Substituting $\mathbb{C} \to \mathbb{C}_Y$, $\tau_l \in \mathbb{C}_Y^{\lceil k}$ contradicts with $\tau_l \notin \mathbb{C}_Z$. Thus, τ_l must be confirmed with arbitrarily high probability $1 - \mathsf{negl}(k)$ with the security parameter k. Hence the theorem. $\qquad \square$

In the case $\tau_o \notin \mathcal{V}_{\mathbb{C}_Y'^{\lceil k}}$ where the offline transaction τ_o is turned out to be invalid later on with respect to the payee's evolved localchain $\mathbb{C}_Y' (\succeq \mathbb{C}_Y^{\lceil k})$, this must be the case where the tamper-proof wallet assumption is broken and τ_o is found to be an overspent transaction. Even in this case, the preloading transaction τ_l must still be confirmed with $1 - \mathsf{negl}(k)$. Therefore, the $proof = \mathsf{Sign}(sk_w; \tau_o, \tau_l)$ still satisfies the following 5 of all 6 conditions in (1) for all honest player $X \in \mathcal{H}$ with $1 - \mathsf{negl}(k)$.

$$
\begin{cases}
cert_T \text{ is issued by a trustworthy provider} \\
\mathsf{Verify}(PK_T; proof) = 1 \\
\tau_o \text{ is a transaction of a form } \mathsf{Sign}(sk_W; w \to \cdot, b_o) \\
\tau_l \text{ is a transaction of a form } \mathsf{Sign}(\cdot; \cdot \to w, b_l) \\
\tau_l \in \mathbb{C}_X{}^{\lceil k}
\end{cases}
$$

This fact convinces all honest players. Given τ_o is invalid with respect to $\mathbb{C}'_Y$, that is, $\tau_o \notin \mathcal{V}_{\mathbb{C}'^{\lceil k}_Y}$, the redeeming transaction $\tau_r = \mathsf{Sign}(sk_Y; proof, \mathsf{cancel}\ \tau_o)$ becomes valid with respect to $\mathbb{C}_X \succeq \mathbb{C}'^{\lceil k}_Y$ for all $X \in \mathcal{H}$ with arbitrarily high probability $1 - \mathsf{negl}(k)$. The trustworthy provider of the tamper-proof wallet or an insurance company might compensate Y for the damage of b_o after τ_r is confirmed.

5   Conclusion

In this paper, we have shown that, with light-weight tamper-proof wallets, completely decentralized offline payment is possible without any modification to the existing Bitcoin network. Our protocol requires the coin pre-loading transaction is confirmed and its block is delivered to every possible payee before the first offline payment is made. This should be the best possible for Bitcoin network.

Lastly, we thank anonymous reviewers for their valuable comments.

References

1. Dmitrienko, A., Noack, D., Yung, M.: Secure wallet-assisted offline Bitcoin payments with double-spender revocation. In: ASIACCS (2017)
2. Garay, J., Kiayias, A., Leonardos, N.: The Bitcoin backbone protocol with chains of variable difficulty. In: Katz, J., Shacham, H. (eds.) CRYPTO 2017. LNCS, vol. 10401, pp. 291–323. Springer, Cham (2017). https://doi.org/10.1007/978-3-319-63688-7_10
3. Garay, J., Kiayias, A., Leonardos, N.: The Bitcoin backbone protocol: analysis and applications. In: Oswald, E., Fischlin, M. (eds.) EUROCRYPT 2015. LNCS, vol. 9057, pp. 281–310. Springer, Heidelberg (2015). https://doi.org/10.1007/978-3-662-46803-6_10
4. Karame, G.O., Androulaki, E., Capkun, S.: Double-spending fast payments in Bitcoin. In: CCS, pp. 906–917. ACM (2012)
5. Lind, J., Eyal, I., Pietzuch, P.R., Sirer, E.G.: Teechan: payment channels using trusted execution environments. https://arxiv.org/abs/1612.07766 (2016), https://arxiv.org/pdf/1612.07766.pdf. Accessed 9 Mar 2017

6. Nakamoto, S.: Bitcoin: a peer-to-peer electronic cash systems, November 2008. https://bitcoin.org/bitcoin.pdf
7. Pass, R., Seeman, L., Shelat, A.: Analysis of the blockchain protocol in asynchronous networks. In: Coron, J.-S., Nielsen, J.B. (eds.) EUROCRYPT 2017. LNCS, vol. 10211, pp. 643–673. Springer, Cham (2017). https://doi.org/10.1007/978-3-319-56614-6_22

Proof-of-Work Sidechains

Aggelos Kiayias[1,3] and Dionysis Zindros[2,3(✉)]

[1] University of Edinburgh, Edinburgh, UK
akiayias@inf.ed.ac.uk
[2] National and Kapodistrian University of Athens, Athens, Greece
dionyziz@di.uoa.gr
[3] IOHK, Hong Kong, China

Abstract. During the last decade, the blockchain space has exploded with a plethora of new cryptocurrencies, covering a wide array of different features, performance and security characteristics. Nevertheless, each of these coins functions in a stand-alone manner, independently. Sidechains have been envisioned as a mechanism to allow blockchains to communicate with one another and, among other applications, allow the transfer of value from one chain to another, but so far there have been no decentralized constructions. In this paper, we put forth the first side chains construction that allows communication between proof-of-work blockchains without trusted intermediaries. Our construction is generic in that it allows the passing of any information between blockchains. Using this construction, two blockchains can be connected in a "two-way peg" in which an asset can be transferred from one chain to another and back. We pinpoint the features needed for two chains to communicate: On the source side, a proof-of-work blockchain that has been *interlinked*, potentially with a velvet fork; on the destination side, a blockchain with smart contract support. We put forth the smart contracts needed to implement these sidechains and explain them in detail. In the heart of our construction, we use a recently introduced cryptographic primitive, Non-Interactive Proofs of Proof-of-Work (NIPoPoWs).

1 Introduction

Bitcoin [13] is the most successful *cryptocurrency* to date. It introduced *blockchains*, a of cryptographic consensus protocol in which *transactions* are organized into *blocks* which are put in a mutually agreed sequence despite the presence of adversaries. Consensus is achieved via *proof-of-work* [4] which is the precondition for block validity. Transactions moving value within blockchains have been proven to be secure and that consensus is eventually achieved, cf. [5,6,14].

Ethereum [3] extends Bitcoin's functionality introducing Turing-complete *smart contracts* programmed in languages like Solidity which run on top of the Ethereum Virtual Machine [18]. These contracts execute autonomously. The smart contracts are confined to access data only within the blockchain itself, such as previous transactions and blocks. Access to external data requires a trusted third party or group thereof to vouch for the data validity [23].

Research partially supported by H2020 project PRIVILEDGE # 780477.

Sidechains [1] are a mechanism for cross-chain communication in blockchains. They allow smart contracts on one blockchain to receive and react to *events* taking place on another blockchain without the need of trusted parties. Despite their widely agreed usefulness there exist no constructions that are decentralised and efficient at the same time.

Our Contributions. In this paper, we introduce the first trustless construction for proof-of-work sidechains. We describe how to build generic communication between blockchains. As one application, we give the construction of a *two-way pegged* asset which can be moved from one blockchain to another while retaining its nature. We provide a high-level construction in Solidity. Our construction works across a broad range of blockchains requiring only two underlying properties. First, that the *source* blockchain is a proof-of-work blockchain supporting Non-Interactive Proofs of Proof-of-Work (NIPoPoWs), a cryptographic primitive which allows constructing succinct proofs *about* events which occur in a proof-of-work blockchain and which was recently introduced in [12]. Support for NIPoPoWs can be introduced to practically any work-based cryptocurrency such as Bitcoin and Ethereum without a hard or soft fork. Second, that the *target* blockchain is able to validate such proofs through smart contracts such as, e.g., Ethereum or Ethereum Classic. To our knowledge, we are the first to provide such a construction in full.

Related Work. Sidechains were introduced as a Bitcoin upgrade mechanism by Back et al. [1]. They proposed introducing a new *child* blockchain which implements a new protocol version, with which assets are *2-way pegged*. The *firewall* property was articulated. No complete construction of the protocol was given. Their paper hints at the need for "*efficient SPV proofs*" (Appendix B) in future work, which we implemented here. We use the term *sidechains* in a more general notion than in their work. Our sidechains allow communication between *stand alone* blockchains and also convey *any* information, not just transfers of value. In our work, a blockchain is a sidechain of another chain if it can react to events on that chain, and so the relationship can be symmetric.

Polkadot [19], *Tendermint, Cosmos* [2], *Liquid* and *Interledger* [7] also build cross-chain transfers. Their validation relies on a trusted committees, federations or is left unspecified. *Drivechains* and *rootstock* are sidechain proposals which require miners of both chains to be aware of both networks. In our scheme, miners remain agnostic to the existence of other chains and connect only to one network. *BTCRelay* is a trustless mechanism relaying information one-way from Bitcoin to Ethereum, in which miners are connected to their network only. BTCRelay requires the transmission of the entirety of the source blockchain headers into the target blockchain. Our proposal only requires data logarithmic in size of the source blockchain. This stems from the *succinctness* property of the NIPoPoW scheme. Other related work includes Plasma [15], XCLAIM [21], PeaceRelay, COMIT [9], and NOCUST [10] and Dogethereum.

2   Overview

We wish to transfer assets from one blockchain to another and then back. When assets can be transferred from one blockchain to another but not back, we call it a *one-way peg*. If assets can also be moved back, we call it a *two-way peg*. In each individual transfer of an asset, we have a particular *source blockchain*, from which the asset is moved, and a particular *target blockchain*, to which the asset is moved. In a sidechain setting of two blockchains that are two-way pegged, both blockchains can function as a source and a target blockchain for different transfers.

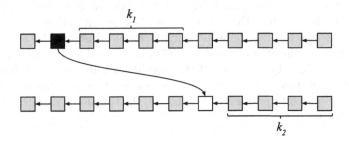

Fig. 1. Basic information transfer between two blockchains

While the motivation for the construction is to be able to move assets from one blockchain to another, we generalize the notion of sidechains from this strict setting. In general, we would like the target blockchain to be able to react to any *event* that occurs on the source blockchain. Such events can be the fact that a transaction with a particular TXID took place, that a certain account was paid a certain amount of money, or that a particular smart contract was instantiated. Our sidechain construction allows the target blockchain to react to events that took place on the source blockchain. This reaction can be implemented in its target blockchain smart contracts. We describe our construction in pseudocode similar to Ethereum' *Solidity*. In Solidity, *events* can be fired arbitrarily from within a smart contract and do not have a semantic interpretation. In this setting, events are defined by Solidity using the event type and have an *event name*, a *contract address* which fired them, as well as certain parameter values. A contract can elect to fire an event with any name and any parameters of its choice by invoking the EMIT command.

A high-level overview of cross-chain event transmission is shown in Fig. 1. The process is as follows. First, an event is fired in the source blockchain, shown at the top. This could be any event that can be emitted using Ethereum's EMIT command. This event firing is caused by a certain transaction which is included at a certain block, indicated in black at the top. This block is then buried under k_1 subsequent blocks within the source blockchain, where the k_1 parameter is a security parameter of the scheme depending on the specific parameters of the source blockchain [5]. As soon as this confirmation occurs, the target blockchain can react to the event, shown at the bottom. This reaction occurs in a transaction which is included in a block within the target blockchain, illustrated in white. As usual, the block needs to be confirmed by waiting for k_2 blocks to be mined on top of it. It is possible that $k_1 \neq k_2$ because of different blockchain parameters such as a difference in block generation time or network synchrony.

Using this basic functionality of event information exchange between blockchains, we can construct two-way pegged sidechains. In such a construction, an asset that exists on one blockchain will gain the ability to be *moved* to a different blockchain and back. We will use the example of moving ether, the native asset of the Ethereum blockchain, from the Ethereum blockchain into the Ethereum Classic blockchain and back. Such an action is different from *exchanging* ether (ETH), the native token of the Ethereum blockchain, with ether classic (ETC), the native token of the Ethereum Classic blockchain. Instead, the asset retains its nature; it maintains its price and its ability to be used for the same purposes, while being governed by the rules of the new blockchain, such as different performance, fees, features, or security guarantees. Furthermore, no counterparty or market is required to perform the exchange; the transfer is something a party can do on its own.

3   Construction

Cross-Chain Certificates

For our construction, we use a primitive called Non-Interactive Proofs of Proof-of-Work recently introduced in [12]. Non-Interactive Proofs of Proofs-of-Work are cryptographic protocols which implement a *prover* and a *verifier*. The prover is a *full node* on the *source blockchain*. The verifier does not have access to that blockchain, but knows the source genesis block $\mathcal{G}$. The prover wants to convince the verifier that an *event* took place in the source blockchain; for instance, a smart contract method was called with certain parameters or that a payment was made into a particular address. Whether such an event took place can easily be determined if one inspects the whole blockchain. However, the prover wishes to convince the verifier by only sending a *succinct proof*, a short string which does not grow linearly with the size of the source blockchain, but, rather, *polylogarithmically*. The verifier must not be fooled by *adversarial provers* who provide incorrect proofs claiming that an event happened while in fact it didn't, or that it didn't while in fact it did. These adversaries can also mine blocks, but the honest parties are assumed to control the majority of computational power on both the source and the target blockchain networks. To withstand such attacks, the verifier accepts multiple proofs, at least one of which is assumed to have been honestly generated (this assumption is necessary in standard blockchain protocols in general [8,20]). Comparing these proofs against each other, the verifier extracts a reliable truth value corresponding to the same value it would deduce if it were to be running a full node on the blockchain itself. This property is the *security* of NIPoPoWs proven in [12].

The NIPoPoWs construction talks about *predicates* evaluated on block-chains, but we are interested in *events*. We can translate from events to predicates provable with NIPoPoWs. Specifically, given a genesis block $\mathcal{G}$, a smart contract address addr, an event name Event, and a series of event parameter values $(\mathsf{param}_1, \mathsf{param}_2, \cdots, \mathsf{param}_n)$, the predicate e we wish to check for truth is the following: *Has the event named* Event *been fired with parameters* $(\mathsf{param}_1, \mathsf{param}_2, \cdots, \mathsf{param}_n)$ *by the smart contract residing in address* addr *on the blockchain with genesis block $\mathcal{G}$ at least k blocks ago?* This predicate is (1) *monotonic*, meaning that it starts with the value false and, if it ever becomes true, it cannot ever change its value back as the blockchain grows; (2) *infix-sensitive*, meaning that its truth value can be deduced by inspecting a polylogarithmically-bound number of blocks on the blockchain (in our case one block, within which the event firing was confirmed); and (3) *stable*, meaning that, if one party deduces that its value is true, then soon enough *all* parties will deduce that its value is true. This last property stems from the requirement that the event be buried under k blocks ensuring a blockchain reorganization up to k blocks ago cannot affect the predicate's value.

In order to determine whether an event took place, the NIPoPoW verifier function $\mathsf{verify}^{\mathcal{G},e}_{k,m}(\mathcal{P})$ accepts the event description in the form of a blockchain predicate e, which we gave above, the genesis block of the remote chain $\mathcal{G}$, as well as two security parameters k and m. These security parameters can be constants specified when the sidechain system is created (concrete values for these are given in [12]). Subsequently, the NIPoPoW verifier accepts a set of *proofs* $\mathcal{P} = \{\pi_1, \pi_2, \cdots, \pi_n\}$ which it compares and extracts a truth value for the predicate: Whether the event has taken place in the remote blockchain or not. As long as at least one *honestly generated* proof π_i is provided, the verifier's security ensures that the output will correspond to whether the event actually occurred.

Our protocol works as follows. Whenever an event of interest occurs on the source blockchain, the occurence of this event is observed by a source blockchain honest node, who generates a NIPoPoW about it. The target blockchain contains a smart contract with a method to accept and verify the veracity of this proof. The node can then submit the proof to the smart contract by broadcasting a transaction on the target blockchain. As soon as the proof is validated by the smart contract, the target blockchain can elect to react to the event as desired.

Adoption Considerations. Our construction has certain prerequisites for both the source and the target blockchain before it can be adopted. In the case of bidirectionally connected blockchains, both of them must satisfy the source and the target blockchain prerequisites.

- **The source blockchain** needs to support *proofs* about it, which requires augmenting it with an *interlink* vector, the details of which can be found in [11]. This interlink vector can be added to a blockchain using a *user-activated velvet fork* [12,22], which is performed without miner awareness and does not require a hard or soft fork. However, only events occuring *after* the velvet fork can be proven. New blockchains can adopt this from genesis.

– **The target blockchain** needs to be able to run the above verify function. This function can be programmed in a Turing-complete language such as Solidity. If the source blockchain proof-of-work hash function is available as an opcode or pre-compiled smart contract within the target blockchain's VM the way, e.g., Bitcoin's SHA256 hash function is available in Solidity, the implementation can be more gas-efficient.

Blockchain Agnosticism. We underline the remarkable property that miners and full nodes of the target blockchain do not need to be aware of the source blockchain at all. To them, all information about the source blockchain is simply a string which is passed as a parameter to a smart contract and can remain *agnostic* to its semantics as a proof. Additionally, miners and full nodes of the source blockchain do not need to be aware of the target blockchain. Only the parties interested in facilitating cross-chain events must be aware of both. Those untrusted facilitators need to maintain an SPV node on the source blockchain about which they generate their NIPoPoW. To broadcast their proof on the target blockchain, they connect to target blockchain nodes and send the transaction containing the NIPoPoW. Blockchain agnosticism allows users to initiate cross-chain relationships between different blockchains *dynamically*, as long as the blockchains in question satisfy the above prerequisites.

Cross-Chain Events

We give our crosschain construction in Algorithm 1. Initially, our communication will be unidirectional. In the next section, we use two unidirectional channels to establish bidirectional communication. This smart contract runs on the target blockchain and informs it about events that took place in the source blockchain. It is parameterized by three parameters: k and m are the underlying security parameters of the NIPoPoW protocol. The value z is a *collateral* parameter, denominated in ether (or the native currency of the blockchain in which the execution takes place) and is used to incentivize honest participants to intervene in cases of false claims. The contract utilizes the NIPoPoW verify function parameterized by the event e, the remote genesis block G and the security parameters k and m. We do not give an explicit implementation of verify, as it can be implemented in a straightforward manner by translating the pseudocode listing of [12]. For our purposes, it suffices to treat it as a black box which, given a set of proofs, at least one of which is honestly generated, returns the truth value of the respective predicate.

The contract allows detecting remote blockchain events and can be *inherited* by other contracts that wish to adopt its functionality. It works as follows. First, the initialize method is called exactly once to configure the contract, passing the *hash* of the genesis block of the remote chain which this contract will handle. This method is internal and can only be called by the contract inheriting from it.

Users of the contract can check it has been configured with the correct genesis block prior to using it. We note that, while our algorithm does not reflect this to keep complexity low, it is possible to have a contract interact with *multiple* remote chains by extending it to include multiple geneses.

Algorithm 1. The smart contract skeleton that enables checking cross-chain proofs about events.

1: **contract crosschain**$_{k,m,z}$
2:     finalized-events $\leftarrow \emptyset$; events $\leftarrow \emptyset$
3:     **internal function** initialize($\mathcal{G}_{\text{remote}}$)
4:         $\mathcal{G} \leftarrow \mathcal{G}_{\text{remote}}$
5:     **end function**
6:     **payable function** submit-event-proof(π, e)
7:         **if** msg.value $< z$ **then**   ▷ Ensure sufficient collateral
8:             **return** $\bot$
9:         **end if**
10:         **if** events[e] $= \bot \wedge$ verify$_{k,m}^{e,\mathcal{G}}(\{\pi\})$ **then**
11:             events[e] $\leftarrow$ {expire: block.number $+ k$, proof: π, author: msg.sender}
12:         **end if**
13:     **end function**
14:     **function** finalize-event(e)
15:         **if** events[e] $= \bot \vee$ block.number $<$ events[e].expire **then**
16:             **return** $\bot$
17:         **end if**
18:         finalized-events $\leftarrow$ finalized-events $\cup \{e\}$
19:         author $\leftarrow$ events[e].author
20:         events[e] $\leftarrow \bot$
21:         author.send(z)   ▷ Return collateral
22:     **end function**
23:     **function** submit-contesting-proof(π^*, e)
24:         **if** events[e] $= \bot \vee$ block.number $\geq$ events[e].expire **then**
25:             **return** $\bot$
26:         **end if**
27:         **if** $\neg$verify$_{k,m}^{e,\mathcal{G}}(\{\text{events}[e].\text{proof}, \pi^*\})$ **then**   ▷ Original proof was fraudulent
28:             events[e] $\leftarrow \bot$
29:             msg.sender.send(z)   ▷ Pay collateral to contester
30:         **end if**
31:     **end function**
32:     **function** event-exists(e)
33:         **return** $e \in$ finalized-events
34:     **end function**
35: **end contract**

The lifecycle of an event submission is illustrated in Fig. 2. When an event has taken place in the source blockchain, any source blockchain SPV node, the *author*, can inform the crosschain contract about this fact by generating a NIPoPoW π claiming that the event took place based on their current view of the source blockchain. This proof can then be submitted to the target blockchain by calling the submit-event-proof function and passing it the proof π and the event predicate e. The submission is accompanied by a collateral payment z. If the author is honest, this collateral will be returned to her later. The submit-event-proof function runs the NIPoPoW verify algorithm to check that the proof π is well-formed and that it claims that the predicate is true. It then stores the proof for later use. It also stores the address of the *author* and an *expiration block number*.

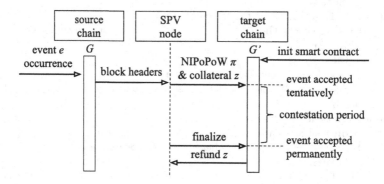

Fig. 2. A sequence diagram showing the actions of the untrusted SPV node when communicating with both blockchain networks and the lifecycle of an event submission

Upon submission of a proof to the submit-event-proof function, the event is *tentatively accepted* for a *contestation period* of k blocks, during which any other party, the *contester*, can provide a counter-proof showing that the original proof was fraudulent. The contester can call the submit-contesting-proof function passing it the contesting proof π^* and the event predicate e. The function runs the NIPoPoW verify algorithm to compare the original proof events[e].proof against the contesting proof π^*. If the verification algorithm concludes that the original proof was fraudulent, the tentatively accepted event is abandoned and the collateral is paid to the contester.

Otherwise, when the contestation period has expired without any valid contestations, the author can call the finalize-event function. This function changes the acceptance of the event from tentative to *permanent* by including it in the finalized-events set and returns the collateral to the author. Finally, the event-exists function can be used by the inheriting contract to check if an event has been permanently accepted. The target blockchain state during this execution is shown in Fig. 3. The source blockchain's event included in the black box, upon sufficient confirmation by k_1 blocks (not shown), is transmitted to the target blockchain at the bottom. The target blockchain includes the event *tentatively* in block 1 until a contestation period of k_2 has passed; the event is included *permanently* in block 2; subsequently, permanent inclusion needs to be confirmed with k_2 further blocks.

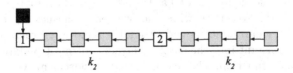

Fig. 3. The target blockchain state during event submission

Two-Way Pegged Sidechains

Having created the generic crosschain contract, we now build two-way pegged sidechains on top. For concreteness, we use the example of transferring ether (ETH), the native currency of the Ethereum blockchain, to the Ethereum Classic blockchain, and back. We note that this example is arbitrary and for illustration. Our construction can be used between any work-based blockchains satisfying the prerequisites detailed above.

When ether is moved to the Ethereum Classic blockchain, it will be represented as an ERC20 token[1] within Ethereum Classic. Let this custom token be called ETH20. The asset retains its nature as it moves from one blockchain to another if it is always possible to move ETH into ETH20 and back at a one-to-one rate. The economic reason is that the price of ETH and ETH20 on the market will necessarily be the same. If the price of ETH were to ever be significantly above the price of ETH20 in the market, then a rational participant would exchange their ETH20 for ETH using sidechains and sell their ETH on the market instead, and vice versa. There can be a small discrepancy in the two prices which stems from two different factors: First, the fees needed for a crosschain transfer; and second, the temporary market fluctuations that can occur during the limited time needed to perform the cross chain transfer $(k_1 + 2k_2)$. If we assume the price fluctuation (of ETH20 denominated in ETH) per unit of time is bounded, then the market price difference between ETH and ETH20 at any moment in time can be bounded by the sum of these two factors.

---

[1] The ERC20 standard [17] defines an interface implementable by smart contracts that enables holding and transferring custom fungible tokens such as ICO tokens.

The sidechain smart contracts are presented in Algorithm 2. These smart contracts both extend the crosschain smart contract of Algorithm 1. Furthermore, sidechain$_2$ also inherits basic ERC20 functionality which allows token owners to transfer the token [16]. The sidechain$_1$ contract will be instantiated on Ethereum, while the sidechain$_2$ contract will be instantiated on Ethereum Classic. Suppose the genesis block hash of Ethereum is $\mathcal{G}_1$ and of Ethereum Classic is $\mathcal{G}_2$. We will use the genesis block hash of each blockchain as its unique identifier.

The two smart contracts both contain an initialize method which accepts the hash of the remote blockchain as well as the address of the remote smart contract it will interface with. Note that, while the two genesis hashes can be hard-coded into the respective smart contract code itself, the remote contract address cannot be built-in as a constant into the smart contract, but must be later specified by calling the initialize function. The reason is that, if sidechain$_1$ were to be created on $\mathcal{G}_1$, it would require the address of sidechain$_2$ to exist prior to its creation, and vice versa in a circular dependency. Therefore, the two contracts must first be created on their respective blockchain to obtain addresses, and then their initialize methods can be called to inform each contract about the address of the other. Specifically, first the contract sidechain$_1$ is created on $\mathcal{G}_1$ to obtain its instance address which we also denote sidechain$_1$. Then the second contract, sidechain$_2$, is created on $\mathcal{G}_2$ to obtain its address sidechain$_2$. Subsequently, the initialize function of sidechain$_1$ is called, passing it $\mathcal{G}_2$ and the address sidechain$_2$. Finally, initialize is called on sidechain$_2$, passing it $\mathcal{G}_1$ and the address sidechain$_1$. These initialization parameters are stored by the respective smart contracts for future use. As the crosschain contract requires, the initialize method can only be called once. Any user wishing to utilize this sidechain is expected to validate that the contracts have been set up correctly and that initialize has been called with the appropriate parameters.

sidechain$_1$ contains a deposit function which is *payable* in the native asset of Ethereum, ETH. When a user pays ETH into the deposit function, the funds are held by the smart contract and can later be used to pay parties who wish to *withdraw*, an operation performed by calling the withdraw function. sidechain$_2$ contains similar deposit and withdraw functions which, however, do not pay in the native currency of Ethereum Classic, but instead maintain a balance mapping akin to a typical ERC20 implementation. The balance is updated when a user deposits or withdraws.

Algorithm 2. An asset transferring contract between $\mathcal{G}_1$ and $\mathcal{G}_2$

```
1:  contract sidechain₁ extends crosschain_{k,m,z}
2:      initialized ← false; ctr ← 0
3:      function initialize(𝒢₂, sidechain₂)
4:          if ¬initialized then
5:              crosschain.initialize(𝒢₂)   ▷ Initialize with the remote chain genesis block
6:              initialized ← true
7:              this.sidechain₂ ← sidechain₂
8:          end if
9:      end function
10:     payable function deposit(target)
11:         ▷ Emit an event to be picked up by remote contract
12:         ctr += 1
13:         emit Deposited₁(target, msg.value, ctr)
14:     end function
15:     function withdraw(amount, target, ctr)
16:         ▷ Validate that event took place on remote chain
17:         if ¬event-exists((sidechain₂, Deposited₂, (amount, target, ctr))) then
18:             return ⊥
19:         end if
20:         msg.sender.send(amount)
21:     end function
22: end contract
23: contract sidechain₂ extends crosschain_{k,m,z}; ERC20
24:     mapping(address ⇒ int) balances
25:     initialized ← false; ctr ← 0
26:     function initialize(𝒢₁, sidechain₁)
27:         if ¬initialized then
28:             crosschain.initialize(𝒢₁)
29:             initialized ← true
30:             this.sidechain₁ ← sidechain₁
31:         end if
32:     end function
33:     function deposit(target, amount)
34:         if balances[msg.sender] < amount then
35:             return ⊥
36:         end if
37:         balances[msg.sender] −= amount          ▷ Charge account of sender
38:         ctr += 1
39:         emit Deposited₂(target, amount, ctr)
40:     end function
41:     function withdraw(amount, target, ctr)
42:         if ¬event-exists((sidechain₁, Deposited₁, (amount, target, ctr))) then
43:             return ⊥
44:         end if
45:         balances[target] += amount              ▷ Credit target account
46:     end function
47: end contract
```

Moving funds from the Ethereum blockchain into the Ethereum Classic blockchain works as follows. First, the user pays with ETH to call the deposit function of sidechain$_1$ which resides on $\mathcal{G}_1$, passing the target parameter which indicates their address in the Ethereum Classic blockchain that they wish to receive the money into. This call emits an event, Deposited$_1$ which contains the necessary data: the target, the amount paid, as well as a nonce ctr to allow for future payments of the same amount to the same target. When the event has been emitted and buried under k_1 blocks within the Ethereum blockchain, the user produces an Ethereum NIPoPoW π_1 about the predicate e_1 which claims that the event Deposited$_1$ has been emitted in blockchain $\mathcal{G}_1$ with the particular parameters by the contract residing at address sidechain$_1$.

Subsequently, the user calls the submit-event-proof function of sidechain$_2$ (which is inherited from the crosschain contract), passing the NIPoPoW π_1 and the event predicate e_1 and paying collateral z, which registers e_1 on sidechain$_2$ as tentative. Because the user is honest, no adversary can produce a π_1^* which disproves their claim during the dispute period, and therefore the user waits for k_2 blocks for the contestation period to expire without any successful contestations. She then calls the finalize-event function for e_1 and receives back the collateral z, marking the event permanent. Finally, she calls the function withdraw of sidechain$_2$, passing it the same parameters that e_1 was issued with. The withdraw function checks that e_1 exists using the event-exists method, which will return true. The user is then credited with amount in their ETH20 balance stored in balances[target]. This increment in balance creates brand new ETH20 tokens. The withdraw function also stores the signature of the event parameters that have been spent to avoid replay attacks, which is not shown here for algorithm brevity.

The user can then transfer their ETH20 tokens by utilizing the functionality inherited from the ERC20 contract. When some (not necessarily the same) user is ready to move some (not necessarily the same) amount of ETH20 from the Ethereum Classic blockchain back into ETH on the Ethereum blockchain, they follow the reverse procedure: They call the withdraw function of sidechain$_2$ which ensures their ERC20 balance is sufficient, deduces the requested amount, and fires an event e_2 as before. At this point, these particular ETH20 tokens are destroyed by the balance deduction. Once e_2 is confirmed in $\mathcal{G}_2$, the user produces the NIPoPoW π_2 about e_2 which claims a payment was made within $\mathcal{G}_2$. That proof is then submitted to sidechain$_1$ by calling the submit-event-proof and finalize-event functions as before. Last, the user calls the withdraw function of sidechain$_1$, which uses the event-exists function which will return true, finally paying back the user the respective amount of ETH. Because the only way to create ETH20 tokens in sidechain$_2$ is by depositing ETH into sidechain$_1$, there will always exist a sufficient balance of ETH owned by the sidechains$_1$ smart contract to pay for any requested withdrawals.

Suppose now that an adversarial user makes a false claim that an event e took place in $\mathcal{G}_1$ and posts a relevant NIPoPoW π in $\mathcal{G}_2$. If an honest party is monitoring the chain $\mathcal{G}_2$ for the appearance of NIPoPoWs and the chain $\mathcal{G}_1$ for the firing of events, the fraudulence of π will be immediately obvious to them. They can subsequently generate a contesting NIPoPoW π^* providing a counter-claim that e did not occur. The honest party will broadcast this transaction at the beginning of the contestation period. Due to the *liveness* property of $\mathcal{G}_2$, the honest party will manage to include this transaction into $\mathcal{G}_2$ within one of the blocks before the end of the contestation period. The collateral z must be sufficient to incentivize an honest party to monitor $\mathcal{G}_1$ and $\mathcal{G}_2$ simultaneously, pay for transaction fees and ensure the time needed to generate a NIPoPoW π^* is small as compared to block generation time. The argument for $\mathcal{G}_2$ is analogous.

Conclusion. We gave the first trustless Proof-of-Work sidechain construction based on the NIPoPoWs primitive. We detailed the implementation of the verifier in the form of a Solidity smart contract. We described how cross-chain events can be used to give rise to two-way pegging, the original sidechains vision, and argued for the need of cryptoeconomic collateral to disincentivise dishonest behavior. Finally, we argued about the feasibility of our proposal and gave the prerequisites for its adoption.

References

1. Back, A., et al.: Enabling blockchain innovations with pegged sidechains (2014). http://www.opensciencereview.com/papers/123/enablingblockchain-innovations-with-pegged-sidechains
2. Buchman, E.: Tendermint: Byzantine fault tolerance in the age of blockchains. Ph.D. thesis (2016)
3. Buterin, V., et al.: A next-generation smart contract and decentralized application platform. White paper (2014)
4. Dwork, C., Naor, M.: Pricing via processing or combatting junk mail. In: Brick-ell, E.F. (ed.) CRYPTO 1992. LNCS, vol. 740, pp. 139–147. Springer, Heidelberg (1993). https://doi.org/10.1007/3-540-48071-4_10
5. Garay, J., Kiayias, A., Leonardos, N.: The bitcoin backbone protocol: analysis and applications. In: Oswald, E., Fischlin, M. (eds.) EUROCRYPT 2015. LNCS, vol. 9057, pp. 281–310. Springer, Heidelberg (2015). https://doi.org/10.1007/978-3-662-46803-6_10. Updated version at http://eprint.iacr.org/2014/765
6. Garay, J., Kiayias, A., Leonardos, N.: The bitcoin backbone protocol with chains of variable difficulty. In: Katz, J., Shacham, H. (eds.) CRYPTO 2017. LNCS, vol. 10401, pp. 291–323. Springer, Cham (2017). https://doi.org/10.1007/978-3-319-63688-7_10
7. The Interledger Payments Community Group: Interledger protocol v4. https://interledger.org/rfcs/0027-interledger-protocol-4/draft-5.html
8. Heilman, E., Kendler, A., Zohar, A., Goldberg, S.: Eclipse attacks on bitcoin's peer-to-peer network. Cryptology ePrint Archive, Report 2015/263 (2015). http://eprint.iacr.org/2015/263
9. Hosp, J., Hoenisch, T., Kittiwongsunthorn, P.: COMIT: cryptographically-secure off-chain multi-asset instant transaction network. https://www.comit.network/doc/COMIT%20white%20paper%20v1.0.2.pdf, 2017
10. Khalil, R., Gervais, A.: Nocust-a non-custodial 2nd-layer financial intermediary. Technical report, Cryptology ePrint Archive, Report 2018/642 (2018). https://eprint.iacr.org/2018/642

11. Kiayias, A., Lamprou, N., Stouka, A.-P.: Proofs of proofs of work with sublinear complexity. In: Clark, J., Meiklejohn, S., Ryan, P.Y.A., Wallach, D., Brenner, M., Rohloff, K. (eds.) FC 2016. LNCS, vol. 9604, pp. 61–78. Springer, Heidelberg (2016). https://doi.org/10.1007/978-3-662-53357-4_5
12. Kiayias, A., Miller, A., Zindros, D.: Non-interactive proofs of proof-of-work (2017)
13. Nakamoto, S.: Bitcoin: a peer-to-peer electronic cash system (2008)
14. Pass, R., Seeman, L., Shelat, A.: Analysis of the blockchain protocol in asynchronous networks. In: Coron, J.-S., Nielsen, J.B. (eds.) EUROCRYPT 2017. LNCS, vol. 10211, pp. 643–673. Springer, Cham (2017). https://doi.org/10.1007/978-3-319-56614-6_22
15. Poon, J., Buterin, V.: Plasma: scalable autonomous smart contracts. White paper (2017)
16. Inc Smart Contract Solutions: Openzeppelin crowdsale contract (2017). https://github.com/OpenZeppelin/openzeppelin-solidity/blob/v2.0.0-rc.1/contracts/token/ERC20/ERC20.sol
17. Vogelsteller, F., Buterin, V.: Erc 20 token standard (2015). https://github.com/ethereum/EIPs/blob/master/EIPS/eip-20.md
18. Wood, G.: Ethereum: a secure decentralised generalised transaction ledger. Ethereum Project Yellow Paper **151**, 1–32 (2014)
19. Wood, G.: Polkadot: vision for a heterogeneous multi-chain framework (2016)
20. Karl, W., Arthur, G.: Ethereum eclipse attacks. Technical report, ETH Zurich (2016)
21. Zamyatin, A., Harz, D., Lind, J., Panayiotou, P., Arthur, G., Knottenbelt, W.J.: Xclaim: interoperability with cryptocurrency-backed tokens
22. Zamyatin, A., Stifter, N., Judmayer, A., Schindler, P., Weippl, E., Knottenbelt, W.J.: A wild velvet fork appears! Inclusive blockchain protocol changes in practice. In: Zohar, A., et al. (eds.) FC 2018. LNCS, vol. 10958, pp. 31–42. Springer, Heidelberg (2019). https://doi.org/10.1007/978-3-662-58820-8_3
23. Zhang, F., Cecchetti, E., Croman, K., Juels, A., Shi, E.: Town crier: an authenticated data feed for smart contracts. In: Edgar, R.W, Stefan, K., Christopher, K., Andrew C.M., Shai, H. (eds.) ACM CCS 2016, pp. 270–282. ACM Press (2016)

You Sank My Battleship! A Case Study to Evaluate State Channels as a Scaling Solution for Cryptocurrencies

Patrick McCorry[1](✉), Chris Buckland[1], Surya Bakshi[2], Karl Wüst[3], and Andrew Miller[2]

[1] King's College London, London, UK
stonecoldpat@gmail.com
[2] University of Illinois at Urbana Champaign, Champaign, USA
[3] ETH Zurich, Zurich, Switzerland

Abstract. Off-chain protocols (or so-called Layer 2) are heralded as a scaling solution for cryptocurrencies. One prominent approach, state channels, allows a group of parties to transact amongst themselves and the global blockchain is only used as a last resort to self-enforce any disputed transactions. To evaluate state channels as a scaling solution, we provide a proof of concept implementation for a two-player battleship game. It fits a category of applications that are not considered reasonable to execute on the blockchain, but it is widely perceived as an ideal application for off-chain protocols. We explore the minimal modifications required to deploy the battleship game as a state channel and propose a new state channel construction, Kitsune, which combines features from existing constructions. While in the optimistic case we demonstrate the battleship game can be played efficiently in a state channel, the requirement for unanimous off-chain agreement introduces new economic and time-based attacks that can render the game as unreasonable to play.

1 Introduction

Since 2009, we have witnessed the rise of cryptocurrencies as the market capitalisation for all cryptocurrencies peaked to $1 trillion US dollars in December 2017. While Bitcoin was the first cryptocurrency designed to support financial transactions, another prominent cryptocurrency called Ethereum has emerged for executing programs called smart contracts. The promise of smart contracts is to support the execution of applications without human oversight or a central operator. Some applications proposed include decentralised (and non-custodial) token exchanges, publicly verifiable gambling games without dealers, auctions for digital goods without auctioneers, boardroom electronic voting without tallying authorities, etc.

Cryptocurrencies do not yet scale. Bitcoin can support approximately 7 transactions per second and Ethereum can support around 13 transactions per second. The lack of scalability is one of the primary hurdles preventing global adoption

© International Financial Cryptography Association 2020
A. Bracciali et al. (Eds.): FC 2019 Workshops, LNCS 11599, pp. 35–49, 2020.
https://doi.org/10.1007/978-3-030-43725-1_4

of cryptocurrencies as the network's transaction fee typically become unaffordable for most users whenever the transaction throughput ceiling is reached (i.e. the average fee in Bitcoin reached $20 in December 2017). The community is pursuing three approaches to scale the network which include new blockchain protocols, sharding the blockchain and off-chain protocols. New blockchain protocols can strictly increase the network's throughput [13,26,27], whereas sharding can be used to distribute transactions into processing areas such that peers only validate transactions that interest them [1,18,20]. However there is a trade-off between increasing the network's transaction throughput to support a larger userbase in terms of affordable fees, and the number of validators with the necessary computational resources to validate every transaction [16].

An alternative scaling approach consists of off-chain solutions to reduce the number of transactions processed by the blockchain. It lets a group of parties deposit coins in the blockchain for use within an off-chain application. Afterwards all parties can transact amongst themselves without interacting with the global network and the deposited coins are re-distributed depending on the application's outcome. Two proposals include an alternative blockchain (i.e. a sidechain) or a channel. A sidechain has block producers (i.e. miners or a single operator) for deciding the order of transactions and users who publish transactions for inclusion. There are several sidechain protocols [2,9] which bootstrap from Bitcoin (including a live network by RSK), whereas Plasma [23] and NOCUST [17] are non-custodial sidechains which bootstrap from Ethereum for financial transactions. While sidechains are a promising off-chain solution, they still require a blockchain protocol which has a transaction throughput ceiling.

On the other hand, a channel can be considered an n of n consensus protocol as all parties collectively authorise the state of an application amongst themselves. There is no blockchain protocol and all parties only store the most recently authorised state of the application. Channels first emerged in Bitcoin to support one-way payments between two parties [8,28], but has since evolved in Bitcoin towards the development of an off-chain payment network [24] by several companies including Blockstream, LND and ACINQ. At the same time, several proposals [4,5,10,11,19,21,22] collectively extend the capability of a channel to support a group of parties to execute a smart contract (i.e. a program) amongst themselves as opposed to simply payments. A state channel promises instant finality for every transaction and no transaction fees as there is no operator to reward. Channels are also self-enforcing as each party is protected against a full collusion of all other parties and in terms of scalability the throughput is only restricted by the network latency between the parties. The Ethereum Foundation has donated over $2.7 m [14] and the Ethereum Community Fund has donated $275k [15] to further explore state channels as a scaling solution.

In this paper, we present an empirical evaluation in the form of a case study for a single-application state channel which must be a viable scaling option before a network of state channels is conceivable. To aid this evaluation we have designed a two-player battleship game as a smart contract. An application like battleship is not typically considered viable to execute via the blockchain due to the quantity of transactions required and in our experiment we confirm this perception as the financial cost is between $16.27 and $24.05. However, state channels are perceived as a potential scaling solution to allow applications like battleship to be executed over the blockchain. Our contributions are as follows:

- We explore the minimal modifications required to deploy a single-application smart contract as a state channel and propose a template of modifications that can be adopted by others deploying state channels.
- We present a new state channel construction, Kitsune, which is application-agonostic, supports n parties and allows the channel to be turned off such that the application's progress can continue via the blockchain. This combines the constructions from [6, 10, 21, 22].
- We provide a proof of concept implementation to evaluate deploying applications within a state channel. This experiment highlights the worst-case scenario of state channels and how it potentially renders applications like battleship as unreasonable to deploy within a state channel.

2 Background

In this section, we provide background information about smart contracts and how the concept of a channel has evolved.

2.1 Smart Contracts

A smart contract can be viewed as a trusted third party with public state. It has a unique address on the network, it is instantiated based on the code supplied at the time of its creation, and all execution can be modelled as a state machine. Every transaction executes a command and this transitions the state machine $state_{i+1} = transition(state_i, cmd)$. All parties must replicate the program's entire execution in order to verify the blockchain and join the network. This mass-replication self-enforces a smart contract's correct execution and also implies that all data for the smart contract must be publicly accessible. Finally all computation by a smart contract is measured using a metric called gas and the sender of a transaction sets a desired gas price. The amount of gas used by a contract invocation multiplied by the gas price sets the transaction fee for incentivising a miner to include this transaction in their block.

2.2 Evolution of Channel Constructions

We present a high-level overview of a channel before exploring the evolution of channel constructions from Bitcoin for financial transactions to Ethereum for executing arbitary smart contracts.

High Level Overview. A channel lets n parties agree, via unanimous consent, to new states that could be published to the blockchain. As a result parties can transact amongst themselves instead of interacting via the global network. To set up, each party in the group must lock coins in the underlying blockchain for the channel. Afterwards all parties collectively execute state transitions and exchange signatures to authorise every new state (i.e. the balance of all parties, the state of a smart contract, etc.). If a single party does not co-operate to authorise a valid state transition, then the underlying blockchain is trusted to resolve disputed transactions and self-enforce the state transition. In the case of Bitcoin, the blockchain gurantees *the safety of coins for the online parties*, whereas in the case of a smart contract in Ethereum it also guarantees *liveness such that an application will always progress and eventually terminate.*

Payment Channels. Spilman proposed *replace by incentive* which is the first state replacement technique for a channel. It is designed for one-way payments from a sender to receiver [28] and the receiver is responsible for publishing the state that pays them the most coins. To support bi-directional payments, Decker proposed *replace by time lock* which decrements the channel's expiry time whenever the payment direction changes [8]. However both state replacement techniques require an expiry time which restricts the total number of transactions that can occur. Poon and Dryja proposed a third state replacement technique called *replace by revocation* for Lightning Channels [24]. It requires both parties to authorise each other's copy of the new state before sharing secrets to revoke the previously authorised state. Crucially, it introduced the concept of a dispute process where one party publishes an authorised state to close the channel and the blockchain provides a fixed dispute period for the counterparty to prove the published state is invalid. Raiden proposed the first payment channel construction for Ethereum which is effectively a pair of replace by incentive channels [25]. Unlike in Bitcoin, this construction has no expiry time and does not restrict the total number of payments within the channel, but it is still restricted to two parties and the channel's state only considers the balance of both parties.

State Channels. Both Sprites and Perun independently proposed a new state replacement technique called *replace-by-version* [10,22], but there is a subtle difference. Sprites introduced a *command transition state channel* which supports n parties and it always remains open. Its dispute process lets one party trigger a dispute by submitting a state, its version and a list of signatures to prove this state was authorised by every party. All parties are provided a fixed time period to submit commands and every accepted command is simply executed via the blockchain after the dispute process has expired. Perun introduced a *closure state channel* which supports 2 parties. It lets the channel close and for the application's execution to continue via the blockchain. Its dispute process can be triggered if one party submits a fully authorised state. All parties are provided a fixed time period to submit states with larger versions and after the dispute process the state with the largest version is considered the final off-chain agreed state. Pisa modified the Sprites construction such that a commitment (i.e. hash) of the new state is signed instead of the plaintext state, but the state channel is still responsible for accepting commands in plaintext. Perun and Counterfactual extend the concept of a state channel in two ways [5,10] First, they proposed the state within a channel can be organised in a hierarchy to support multiple-applications and the dispute process for one application does not impact other applications in the channel. Second, they proposed virtual channels which allow two parties without a direct and established channel to connect with each other using a network of channels. This requires all channels along the route to lock up collateral while the virtual channel is open.

3   Kitsune State Channel Construction

We propose, Kitsune, the first application-agnostic state channel construction SC. Kitsune focuses on the dispute process and it only considers the list of parties, signatures, a hash of the final state, and the version number. Like Sprites, it is designed to support n parties and follows the same dispute model of triggering a dispute, submitting evidence and then finally resolving the dispute. Like Perun, it simply focuses on deciding the final agreed off-chain state to close the channel. Finally we also propose an application template AC which will lock and unlock an application into a state channel upon the approval of all parties.

3.1   Overview of Kitsune

Briefly, all parties must approve to lock the application using AC.lock which disables all functionality and instantiates the state channel contract. All parties continue the application's execution off-chain by collectively signing the hash of every new state alongside an incremented version. The channel can be co-operatively turned off using SC.close, or any party can trigger the dispute process using SC.trigger. If triggered, all parties have a fixed time period to publish the state hash with the largest version using SC.setstatehash. After the dispute process has expired, any party can resolve the dispute using SC.resolve which stores the final state hash with the largest version. Any party can unlock the application by submitting the entire state in plaintext using AC.unlock. The application will hash the enite state, fetch the final state hash from the state channel contract using SC.getstatehash, and compares both hashes. If satisified, the full state is stored and all functionality in the application contract is re-enabled to permit executing it via the blockchain.

3.2   Kitsune State Channel Contract

We provide an overview of the state channel contract for Kitsune before discussing how to instantiate it, how parties collectively authorise new states off-chain and how the dispute process is used to confirm the final state hash.

Overview of the State Channel Contract. The state channel can be in one of three states which are status := {ON, DISPUTE, OFF}. All parties can collectively authorise new states for the application when the state channel is set as status := ON. Any party can trigger a dispute which sets the state as status := DISPUTE and this provides a fixed time period for all parties to submit an authorised state hash (and its corresponding version). Once the dispute is resolved or if the channel is closed co-operatively, then the state is set to status := OFF and this determines the final state hash for the application. If the channel is closed due to the dispute process, then a dispute record is stored which includes the starting time and finishing time for the dispute t_{start}, t_{end} and the final version i.

Creating the Channel. The application contract AC is responsible for instantiating the state channel contract with the list of participants $\mathcal{P}_1, ..., \mathcal{P}_n$ and the dispute timer $\Delta_{dispute}$. The state channel is set as status := ON and the application contract's functionality is disabled.

Authorising Off-Chain State Hashes. A command cmd is a function call within the application contract. Any party $\mathcal{P}$ can select a command cmd and propose a new state transition $state_{i+1} := transition(state_i, cmd)$. The new state is hashed with a blinding nonce[1] $hstate_{i+1} := H(state_{i+1}, r_{i+1})$ and signed $\sigma_{\mathcal{P}} := Sign(hstate_{i+1}, i + 1)$. To complete the state transition, the party sends $cmd, hstate_{i+1}, state_{i+1}, r_{i+1}$ and $\sigma_{\mathcal{P}}$ to all other parties for their approval. All other parties in the channel verify the state transition before authorising it. To verify, each party re-computes the transition $state'_{i+1} := transition(state_i, cmd)$ and state hash $hstate'_{i+1} := H(state'_{i+1}, r_{i+1})$. Then each party verifies the signature $VerifySig(\mathcal{P}, (hstate'_{i+1}, i+1), \sigma_{\mathcal{P}})$ and that the version is the largest received so far. If satisfied, each party signs the state hash $\sigma_k := Sign(hstate_{i+1}, i + 1, SC, AC)$ and sends this signature to all other parties. A new state hash is only considered valid when each party has received a signature from every other party. If one party does not receive all signatures by a local time-out, then this party can trigger the dispute process to turn off the channel, unlock the application and continue its execution via the blockchain.

Dispute Process. Any party can trigger the dispute process using SC.trigger. This self-enforces the dispute time period $t_{start} := t_{now}, t_{end} := t_{now} + \Delta_{dispute}$ and sets status := DISPUTE. All parties can submit the latest state hash, its version and the list of signatures to prove it was authorised using SC.setstatehash. The state channel contract SC only stores $hstate_i$ if it is signed by all parties and it has the largest version i received so far. After the dispute period has expired, any party can resolve it using SC.resolve. This sets status := OFF, stores a dispute record (t_{start}, t_{end}, i) and allows the application contract AC to fetch the final state hash $hstate_i$.

Co-operative Close. All parties can sign $\sigma_{\mathcal{P}} := Sign_{\mathcal{P}}('close', hstate_i, i, SC)$ and submit it to the state channel using SC.close. This stores the state hash $hstate_i$, its version i and sets status := OFF. No dispute is recorded in the contract.

---

[1] The blinding nonce is used for state privacy if resolving disputes is outsourced to an accountable third party as proposed by Pisa [21].

3.3   Application Contract Template

We present an application template that can be applied to easily add state channel support to an existing smart contract. It demonstrates how to lock all functionality in the application for use in the state channel and how to unlock all functionality to permit the application's execution to continue via the blockchain.

Overview of Template. After modifications, the application contract must explicitly record a list of participants $\mathcal{P}_1, ..., \mathcal{P}_n$, a dispute timer Δ_{dispute}, whether the state channel has been instantiated instantiated := {YES, NO} and if so it also stores the state channel's address SC. All functions within the application require a new pre-condition to check whether the state channel is instantiated and should only permit execution if instantiated = NO. Finally the application must include two new functions AC.lock that instantiates the state channel upon approval of all parties and AC.unlock that verifies a copy of the full state before re-enabling the application.

Lock Application Contract. All parties must agree to create the state channel by signing (ON, AC, Δ_{dispute}, lockno), where ON signals turning on the channel, lockno is an incremented counter to ensure freshness of the signed message and Δ_{dispute} is the fixed time period for the dispute process. Any party can call AC.lock with the list of signatures $\Sigma_{\mathcal{P}}$, Δ_{dispute} and lockno to turn on the state channel. The application contract AC verifies all signatures and that lockno represents the largest counter received so far. If satisfied, AC sets instantiated := YES and this disables all functionality within the application. Next AC creates the state channel contract SC which sets the list of participants $\mathcal{P}_1, ..., \mathcal{P}_n$ and the dispute timer Δ_{dispute}. Finally AC stores the state channel address SC.

Unlock Application Contract. After the dispute process has concluded in SC, one party must send state_i', r_i' using AC.unlock before the functionality can be re-enabled. The application contract verifies that state_i' indeed represents the final state by computing $\text{hstate}_i' := H(\text{state}_i', r_i')$, fetching the final state hash hstate_i from SC using SC.getstatehash and checking $\text{hstate}_i' = \text{hstate}_i$. If satisfied, AC stores state_i' and re-enables all functionality by setting instantiated := NO. Of course, if there is no activity within the state channel, then the state channel contract's dispute process can expiry without a submitted hstate_i. In this case, the application contract verifies the state channel returns $\emptyset$ and re-enables all functionality without modifying the existing state.

4   Applying the Application Template for Battleship

We explore how to apply the application template from Sect. 3.3 to a contract like battleship[2] such that it can be deployed within a state channel. Next we discuss workarounds (and pitfalls) discovered while building our proof of concept.

---

[2] Our battleship contract will be presented in an online version of this paper.

4.1   Minimal Modifications for a State Channel

We present how to modify the battleship contract before deployment in order to support state channels. This tracks whether a state channel was instantiated, the lock/unlock functionality to instantiate the state channel, a new pre-condition for every function in the game and how to handle functionality with side-effects in the off-chain contract.

Applying the Application Template. The application contract stores the dispute timer and a counter instance to track the number of times the state channel is turned on. It sets instantiated := NO and both players P_1, P_2 for use by the state channel. The pre-condition **discard if** instantiated = YES is included in every function except BS.unlock. If the pre-condition is satisfied, then all future transactions that interact with this function will fail. This disables all functionality within the application contract if it is locked and the state channel is turned on.

Lock and Unlock Functions. The lock function BS.lock requires a signature from both parties P_1, P_2 to authorise creating the state channel which is denoted as $\sigma_P^{lock} := \text{Sign}_P('lock', \text{chan}_{ctr}, \text{round}, \text{BS})$. Once the state channel is turned on, the battleship contract sets instantiated := YES, it creates a new state channel contract SC with the list of participants P_1, P_2 and the dispute timer $\Delta_{dispute}$. The unlock function BS.unlock allows any party to submit the final game state_i alongside the nonce r after the dispute process is resolved in the state channel contract. The battleship contract verifies if it corresponds to the final state hash accepted by the state channel contract using $H(\text{state}, r) == \text{SC.getstatehash}$. If successful, the full state is stored and the flag instantiated is set as NO. This re-enables all functionality in the battleship contract.

4.2   Workarounds for State Channel

Off-chain Contract. Our proof of concept requires each player to deploy an off-chain version of the battleship contract to a local blockchain to replicate (and verify) the execution of all state transitions. Without modifying the local blockchain instance, both the off-chain and on-chain battleship contracts have different addresses. This poses problems for our fraud proofs if a message is signed for the off-chain contract address as it will not be valid when the on-chain contract is re-activated. To alleviate this issue, we sign two messages for the on-chain and off-chain contract. However there is an upcoming new consensus rule [3] to deterministically derive the contract's address which simplifies deploying an off-chain contract with the same address.

Loss of a Global Clock. Both parties no longer share a global clock within the channel to self-enforce time-based events. We propose two approaches to handle time-dependent events. First, the time $t_{challenge}$ can be set by the player proposing a new state and the counterparty must verify the proposed time is within a range (i.e. a few minutes, or n blocks) before mutually authorising it. It must take into account the time required to turn off the channel via the dispute process and the time to initiate/settle the dispute such that $t_{challenge} := t_{now} + \Delta_{challenge} + \Delta_{dispute} + \Delta_{extra}$. An alternative approach is to set $t_{challenge}$ as $\perp$ for all updates within the state channel. Instead the time $t_{challenge}$ is set by battleship contract when it is re-activated in the blockchain using BS.unlock and if the game is in a relevant phase.

No External Interaction or Side-Effects. We define a side-effect as a state update that relies on an environmental variable or external interaction with another contract. This is because the side-effects will not persist when the application is re-activated on the blockchain. Some examples in Ethereum include the environment variables msg, block, tx, and transfering coins to another contract. All functions with side-effects should be deleted or disabled in the off-chain contract which for battleship includes the auxiliary functions BS.deposit and BS.withdraw.

Authenticating Transaction Signer and Replay Protection. The battleship contract relies on msg.sender to authenticate the immediate caller as the transaction signer. This requires the party to sign a transaction for execution in the counterparty's local blockchain. Ethereum transactions have a chain_id to prevent transactions signed for one blockchain being replayed to another blockchain. The counterparty can verify the transaction has set chain_id and it is destined for the off-chain contract address before executing it in their local blockchain. Finally the off-chain contract can also include a new BS.getstate to return the full state and the corresponding hstate, i.

Persistent Race Conditions. The gameplay for battleship is turn-based and it is clear which player is responsible for proposing every new state. Setting up the game using BS.select or BS.begingame has no order and both players may concurrently propose a state transition for the same version. In our case, both players can use a deterministic rule to resolve the race condition (i.e. $\mathcal{P}_1$ proposed state has priority) as the order of execution has no impact on the game's outcome. This highlights that race conditions in the underlying application are reflected in the state channel and can result in the state channel being turned off if the order of execution has an impact on the application's outcome.

Limitations Due to the EVM. The mapping data structure in Solidity for the Ethereum contract environment poses problems for the state channel as it cannot simply delete all key-value pairs. If a key-value pair is set to $\perp$ within the state channel, then this over-write must also occur when the full state is sent to the contract. Otherwise, the key-value pair will persist in the application contract after the state channel is turned off. For example, if a party's balance is set to $\perp$ off-chain, but this isn't reflected in the on-chain contract, then this party can withdraw more coins than they deserve.

Table 1. Costs of running the battleship game within the state channel. We have approximated the cost in USD (\$) using the conversion rate of 1 ether = \$306 and the gas price of 2.6 Gwei which are the real world costs in September 2018.

Step	Purpose	Gas Cost	\$\$
Battleship game			
1	Create BattleshipCon without State Channel	10,020,170	7.97
2	Deposit (BS.deposit)	44,247	0.04
3	Place bet (BS.placebet)	34,687	0.03
4	Select counterparty's ships (BS.select)	422,894	0.34
5a	Ready to play (BS.begingame)	47,651	0.04
5b	Do not play (BS.quitgame)	388,805	0.31
6	Attack (BS.attackcell)	69,260	0.06
7a	Reveal cell (BS.opencell)	73,252	0.06
7b	Reveal ship (BS.sunk)	111,372	0.09
8	Open ships (BS.openships)	159,748	0.13
9	Finish game (BS.finish)	275,521	0.22
10	Withdraw (BS.withdraw)	36,674	0.03
11	Fraud: Ships at same cell (BS.celltwoships)	280,766	0.22
12	Fraud: Declared not hit (BS.declarednothit)	284,261	0.23
13	Fraud: Declared not miss (BS.declarednothit)	284,654	0.23
14	Fraud: Declared not sunk (BS.declarednotsunk)	312,481	0.25
15	Fraud: Attack same cell (BS.attacksamecell)	100,861	0.08
16	Challenge period expired (BS.expiredchallenge)	75,349	0.06
State channel			
17	Create BattleshipCon with State Channel	13,607,0695	10.83
18	Lock (BS.lock)	991,617	0.79
19	Trigger dispute (SC.trigger)	84,106	0.07
20	Set state hash (SC.setstatehash)	70,035	0.06
21	Resolve (SC.resolve)	89,745	0.07
21	Co-operative turnoff (SC.close)	90,354	0.07
22a	Unlock (BS.unlock)	725,508	0.6
22b	Unlock (No Activity) (BS.unlock)	51,454	0.04
Aggregated statistics			
Turn state channel on and off		1,961,011	1.56
Average case for game		20,451,633	16.27
Worst case for game		30,237,372	24.05

Table 2. Time taken to propose, verify and acknowledge new state transitions, measured in milliseconds (ms) and calculated as an average over 100 runs.

Purpose	Propose	Verify	Acknowledge
Place bet (BS.placebet)	232.18	212.23	0.44
Select counterparty's ships (BS.select)	330.59	304.70	0.44
Ready to play (BS.begingame)	243.70	224.51	0.44
Attack (BS.attackcell)	267.09	243.69	0.35
Reveal cell (BS.opencell)	268.93	248.51	0.40
Reveal ship (BS.sunk)	291.25	276.97	0.38
Open ships (BS.openships)	288.75	258.70	0.35
Finish game (BS.finish)	376.05	349.20	0.30

5 Proof of Concept Implementation

We present a proof of concept implementation for our battleship game within a state channel[3]. The experiment was performed using a Dell XPS 13 with Intel Core i5-7200U CPU @ 2.50 GHz processor and 8GB LPDDR3 on a private Ethereum node using Ganache. In the following we discuss Table 1 which outlines the gas costs for our proposed modifications and Table 2 which presents a timing analysis to propose, verify and acknowledge a state transition within the channel.

Our experiment involves three contracts which includes the unmodified battleship contract (Step 1), the battleship contract after applying the application template (Step 15) and the state channel contract (Step 16). Deploying both the modified and unmodified battleship contract highlights the cost for modifying an application contract to support a state channel is approximately 1 million gas. A single game of battleship (Steps 4–9) via the blockchain costs $16.27 (approx 20 million gas) where each player takes 65 shots[4]. In the worst case, the game requires one player to take 99 shots, and the counterparty to take 100 shots. This worst-case costs $24.05 (approx 30 million gas) to finish the game. Locking the battleship game, creating the state channel, performing the dispute process costs and unlocking the battleship game costs $1.56 (approx 1 million gas). The cost for each fraud proof is presented in Steps 11–14 and only one fraud proof is required per game to prove the counterparty has cheated.

All timings in Table 2 are approximations. We focus on the time taken to propose a new state transition, the time required for the counterparty to verify a state transition and for the initial proposer to verify the signed new state which is an acknowledgement from the counterparty that the state transition is complete. Proposing a new state takes between 232–376 ms. This includes creating and signing a transaction at 12 ms, executing the transaction within

---

[3] Anonymous code: https://www.dropbox.com/s/o5s5k662h9lqlk4/Battleship.zip?dl=0.

[4] This number of shots is based on the better than random algorithm in [7].

a local blockchain which is between 35–179 ms (i.e. it depends on the function executed), retrieving the full new state from the local blockchain at 172 ms, preparing a transaction for the counterparty and signing the full state's hash at 15 ms. The state hash and signature is sent to the counterparty which incurs typical network latency. The counterparty takes between 212–349 ms to verify a state transition which includes verifying the received transaction's signature (and checking it is destined for the off-chain contract) at 8 ms, executing the received transaction within the local blockchain which is between 34–163 ms, retrieving the full new state from the local blockchain at 171 ms, verifying the signature for the received state hash and verifying it matches the newly computed state hash at 0.4 ms, and finally signing the new state hash at 4 ms. The counterparty sends the corresponding signature for the new state hash back to the proposer which incurs typical network latency. Finally the proposer must verify the signature from the counterparty which takes 0.4 ms. Overall, while the timings are reasonable for real-world use, the most expensive operations involve interacting with the Ganache client.

6   Discussion and Future Work

Supporting Third Party Watching Services. To alleviate the security assumption that all parties must remain online and synchronised with the blockchain to watch for disputes, PISA [21] proposed that parties can hire an accountable third party to watch the channel on their behalf. The application-agnostic design of the new state channel construction Kitsune is beneficial to PISA as the accountable third party is only required to verify the state channel contract's bytecode (and not the application) before accepting a job from the customer. Tthe accountable third party only requires a signature from every party in the channel $\Sigma_{\mathcal{P}}$, the state hash hstate and the version i to resolve disputes on the customer's behalf.

Funfair Dilemma. There is a chicken-and-egg problem on whether state channels should create and destroy applications off-chain, or if the state channel should first require an application to already exist on the blockchain. Perun and Counterfactual advocate for the former to minimise the up front cost of creating the channel, whereas Funfair are pursing the latter to minimise cost of resolving a dispute as only the application's state is kept off-chain. Fundamentally both approaches have a different trust assumption on the likelihood one party will trigger a dispute and whether the financial cost to resolve a dispute can interfere with the application. This dilemma can be summed up in a single question:

If the player is about to win a $10 bet, but the counterparty has stopped responding in the channel, then is it worthwhile for the player to turn off the channel, complete the dispute process, re-activate the application and win the bet via the blockchain if this process costs $100?

To evaluate this dilemma, our case study highlights that it costs $1.56 to resolve the dispute and submit the full game state to the contract which is an affordable (and reasonable) cost. However it does not consider the cost to deploy and instantiate the battleship game at $7.97, the continued cost for both players to play battleship or the remaining time required to finish playing it.

Dominant Strategy to Force-Close. Let's consider the worst-case for battleship. Both players set up the game with an expectation to play it within the state channel, but afterwards one player triggers a dispute to turn off the channel and the game must be finished via the blockchain. To play the entire game costs between $16.27 to $24.05 and every move requires a reasonable time period for moves to be accepted into the blockchain. If it is set to 5 min per move and the game requires 200 transactions, then the game may take several hours (i.e. 16 h) to complete. This can be considered a dominant strategy by an adversarial player as it is likely rational players will simply forfeit their deposit (and bet) to quit the game early.

Inducing Cooperative Behaviour. There is no mechanism to distinguish why a channel broke down, i.e. a blockchain cannot distinguish if Alice refused to sign and send Bob the latest state, or if Bob claims that he did not received a signed update. This makes it non-trivial to build a reputation system as it is unclear which party was at fault for the channel's failure and if any reasonable action can be taken to penalise the party at fault. To workaround the inability to identify the misbehaving party, future work must focus on how to induce cooperative behaviour amongst all parties in the channel. Any mechanism should not let an adversarial player to force-close a channel to their advantage (i.e. expecting rational players to simply give up). On the other hand, it must be careful not to discourage honest parties from closing the channel and continuing the application's execution via the blockchain.

Self-inspection of Blockchain Congestion. On 6th January 2018, we witnessed the network's transaction fee spike to 95,788,574,583 wei [12][5] as the network became congested due to a significant increase in transaction throughput. Congestion impacts state channels as it increases the cost for resolving disputes (i.e. $57.58 for battleship) and continuing the application's execution (between $599 and $886 for battleship). If the increased transaction fees are not paid, then it is probable that a transaction will not be accepted into the blockchain within the dispute time period. Future work should focus on a new operation code (i.e. CheckCongestion()) that can retrospectively self-inspect the previous k of n blocks to determine if it was affordable for an honest party's transaction to be accepted into the blockchain. This could be used to extend the time period for resolving disputes and let players wait until the network is no longer congested before continuing the application's execution.

---

[5] The congestion was caused by a popular game called Cryptokitties.

What to Consider Before Deploying a State Channel. State channels require unanimous consent for an application's execution to progress off-chain. This implies an all parties should be involved throughout the entire application's execution or permit parties to leave via the blockchain without closing the channel. The developer must take care to ensure the application can gracefully handle (or remove) all race conditions. As well, they must be mindful the off-chain state size does not grow significantly which may prevent its publication to the blockchain. The application should be self-contained, not rely on any side-effects, and explicitly consider how to handle time-based events. Finally to guarantee liveness, it must always be reasonable to continue an application's execution via the blockchain.

Applicable Applications. Our case study demonstrates that applications like battleship are not suitable for state channels due to the liveness requirement. Instead it appears that state channels are only useful for applications that are already suitable for execution via the blockchain and it only involves a small number of parties who can remain online throughout the application's life-time. It is also beneficial if all parties want to repeat the application's execution more than once such that the additional overhead to set up the channel costs less than simply executing it via the blockchain. Some potential applications include payments, casino games, boardroom elections and auctions. We conclude that a state channel should be viewed as an optimistic scaling approach only if all parties are willing to cooperate.

References

1. Al-Bassam, M., Sonnino, A., Bano, S., Hrycyszyn, D., Danezis, G.: Chainspace: a sharded smart contracts platform. arXiv preprint arXiv:1708.03778 (2017)
2. Back, A., et al.: Enabling blockchain innovations with pegged sidechains (2014)
3. Buterin, V.: EIP 1014: Skinny CREATE2. https://eips.ethereum.org/EIPS/eip-1014. Accessed 08 Sept 2018
4. Close, T., Stewart, A.: Force move games. https://magmo.com/force-move-games.pdf. Accessed 08 Sept 2018
5. Coleman, J., Horne, L., Xuanji, L.: Counterfactual: generalized state channels (2018)
6. Croman, K.: On scaling decentralized blockchains. In: Clark, J., Meiklejohn, S., Ryan, P.Y.A., Wallach, D., Brenner, M., Rohloff, K. (eds.) FC 2016. LNCS, vol. 9604, pp. 106–125. Springer, Heidelberg (2016). https://doi.org/10.1007/978-3-662-53357-4_8
7. DataGenetics: Battleship. http://www.datagenetics.com/blog/december32011/. Accessed 08 Sept 2018
8. Decker, C., Wattenhofer, R.: A fast and scalable payment network with Bitcoin duplex micropayment channels. In: Pelc, A., Schwarzmann, A.A. (eds.) SSS 2015. LNCS, vol. 9212, pp. 3–18. Springer, Cham (2015). https://doi.org/10.1007/978-3-319-21741-3_1
9. Dilley, J., Poelstra, A., Wilkins, J., Piekarska, M., Gorlick, B., Friedenbach, M.: Strong federations: an interoperable blockchain solution to centralized third-party risks. arXiv preprint arXiv:1612.05491 (2016)

10. Dziembowski, S., Eckey, L., Faust, S., Malinowski, D.: PERUN: virtual payment channels over cryptographic currencies. Technical report, IACR Cryptology ePrint Archive, 2017: 635 (2017)
11. Dziembowski, S., Faust, S., Hostáková, K.: General state channel networks. Cryptology ePrint Archive, Report 2018/320 (2018). https://eprint.iacr.org/2018/320
12. Etherscan. Ethereum gas price.: https://etherscan.io/chart/gasprice. Accessed 08 Sept 2018
13. Eyal, I., Gencer, A.E., Sirer, E.G., Van Renesse, R.: Bitcoin-NG: a scalable blockchain protocol. In: NSDI, pp. 45–59 (2016)
14. Ethereum Foundation: Ethereum foundation grants update - wave III. https://blog.ethereum.org/2018/08/17/ethereum-foundation-grants-update-wave-3/. Accessed 08 Sept 2018
15. Ethereum Community Fund: Meet the grantees ECF class of 2018 Part II. https://medium.com/ecf-review/meet-the-grantees-ecf-class-of-2018-part-ii-ff46a284a0b1. Accessed 08 Sept 2018
16. Gervais, A., Karame, G.O., Wüst, K., Glykantzis, V., Ritzdorf, H., Capkun, S.: On the security and performance of proof of work blockchains. In: Proceedings of the 2016 ACM SIGSAC Conference on Computer and Communications Security, pp. 3–16. ACM (2016)
17. Khalil, R., Gervais, A.: Nocust-a non-custodial 2nd-layer financial intermediary
18. Kokoris-Kogias, E., Jovanovic, P., Gasser, L., Gailly, N., Syta, E., Ford, B.: OmniLedger: a secure, scale-out, decentralized ledger via sharding. In: 2018 IEEE Symposium on Security and Privacy (SP), pp. 583–598. IEEE (2018)
19. ScaleSphere Foundation Ltd.: Celer network: bring internet scale to every blockchain. https://www.celer.network/doc/CelerNetwork-Whitepaper.pdf. Accessed 08 Sept 2018
20. Luu, L., Narayanan, V., Zheng, C., Baweja, K., Gilbert, S., Saxena, P.: A secure sharding protocol for open blockchains. In: Proceedings of the 2016 ACM SIGSAC Conference on Computer and Communications Security, pp. 17–30. ACM (2016)
21. McCorry, P., Bakshi, S., Bentov, I., Miller, A., Meiklejohn, S.: Pisa: arbitration outsourcing for state channels. IACR Cryptology ePrint Archive, 2018:582 (2018)
22. Miller, A., Bentov, I., Kumaresan, R., McCorry, P.: Sprites: payment channels that go faster than lightning. CoRR abs/1702.05812 (2017)
23. Joseph P., Buterin, V.: Plasma: scalable autonomous smart contracts. White paper (2017)
24. Poon, J., Dryja, T.: The Bitcoin lightning network: scalable off-chain instant payments. Draft version 0.5, 9:14 (2016)
25. Raiden: Raiden network. https://github.com/raiden-network/raiden-contracts/blob/d3c30e6d081ac3ed8fbf3f16381889baa3963ea7/raiden_contracts/contracts/TokenNetwork.sol. Accessed 08 Sept 2018
26. Sompolinsky, Y., Lewenberg, Y., Zohar, A.: SPECTRE: a fast and scalable cryptocurrency protocol. IACR Cryptology ePrint Archive, 2016:1159 (2016)
27. Sompolinsky, Y., Zohar, A.: Secure high-rate transaction processing in Bitcoin. In: Böhme, R., Okamoto, T. (eds.) FC 2015. LNCS, vol. 8975, pp. 507–527. Springer, Heidelberg (2015). https://doi.org/10.1007/978-3-662-47854-7_32
28. Spilman, J.: [Bitcoin-development] anti Dos for tx replacement. https://lists.linuxfoundation.org/pipermail/bitcoin-dev/2013-April/002433.html. Accessed 08 Sept 2018

Game-Theoretic Analysis
of an Incentivized Verifiable
Computation System

Mahmudun Nabi[(✉)], Sepideh Avizheh,
Muni Venkateswarlu Kumaramangalam, and Reihaneh Safavi-Naini

University of Calgary, Calgary, AB, Canada
{mahmudun.nabi1,sepideh.avizheh1,munivenkateswarlu.ku,rei}@ucalgary.ca

Abstract. Outsourcing computation allows a weak client to outsource its computation to a powerful server and receive the result of the computation. Verifiable outsourcing enables clients to verify the computation result of untrusted servers. Permissionless distributed outsourcing systems provide an attractive marketplace for users to participate in the system as a problem-giver who needs solution to a problem, or problem-solver who is willing to sell its computational resources. Verification of computation in these systems, that do not assume trusted computational nodes, is a challenging task. In this paper we provide a game-theoretic analysis of an incentivized outsourcing computation system, proposed by Harz and Boman [Harz *et al.* 2018] (HB), at WTSC 2018 (FC Workshop), and show that the system is vulnerable to collusion and Sybil attacks, that result in incorrect solutions to be accepted by the system. We also show that malicious computational node can succeed in polluting the blockchain. We propose modifications to the system that incentivizes honest behavior, and improve the system's correctness guarantee. We provide a high-level analysis of the modified system using our game theoretic approach, and show the effectiveness of the proposed modifications.

Keywords: Outsourcing computation · Verifiable distributed computation · Rational adversaries · Incentivized security

1 Introduction

Outsourcing computation is an intriguing concept that enables clients to expand their computational power when needed. The rise of cloud computing in recent years has been the driving force of outsourcing computation in a variety of settings. Outsourcing to cloud has made computationally expensive applications, such as complex analytics, available to small mobile devices, and has enabled clients to run resource intensive applications by purchasing the required computational resources from cloud providers. In both these cases the user interacts

A. Bracciali et al. (Eds.): FC 2019 Workshops, LNCS 11599, pp. 50–66, 2020.
https://doi.org/10.1007/978-3-030-43725-1_5

with a single cloud provider, and the service is paid for indirectly (e.g. through purchase of a device), or directly, from the cloud. The idea of computation as a commodity that can be bought and sold in a market-place has gained attraction with the development of cryptocurrencies that enable payment for services using blockchains. Outsourcing however has many security and privacy challenges. The outsourcer (O) and the computational nodes (contractors) in general are not mutually trusting, and each party may attempt to subvert the system for their own goals. The most basic security goal of the outsourcer is the correctness of the computation. Verifiable computation enables the outsourcer to verify the correctness of the result using efficient verification algorithms. Cryptographic schemes for verifiable computation [5,10,13] guarantee high level of security but are inflexible and incur heavy computational cost. A second approach is by assuming rational adversaries and designing mechanisms to incentivize honest behavior, and guarantee correctness of the results [2,7,9,12]. These systems however need complex management processes (e.g. managing rewards, punishments, auditing) to arrive at the correct result, and so may not be appealing to average user.

Two recently proposed systems, TrueBit [8,14], and a system proposed by Harz and Boman (HB) [6], attempt to remove this complexity introducing an intermediate layer between the outsourcer and the contractors. The intermediate layer receives a request from the outsourcer, recruits contractors, and runs a public protocol with the guarantee that correct results will be delivered to the outsourcer, and that the contractors are paid for their services. Both systems are implemented in Ethereum platform, and use the trustable computation of Ethereum as the ultimate truth in arriving at the correct result. The goal is to achieve the same correctness guarantee of Ethereum while minimizing the actual request from computation Ethereum. This can be seen as performing computation "off-chain", and use Ethereum to verify the results.

The correctness guarantee in both systems relies on rewards, bounties, jackpots and similar incentives, and assumes rational entities. TrueBit has a detailed white paper that discusses possible attacks, which are further discussed in blog posts, and other platforms. HB paper provides a high level argument about possible attacks and security of the system. None of the systems have formal game theoretic analysis in part due to the complexity of modelling the range of attack goals and colluding strategies in a highly distributed and permissionless systems.

Our Work. Our motivation is to provide game a theoretic framework for analysis of non-permissioned incentivized verifiable computation systems that use an intermediate layer. The variety of attack goals and possible collusions, make this analysis a daunting task. We start with HB, which compared to TrueBit, uses stronger trust assumptions which makes in more amenable to analysis. The HB system, is implemented as the *Arbiter*, an Ethereum smart contract that enforces the execution of the required steps of the verifiable computation process.

In HB, there is an outsourcer, called *problem-giver*, who outsources a computation. Following [2,9], we assume that the outsourced computation is composed of a finite number of atomic operations. Also, we define the inner state of an algorithm as the concatenation of all the input/outputs of the atomic operations of the algorithm. Computational nodes (contractors) are *problem-solvers* and *verifiers*, the former providing a solution to the outsourced computation, and the latter verifying the solution.

Our game theoretic analysis of HB system, although primarily focuses on the *rational* contractors (solver and verifiers) that have well-defined utilities, will also allow us to evaluate security against *irrational* behaviour where contractors are not driven by their utilities. This approach was first considered in [2,9] in which each contractor may behave rationally (*diligent* or *lazy*), or be *honest* or *malicious* irrespective of their utilities. In Sect. 6 we also consider goal driven contractors (irrational and malicious) who are not bounded by a utility function. The goal of these malicious contractors is to corrupt the blockchain.

For rational behaviors, we first derive a payoff matrix for the HB system when each contractor behaves independently (chooses to be diligent or lazy on its own), assuming the same q-algorithm is used by all lazy contractors. Table 2 shows the payoff of a solver and verifier when the set of other verifiers consist of all lazy, all diligent, or a combination of the two. The analysis shows that, depending on the system parameters, for an independent contractor (solver/verifier) being diligent results in the highest utility. To analyze the system, we consider all possible scenario in the system, for instance, one contractor (solver/verifier) being diligent or lazy against the rest of the system that is lazy and, show that being diligent is better for an independent contractor (see Sect. 4.1).

We then consider collusions where the colluding contractors agree to follow a single behavior (diligent or lazy), and share the reward equally. We obtain the system's payoff matrix when the set of N contractors, that are chosen by the Arbiter, consists of a colluding set, and two sets of contractors that are working lazily and diligently, but without any coordination (independently choosing their behaviour). Our analysis shows that, being part of a collusion maximizes a contractor's utility. We also analyze the system for Sybil attacks where a single contractor participate in the system using multiple identities (see Sect. 4.2). Our analysis shows that existing incentive structure of HB system cannot guarantee correct result.

In Sect. 5 we propose modifications to the HB system with the goal of improving the correctness guarantee. These consists of modifications that are necessary to ensure the incentives for diligent behavior to guarantee correct result, and make the system robust against the lazy behavior in both collusion and Sybil attacks. In HB, if all the contractors (independently or colluding) return the same incorrect results, the Arbiter accepts this as a correct result. We propose changes to HB system and show that the modified system alleviates such vulnerabilities and, guarantees high correctness (see Sect. 5). These modifications although improve the correctness of HB system but does not prevent collusion and Sybil attacks. We also propose modifications that would intuitively make the system more socially fair. In particular using the deposits of the lazy contractors to encourage diligent behavior.

Paper Organization: Sect. 2 gives an overview of the HB system, and Sect. 3 presents its game analysis. In Sect. 4, two attacks (collusion and Sybil) using different attack strategies are analyzed. Our modifications of HB system and their analysis are in Sects. 5 and 6, respectively. Section 7 is the related work, and Sect. 8 concludes the paper.

2   HB System

Ethereum is a permissionless blockchain that is known as *consensus computer*, meaning that a computation that is sent to Ethereum will be executed by all agents and as long as more than 50% of agents are honest, the computation result will be correct. To prevent attacks such as denial of service however, Ethereum introduces a gas limit to put a bound on the complexity of the requested computation, and so larger computations must be performed off-chain. HB [6] aims to extend correctness guarantee of Ethereum to off-chain computations.

Table 1. HB incentive structure for different behaviors of a solver and verifier

Verifier V	Solver S	
	Incorrect	Correct
Challenge	S: receives nothing, loses D_s V: receives $v_{fee} + s_{fee}$ + fee shares of all accepting verifiers (accepting verifiers receives nothing, loses D_v)	S: receives s_{fee} + fee shares of all challenging verifiers V: receives nothing, loses D_v (accepting verifiers receives v_{fee})
Accept	S: receives s_{fee} V: receives v_{fee}	S receives s_{fee} V: receives v_{fee}

The entities of the HB system are: *Problem-giver, Problem-solver, Verifier, Arbiter* and the *Judge*. Problem-givers are Ethereum users who outsource their computations for rewards. The solver is a computational contractor who provides computation power to solve computation problems in exchange for receiving a reward, s_{fee}. Verifiers are computational contractors who are contracted to provide computation power to correctly verify the solver's solutions for a reward, v_{fee}, by redoing the computation. Both these types of contractors must pay a deposit to participate in the computation. Arbiter is an Ethereum smart contract that enforces the execution of the required steps of the verifiable computation process. Arbiter acts as an *intermediary* between the problem-giver and the other entities. For each computation request that it receives from problem-giver, Arbiter randomly selects N contractors from the pool of registered contractors, and randomly chooses one as the problem-solver and the remaining $(N-1)$ as verifiers $V = \{v_1, \ldots, v_{N-1}\}$. The solver publishes a solution together with a hashed trace of computation in the form of a Merkle tree to allow efficient checking of the results. The assumption is that the computational steps run by different contractors will produce the same values and so the same hashes. Verifiers also perform the computation and construct their own local hash tree, and publish the solution. The solution that is provided by the solver will be challenged by the verifiers who find inconsistencies between solver's solution and their own. Arbiter compares the provided solutions and initiate a dispute resolution if the solutions do not match, in which case a step-by-step comparison of the hash tree of the solver and a verifier is performed, and inconsistencies will be resolved by sending a random computational step to the Ethereum (Judge). Judge resolves the dispute and find whether the solver's computation is correct or not. If it is correct, the process continues as long as a verifier challenges the solver's solution. After all challenges are resolved, the problem-giver receives the results of the computation. If the solver is found incorrect the computation terminates.HB assumes that *Arbiter, judges and problem-givers are trusted and correctly follow the protocol.* Table 1 shows the distribution of rewards in HB for different behaviors of a solver and verifier.

3   Game-Theoretic Analysis of HB

In HB, a problem-giver outsources its computation to a registered subset of contractors who are randomly selected by Arbiter. The registration fee of the contractors will be returned if they are not caught violating the verifiable computation algorithm. The deposits of the selected contractors will be used as part of rewards and fines that will be applied to the contractors, in addition to the fee which will be paid by the problem-giver to the contractors whose work have not been challenged. We assume a contractor will participate in a computation when the received reward is higher than the cost of performing the task. A rational contractor, solver or verifier, perform the computation honestly as long as the utility of performing the task correctly is greater than doing it otherwise. A *diligent* rational contractor performs the task honestly, and returns the correct result. A *lazy* contractor *uses a tricky algorithm* that can return the correct result with probability q (see Definition 1).

Definition 1 (q-algorithm). *An algorithm, composed of a finite number of atomic operations, is called a* q*-algorithm if it generates the correct solution with probability q, and such that $0 \leq cost(q) < cost(1)$. Here, $cost(q)$ denotes the cost of employing a* q*-algorithm and $cost(1)$ is the cost of the honest computation.*

We assume that the chance of a guessed solution being correct is nearly zero. In HB a solution will be accompanied with the hash tree of the computation steps. Thus even if the q-algorithm can find the solution, the chance of generating the same inner state hashes as the original algorithm, will be *negligible* (i.e., $q \approx 0$). The inner state of an algorithm can be captures at different granularity and will include the computational module input and output. *We also assume all lazy nodes use the same (best) q-algorithm.*

Payoffs When Contractors Behave Independently. We consider a multi-contractor game with one solver s and $N-1$ verifiers $\mathcal{V} = \{v_1, \ldots, v_{N-1}\}, N > 1$, and assume each contractor chooses its behaviour independently. The fee for a solver's correct solution is s_{fee} and so a diligent solver will always receive this fee. The fee for a verifier whose result is accepted by the Arbiter is v_{fee}. If a lazy contractor is caught (with probability $1 - q$), his reward is distributed to contractors who have challenged it.

We first analyze the system *assuming contractors work independently*. Let $u_z^{x,y}(q)$ denotes the *utility function of a contractor of type x, whose behavior is of type y, when there are total z lazy contractors (among the selected contractors) for the given computation*. We use $x \in \{s, v, c\}$, where s denotes the solver, v denotes the verifier and c denotes the colluder, $y \in \{d, \ell\}$ where d and ℓ denote the diligent and lazy behaviors, respectively, and $z \in \{0, 1, \ldots, N\}$. For diligent contractors, $q = 1$, otherwise $q < 1$. Also, the utility of any contractor $u_z^{x,y}(q)$ is linear in the reward and losses. Table 2 shows the utility of contractors.

If a contractor of type x behaves diligently, and challenges a lazy contractor's incorrect solution, its utility will be, $u_z^{x,d}(1) = r + b(1 - q) - cost(1)$, where r denotes the reward for honest computation, $r = s_{fee}$ if $x = s$ or $r = v_{fee}$ if $x = v$, and b will be the additional reward (reward share of the lazy contractor) that a diligent contractor receive by challenging the lazy contractor. A lazy contractor cannot win a challenge against a diligent contractor because Ethereum will be used as the ultimate truth. In HB, a solver can challenge the verifiers, and the verifiers can challenge the solver. But, a verifier cannot challenge the other verifier. If a contractor x is lazy its utility is, $u_z^{x,l}(q) = rq - f(1 - q) - cost(q)$, where f is the fine that a lazy contractor, who is caught, pays for providing an incorrect solution. As long as there is one diligent contractor, the system's final result will be correct and all the lazy contractor will be caught. Table 2 gives the payoff matrix of the game. Using the Table 2, in Sect. 4 we analyze the HB system for collusion and Sybil attacks.

Table 2. The payoff table of a solver against all verifiers, when each contractor (s and v) choose their behaviour (diligent or lazy) independently, assuming all lazy contractors use the same q-algorithm.

Verifiers	Solver	
	Diligent	Lazy
k_2 lazy ($k_3 = N - 1 - k_2$ diligent)	$u_{k_2}^{s,d}(1) = s_{fee} + k_2 v_{fee}(1-q) - cost(1)$ $u_{k_2}^{v,d}(1) = v_{fee} - cost(1)$ $u_{k_2}^{v,l}(q) = v_{fee}q - D_v(1-q) - cost(q)$	$u_{k_2+1}^{s,l}(q) = s_{fee}q - D_s(1-q) - cost(q)$ $u_{k_2+1}^{v,d}(1) = v_{fee} + \frac{s_{fee} + k_2 \cdot v_{fee}}{k_3}(1-q) - cost(1)$ $u_{k_2+1}^{v,l}(q) = v_{fee}q - D_v(1-q) - cost(q)$
All diligent ($k_2 = 0$, $k_3 = N - 1$)	$u_0^{s,d}(1) = s_{fee} - cost(1)$ $u_0^{v,d}(1) = v_{fee} - cost(1)$	$u_1^{s,l}(q) = s_{fee}q - D_s(1-q) - cost(q)$ $u_1^{v,d}(1) = v_{fee} + \frac{s_{fee}}{k_3}(1-q) - cost(1)$
All lazy ($k_2 = N - 1$, $k_3 = 0$)	$u_{N-1}^{s,d}(1) = s_{fee} + k_2 v_{fee}(1-q) - cost(1)$ $u_{N-1}^{v,l}(q) = v_{fee}q - D_v(1-q) - cost(q)$	$u_N^{s,l}(q) = s_{fee} - cost(q)$ $u_N^{v,l}(q) = v_{fee} - cost(q)$

In Table 2, k_2 and k_3 represents the number of independent lazy and independent diligent verifiers, respectively. Note that, row 2 and row 3 in the Table 2 can be obtained by substituting the respective k_2 and k_3 values in row 1. We presented them separately here to show the utilities of all the involved parties in all the possible scenarios.

4   Attacks on HB System

We consider two attacks: (i) *Collusion attack* where multiple contractors who have been selected by the Arbiter, form a collusion. The colluders divide the computation task among themselves, each performing a fraction of the computation and sharing the results to construct a common output. They also share the payment from the system. And, (ii) *Sybil attack* where a single contractor registers under multiple identities in the hope of being selected multiple times in the set chosen by the Arbiter to increase their utility.

4.1   Collusion Attack in HB System

Let k_1 be the collusion group size where $1 < k_1 \leq N$. When $k_1 \neq N$, we also assume that the system may have two other sets of contractors, say k_2, $0 \leq k_2 < N$ who are independently lazy and $k_3 = N - (k_1 + k_2)$, $0 \leq k_2 < N$, who are independently diligent. Note that, for a computation task, the values of k_2 and k_3 are unknown to the collusion group k_1. We consider the following two cases to analyze the collusion attack.

The Solver is in the Collusion. The colluder's set consists of a solver and a set of verifiers. The remaining verifiers may be independently lazy or diligent. The k_1 colluders can either act diligently (i.e. share the computation of the correct algorithm) or lazily (i.e., by sharing the computation cost of the same q-algorithm). Let δ_c be an indicator value, $\delta_c \in \{0,1\}$ defined as, $\delta_c = 1$ if the solution of lazy participant is challenged, and $\delta_c = 0$, if it is not. Table 3 shows the utilities in the game between the colluding contractors (solver and verifiers) and the remaining independent contractors.

Table 3. Utility table for solver-verifier collusion game.

Verifiers	Colluders	
	Diligent	Lazy
k_2 lazy verifiers	$u_{k_2}^{c,d}(1) = r + \frac{k_2 \cdot v_{fee}}{k_1}(1-q) - \frac{cost(1)}{k_1}$ $u_{k_2}^{v,l}(q) = rq - D_v(1-q) - cost(q)$	$u_{k_1+k_2}^{c,l}(q) = rq + r(1-q)(1-\delta_c) - D(1-q)\delta_c - \frac{cost(q)}{k_1}$ $u_{k_1+k_2}^{v,l}(q) = rq + r(1-q)(1-\delta_c) - D(1-q)\delta_c - cost(q)$
k_3 diligent verifiers	$u_{k_2}^{v,d}(1) = r - cost(1)$	$u_{k_1+k_2}^{v,d}(1) = r + \frac{(k_1+k_2) \cdot v_{fee}}{k_3}(1-q) - cost(1)$

We use the table to evaluate *stability of a collusion*. That is, a member of the colluding group will have a higher utility to stay in the collusion. Note that the colluding group also have two behaviour, diligent and lazy. If the colluders behave diligently, the collusion will be stable if the colluders have higher utility than being independent contractors. That is,

- *Case 1*: $u_{k_2}^{c,d}(1) > u_{k_2}^{v,l}(q)$ (when k_2 verifiers are independently lazy), and
- *Case 2*: $u_{k_2}^{c,d}(1) > u_{k_2}^{v,d}(1)$ (when k_3 verifiers are independently diligent).

For a given set of system parameters, we will have $u_{k_2}^{v,l}(q) > u_{k_2}^{v,d}(1)$, or the reverse. So, we choose $u_{k_2}^{c,d}(1) > max\{u_{k_2}^{v,l}(q), u_{k_2}^{v,d}(1)\}$. This gives the following results (using Table 3):

- if $u_{k_2}^{c,d}(1) > u_{k_2}^{v,l}(q)$, we get $k_1 > \frac{cost(1)}{(r+D_v)(1-q)+cost(q)}$, and
- if $u_{k_2}^{c,d}(1) > u_{k_2}^{v,d}(1)$, we get $k_1 > 1$.

This implies that for a given set of system parameters as long as the collusion size is higher than the corresponding k_1, the diligent colluding strategy will have higher pay-off than working independently (diligent or lazy), and so the collusion will be stable.

Similarly, if the colluders behave lazily, to have higher utility than independent contractors, the following should be true:

- *Case 3*: $u_{k_1+k_2}^{c,l}(q) > u_{k_1+k_2}^{v,l}(q)$ (when k_2 verifiers are independently lazy), &
- *Case 4*: $u_{k_1+k_2}^{c,l}(q) > u_{k_1+k_2}^{v,d}(1)$ (when k_3 verifiers are independently diligent).

Using a similar argument as above, a collusion remains stable if the following is satisfied: $u_{k_1+k_2}^{c,l}(q) > max\{u_{k_1+k_2}^{v,l}(q), u_{k_1+k_2}^{v,d}(1)\}$. Using the utilities from Table 3 we get the following results:

- if $u_{k_1+k_2}^{c,l}(q) > u_{k_1+k_2}^{v,l}(q)$, then $k_1 > 1$, and
- if $u_{k_1+k_2}^{c,l}(q) > u_{k_1+k_2}^{v,d}(1)$, $k_1 > \frac{cost(q)}{cost(1)-(1-q)[(N-1)V_{fee}+r+D]}$.

Note that the bounds only depend on the system parameters and so can be computed by a contractor. In other words, a contractor can decide to be independent, or stay in the collusion based on the size of the colluding set. The above analysis leads to the following theorem.

Theorem 1. *(a) For a given set of system parameters, there are values for the colluding set size k_1, for which being diligent, or being lazy has higher utility than being an independent contractor.*

(b) For values of k_1 for which both collusion behaviours (diligent and lazy) allow stable collusion, one can find the best strategy (the strategy with the highest utility) of colluders (diligent or lazy) that maximizes their utility.

Note that based on the system parameters of HB, solver-verifier collusion is possible as long as the collusion size is higher than the corresponding k_1.

In HB, if colluders act diligently when $k_1 < N$, we get $k_1 > \frac{cost(1) - cost(q)}{(r+D)(1-q)}$. Since $cost(q) < cost(1) \leq r$ and $q \approx 0$ (e.g. by using inner state hash [2]), $r + D > cost(1) - cost(q)$. So, $\frac{cost(1) - cost(q)}{(r+D)(1-q)} < max\{1, \frac{cost(1)}{(r+D)(1-q)+cost(q)}\}$. So, in this case, the best strategy is to act diligently. However, when $k_1 = N$, since $\delta_c = 0$ and $q = 0$ (in HB), from Table 3 we get $r - \frac{cost(q)}{k_1} > r - \frac{cost(1)}{k_1}$. So, in this case being lazy is the best strategy.

Collusion of Verifiers Only. Assume that k_1 verifiers are colluding and doing the computation jointly. The colluders may act diligently, or lazily. The remaining contractors, consist of k_2 lazy, and $k_3 = N - (k_1 + k_2)$ diligent, contractors. As the solver is an independent contractor, it may be in the diligent, or in the lazy group. Table 4 shows the payoff of a colluding verifier against the payoff of an independent verifier in each case.

Table 4. Pay-off matrix for verifiers collusion game

Remaining contractors		Colluding verifiers (k_1)	
Solver	Verifiers	Diligent	Lazy
Diligent	k_2 *Lazy*	$u_{k_2}^{(c,d)(s,d)}(1) = v_{fee} - \frac{cost(1)}{k_1}$	$u_{k_1+k_2}^{(c,l)(s,d)}(q) =$ $v_{fee}q - D_v(1-q) - \frac{cost(q)}{k_1}$
	$k_3 - 1$ *Diligent*	$u_{k_2}^{(v,l)(s,d)}(q) =$ $v_{fee}q - D_v(1-q) - cost(q)$ $u_{k_2}^{(v,d)(s,d)}(1) = v_{fee} - cost(1)$	$u_{k_1+k_2}^{(v,l)(s,d)}(q) =$ $v_{fee}q - D_v(1-q) - cost(q)$ $u_{k_1+k_2}^{(v,d)(s,d)}(1) = v_{fee} - cost(1)$
Lazy	$k_2 - 1$ *Lazy*	$u_{k_2}^{(c,d)(s,l)}(1) =$ $v_{fee} + \frac{s_{fee}+(k_2-1)v_{fee}}{k_1+k_3}(1-q) - \frac{cost(1)}{k_1}$	$u_{k_1+k_2}^{(c,l)(s,l)}(q) = v_{fee}q + v_{fee}(1-q)(1-\delta_c) - D_v(1-q)\delta_c - \frac{cost(q)}{k_1}$
	k_3 *Diligent*	$u_{k_2}^{(v,l)(s,l)}(q) =$ $v_{fee}q - D_v(1-q) - cost(q)$ $u_{k_2}^{(v,d)(s,l)}(1) =$ $v_{fee} + \frac{s_{fee}+(k_2-1)v_{fee}}{k_1+k_3}(1-q) - cost(1)$	$u_{k_1+k_2}^{(v,l)(s,l)}(q) = v_{fee}q + v_{fee}(1-q)(1-\delta_c) - D_v(1-q)\delta_c - cost(q)$ $u_{k_1+k_2}^{(v,d)(s,l)}(1) = v_{fee} + \frac{s_{fee}+(k_1+k_2-1)v_{fee}}{k_3}(1-q) - cost(1)$

Using an argument similar to the above case (solver is in the collusion), we will have: $u_{k_2}^{(c,d)(s,d)}(1) > max(u_{k_2}^{(v,l)(s,d)}(q), u_{k_2}^{(v,d)(s,d)}(1))$ and $u_{k_2}^{(c,d)(s,l)}(1) > max(u_{k_2}^{(v,l)(s,l)}(q), u_{k_2}^{(v,d)(s,l)}(1))$.

For colluders behaving lazily a collusion remains stable if the followings are satisfied: $u_{k_1+k_2}^{(c,l)(s,d)}(1) > max(u_{k_1+k_2}^{(v,l)(s,d)}(q), u_{k_1+k_2}^{(v,d)(s,d)}(1))$ and $u_{k_1+k_2}^{(c,l)(s,l)}(1) > max(u_{k_1+k_2}^{(v,l)(s,l)}(q), u_{k_1+k_2}^{(v,d)(s,l)}(1))$.

These give lower bounds on collusion sizes for which colluders will have higher utility with their corresponding strategies, compared to playing independently. From the above analysis it is proved that HB system cannot protect against colluding attacks.

4.2   Sybil Attack in HB System

Consider an attacker who creates K Sybil identities hoping that k_1 of them are selected. Additionally, consider n identities in the system and N of them are selected for a given task. Then K can be estimated as follow: If n and N are large, then the proportion of identities that belongs to the attacker, $\frac{K}{n}$, is equal to the proportion of identities chosen for the given task, $\frac{k_1}{N}$. In another way, $\frac{k_1}{N} = \frac{K}{n}$. So, attacker should create $K = \frac{k_1}{N}n$ identities in order to gets k_1 of them accepted for a given task. Sybil attack can happen when all the selected identities of the Sybil node are verifiers, or it also includes the solver.

We consider two cases: $k_1 < N$ and $k_1 = N$. If $k_1 < N$, we consider k_2 independently lazy verifiers and $k_3 (= N - k_1 - k_2)$ independently diligent verifiers. Otherwise, if $k_1 = N$, $k_2 = k_3 = 0$. Sybil attack can be seen as a realization of collusion attack with the difference that the Sybil attacker must provides deposit for all k_1 identities and will receive all the rewards, and so instead of considering the utility of a member of the collusion, we will consider the utility of the whole colluding. Using the analysis similar to previous section we have the following.

Sybil Identities Includes the Solver. Let $U(a, b)$ represents the total utility of the Sybil attacker for strategy $a \in \{d, l\}$, when $b \in \{0, 1, \dots, N\}$ is the number of identities that are selected by the Arbiter. If the solver is in k_1, then,

- when $k_1 < N$ the total utility for the *diligent* strategy is: $U(d, k_1) = k_1.[r + \frac{k_2 \cdot v_{fee}}{k_1}(1 - q)] - cost(1)$.
- when $k_1 = N$ the total utility for the *lazy* strategy is: $U(l, N) = N.r - cost(q)$

Here, $r = s_{fee}$ for solver (or v_{fee} for verifier), and D is the registration cost (i.e., deposit) by contractor. As these utilities are greater than one diligent identity, Theorem 1 holds, Sybil attack of solver-verifiers is possible.

We note that the probability of $k_1 = N$ will be very small for large values of N, the registration cost of registered identities would become formidable.

Sybil Attack of Verifiers. Analysis of collusion attack showed that for a given k_1, being diligent is the better strategy. Where as a Sybil attacker does not know how the solver would act, so we have two cases:

- If solver is diligent, the total utility for the attacker is: $U(d, k_1) = k_1(v_{fee}) - cost(1)$.
- If solver is lazy, the total expected utility for the attacker is: $U(l, k_1) = k_1[v_{fee} + \frac{s_{fee} + (k_2 - 1)v_{fee}}{k_1 + k_3}(1 - q)] - cost(q)$.

These utilities are higher than the utility of a single diligent identity and using the similar analysis we can show that Sybil attack of verifiers is possible.

4.3   Shortcoming of HB

The above analysis of HB showed that it is vulnerable to both collusion and Sybil attacks. Below are additional shortcoming of the system.

- In HB, when a contractor is lazy and is caught, the diligent contractors who catch the lazy contractor gets its reward shares (additional reward) that is committed by the problem-giver prior to the computation. We suggest that the additional reward should be harvested from the fine that the lazy contractor pays rather than charging the problem-giver.
- In HB, the deposit (D) amount is set by the Arbiter and the contractors pay this amount before the problem-giver requests for a computation to the Arbiter. This deposit works as a commitment to the system and will not be returned to the contractor if it gets caught by cheating. However, as the task difficulty is unknown to the Arbiter, the deposit value set might be so little to ensure the honest computation. The deposit value should be fixed based on the task difficulty.

5   HB+ System

The analysis in of HB showed that it is vulnerable to both collusion and Sybil attacks. In this section, to improve the correctness guarantee of HB system, for the attacks presented in Sect. 4, we propose the following modifications to the original HB system, and we call it *HB+*. Finally, we analyze the effectiveness of these modifications on the HB system.

Random Audit. We propose the following changes to HB system to alleviate the Sybil attack discussed in Sect. 4.2. The idea is, when all the contractors return *same* result, Arbiter randomly audits (i.e., probabilistic auditing) the results using the Judge (Ethereum). The random auditing involves of two parties: the *Arbiter*, who triggers this auditing by sending an intermediary result of a step stored in a Merkle tree and input, if any, to Judge for the given computation. The *Judges*, who are the set of miners in Ethereum, returns a boolean value to Arbiter: If the judge returns *true*, the solver and the verifiers get their reward. Otherwise, the Arbiter penalize the solver and the verifiers by taking away their deposits and reassign the computation to another group of contractors.

Operational Flow of HB+ System. In HB, each contractor commits a deposit to Arbiter for participating in the system that is independent of problem-giver's computation. It may so happen that the deposit amount is much smaller than the reward (that is calculated based on the complexity of the computation) for computing results. Because of this, the system is vulnerable to attacks such as Sybil. For example, within its financial limits, a rational contractor (Sybil attacker) may create multiple identities to increase its chances of being selected for the computation expecting huge rewards. This causes questioning the correctness guarantee of the system. To avoid such scenarios, we propose that the Arbiter should determine the deposit amount independently for each computation requested based on computation complexity. In more detail, the deposit amount should be fixed after receiving the computation request from the problem-giver. Then, the interested contractors commit this fixed deposit and register to the Arbiter for the computation.

HB+ Incentive Structure. In HB, when a diligent contractor challenges an incorrect solution published by a lazy contractor, the diligent contractor receive an additional reward (bonus) for helping the system to catch the cheating contractor and the lazy contractor loses his deposit. The bonus given to the diligent contractor is actually the reward that is originally committed by the problem-giver (when the computation is requested) for the contractor who has been caught for his lazy behavior. Since HB assumes that the problem-givers are rational, they always try to optimize (minimize) their cost (payment) for their requested computation. Therefore, to encourage the problem-givers to use the system often and for social good, we propose to use the deposits paid by the cheating contractors to reward diligent contractors instead of using problem-givers payment.

Based on the proposed idea of using lazy contractors deposits to reward diligent contractors and the probabilistic auditing mechanism presented in Sect. 5, we modify the HB incentive structure (given in Table 1) and present a modified incentive structure in Table 5. To be consistent, in Table 5 we use the notations that are defined already (see Sect. 2) and, with an additional one, β to denote the probability of an Arbiter performing random auditing.

Table 5. New incentive structure of a solver and verifier with different behaviors in the modified HB system

Verifier V	Solver S	
	Incorrect	Correct
Challenge	S losses D_s	S receives $s_{fee} + D_v$
	V receives $v_{fee} + D_s$	V losses D_v
Accept	S receives $s_{fee}(1 - \beta)$	S receives s_{fee}
	S losses $D_s\beta$	
	V receives $v_{fee}(1 - \beta)$	V receives v_{fee}
	V losses $D_v\beta$	

In Table 5, when a solver's incorrect solution is challenged by a verifier, S does not receive reward (s_{fee}) and losses his deposit D_s and (each) challenger (verifier) receives its reward (v_{fee}) with an additional reward, a share of D_s, as a bonus (for example, if there are N_c challengers, then each challenger will get $v_{fee} + D_s/N_c$. If a verifier challenges correct solution of a solver, it losses D_v and does not receive any reward and, S gets his reward and deposits of all the challengers as a bonus. When the results are same, using the Judge, Arbiter verifies the results randomly with probability β. For example, in the Table 5, when the solver's solution is incorrect and the verifier accepts it (i.e., the results are same), both S and V either loss their deposits with probability β or receive their rewards with $(1 - \beta)$ probability.

5.1   Analysis of HB+

Let $\beta \in [0, 1]$ be the probability of auditing by the Arbiter when the returned results are same. We assume that Arbiter sets the deposit D based on the task difficulty. Although each contractor provides the same amount of deposit for participation, we use D_s (solver's deposit) and D_v (verifier's deposit) same as before (in Sect. 3) to distinguish them, where $D = D_s = D_v$. However, in this modified model the usage of the deposit is different than the original HB system. That is instead of burning the deposits of the cheating parties they will be distributed among the honest parties as a bonus. Based on these assumptions and changes, the game pay-off Table 2 of original HB updated and new utilities are shown in Table 6.

Table 6. Pay-off matrix of the modified HB

Verifiers	Solver	
	Diligent	Lazy
All diligent	$u_0^{s,d}(1) = s_{fee} - cost(1)$	$u_0^{s,l}(q) = s_{fee}q - D_s(1 - q) - cost(q)$
	$u_0^{v,d}(1) = v_{fee} - cost(1)$	$u_0^{v,d}(1) = v_{fee} + \frac{D_s}{N-1}(1 - q) - cost(1)$
k lazy N − 1 − k diligent	$u_k^{s,d}(1) = s_{fee} + \frac{kD_v}{N-k}(1 - q) - cost(1)$	$u_k^{s,l}(q) = s_{fee}q - D_s(1 - q) - cost(q)$
	$u_k^{v,d}(1) = v_{fee} + \frac{kD_v}{N-k}(1 - q) - cost(1)$	$u_k^{v,d}(1) = v_{fee} + \frac{D_s+kD_v}{N-1-k}(1-q) - cost(1)$
	$u_k^{v,l}(q) = v_{fee}q - D_v(1 - q) - cost(q)$	$u_k^{v,l}(q) = v_{fee}q - D_v(1 - q) - cost(q)$
All lazy	$u_{N-1}^{s,d}(1) =$ $s_{fee} + (N - 1)D_v(1 - q) - cost(1)$	$u_{N-1}^{s,l}(q) = s_{fee}q + s_{fee}(1 - q)(1 - \beta)$ $-D_s(1 - q)\beta - cost(q)$
	$u_{N-1}^{v,l}(q) = v_{fee}q - D_v(1 - q) - cost(q)$	$u_{N-1}^{v,l}(q) = v_{fee}q + v_{fee}(1 - q)(1 - \beta)$ $-D_v(1 - q)\beta - cost(q)$

Using the above utilities, and the analysis presented in Sect. 4, it can be shown that with the modified utilities presented in Table 6, collusion attack is still possible. But, the possibility of Sybil attack is reduced, because of the probabilistic auditing, even if all sybil identities output the same solution.

5.2   Malicious Contractors

Malicious contractors aim at polluting the blockchain by making the Arbiter accept an incorrect solution. They will collude and share their budgets to harm the system. To have enough, non-negative, balance to participate in the tasks they will act honestly time to time. The following theorem shows the best strategy for malicious contractors.

Theorem 2. *The best strategy for malicious contractors is to all collude when they are selected for a given task.*

Proof. As we have previously shown in Table 6, whenever all contractors reveal the same incorrect solution and when there is no auditing by judges, $\beta = 0$, Arbiter accepts the incorrect solution and the utility of each contractor is, $u_z^{x,m}(0) = r(1 - \beta) = r$.

Theorem 3 shows the bound for the expected false rate which is the number of incorrect solutions broadcasted to blockchain if malicious contractors follow strategy given in Theorem 2.

Theorem 3. *The expected false rate in the system is $p^N(1 - \beta)$, where N is the number of computation services, p, is the prior probability that a contractors is malicious in the system, and β is probability of auditing by the judges.*

Proof. If all the N chosen contractors are malicious they can collude and reveal an incorrect solution. The probability of this case is p^N. However, they may be challenged by judges with probability β if all reveal the same solution. The probability that they are not challenged is $1 - \beta$, therefore the attackers succeed with probability $p^N(1 - \beta)$.

According to Theorem 3, we gain a reduction on the expected false rate proportional to $1 - \beta$ compared to HB. In the next section we compare our result with HB assuming some values for p, N and β.

6   Evaluation and Comparison

Table 7 shows the expected false solutions broadcasted to blockchain in HB+ versus HB. The prior probability of being lazy is selected to be 0.3, 0.5 and 0.7 to facilitate the comparison to HB. According to HB, if solver reveals a wrong solution and verifiers accept it then false solution goes to blockchain; if the probability that a computation service be lazy and output a wrong solution is p, and the number of verifiers is n, then the probability of false solution to be accepted is p^{n+1} $(N = n + 1)$. In our scheme, however, the expected false rate also depends on the probability of auditing; if a task is audited by judges with probability β then the probability of false solution accepted will be $p^{n+1}(1 - \beta)$. For comparison, we have considered β to be 0.1, 0.5, and 0.9. According to table, the probabilistic auditing reduces the expected false percentage proportional to $1 - \beta$. We expect to see more reductions in practice as the auditing time is unknown to computation services.

7   Related Work

In blockchain, transactions must be validated and processed at every node in the network. So, any blockchain system experiences limitations in scalability. Outsourcing computation techniques have been proposed in various papers addressing the scalability and security challenges of a blockchain [6,8,14]. Trust models

Table 7. Comparison between expected false in our scheme and HB.

Prior p	Verifiers n	Expected false [%]			Expected false HB [%]
		$\beta = 0.1$	$\beta = 0.5$	$\beta = 0.9$	
0.3	1	8.1	4.5	0.9	9.0
	2	2.43	1.35	0.27	2.7
	3	0.729	0.405	0.081	0.81
	4	0.2187	0.1215	0.0243	0.243
	5	0.06561	0.03645	0.00729	0.0729
	6	0.019683	0.010935	0.002187	0.02187
0.5	1	22.5	12.5	2.5	25.0
	2	11.25	6.25	1.25	12.5
	3	5.625	3.125	0.625	6.25
	4	2.8125	1.5625	0.3125	3.125
	5	1.40625	0.78125	0.15625	1.5625
	6	0.703125	0.390625	0.078125	0.78125
0.7	1	44.1	24.5	4.9	49.0
	2	30.87	17.15	3.43	34.3
	3	21.609	12.005	2.401	24.01
	4	15.1263	8.4035	1.6807	16.807
	5	10.58841	5.88245	1.17649	11.7649
	6	7.411887	4.117715	0.823543	8.23543

(based on incentive mechanism) [6,8,14] are proposed to off-chain the computations to third parties to inherit transparency and particular trust for implementing smart contracts in permission-less blockchains. ZoKrates [4], shares the same spirit of off-chaining computations to third parties by supplying a non-interactive zero-knowledge proof with the results. Moreover, several works have been proposed to incorporate multiparty computation onto blockchains [1,11]. In addition, Dong *et al.* [3] provide a game theoretical analysis for verifiable outsourced computation in cloud computing that involves blockchain technology. The authors assume only two rational clouds who can collude and later one can secretly deviate from the collusive agreement to maximize their own profit. The authors design smart contracts to sabotage collusion. In case of our analysis, we assume that once collusion is formed, colluders do not deviate from their agreement and the goal is to prevent collusion from happening. Moreover, we have considered both rational and malicious adversaries for our analysis. Finally, their system needs a trusted third party to resolve conflicts where the HB system resolves the dispute through the distributed consensus algorithms (i.e., by using Ethereum as Judge) and removes the need of a trusted third party. In [12] the authors researched the outsourced verification computation from an economics aspect. They provided a general approach based on game theory for optimal contract design for outsourcing computation. They considered the cheating or lazy behavior of the service providers and analyzed it with one and multiple server settings. In the follow up work [7], they identified the optimal settings for the multi-server case when collusion is allowed.

8 Conclusion

Security of incentivized verifiable computation system is an intriguing challenge because of the range of possible attacks and possible collusions. Our goal was to examine the security claims of such an incentivised outsourcing system proposed by Harz and Boman [Harz *et al.* 2018] (HB), at FC WTSC 2018. We analyse the system, considering rational contractors, using a game-theoretic approach and discuss its correctness guarantee considering two attacks, collusion and Sybil. Interestingly, our analysis shows that the incentive structure of HB can not protect the system against these attacks. We propose modifications for HB (HB+) that helps the system to improve its correctness guarantee by motivating diligent behavior in contractors by incentivizing contractors with bonus rewards. We analyse HB+ and show that the modifications alleviates vulnerabilities of the attacks and, guarantee high correctness in results, however it can not prevent the attacks. We also propose to utilize the deposits of lazy contractors to encourage diligent behavior in rational contractors for social fair. Fixing the HB system from collusion and Sybil attacks for any behaviors (diligent and lazy) is however our future work. Finally, we extend our analysis to malicious contractors whose goal is to corrupt the blockchain. We show that HB+ alleviates the expected false rate compared to the original HB system.

References

1. Andrychowicz, M., Dziembowski, S., Malinowski, D., Mazurek, L.: Secure multi-party computations on bitcoin. In: IEEE Symposium on Security and Privacy, pp. 443–458 (2014)
2. Belenkiy, M., Chase, M., Erway, C.C., Jannotti, J., Küpçü, A., Lysyanskaya, A.: Incentivizing outsourced computation. In: Proceedings of International workshop on Economics of networked systems, pp. 85–90. ACM (2008)
3. Dong, C., Wang, Y., Aldweesh, A., McCorry, P., van Moorsel, A.: Betrayal, distrust, and rationality. In: Proceedings of ACM SIGSAC Conference on Computer and Communications Security, pp. 211–227 (2017)
4. Eberhardt, J., Tai, S.: ZoKrates-scalable privacy-preserving off-chain computations. In: IEEE International Conference on Blockchain (2018)
5. Gennaro, R., Gentry, C., Parno, B.: Non-interactive verifiable computing: outsourcing computation to untrusted workers. In: Rabin, T. (ed.) CRYPTO 2010. LNCS, vol. 6223, pp. 465–482. Springer, Heidelberg (2010). https://doi.org/10.1007/978-3-642-14623-7_25
6. Harz, D., Boman, M.: The scalability of trustless trust. In: Zohar, A., et al. (eds.) FC 2018. LNCS, vol. 10958, pp. 279–293. Springer, Heidelberg (2019). https://doi.org/10.1007/978-3-662-58820-8_19

7. Khouzani, M., Pham, V., Cid, C.: Incentive engineering for outsourced computation in the face of collusion. In: Proceedings of WEIS (2014)
8. Koch, J., Reitwiessner, C.: A predictable incentive mechanism for TrueBit. arXiv preprint arXiv:1806.11476 (2018)
9. Küpçü, A.: Incentivized outsourced computation resistant to malicious contractors. IEEE Trans. Dependable Secure Comput. 14(6), 633–649 (2017)
10. Parno, B., Raykova, M., Vaikuntanathan, V.: How to delegate and verify in public: verifiable computation from attribute-based encryption. In: Cramer, R. (ed.) TCC 2012. LNCS, vol. 7194, pp. 422–439. Springer, Heidelberg (2012). https://doi.org/10.1007/978-3-642-28914-9_24
11. Paul, S., Shrivastava, A.: Robust multiparty computation with faster verification time. In: Susilo, W., Yang, G. (eds.) ACISP 2018. LNCS, vol. 10946, pp. 114–131. Springer, Cham (2018). https://doi.org/10.1007/978-3-319-93638-3_8
12. Pham, V., Khouzani, M.H.R., Cid, C.: Optimal contracts for outsourced computation. In: Poovendran, R., Saad, W. (eds.) GameSec 2014. LNCS, vol. 8840, pp. 79–98. Springer, Cham (2014). https://doi.org/10.1007/978-3-319-12601-2_5
13. Setty, S.T., McPherson, R., Blumberg, A.J., Walfish, M.: Making argument systems for outsourced computation practical (sometimes). In: NDSS, vol. 1, p. 17 (2012)
14. Teutsch, J., Reitwießner, C.: A scalable verification solution for blockchains (2017). https://people.cs.uchicago.edu/teutsch/papers/truebitpdf

Sluggish Mining: Profiting from the Verifier's Dilemma

Beltrán Borja Fiz Pontiveros[(⊠)], Christof Ferreira Torres[(⊠)],
and Radu State[(⊠)]

Center for Security, Reliability and Trust, University of Luxembourg,
Luxembourg City, Luxembourg
{beltran.fiz,christof.torres,radu.state}@uni.lu

Abstract. Miners in Ethereum need to make a choice when they receive a block: they can fully validate the block by executing every transaction in order to validate the new state, but this consumes precious time that could be used on mining the next block. Alternatively, miners could skip some of the verification stages and proceed with the mining, taking the risk of building on top of a potentially invalid block. This is referred to as the verifier's dilemma.

Although the gas limit imposed on Ethereum blocks mitigates this attack by forcing an upper bound on the time spent during verification, the slowdown that can be achieved within a block can still be enough to have an impact on profitability.

In this paper we present a mining strategy based around sluggish contracts; these computationally intensive contracts are purposely designed to have a slow execution time in the Ethereum Virtual Machine to provide an advantage over other miners by slowing their contract verification time.

We validate our proposed mining strategy by designing and evaluating a set of candidate sluggish smart contracts. Furthermore, we provide a detailed analysis that shows under which conditions our strategy becomes profitable alongside a series of suggestions to detect this type of strategy in the future.

Keywords: Ethereum · Smart contracts · Mining strategy · Security · Cryptocurrencies

1 Introduction

Ethereum is a blockchain protocol which keeps a record of state transition transactions and the state of the Ethereum Virtual Machine (EVM): a stack-based run-time environment designed for smart contracts, programs that are executed in a distributed and decentralised fashion across the Ethereum network [23]. This turned the Ethereum blockchain into a global decentralised computing platform. As of December 2018 its market capitalisation is evaluated at over $10 Billion, making it third in volume after Bitcoin and Ripple.

© International Financial Cryptography Association 2020
A. Bracciali et al. (Eds.): FC 2019 Workshops, LNCS 11599, pp. 67–81, 2020.
https://doi.org/10.1007/978-3-030-43725-1_6

The EVM currently supports over 150 instructions, commonly referred to as opcodes. Each of these opcodes performs a different operation on the stack of the EVM. Smart contracts are usually developed using a dedicated high-level programming language such as Solidity [19], which afterwards gets translated into a sequence of opcodes. Each opcode has an assigned gas cost, which represents the amount of resources required to use this operation. Although ideally each operation should take a similar amount of time per gas consumed, due to the need of having cheap, yet CPU intensive operations such as hash calculations, means some opcodes are considered to be under-priced.

At the time of writing, Ethereum achieves consensus through a proof-of-work algorithm similar to Bitcoin. However, one of the reasons why Ethereum became so popular among casual miners, was thanks to their choice of a memory-hard proof-of-work algorithm: Ethash [10]. The algorithm was designed to be ASIC-resistant and thus to only be run using commodity hardware such as CPUs or graphics cards. During block validation, miners are expected to execute each transaction to calculate the new state and validate the block. This however poses a problem: if they choose to validate a block upon receipt, they need to spend time running the transactions that could be used to create the next block; however if they do not validate the block and proceed mining on top of it, they have a risk of building on top of an incorrect block. This is known as the verifier's dilemma [14]. If however a miner were to gain an edge by being able to execute the validation faster than other miners, they would be able to begin work ahead of other miners and thus gain a competitive advantage. In this paper we present a mining strategy for the Ethereum network, built around this verification process of blocks by miners.

We propose a strategy that deploys a *sluggish* smart contract: a purposely designed slow execution contract for which we have a simplified, faster version available. We then create a new block with a transaction executing this sluggish contract in order to slow down other miners during block validation. The difference here is that we run the optimised version to create our block, while other miners will run the under-optimised version. This will gain us time and increase our chances to build the next block by having additional time over other miners in the network. The paper is structured as follows: In Sect. 2, we present a summary of some of the related work currently available. In Sect. 3, we present the methodology of our proposed mining strategy, with a step-by-step description. In Sect. 4, we evaluate our mining strategy as a Markov Decision Process and extract the viability conditions. In Sect. 5, we proceed to evaluate our strategy by extracting and evaluating past and current Ethereum settings and show that our strategy is viable under certain conditions. Finally in Sect. 6, we present some conclusions of our work with some suggestions on potential future work.

2   Related Work

Since its release in 2015 [23], a lot of research has been produced around Ethereum, spanning across multiple rapidly developing areas, as shown in the work performed in [21].

The evaluation of different mining strategies and the game theory behind it is a very active domain within the Bitcoin research community [12]. Modelling the mining process as a Markov Decision Process was performed in [9], where the authors simulated a selfish mining strategy and assessed its efficiency with respect to the standard behaviour. Additional work continued along these lines, modelling additional strategies and assessing their viability [16].

The verifier's dilemma was first introduced in [14]; the authors suggest a 'divide and conquer' solution by dividing computationally intensive transactions into multiple smaller transactions, spread across multiple blocks. In [20] the authors proposed a system named TrueBit. It provides an alternative to Ethereum's need to replicate calculations in every node by reducing it to a small set of entities. This would prevent computationally intensive contracts to slow down the network. In [7] the authors suggest moving some of the work off-chain while providing guarantees under a threat model that includes selfish nodes.

In addition to computationally intensive transactions that may cause denial-of-service attacks (DoS), there are also numerous vulnerabilities that are caused due to developers programming bad code. These vulnerabilities range from smart contract specific ones such as reentrancy and transaction order dependence (TOD)[13] to classic vulnerabilities such as integer overflows [22]. Finally, several attacks on the peer-to-peer network of Bitcoin and Ethereum have been proposed in order to reduce the computational power required to reach the majority vote in the consensus algorithm [11].

3   Methodology

In this section, we describe how our mining strategy works, the preparation steps required to deploy it and finally an evaluation of when this strategy becomes more profitable than the default mining strategy.

3.1   Sluggish Mining Strategy

In Ethereum the final block reward obtained by miners can be divided into three sub rewards:

- Block creation reward (R_{blck}): A static reward initially set to 5 Ether, which has been lowered in October 2017 [1] to 3 Ether and is expected to be lowered once again to 2 Ether with the release of [17].
- Gas reward (R_{gas}): This includes the transaction fees, consisting of all the gas that has been spent during execution of the transactions in the block. This is to outset the time and effort spent on validating the block, as defined in the consensus protocol. The overall reward obtained depends on the gas price offered by the transactions, and the transaction load of the network. Like in the Bitcoin protocol, it is expected to have this reward eventually replace the block creation reward entirely.

– Uncle reward (R_{uncle}): If any uncles (stale blocks) are included in the created block, providing an additional reward of $\frac{1}{32}$ of the current block creation reward. A maximum of 2 uncles are allowed per block.

The main idea behind the sluggish mining strategy is to forfeit the gas reward obtained from executing and including other users transactions (R_{gas}), and instead create a transaction designed to use all the gas available in a block and send it to a smart contract purposefully designed to be as slow as possible to execute. In addition to being slow, the state change caused to the Ethereum blockchain must be predictable or basically unchanged, such that the attacker does not require to run the contract himself. In order to ensure we do not waste time validating our transaction, we simply replace the pointer in our database from our sluggish smart contract (SSC) to an identical optimised smart contract (OSC) with an identical state transition function while being optimised for a negligible execution time. This can be seen in Fig. 1.

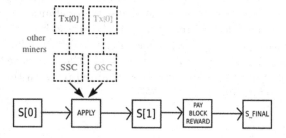

Fig. 1. Using OSC allows for a faster state transition than using SSC.

The purpose of this sluggish contract is to gain an advantage over other miners by having them execute this slow contract during the block validation phase. This will allow the attacker to gain an advantage in terms of time as compared to other miners on the next block, at the expense of the fee rewards not taken to accommodate for our transaction. This strategy makes the assumption that other nodes validate a received block before starting work on the next block although it is possible that miners simply skip the validation stage and proceed to the block creation stage of the next block without wasting time on our contract. As discussed before, this is part of the verifier's dilemma.

The following assumptions are made in our mining strategy:

– Executions times are similar between different architectures. With the rise of specialised hardware such as FPGAs and ASICs purposely built for specific tasks, this condition might not hold in the future.
– We assume that miners will validate a block before beginning the mining process on top of it. However, in practice the validation could be simplified by verifying soley the previous hash without executing the transactions. This would mean that no slow down effect would be caused by our sluggish contract.

- We treat miners as purely rational agents wanting to maximise their revenue given the current mining conditions. We do not investigate on any effects such a mining strategy could have on the value of Ethereum. This could be seen as an attack (and thus trust in the system lowered).
- We do not take into consideration the network delays in block propagation. However, it should be noted that our strategy could yield blocks with only one single transaction, hence producing small size blocks and therefore susceptible for faster propagation.

The steps required to deploy this strategy are as follows:

1. The design of a sluggish smart contract i.e. a contract that shows a dreadful execution time.
2. The deployment of the sluggish smart contract and modification to the client in order to avoid or replace the execution of our sluggish smart contract.
3. The mining and broadcast of a block which includes a transaction executing our sluggish smart contract.

In the following subsections we will explain the design and deployment of sluggish smart contracts in greater detail.

Sluggish Contract Design. The first step is to design a sluggish smart contract. The purpose of this contract is to maximise the time taken to execute, given a fixed amount of gas. Although the Ethereum community goes to great lengths to ensure that the gas cost of each opcode reflects its computational time expense, there are always exceptions or opcodes that fail to reflect their real cost, leading to attacks such as the one that took place in mid 2017, leading to a hard fork [3], which caused the following opcodes to change their gasprice: $EXTCODESIZE$ and $EXTCODECOPY$ from 20 to 700, $BALANCE$ from 20 to 400, $SLOAD$ from 50 to 200, $CALL$, $DELEGATECALL$, $CALLCODE$ from 40 to 700 and finally $SEFLDESTRUCT$ from 0 to 5000. Despite these readjustments to the opcode pricing we show in this work that our strategy remains viable. In summary, we want our sluggish contract to satisfy the following criteria:

1. We need to be able to precompute the state change that our contract has on the EVM world state, without actually executing it.
2. The contract needs to be as slow as possible given the maximum amount of gas that can be consumed inside a block, known as the *gaslimit*. This limit is currently set to about 8 million.

Algorithm 1 provides a very simple and generic design, where $OPCODE$ may be replaced by any particular opcode that has a major impact on the execution time. The algorithm takes as input an opcode and the opcode's input values. As described in Sect. 2, there have already been numerous studies and benchmarks regarding the under-pricing of several EVM opcodes [5,6] and based on the literature we selected the following opcodes in order to affect either the CPU or the access to I/O:

Algorithm 1. Sluggish Smart Contract

Input: (OPCODE, INPUT)
Output: 0
1: Push INPUT onto the stack
2: Execute OPCODE
3: **if** gas left > 0 **then**
4:     Jump to line 1
5: **end if**
6: **return** 0

---

1. **CPU Bound:** The goal of CPU bound sluggish contracts is to ensure that the CPU remains busy as possible during the contract execution. Two opcodes were selected:
   - *SHA3* (0 × 20): This opcode computes the Keccak-256 hash [23] and has a gas cost of 30 + 6 * (size of input in words). It pops two values from the stack, the memory offset p and the size n, and finally pushes the result onto the stack.
   - *EXP* (0 × 0a): This opcode computes the exponential on two values popped from the stack, the base b and the exponent e. If e is 0 then the gas used is 0. If e is greater than 0, then the gas used is 10 + 50 * a factor related to the size of the log of the exponent. It should be noted that the factor gas cost of EXP has already been increased from 10 to 50 [2].
2. **I/O Bound**: As described in the previous section, operations dealing with peristent storage have always been tricky to price. We test two of the most common opcodes:
   - *SLOAD* (0 × 54): This opcode loads a value from storage. Storage in Ethereum is implemented as a key-value store. The opcode takes as input the storage location (key) and returns the value associated to this location. It has a cost of 200 gas.
   - *SSTORE* (0 × 55): This opcode stores a value into storage. The gas cost is 20,000, if the storage value is set from a zero value to a non-zero value. Otherwise, the gas cost amounts to 5,000.

The sluggish smart contracts used during our experiments were formed using the layout defined in Algorithm 1 and the opcodes listed above. Given that some EVM client implementations have optimisations for simple input values such as 0 and 1, we decided to use input values of 15 instead (0xe); these contracts can be seen in Figs. 2, 3, 4, 5, alongside their corresponding sequence of opcodes and bytecode. The evaluation of the total delay obtained can be seen in Sect. 5.

Contract Deployment. Smart contracts are deployed on the blockchain via transactions. A transaction has a base fee of 21,000 gas. The cost of deploying our sluggish smart contract has a minimum fee of 32,000 gas for the *CREATE* opcode. This is meant to cover the cost of performing an elliptic curve operation to recover the sender address from the signature in addition to the cost

SHA3	EXP	SLOAD	SSTORE
JUMPDEST 1 gas	JUMPDEST 1 gas	PUSH 0 3 gas	JUMPDEST 1 gas
PUSH 0 3 gas	PUSH 0 3 gas	JUMPDEST 1 gas	PUSH 1 3 gas
PUSH 0 3 gas	PUSH 0 3 gas	SLOAD 200 gas	PUSH 0 3 gas
SHA3 30 gas	EXP 60 gas	PUSH 222 3 gas	SSTORE 5000 gas
POP 2 gas	POP 2 gas	GAS 2 gas	PUSH 20028 3 gas
PUSH 60 3 gas	PUSH 60 3 gas	GT 3 gas	GAS 2 gas
GAS 2 gas	GAS 2 gas	PUSH 2 3 gas	GT 3 gas
GT 3 gas	GT 3 gas	JUMPI 10 gas	PUSH 0 3 gas
PUSH 0 3 gas	PUSH 0 3 gas	STOP 0 gas	JUMPI 10 gas
JUMPI 10 gas	JUMPI 10 gas		STOP 0 gas
STOP 0 gas	STOP 0 gas		

Bytecode:	Bytecode:	Bytecode:	Bytecode:
5b6000600020506	5b600060000a506	60005b5460de	5b6001600055614
03c5a1160005700	03c5a1160005700	5a1160025700	e3c5a1160005700

Fig. 2. SHA3 (CPU)   **Fig. 3.** EXP (CPU)   **Fig. 4.** SLOAD (I/O)   **Fig. 5.** SSTORE (I/O)

of the disk and bandwidth space of storing the transaction. In addition to the contract creation, we also must pay another 200 gas per byte of the contract's bytecode [23]. The largest contract in our test set had a size of 14 bytes, meaning that the cost of deploying our largest contract would haven been in total 54,800 gas. Considering an average gas limit of 8 million per blocks, the deployment costs solely represent 0.68% of the total amount of gas that can be used by a block.

4   Mining Strategy Evaluation

In order to evaluate our proposed mining strategy, we use a Markov Decision Process to model the mining process using a similar notation to the models proposed in [9] and [15]. As in the other models, we do not take the block propagation time into consideration. Figure 6 shows that once we have created a block (state M_1), we gain a slight advantage of $\gamma \cdot \alpha$ over the other miners. This is due to the slow execution time of the sluggish smart contract that get executed by the other miners during validation.

We can now calculate the steady-state distribution of our Markov Process to determine the overall gain in computational power obtained in the long run by our strategy. The steady-state distribution can be calculated using:

$$\pi \cdot \mathbf{P} = \pi \tag{1}$$

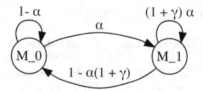

M_0: State when failed to create previous block.
M_1: State when created previous block.
α: Hashing power ratio of the miner.
γ: Ratio of the delay with respect to the block time.

Fig. 6. Markov decision process for sluggish mining

And substituting the values from our model we have that:

$$\begin{bmatrix} \pi_0 & \pi_1 \end{bmatrix} \begin{bmatrix} 1-\alpha & \alpha \\ 1 - \alpha \cdot (\gamma + 1) & \alpha \cdot (\gamma + 1) \end{bmatrix} = \begin{bmatrix} \pi_0 & \pi_1 \end{bmatrix} \tag{2}$$

$$\begin{cases} \pi_0 = \pi_0 \cdot (1 - \alpha) + \pi_1 (1 - \alpha \cdot (\gamma + 1)) \\ \pi_1 = \pi_0 \cdot \alpha + \pi_1 \cdot \alpha \cdot (\gamma + 1) \\ \pi_0 + \pi_1 = 1 \end{cases} \tag{3}$$

$$\pi = \begin{bmatrix} 1 - \frac{\alpha}{1 - \alpha \cdot \gamma} & \frac{\alpha}{1 - \alpha \cdot \gamma} \end{bmatrix} \tag{4}$$

As a result of our sluggish contract, our overall ratio of the total hashing power of the system has increased from α to $\frac{\alpha}{1 - \alpha \cdot \gamma}$. This gain in hashing power however comes at the cost of forfeiting the reward obtained through transaction fees. Every time a block is successfully mined, a transition into state M_1 occurs. In order to determine when our sluggish mining strategy is more lucrative than honest mining, we solve the inequality shown below:

$$\frac{\alpha}{1 - \alpha\gamma} \cdot \frac{R_{blck}}{t_{blck}} \geq \frac{\alpha}{t_{blck}} \cdot (R_{blck} + R_{fees}) \tag{5}$$

where R_{blck} is the block reward, R_{fees} is the transaction fees (average) and $\gamma = \frac{timedelay}{blocktime}$. Once the inequality is solved we can isolate the variables such that we can determine the requirements needed for our strategy to become profitable:

$$transaction fees \leq \frac{R_b \cdot \alpha \cdot \gamma}{1 - (\alpha \cdot \gamma)} \tag{6}$$

So given a miner with 15% of the total hashing power, a sluggish contract execution of about 3 s ($\gamma \approx 0.2$) and using the current static block reward of 3 Ether, we find that if the average transaction reward fees obtained from a block are below 0.0963 Ether, our strategy becomes viable.

5   Experimental Results

In this section we describe the experiments that we performed and the evaluation of the results. The experiments were conducted using a MacBook Pro (13-inch, 2016) with a 2.9 GHz Intel Core i5 Processor and 8 GB 2133 MHz LPDDR3 of Memory. Although the results might vary slightly between different machines, as mentioned in Sect. 3, we expect similar slowdowns on other machines as well. The average block time in Ethereum is 14.5 s.

5.1   Ethereum Clients

In order to ensure that our slow down is as effective as possible, we executed our contracts using the EVM implementation of the two most popular Ethereum clients at the time of writing: *Geth* and *Parity*. In particular we tested our contracts on the following two client versions: `geth v1.8.17` and `parity v2.0.9`.

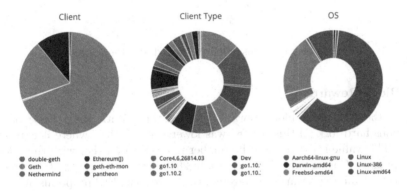

Fig. 7. Distribution of Ethereum clients, versions and OS.

While there are other clients and versions in use, as can be seen in Fig. 7, without selection we cover over 88% of the clients based on the data collected in [8].

5.2   Transaction Fees

The average transaction fees per block can vary quite drastically from day to day based on the current transaction backlog in the system, as can be seen in Fig. 8. For the purposes of our work, we calculated the average transaction fee for the blocks published during the month of January and November:

- January 2018: $\mu = 0.15$ *Ether/block*
- November 2018: $\mu = 0.08$ *Ether/block*

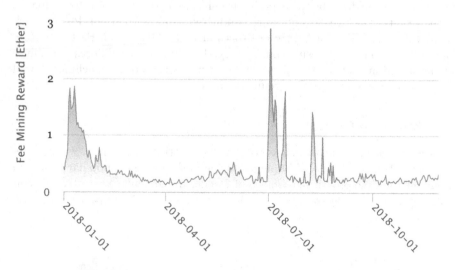

Fig. 8. Average transaction fees based on Etherscan [8]

5.3   Block Reward

Initially the Ethereum block reward was 5 Ether. With the release of the Metropolis hard fork [1] this reward was lowered to 3 Ether, where it currently stands. This value is expected to be further reduced to 2 Ether with the release of the planned Constantinople hard fork in 2019 [18]. Although the trend seems to be to have mining rewards be lowered, there are some EIP proposals advocating a raise in incentives for miners, such as the EIP1227 which seeks to restore the reward to 5 Ether. Therefore for the purposes of our tests we will take these three possible block reward values into consideration: 2, 3 and 5 Ether.

5.4   Sluggish Contract Execution Times

In order to calculate the slow down caused by our contracts we used the EVM stand-alone implementations: evm available in Geth and `parity-evm` available in Parity. This allows us to test and measure the execution time of our contracts without the need to deploy them on a test network. The commands used in our tests are:

```
$ time evm --gas 8000000 --code 5b60ff60ff2050603c5a1160005700 r0un
$ time evm --gas 8000000 --code 5b60ff60ff0a50603c5a1160005700 run
$ time evm --gas 8000000 --code 60005b5460de5a1160025700 run
$ time evm --gas 8000000 --code 5b6001600055614e3c5a1160005700 run

$ time parity-evm --gas 8000000 --code 5b60ff60ff2050603c5a1160005700
$ time parity-evm --gas 8000000 --code 5b60fe60fe0a50603c5a1160005700
$ time parity-evm --gas 8000000 --code 60005b5460de5a1160025700
$ time parity-evm --gas 8000000 --code 5b6001600055614e3c5a1160005700
```

Listing 1.1. CMDs used for experiments

We ran each command 100 times and then averaged the results, obtaining the following average slow downs in seconds:

	Geth	Parity
SHA3	0.15 s	2.52 s
EXP	1.21 s	3.42 s
SLOAD	0.03 s	1.13 s
SSTORE	0.02 s	0.29 s

The slowest contract, given a maximum of 8 million gas to run, appears to be the contract based on the EXP opcode, by quite a large margin for both Geth and Parity. This seems to suggest that the opcode is under-priced, as already explored in [4]. The difference between the execution times in Geth and Parity might indicate some issue in the implementation of the exponentiation function in Parity. An inspection of their code shows that both clients include shortcuts for specific values of the base and exponent ($x^0 = 1$, for example). Interestingly enough, both appear to implement the same technique, namely exponentiation by squaring, by using a left to right binary representation.

5.5 Evaluation

We would need to know the distribution of computational power of every single Ethereum client, in order to determine the overall slow down on the entire Ethereum network caused by our sluggish smart contract execution. Since we lack this information, we can only provide the lower and upper bounds of our attack. In the best case scenario for our strategy, all our nodes will be using Parity, while in the worst case, all will be using Geth. This can be seen in Figs. 10 and 11, by the vertical delimiters.

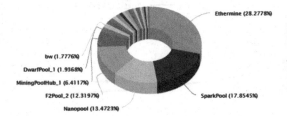

Ethermine (28.2778%)
bw (1.7776%)
DwarfPool_1 (1.9368%)
MiningPoolHub_1 (6.4117%)
F2Pool_2 (12.3197%)
Nanopool (13.4723%)
SparkPool (17.8545%)

Rank	Name	Blocks
1	Ethermine	28.2778%
2	SparkPool	17.8545%
3	Nanopool	13.4723%
4	F2Pool	12.3197%
5	MiningPoolHub	6.4117%

Fig. 9. Mining pools hashing power distribution [8] as of December 2018.

If we use the number of blocks mined to estimate the total hashing power of a mining pool and their names as given in Etherscan [8], we can extract the values shown in Fig. 9 for the first week of December 2018.

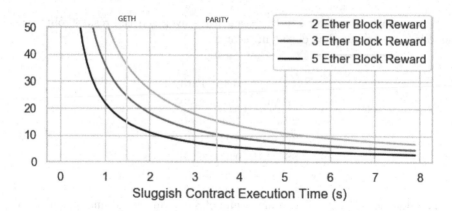

Fig. 10. Sluggish mining inequality for a transaction fee of 0.08 *Ether/block*.

Given the Ethereum settings described above, we can now define the conditions under which our strategy becomes viable using the equations shown in Sect. 4.

With an average transaction fee of 0.08 Ether we find that our strategy becomes viable under the conditions shown in Fig. 10. Each of the vertical lines represent the boundaries for our strategy to become viable (as described before, depending on the composition of mining clients), and any value above the block reward curve. This means that with a block reward of 3 Ether, any computational power above 10% and 24% would benefit from a switch to sluggish mining. These margins rise to 15%–35% for a block reward of 2 Ether, and become as low as 8% to 15% in the case of a 5 Ether block reward. Given the data shown in Fig. 9, this suggests that the top 4 mining pools could currently benefit from our approach.

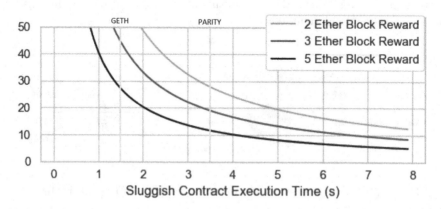

Fig. 11. Sluggish mining inequality for a transaction fee of 0.15 *Ether/block*.

However, if we assume a higher average transaction fee of 0.15 Ether, as seen in Fig. 11, then the strategy only becomes viable for mining pools with a hashing power between 20% and 45%, and hence only becoming viable for the Ethermine mining pool.

Moreover, once Constantinople is released and assuming the block reward does indeed drop, it would further reduce the viability of our strategy for mining pools with a hashing power within the range of 15% to 35%. However, it serves to highlight how a change in incentives for miners at the reward level can have such a drastic effect on their optimal strategy.

Although this strategy could be interpreted as a type of resource exhaustion attack, it is not significant enough to become apparent by miners. In order to ensure this strategy is not implemented to the potential detriment of the Ethereum community the best way is to ensure that the economic incentive is never there. We propose four ways to ensure this:

1. Reduce the block reward and therefore force mining pools to include transactions if they wish to continue make profit.
2. Increase the transaction fees by including a fee that compensates the mining pool.
3. A safeguard for this strategy would be to simply add these conditions to the benchmarking process of EVM opcodes, to ensure it never becomes a viable mining strategy for any mining pool by adequately pricing their opcodes.
4. Shift to another consensus mechanism such as proof-of-stake (PoS), in which having a delay in the execution time does not have such a tremendous impact as in PoW based mining. This is because there is no arms race with regard to who gets to mine the next block.

A scan of all transactions for each block would have to be done in order to determine if this type of mining strategy is already being used by mining pools. If at every block there is a transaction sent to a contract which fills up the remainder of that blocks remaining gas (and this same address is used across multiple blocks) then this could be an indicator for the deployment of our strategy.

6   Conclusions

In this work we have shown that sluggish smart contracts that aim at gaining an advantage over other miners who are validating received blocks before starting to create a new block, is a viable mining strategy provided certain conditions are met. We evaluated our strategy given current Ethereum conditions and shown that it would be a viable strategy for the top mining pools. Given that no user transactions are added to these 'sluggish blocks', the overall usefulness of the Ethereum network lowers, meaning that it might not be in a miners best interest to implement this strategy.

We have also shown that given the expected Ethereum changes in the pipeline, this type of strategy will be less useful in the future. In addition, we also provided a series of mechanisms for detecting this behaviour and how to ensure that this strategy does not become a profitable strategy in the future.

In this work we have shown that our mining strategy is viable by creating a block that is composed of one transaction sent to the sluggish contract. However a mining pool could instead include a series of normal pending transactions as the standard behaviour and make use of the remaining block gas by injecting a transaction that invokes a sluggish contract.

In future work it would be interesting to see if this type of strategy could be applied with different consensus mechanisms. For example the delay caused by computationally intensive contracts could be used in a proof-of-stake mechanism as an attack: given that miners have a certain time frame to create and broadcast a block, a long enough delay caused by the validation of the previous block could cause them to miss the window and therefore effectively to lose money.

References

1. Schoedon, A., Buterin, V.: Metropolis Difficulty Bomb Delay and Block Reward Reduction (2017). https://github.com/ethereum/EIPs/blob/master/EIPS/eip-649.md. Accessed December 2018
2. Buterin, V.: EXP cost increase (2016). https://github.com/ethereum/EIPs/blob/master/EIPS/eip-160.md. Accessed November 2018
3. Buterin, V.: Ethereum Improvement Proposal: Gas cost changes for IO-heavy operations (2017). https://github.com/ethereum/EIPs/blob/master/EIPS/eip-150.md. Accessed December 2018
4. Buterin, V.: Blockchain resource pricing (2018)
5. Chen, T., Li, X., Luo, X., Zhang, X.: Under-optimized smart contracts devour your money. In: 2017 IEEE 24th International Conference on Software Analysis, Evolution and Reengineering (SANER), pp. 442–446. IEEE (2017)
6. Chen, T., et al.: An adaptive gas cost mechanism for ethereum to defend against under-priced DoS attacks. In: Liu, J.K., Samarati, P. (eds.) ISPEC 2017. LNCS, vol. 10701, pp. 3–24. Springer, Cham (2017). https://doi.org/10.1007/978-3-319-72359-4_1
7. Das, S., Ribeiro, V.J., Anand, A.: Yoda: enabling computationally intensive contracts on blockchains with byzantine and selfish nodes. arXiv preprint arXiv:1811.03265 (2018)
8. Etherscan: Etherscan, the Ethereum Block Explorer (2018). https://etherscan.io/. Accessed December 2018
9. Eyal, I., Sirer, E.G.: Majority is not enough: bitcoin mining is vulnerable. Commun. ACM **61**(7), 95–102 (2018)
10. Foundation, E.: Ethash, December 2018. https://github.com/ethereum/wiki/wiki/Ethash
11. Heilman, E., Kendler, A., Zohar, A., Goldberg, S.: Eclipse attacks on bitcoin's peer-to-peer network. In: USENIX Security Symposium, pp. 129–144 (2015)
12. Kiayias, A., Koutsoupias, E., Kyropoulou, M., Tselekounis, Y.: Blockchain mining games. In: Proceedings of the 2016 ACM Conference on Economics and Computation, pp. 365–382. ACM (2016)
13. Luu, L., Chu, D.H., Olickel, H., Saxena, P., Hobor, A.: Making smart contracts smarter. In: Proceedings of the 2016 ACM SIGSAC Conference on Computer and Communications Security, pp. 254–269. ACM (2016)

14. Luu, L., Teutsch, J., Kulkarni, R., Saxena, P.: Demystifying incentives in the consensus computer. In: Proceedings of the 22nd ACM SIGSAC Conference on Computer and Communications Security, pp. 706–719. ACM (2015)
15. Nayak, K., Kumar, S., Miller, A., Shi, E.: Stubborn mining: generalizing selfish mining and combining with an eclipse attack. In: 2016 IEEE European Symposium on Security and Privacy (EuroS&P), pp. 305–320. IEEE (2016)
16. Sapirshtein, A., Sompolinsky, Y., Zohar, A.: Optimal selfish mining strategies in bitcoin. In: Grossklags, J., Preneel, B. (eds.) FC 2016. LNCS, vol. 9603, pp. 515–532. Springer, Heidelberg (2017). https://doi.org/10.1007/978-3-662-54970-4_30
17. Savers, N.: Hardfork Meta: Constantinople (2018). https://eips.ethereum.org/EIPS/eip-1013. Accessed December 2018
18. Schoedon, A.: Constantinople Difficulty Bomb Delay and Block Reward Adjustment (2017). https://github.com/ethereum/EIPs/blob/master/EIPS/eip-1234.md. Accessed December 2018
19. Solidity: Solidity 0.5.1 documentation, December 2018. https://solidity.readthedocs.io/en/v0.5.1/
20. Teutsch, J., Reitwießner, C.: A scalable verification solution for blockchains (2017)
21. Tikhomirov, S.: Ethereum: state of knowledge and research perspectives. In: Imine, A., Fernandez, J.M., Marion, J.-Y., Logrippo, L., Garcia-Alfaro, J. (eds.) FPS 2017. LNCS, vol. 10723, pp. 206–221. Springer, Cham (2018). https://doi.org/10.1007/978-3-319-75650-9_14
22. Torres, C.F., Schütte, J., State, R.: Osiris: hunting for integer bugs in ethereum smart contracts. In: Proceedings of the 34th Annual Computer Security Applications Conference, pp. 664–676. ACSAC 2018, ACM, New York (2018). https://doi.org/10.1145/3274694.3274737, http://doi.acm.org/10.1145/3274694.3274737
23. Wood, G.: Ethereum yellow paper (2014)

Short Paper: Deploying PayWord on Ethereum

Muhammad Elsheikh, Jeremy Clark$^{(\boxtimes)}$, and Amr M. Youssef

Concordia University, Montreal, Canada
pulpspy@gmail.com

Abstract. We revisit the 1997 PayWord credit-based micropayment scheme from Rivest and Shamir. We observe that smart contracts can be used to augment this system, apply to 'claim or refund' paradigm of cryptocurrencies to remove the counter-party risk inherent in PayWorld, and use a smart contract to 'staple' real value (in Ether) to payments in the system. Our implementation is more concise than any Ethereum payment channel we are aware of and the offline payments are very compact values (264 bits). It only uses hash functions and not digital signatures. EthWord becomes cheaper than standard Ethereum transfers when more than 16 payments between the same participants are made and appears to maintain its advantage for up to 1000+ transactions, at which point signature-based payments become cheapest. The main drawback of EthWord is the moderate gas price of using the system—despite dropping signatures, it is still priced out of the micropayments use-case. Like any payment channel, requires only two on-blockchain function calls to open and close the channel, while allowing the rest to be made off-blockchain.

1 Introduction

PayWord is a credit-based payment system, envisioned for small payments proposed by Rivest and Shamir [22]. The mechanics we will turn to later, but for now, the reader can think of tokens being issued that have some value. The key advantage of PayWord is its efficiency and succinctness drawn from using only hash functions. A limitation of PayWord is that tokens do not have inherent value; their value is based on the trust assumption that a counter-party will honour the value ascribed to them. With Ethereum, we can fix this issue by stapling cryptocurrency to the token through the use of a smart contract. Finally, while Ethereum already has internal functionality for payments, EthWord enables payments to be made off-blockchain and settled once on-blockchain.

This transformation turns PayWord from a trust-based credit system to an escrow-based payment system; not unlike offline payment channels and networks being proposed for Bitcoin (*e.g.*, the Lightning Network [20]). It is known that an Ethereum-based payment channel will be less complex than a Bitcoin one, since most of the complexity of Bitcoin-based payments channels comes from Bitcoin's limited scripting language [13]. EthWord is a uni-directional payment channel that can be chained into a payment network and has very compact

A. Bracciali et al. (Eds.): FC 2019 Workshops, LNCS 11599, pp. 82–90, 2020.
https://doi.org/10.1007/978-3-030-43725-1_7

(*e.g.*, 256-bit) payments. It thus might be an interesting primitive to enhance in the same ways other payment channels [4,20] have been: adding features [10], increasing efficiency [6,15], and adding transactional privacy [7,8,12,23].

2 Background

Beginning in the 1980s, a significant amount of the cryptographic literature has been devoted to the design of e-cash systems. In the 1990s, many startups worked toward deployment of this technology but most ultimately failed [17]. By late 2008, when Bitcoin was first proposed [16], innovation on both the academic and commercial side of digital cash had dried up. Now Bitcoin's success has breathed new life into the field: cryptocurrencies have billion dollar market capitalizations and academic conferences like *Financial Cryptography* are again publishing papers on financial cryptography.

At first glance, Bitcoin seems like a major departure from the e-cash systems from the 80s and 90s. In reality, its 'academic pedigree' is a novel combination of pre-existing ideas [18]. Similarly, researchers are re-discovering long lost ideas from the e-cash literature and finding new ways to apply them in a blockchain world. For example, blinded coins were a staple of e-cash [3] that re-emerge, along with accumulators [24], in post-Bitcoin systems like zcash [14,25]. Enabling micropayments through lottery-based probablistic payments of macropayments was explored in the 90s [9,21,27] and re-emerged for Bitcoin [19]. In this paper, we 're-discover' the 1997 payment system PayWord from Rivest and Shamir [22].

3 Preliminaries

Hash Chains. A hash chain [11] is constructed by iteratively applying a public one-way hash function $H()$ on a random value s. Let the notation $H^{i+1}(s) = H(H^i(s))$. A hash chain of length $n+1$ is:

$$\langle s, H(s), H^2(s), H^3(s), \ldots, H^{n-1}(s), H^n(s) \rangle$$

where s (technically equivalent to $H^0(s)$) is called the *seed* and $H^n(s)$ is called the *tip*. Given the hash is preimage resistant against a computationally bounded adversary, knowing some value in the chain $H^x(s)$ does not reveal any values 'up' the chain from it, including the seed: $\langle s, \ldots, H^{x-1}(s) \rangle$. Conversely the value $H^x(s)$ can be iteratively hashed to produce the rest of the values 'down' the chain ending up producing the tip value.

Recognition. If Alice meets Bob at a party, Bob can give the tip of a chain to Alice as a token [1]. Later when Bob meets Alice again, he can provide $H^{n-1}(s)$ as proof he is the same person that gave her the token. On the subsequent visit, he provides $H^{n-2}(s)$ and so on for n visits. Of course, Bob could more directly provide Alice with his public key and sign messages each visit, however hash chains avoid the relatively expensive public key operations of a signature.

Payments. In PayWord, recognition is used for credit-based payments. A Pay-Maker generates a length $n + 1$ hash chain and provides a signed[1] tip to a PayTaker. They agree that each preceding value in the hash chain has a specified unit of value owed to the PayTaker by the PayMaker. For example, say n is 100 and the value of each hash in the chain is a \$1 debt owed to the PayTaker. To expense \$27, the PayMaker provides $H^{n-27}(s)$ to the PayTaker who will verify that hashing it 27 times produces the signed tip. The PayMaker can increase the amount by sending further hashes, up to \$100 (the *capacity*), after which, the payment channel is *exhausted* and must be reinitiated.

Payment Channels. Payment channels were reconceived for Bitcoin [4,20] to offer offline payments between Alice, Bob, and possibly with some intermediaries relaying transactions. In Bitcoin, payment channels work the same as EthWord (in other words, EthWord *is* a payment channel) but involve setting up a number signed transactions (some pushed to the blockchain and others held in reserve) and the payments themselves are one or more full and signed Bitcoin transaction. While EthWord is a payment channel, it is a simple one. It can only send payments from the PayMaker to the PayTaker (thus it is *unidirectional*) and it can only send payments in increasing amounts (thus it is *monotonic*). Making a bidirectional payment channel, where payment values can be increased and decreased arbitrarily, is interesting future work.

Pay50. A recent blog post by Di Ferrante argues for the simplicity of Ethereum-based payment channels (relative to Bitcoin) and he offers a '50 lines of code' Solidity implementation of a uni-directional, monotonic channel we will name Pay50 for the purposes of this paper [5]. As a deliberate barebones implementation, it is simple and it relies on offline payments to be signed by the sender. We describe it further in the next section.

4   EthWord Implementation

EthWord is a line-by-line replication of Pay50, replacing the use of digital signatures with hash functions as described in the original PayWord proposal. We slightly modernize Pay50 to make it compliant with changes introduced in the Solidity language.[2] We replicate Pay50 to enable an isolated comparison between a signature-based approach (Pay50) and hash-based (EthWord) approach.

The primary issue with PayWord is that payments have no actual value and only represent an agreement to pay. In EthWord, we staple Ethereum's internal currency ether (ETH) to the payments through a smart contract to give them real value. Thus EthWord eliminates the counter-party risk in accepting payments that is inherent in PayWord, and this is only possible because payments are backed by both a digital currency and a decentralized execution environment.

Both Pay50 and EthWord follow the standard paradigm used in the literature to eliminate counterparty risk (sometimes called *claim-or-refund* [2]). If Bob

---

[1] The signature is only for non-repudiation, not for future authentication.

[2] Source code: https://github.com/MadibaGroup/2017-EthWords.

1. The PayMaker runs the constructor of **EthWord**.
2. The PayMaker opens the contract by specifying the identity of PayTaker, the validity period of the channel, how much each hash is worth, and funds the contract. The PayMaker will send the contract address to PayTaker.
3. The PayTaker will check the parameters of the contract to ensure it is funded, how long she has to settle the account before the PayMaker can withdraw his deposited funds, and the total amount of the deposited funds. When satisfied, she stores the hashchain tip offline.
4. Offline, the PayMaker will make payments by sending hash values. The PayTaker will check that the value iteratively hashes to the tip for a correct number of iterations corresponding to amount of payment she expects. If PayMaker wants to make successive payments, they send a new hash that represents the new total amount to be paid to the PayTaker.
5. At any time while the contract is open, PayTaker can submit a hash value and receive the appropriate payment. If the PayTaker has not run this function and the validity period expires, the PayMaker can withdraw all the money in the contract and close it.

Protocol 1: The on-blockchain and off-blockchain steps in **EthWord** payments

(the PayMaker) wants to send up to X ETH to Alice (the PayTaker), he prepays by loading X ETH into a smart contract that the PayTaker can withdraw from when specified conditions are met. The PayMaker also sets a deadline for the PayTaker to withdraw, after which he can release the escrowed funds back to himself. The PayTaker checks that the contract is properly formed and funded; only then will she accept payments from the PayMaker.

4.1   **EthWord** Code Design

As **EthWord** is a modification of **Pay50**, we will discuss the design of both in parallel. Both use the constructor to initially setup the contract. In addition, they have two functions that both close the channel: one is used by the PayTaker to claim a payment and other is used by the PayMaker to dissolve the contract after it has timed out. **EthWord** is summerized in Protocol 1. The constructor for both **Pay50** and **EthWord** establishes the core components of the contract:

- PayTaker: `msg.sender` for the contract creation.
- PayMaker: an address passed into the constructor.
- Total available funds: the constructor allows an amount of Ether to be transferred to the payment channel contract (the constructor is marked `payable`).
- Timeout: a validity period passed into the constructor. The contract also stores the block timestamp of when the constructor was run. These values are added together and when they exceed any future block timestamp, the self-destruct function is permitted to run allowing the PayMaker a refund.

Table 1. Function cost. Since closeChannel is dependent on how long the hash chain is for the claimed payment, we shows costs for length 50 and length 100.

EthWord Function	Gas	ETH	USD
Channel	318 953	0.00539	$0.689
closeChannel (50)	18 757	0.00033	$0.042
closeChannel (100)	21 907	0.00038	$0.049

Note that as implemented, the timeout functionality in both is timestamp dependent which could enable the PayMaker to refund earlier than allowed, or alternatively be locked out from refunding, as a result of miner manipulation of the timestamps. This is feasible for adjustments of approximately 900 s. Therefore, the contract timeout should be considered 'fuzzy' or imprecise.

For EthWord specifically (not Pay50), the constructor also establishes the payword tip and the amount of Ether each payword is worth. Consider a contract that holds 1.00 ETH in escrow and the PayTaker supplies proof that they are entitled to, say, 0.45 of the 1.00 ETH by invoking this function. For Pay50, the proof is the claimed amount as signed by PayMaker and the contract validates the signature. For EthWord, it is a payword (*i.e.*, the output of a hash function). In this case, the PayMaker might make a hash-chain of length 100, construct the contract with the tip, specify the value of each hash as 0.01 ETH, and funds the contract with 1.00 ETH.

Note that the contract does not care about the length of the hash chain because there is no simple way (nor reason) for the PayTaker to actually verify the length of the hash-chain. If it is too short, then PayMaker cannot make payments after a certain point. If it is longer, than PayTaker needs to stop accepting payments in excess of what she has verified to the contract to hold. Similarly, since the length of the hashchain is unknown to PayTaker, the contract does not require a specific amount to be funded. The PayTaker will just treat this amount as the maximum.

The PayMaker can make an offline payment to the PayTaker by sending a hash (again see Protocol 1). Note that the hash is in no way bound to the identity of the PayTaker—the smart contract binds the use of the hash to the PayTaker. Next, note that technically the PayTaker can compute the chain and submit any hash from this chain to claim(), however they are incentivized to send the most valuable hash. For this same reason, the PayMaker can then later 'up the payment' by sending a more valuable hash to the PayTaker. This can be repeated until the PayMaker runs out of hashes or PayTaker wants to run claim(). This is called *replace-by-incentive* [13] in the payment channel literature.

4.2   Evaluation

Footprint. Relative to Pay50, EthWord does not add to the lines of code; in fact, it even shaves a few off. The more important property is the size of the

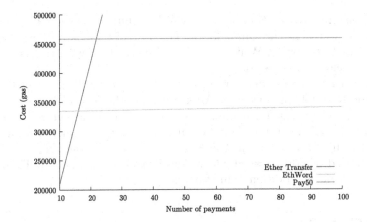

Fig. 1. The total gas cost of running the payment channels EthWord, Pay50, and the internal Ether Transfer as a function of the number of payments. Internal transfers are most economical up to 16 transactions, then EthWord is most economical, and we extrapolate that Pay50 (at a gas cost of around 460 000) will only become more economical when the transactions exceed 1000.

payment sent to the receiver; this is reduced from a digital signature to a hash or from 776 bits to 264 bits. Note that it is even possible to reduce EthWord to 256-bits; an extra 8 bit value representing the length of the hash from the tip is included for a more convenient loop.

Gas Costs. As of January 15th, 2019, the weighted average price of 1 gas is 17.26×10^{-9} ETH[3] and the exchange rate of 1 ETH to USD is \$127.85.[4] Table 1 shows the gas costs of each function in EthWord if run successfully. The cost of the claim function includes checking if the provided payment (hash) is part of the hash chain (if when iteratively hashed, it results in the tip value). Thus the cost of claiming will vary on how many times the hash must be iterated. For example, consider a channel with 100 payment values worth 0.01 ETH each. Running claim on the payment value representing 0.05 ETH will require hashing the value 5 times. The payment value of 0.95 ETH will require 95 hashes.

Figure 1 shows the total gas cost of running the payment channels EthWord, Pay50, and the internal ether transfer as a function of the number of payments (from 1 to 100). At 100, the cost by EthWord is 334 236 which is still about 30% less than the cost of running Pay50 that must verify a digital signature (*i.e.*, Pay50 uses Solidity's `ecrecover` with some additional processing logic).

Contract Security. As mentioned above, the contract depends on timestamps for allowing a refund after an elapsed time. Further, once the contract is refundable, the PayTaker can still close the contract and receive payment assuming they have a payment proof. If PayTaker and PayMaker try to close the contract

---

[3] https://ethgasstation.info/.
[4] https://coinmarketcap.com/.

at the same time, transaction ordering will be arbitrary, subject to a gas auction, and subject to miner manipulation. For both of these issues, the PayTaker simply needs to be aware. Well before the timeout, the PayTaker has exclusive control over closing the contract.

Last, consider a case where the PayTaker is given a payment of 0.45 ETH from a contract holding 1.00 ETH. After receiving the 0.45 ETH at the address of the PayTaker (call it T), note that T may be a contract address and if so, it's fallback function will be allowed to run. Logically, this function could recall close and result in an addition 0.45 ETH—a reentrancy attack. The mitigation is the standard one: using send which does provide enough gas to T's fallback function to make an additional function call.

5   Discussion

Forming payment networks. Consider a third party, in addition to the PayMaker and the PayTaker, called an intermediary. If PayMaker establishes an EthWord channel with the intermediary and the intermediary establishes an EthWord channel with PayTaker, and both channels use the same tip, then payments can be routed through the intermediary without trusting it. This requires one small modification: PayTaker can run closeChannel() in both contracts. It can also admit further modifications: for example, the intermediary might modify closeChannel() so that it keeps some fraction of the total payout as a fee.

Porting to Bitcoin. Bitcoin's scripting language is purposely limited, compared to Ethereum, to ensure scripts execute efficiently and support Bitcoin's core functionality of digital money. Many PayWord components are supported in Bitcoin script, including but not limited to locking transactions with a hash image that requires a pre-image to spend; and the ability to iteratively hash elements. However it does support looping nor dynamically changing how an output can be split. A moderate extension to Bitcoin's scripting language could enable PayWord on Bitcoin; one proposal is MicroBTC [26].

Micropayments. With a total gas cost (to construct, open, and claim within a contract) of $0.75 or more, EthWord (or other Ethereum-based payment networks) are not suitable for true micropayments. Even to send $100 of value, it represents a 0.75% fee. The simplest internal Ethereum transaction costs 21 000 gas so EthWord will have to replace 16 transactions to pay for itself.

Prepaying. A limitation that underlies almost all payment channels is the fact that payments have to be *prepaid*. Without some broader economic infrastructure, payment channels are similar to using prepaid cards, something we expect compensation for (generally, customers pay for credit; preloading a card or account is giving the merchant credit which the merchant should pay for[5]). If Alice were to pay all her bills for a single year using EthWord (or other payment

---

[5] For example, a $50 Apple Store prepaid card might sell for $40 or using a preloaded Starbucks app might result in rewards that can be redeemed for future purchases.

channel), she would have to have enough Ether for an entire year on the first day of the year. For many people, this would be a cash flow issue.

Trickling. One issue in payments is fairness or fair exchange. When the payment is made on-blockchain for a token that is already on-blockchain, the swap of payment for token can be made atomic. However when the purchase is off-blockchain, either the purchased good or the payment has to be released first, leading to counter-party risk. Some purchases are divisible (*e.g.,* electricity purchased to charge an electric car) and in these cases, payment channels like EthWord are useful for *trickling* small payments in exchange for small divisions of the purchased good. If one party unfairly aborts, the value that is forfeited is small and bounded. Trickling can also be used for sending funds via an untrusted intermediary when the payment network approach cannot be used—*e.g.,* if the intermediary is a mixing service that is anonymizing the payment stream amongst other indistinguishable output payment streams.

References

1. Anderson, R., Bergadano, F., Crispo, B., Lee, J.-H., Manifavas, C., Needham, R.: A new family of authentication protocols. SIGOPS Oper. Syst. Rev. **32**(4), 9–20 (1998)
2. Bentov, I., Kumaresan, R.: How to use bitcoin to design fair protocols. In: CRYPTO (2014)
3. Chaum, D.: Blind signatures for untraceable payments. In: CRYPTO (1982)
4. Decker, C., Wattenhofer, R.: A fast and scalable payment network with bitcoin duplex micropayment channels. In: SSS (2015)
5. Di Ferrante, M.: Ethereum payment channel in 50 lines of code. Medium (2017)
6. Dziembowski, S., Eckey, L., Faust, S., Malinowski, D.: Perun: virtual payment channels over cryptographic currencies. IACR ePrint (2017)
7. Green, M., Miers, I.: Bolt: anonymous payment channels for decentralized currencies. In CCS (2017)
8. Heilman, E., Alshenibr, L., Baldimtsi, F., Scafuro, A., Goldberg, S.: Tumblebit: an untrusted bitcoin-compatible anonymous payment hub. In: NDSS (2017)
9. Jarecki, S., Odlyzko, A.: An efficient micropayment system based on probabilistic polling. In: Financial Cryptography (1997)
10. Khalil, R., Gervais, A.: Revive: rebalancing off-blockchain payment networks. In: CCS (2017)
11. Lamport, L.: Password authentication with insecure communication. CACM **24**(11), 770–772 (1981)
12. Malavolta, G., Moreno-Sanchez, P., Kate, A., Maffei, M., Ravi, S.: Concurrency and privacy with payment-channel networks. In: CCS (2017)
13. McCorry, P., Möser, M., Shahandasti, S.F., Hao, F.: Towards bitcoin payment networks. In: Information Security and Privacy (2016)
14. Miers, I., Garman, C., Green, M., Rubin, A.D.: Zerocoin: anonymous distributed e-cash from bitcoin. In: IEEE Symposium on Security and Privacy (2013)
15. Miller, A., Bentov, I., Kumaresan, R., McCorry, P.: Sprites: payment channels that go faster than lightning. CoRR, abs/1702.05812 (2017)
16. Nakamoto, S.: Bitcoin: a peer-to-peer electionic cash system. Unpublished (2008)

17. Narayanan, A., Bonneau, J., Felten, E.W., Miller, A., Goldfeder, S.: Bitcoin and Cryptocurrency Technologies. Princeton (2016)
18. Narayanan, A., Clark, J.: Bitcoin's academic pedigree. CACM **60**(12), 770–772 (2017)
19. Pass, R., Shelat, A.: Micropayments for decentralized currencies. In: CCS (2015)
20. Poon, J., Dryja, T.: The bitcoin lightning network: scalable off-chain instant payments (2015)
21. Rivest, R.L.: Electronic lottery tickets as micropayments. In: FC (1997)
22. Rivest, R.L., Shamir, A.: PayWord and MicroMint: two simple micropayment schemes. In: Security Protocols (1996)
23. Roos, S., Moreno-Sanchez, P., Kate, A., Goldberg, I.: Settling payments fast and private: efficient decentralized routing for path-based transactions. In: NDSS (2018)
24. Sander, T., Ta-Shma, A.: Auditable, anonymous electronic cash. In: CRYPTO (1999)
25. Sasson, E.B., et al.: decentralized anonymous payments from bitcoin. In: IEEE Symposium on Security and Privacy (2014)
26. Wan, Z., Deng, R.H., Lee, D., et al.: MicroBTC: efficient, flexible and fair micropayment for bitcoin using hash chains. J. Comput. Sci. Technol. **34**, 403–415 (2019). https://doi.org/10.1007/s11390-019-1916-x
27. Wheeler, D.: Transactions using bets. In: Security Protocols (1997)

SoK: Development of Secure Smart Contracts – Lessons from a Graduate Course

Monika di Angelo[1,2]([⊠]) [iD], Christian Sack[1], and Gernot Salzer[1,2] [iD]

[1] Technische Universität Wien, Vienna, Austria
{monika.diangelo,christian.sack,gernot.salzer}@tuwien.ac.at
[2] Eurecom, Biot, France

Abstract. Smart contracts are programs on top of blockchains and cryptocurrencies. This new technology allows parties to exchange valuable assets without mutual trust, with smart contracts controlling the interaction between the parties. Developing smart contracts, or more generally decentralized applications, is challenging. First, they run in a concurrent environment that admits race conditions; adversaries may attack smart contracts by influencing the order of transactions. Second, the required functionality is often based on roles and states. This proves to be difficult to implement in current smart contract languages. Third, as a distinctive feature, smart contracts are immutable, hence bugs cannot be corrected easily. At the same time, bugs may cause (and have already caused) tremendous losses; they are to be avoided by all means.

This paper discusses our approach of *teaching* the development of secure smart contracts on the Ethereum platform at university level. This is a challenging task in many respects. The underlying technologies evolve rapidly and documentation lags behind. Available tools are in different stages of development, and even the most mature ones are still difficult to use. The development of secure smart contracts is not yet a well-established discipline. Our aim is to share our ideas, didactic concept, materials, insights, and lessons learned.

Keywords: Smart contract · Secure development · University course · Ethereum · Solidity

1 Introduction

Smart contracts were envisioned by Nick Szabo about 20 years ago [27,28] as computer programs automating the exchange of digital assets, which may be linked to non-digital objects or values. Smart contracts became effectively alive with the advent of cryptocurrencies. While playing only a limited role in Bitcoin, they are an essential ingredient of platforms like Ethereum [12].

Cryptocurrency-based smart contracts run on peer-to-peer networks that consist of mutually distrusting nodes (so-called miners) ideally operating in a decentralized manner. There is no need for an external trusted authority, miners execute smart contracts in an autonomous fashion.

© International Financial Cryptography Association 2020
A. Bracciali et al. (Eds.): FC 2019 Workshops, LNCS 11599, pp. 91–105, 2020.
https://doi.org/10.1007/978-3-030-43725-1_8

1.1 Characteristics of Smart Contracts

The main characteristics of smart contracts are: *immutability* (as long as the community does not decide otherwise), *transparency* (when the ledger is open), provisioning of a *digital service* (or the digital mapping of a service), an *interface to the outside world* to enable interaction with it, *no central control/supervision* of transactions and contract execution, and for the contracting parties *no necessity to reveal their identities* to anyone.

Because of these properties smart contracts promise to be of use for applications requiring trustless computation, observability, tamper evidence, and decentralization. *Trustless computation* means autonomous execution of the program as well as no need for a trusted (third) party. Instead, trust is put in the ledger that keeps track of the exchange of assets. Smart contracts draw from the transparency technology of the underlying cryptocurrency, providing *observability and tamper evidence* as a trust base. *Decentralization* means that the system as a whole should not suffer from a single point of failure, and again should not rely on anything that needs to be trusted.

Application areas where such requirements may be desirable and useful are for example notary services, open government, insurance services, supply chain management, copyright management, and FinTech. Applications based on smart contracts are still in their infancy, with the most successful ones being initial coin offerings (ICOs) and collectibles like CryptoKitties [6].

1.2 Reasons for a University Course

Distributed applications (Dapps) use smart contract as backend to implement part of the business logic and to store critical data. Developing such Dapps is not just about learning another script language for smart contracts, but brings in considerable complexities that result e.g. from the concurrency, transparency, and immutability of transactions. Failing to acknowledge these complexities led to a situation where smart contracts are more famous for bugs and money losses than for success stories.

At the same time start-ups and traditional companies (like financial institutions and energy providers) jump on the bandwagon and urgently search for programmers able to develop Dapps that handle valuable assets reliably. This need is complemented by a massive interest of computer science students in this apparently hot topic. From a didactic point of view, smart contracts and blockchains are a worthwhile subject as they relate to many topics in computer science, like security, concurrency, cryptographic protocols, randomness, advanced algorithms, data structures, and formal verification.

1.3 Interesting Courses Online and at Other Universities

Among the available university based courses on Bitcoin, blockchains, and cryptocurrencies, the most prominent one is [19], a highly recommended book with a great accompanying online course.

For smart contracts in particular, information on held or available courses is scarce. The authors of [7] were the first to document the teaching of smart contracts as a university course. They report "several typical classes of mistakes [undergraduate] students made, suggest ways to fix/avoid them, and advocate best practices for programming smart contracts." The main problems were failure to encode the state machine properly, failure to use cryptography, misaligned incentives, and Ethereum specifics. This can be regarded as a reference course. For their lab they used Serpent, a high level programming language in the Ethereum world. Their pedagogical approach of "build, break, and amend your own program" seemed to be beneficial to teach adversarial thinking. As a conclusion about smart contracts, they arrived at "designing and implementing them correctly was a highly non-trivial task".

Outside academia and free to use on the internet, there are two projects which we consider well done and worthwhile. *Ethernaut* [20] is a war game, where vulnerabilities of smart contracts need to be exploited to advance. The instructive challenges have different levels of difficulty that are indicated accordingly. To succeed one has to understand known vulnerabilities and to apply the gained insights when using the provided tools. The online tutorial *CryptoZombies* [15] provides a nice gamification of how to develop smart contracts. It introduces the programming language Solidity in several steps, while jumping right into matters. By forming an army of zombies, one learns to program a suite of contracts similar to the popular CryptoKitties [6]. Finally, one is instructed on how to build a Dapp around the zombie contracts.

1.4   Added Value of This Paper

Teaching a subject like smart contracts that is new and in flux poses several challenges. There are no reference courses that may serve as a blue-print; the essence of secure smart contract programming has to be distilled from many sources. Moreover, the tools and techniques for the development of Dapps are still evolving and need to be evaluated regarding their suitability for teaching. When preparing the course, we came across a single report about a similar endeavor [7], which was helpful but at the same time already partly outdated.

The purpose of this report is to pass on our findings and experience in order to inspire and aid teachers designing similar courses as well as to identify difficulties encountered during the development of smart contracts. To this end, we present an analysis of the students' development efforts, a discussion of useful resources and tools, and a critical reflection of our experiences.

Furthermore, we contribute to defining the need for specific and qualifying university courses on blockchain and smart contracts programming. Based on the students' answers and feedback, we present insights into problems faced by researchers and developers when dealing with smart contracts. We elaborate on the issues encountered and provide several suggestions.

1.5 Roadmap

In the next section we present our course design in detail and the course setup. The lessons learned including an analysis of the students' development efforts is provided in Sect. 3. In Sect. 4 we discuss our approach, and in Sect. 5 we draw our conclusions about smart contract development and note further challenges.

2 Course Design

For the course design, we first define basic details like learning outcomes and content. Subsequently, we summarize the considered body of knowledge on which we base the learning activities. Then we present the assignments in detail.

2.1 Characteristics

Learning Outcomes. The aim of the course is that students gain knowledge and skills in the following areas.

Technological foundations: Understand the technological basis of smart contracts, like the blockchain, the Ethereum virtual machine (EVM), and the execution of smart contracts by miners.

Programming languages and tools: Use the languages, tools, and technologies for developing smart contracts and for interacting with them, like Solidity, Remix, Truffle, Geth, and Web3.js.

Security and privacy issues: Recognize and avoid security and privacy issues resulting either from the technology or from poor programming practices.

Smart contracts and Dapps: Develop secure smart contracts and Dapps involving tokens and cryptocurrencies.

Course Contents. In the lectures we recap the cryptographic basics as needed to understand cryptocurrencies and blockchain mechanics, explain the basic concepts of smart contracts, describe Ethereum in detail, highlight the peculiarities of scripting in Solidity, present the basics of the EVM as well as its relation to Solidity, and discuss current approaches to verification of smart contracts. The workshops cover tools and introductory exercises. The challenges address known vulnerabilities. Tokens and their usage as well as specific programming techniques are essential parts of the two projects.

Target Audience. Smart contracts and Dapps constitute advanced topics in computer science that presuppose knowledge in areas like algorithms, programming, web computing, and security. Therefore we devised *Smart Contracts* as an elective course in the master programmes of computer science and business informatics. Students without a background in Bitcoin and blockchain technology are referred to [19] and the accompanying video lectures.

2.2 Body of Knowledge

Smart Contracts. We start with Nick Szabo's ground breaking ideas on smart contracts [27,28] and Princeton's great introductory book and online course on cryptocurrencies [19]. The research perspectives and challenges for cryptocurrencies in [4] are worth considering, too. Regarding the Ethereum world, we refer to the Ethereum basics [12,31] and Buterin's blockchain and smart contract mechanism design challenges [29], as well as the overview of scripting languages in [24]. Furthermore, the article [26] with a legal perspective and the presentation [14] with a programming point of view offer additional perspectives on the topic. For platforms and use cases, [2] provides an interesting empirical analysis of smart contracts regarding platforms, applications, and design patterns, whereas [23] discusses decentralized applications. The challenges and new directions for blockchain-oriented software engineering in [22] provided useful insights, as did [17] with their elaboration on validation and verification of smart contracts.

Security Issues. [1] presents a useful survey of attacks on Ethereum smart contracts, whereas [16] not only investigates the security of smart contracts deployed on the Ethereum main chain, but also proposes to use symbolic execution (as implemented in the tool Oyente) to make contracts less vulnerable. [3] presents a declarative domain-specific language (Findel) to add security to financial agreements handled by smart contracts. The blog post [13] provides a guide to auditing smart contracts and reviews relevant attacks.

Last Minute Contributions. As smart contracts are a lively field, interesting work kept appearing throughout the course. This includes the collection of coding patterns [30] with proposals how to mitigate typical attacks. The authors of [8] encourage best practices to mitigate detrimental software behavior and argue for specific "Blockchain Software Engineering" since existing approaches seem insufficient for the particular needs of smart contract development.

2.3 Learning Activities

The course activities comprised lectures, workshops, and assignments, accompanied by a moderated discussion forum and email support.

Lectures. The main intention of the lectures was to cover new material deemed necessary to achieve the learning outcomes. While the usual course format is lectures with accompanying assignments, we deliberately added a workshop component.

Workshops. The intent of the workshops was to alleviate the frustration associated with using a range of new tools, and to close gaps in the understanding of the presented material. The students brought their own laptops to gain hands-on experience. We first demonstrated the handling of selected tools and assisted with initial problems arising from the partly unstable tool chain and the incomplete documentation. Then, we focused on small ad-hoc tasks to make sure everyone was familiar with the operations and concepts required for the upcoming assignments. The workshops also served the purpose of discussing sample solutions after the submission deadlines.

Assignments. The assignments were intended to provide students with practical experience regarding the implementation of smart contract, to let the students apply the newly gained skills and knowledge, and for us to get feedback on the progress of students regarding their understanding of the essential concepts.

The assignments started with the online tutorial *CryptoZombies* [15] (see Sect. 1.3) in order to provide an entertaining introduction into programming in Solidity. Subsequently, eight security challenges had to be solved, with the intention to get the students to understand known vulnerabilities and to motivate the need for secure smart contract development.

Finally, there were two constructive tasks. For the guided project "beer bar" we provided a clear specification and an abstract Solidity contract including comments for the parts to be implemented by the students. The final project had a free topic and just a few constraints.

Ether was only available in limited quantities to raise awareness that it is a costly resource. Next to a regular supply of Ether which was sufficient to solve the assignments, it was also handed out as a reward for participation in the workshop tasks, and upon request.

2.4   Assignments in Detail

Challenges. The eight security challenges (inspired by Ethernaut [20]) are packed into a story in which the main character is a software developer. For each challenge the task is to deplete the provided contract by finding and successfully exploiting one or more security issues. The challenges address known vulnerabilities concerning the fallback function, a misnamed constructor, math issues like overflow, forced transfer of Ether, reentrancy, hidden variables, delegatecall, insecure contract interaction, failing transactions, and randomness.

Beer Bar. This assignment consists of four constructive sub-tasks.

Task 1. The students implement a *bar token* that is not divisible, but mintable and burnable. Furthermore, they make sure that tokens cannot get lost by sending them accidentally to contracts that are not set up for accepting them. The concept of tokens as well as standard token contracts [21] were introduced in the workshop. To solve this task the students customize an ERC223 token.

Task 2. The students implement a *beer bar* that uses the bar token from Task 1. We provide the interface as well as a skeleton contract with in-line comments that describe the functionality to be implemented, like opening and closing the bar, setting the beer price and the bar token to be accepted, and the processing of beer orders. For modeling the roles of bar owners and bar keepers, the students use the RBAC contract [21].

Task 3. The students extend the bar to a *song voting bar* where customers can vote for the songs to be added to the playlist, with an additional role DJ.

Task 4. We provide a simple web interface in Javascript that uses `web3.js` to communicate with the contract of the beer bar. The students extend the interface to interact with their song voting bar.

Final Project. For the final project, the students are encouraged to choose a topic of their own. If lacking inspiration, they may extend the beer bar. The final project is graded with respect to the following criteria.

- Use of mappings, `RBAC`-roles, modifiers, Ether, tokens, correct math.
- Some (minimalistic) web interface for interacting with the contract.
- The contracts should not make any Ether or tokens inaccessible.
- The contracts should not exhibit any of the vulnerabilities discussed in the security challenges before.
- Quality of the documentation specifying the contract and the web interface.

The following aspects give an additional bonus: original choice of topic, commitment schemes for guarding secrets (like bids or game moves), deposits to prevent aborts or reverts of games, timeouts to ensure the termination of moves or games, and good randomness.

2.5   Technical Setup

The technical setup of the course consists of a Linux server providing an Ethereum blockchain and a block explorer, as well as a separate client for the lecturers and the students (Linux, MacOS, and Windows). As implementation languages we use *Bash, Javascript, Solidity,* and *Html.*

Ethereum Blockchain. Geth [11] runs a private chain with proof of authority (POA). The geth client (miner) has to be configured such that it can handle sufficiently many concurrent connections to give all students access in parallel. Moreover, it turned out that we need a high block gas limit for publishing the challenges (see below).

Block Explorer. We developed our own block explorer consisting of a single Html page and some programs in Javascript. When the user opens the block explorer in a browser it connects to the local geth instance to load the chain data. As a result, the user sees the local synchronized state of the blockchain, reducing the network load on our server. A filter allows the students to restrict their view to the transactions they are actually involved in. This helps in situations where several students are active at the same time (like during workshops).

Administration of Students and Assignments via the Blockchain. We deployed several contracts on our blockchain to manage the submission of assignments and the interaction with and between students.

The *address book* provides a unique mapping between student ids and Ethereum addresses (one *public* address per student); moreover, it maintains a list of several *private* Ethereum addresses per student. The public address is used e.g. for interactions between students and for transferring Ether.

The addresses of personalized copies of challenges and of contracts submitted by a student are stored as private addresses, only known to a single student and to the lecturers.

The *Ether tap* regularly transfers small amounts of Ether to all public addresses. Moreover, in case of mishaps (like transferring accidentally all Ether to the zero address) students may request limited amounts of Ether from this contract.

The *alias directory* allows the students to specify a string to be used in place of their name. This alias is later used for displaying live progress visualizations and feedback (e.g. who has already solved a task) and rankings (like the time needed to solve a challenge).

A *base contract* is inherited by each personalized copy of a challenge. It adds private variables that ensure that the students can only interact with their own copy, and that the challenge can be turned off after the deadline.

Client for Lecturers. The client for lecturers is a geth client with console scripts attached to it. It automatically prints each transaction as it occurs, improving readability by translating the involved addresses to names. The scripts provide functions for easy maintenance and observation during the course. As an example, the function `balances` identifies students who have spent most of their Ether. Other scripts deploy a challenge for a single student or groups of addresses, whereby certain values in each instance can be varied randomly to personalize the challenge for each student.

Client for Students. The client for the students is a geth client connecting automatically to the private course chain. It includes the abstract binary interface (ABI) and the deployment address of the address book such that students can access their private and public addresses in a symbolic way.

3   Lessons Learned from the Students' Submissions

3.1   Beer Bar

It turned out to be difficult for some students (25%) to accept only their own tokens (and not arbitrary ones). After the submission deadline, we addressed this issue in the workshop. We reopened the submission for the beer bar to admit corrections, because we felt this token aspect was too important to miss.

3.2   Final Project

After teaching known vulnerabilities by means of security challenges to motivate secure smart contracts, and after showing best practice examples, we were interested to see which topics the students would choose for their final project and how they would implement them.

The final project was handed in by 44 students. Most students addressed the *homo ludens* by implementing some sort of game (14), gambling (13), betting (5), or lottery (3). Three students opted for a shop. The remaining six students came up with extra-ordinary topics, namely *cash register functionality that conforms to local law, untraceable and unlinkable voting (using a ring signature), smart marketplace, data saver, trusted recommender,* and *betterSpotify.*

The effort put into the final project varied. 14 students pragmatically extended their implementation of the beer bar or transformed it into a shop of similar structure. Several students skipped the web interface (10) or documented their project poorly (6). At the other end, about half of the students went at great lengths to provide a rounded-off project, paying also attention to details.

The students encountered several difficulties in their implementation efforts. Our insights are broken down with respect to the requirements for the project.

Roles, Modifiers, Require Statements. These elements posed no problems. They are mentioned first in the initial tutorial on Solidity, CrytoZombies, and then are repeatedly used throughout the challenges and in the guided project.

Data Structures. Many students wanted to iterate over arrays. We explained during the course that loops over potentially growing ranges should be avoided as the execution may eventually exceed the gas limit and fail (apart from becoming more and more expensive). Not being able to iterate over mappings required time to get used to. Deciding which part of the data and the program logic should be put on-chain and which one off-chain remained an issue.

Correct Math. It was easy for the students to understand the problems of overflows and wrap-arounds and to take precautions.

Token Usage. Even though we put an emphasis on tokens and their correct usage, some students had troubles. This was particularly true for ERC223 tokens and the idea of the token fallback function. These concepts presumably need more time, explanations, and exercises.

Commitments. The correct usage of commitments needs basic security knowledge that we did not teach, just briefly summarized. Most students did not require commitments for their final project. Several students (13) employed them correctly, a few tried but failed.

Stages/Phases. The usage of stages or phases in order to ensure the correct ordering of transactions did not pose any problems.

Randomness. Good randomness within smart contracts is generally tricky. We only covered it superficially. Most projects did not require (good) randomness. Some students made serious attempts, most of them (9) succeeded.

Private Variables. Even though we covered private variables in the workshops and the challenges, quite a few students had problems with them. The keyword *private* and the missing getter function seemed to make them blind to the fact that the variables could still be inspected from the outside. Apparently, private variables represent new and unexpected material that needs more exercises.

It might also be worthwhile to modify the syntax of Solidity by replacing the misleading keyword by another one, maybe *local* or *internal*.

Deposits/Timeouts. The usage of deposits or timeouts to handle unfair game aborts or stalling did not pose any problems.

Web User Interface. Students with little prior knowledge of web scripting had a difficult time implementing a basic web interface for their contracts, even though we provided an exemplary one for the bar contract. If this is to be an integral part of the course, it definitely needs more coverage or prior knowledge.

3.3   Tools

All students initially used Remix, and most of them stayed with this browser IDE. Some additionally tried Remixd to access the local file system; this add-on, however, did not prove stable and lead to the destruction of files in two cases.

Some students switched to the Truffle framework because of its promise of more structured testing and better handling of multi-contract projects. Testing is generally an issue with little or unstable support by the tools. A problem with Truffle was that a new version became available during the course that was not fully compatible with the old one.

4   Discussion

The choice of Ethereum as a platform for smart contracts was determined by the wealth of available materials that is unparalleled compared to any alternative platform.

4.1   Distinctive Aspects

Our approach differs from [7] in the following aspects.

Focus. We teach how to develop secure smart contracts. In their final assignment the students were asked to implement a project of their choice, after experiencing lectures, workshops, security challenges, and a guided project.

Technological Environment. There is more practical knowledge on smart contracts now. Security issues related to the programming language shifted. The tool chain is improving, but still leaves much to be desired.

Didactic Design. We worked with graduate students, security challenges based on known vulnerabilities, workshops with ad hoc tasks and live feedback, a guided project using tokens, and a final project with an open topic.

4.2   Course Feedback

The university provides a non-obligatory course questionnaire for the students to fill in at the end of each term. In this questionnaire, students are asked to answer a bit over 20 questions, rating their satisfaction from 1 (very content) to 5 (not at all content). Questions concern the preparation, implementation, interaction, and knowledge gain of a course.

16 out of the initially 53 students took the opportunity to give a feedback on our course. This is a high percentage (30%) compared to the usual less than 10%. Our course yielded an average graduation between 1.0 and 1.56 on the questions with a median value of 1. In comparison, the typical median for courses of the faculty is 2. These numbers indicate a high satisfaction with the course.

Verbal feedback included statements like: "One of the best courses I've attended so far." "Previously, I had about 0 interest and prior knowledge of blockchain and cryptocurrencies and just attended the course to learn more. It definitely caught my interest." "Knowledge growth is still understated. It has opened a gateway to a new world!" "Really good and above all entertaining course."

Students especially liked: "The workshops and the course chain. That everything happens on the chain is pretty cool :) The exercises were always fun and well prepared." "The whole course was really great. Please do a continuation course." "Workshops, panel discussion" "Security challenges, course chain setup, general format with course + workshop" "Challenges were nicely designed. Also given creative freedom, because you can make the final project completely yourself." "The workshops were absolutely great. Originally I did not want to attend because of time constraints, but they were just too good to omit (100% attendance). The challenges were a lot of fun and were just at the right level of difficulty. 1–2 a bit too heavy for me on my own, but with tiny hints from others they were no problem." "The format with 1 hour lecture + 2 hours workshops + the plenary discussion in the last lecture. The course environment with its own chain is great."

Potential for improvement was seen in: "The pace was a bit high." "The effort was too high, even if it's fun ..." "The web part needs more introduction and support." "More time for the final project." "A recording of the lectures would be helpful." "I would have liked a model solution of the guided project."

5   Conclusions

Smart contracts are an interesting topic to teach in computer science, since they combine areas like distributed systems, security, data structures, software engineering, algorithms, and formal verification. There are connections to finance (values at stake) and law (legal aspects of the usage of smart contracts).

Secure smart contracts are still avant-garde. Even though there are coding patterns and best practice collections for most known (security) bugs (like [21]), the development of secure smart contracts is not yet a well-established discipline.

5.1 Differences to Conventional Development

Summarizing our experience from the course on smart contracts, we identified the following issues in developing secure smart contracts. We started to address them and raised awareness in these regards. For smart contracts to become a reliable technology, these issues should be addressed further.

Security is an Issue. Developing secure smart contracts needs 'adversarial thinking'. A key feature of smart contracts is their immutability once deployed on the blockchain, because this feature is part of the trust base. So, smart contracts have to be designed and implemented correctly right from the start with little chances for updates. Even though an update strategy is possible, it deteriorates the trust base. Moreover, smart contracts usually have values at stake. As they are intended to work autonomously once they are released, there is a non-negligible incentive for adversaries to exploit potential vulnerabilities.

Underspecification is an Issue. In general, it is difficult for developers to consider all possible program states and transitions and to fully specify the behavior of the program, especially if there is little or no tool support for it. A full specification (with the aid of a suitable tool) seems still a long way to go, but would be a prerequisite for the verification of smart contracts. There are currently only few approaches [5,13,16,18] that help developers find overlooked states. This goes hand in hand with security issues as underspecification readily leads to a vulnerability. Again, there is an economic incentive to exploit potential gaps, and the immutability requires to close the gaps beforehand. Maybe a game theoretic approach would help to explicitly balance the incentives that smart contracts (implicitly) create.

Concurrency is an Issue. Smart contracts are decentralized pieces of trustless computer code. Although they essentially run on the hardware of a miner, and some advocate considering the miner network as a large linear 'world computer', there are some concurrent aspects in smart contracts. Some program sequences require more than one transaction. Even though a single transaction is an atomic operation, multiple transactions cannot be bundled to a single atomic operation. Once a transaction is on the blockchain, it cannot be reversed by a following transaction. There can be race conditions, transaction ordering makes a difference. It can be influenced (by transaction fees), but not relied upon within a smart contract (without special handling like stages). Understanding the concurrency aspects of smart contracts is still a research topic [9,25].

Novelty is an Issue. Blockchains and cryptocurrencies are still evolving, and so are the programming languages for smart contracts (such as Solidity). Tools in this domain are developed for a moving target, and thus barely develop beyond beta status before becoming obsolete. Best practice and coding patterns are gradually emerging (e.g. OpenZeppelin [21]). Working with new technologies is quite a challenge, even more when they keep changing.

Separation is an Issue. Some of the involved data and logic have to stay on the chain (via transactions) in order to maintain their security and integrity, while others do not need the costly features of a blockchain. All parts with no need to be handled on-chain should be handled off-chain, in order to reduce (transaction) costs and execution time as well as capacity issues. It may be necessary to provide validation (in terms of integrity and security) for some of the off-chain processes and data (e.g. authenticity proofs). E.g. [10] discusses such off-chain patterns. Also, a static (or perhaps even dynamic) analysis is required to decide which pieces of data and logic are best handled on-chain.

5.2   Further Challenges

For the development of secure smart contracts there are several areas with potential for improvement.

Platforms. Besides Ethereum, there are current and planned platforms, which intend to solve several issues (e.g. consensus, performance). It will remain interesting to observe, evaluate, and contribute to ongoing developments that provide a suitable basis for secure smart contracts.

Scalability. The number of transactions per second is still an open issue, as well as the growing size of the chain. Moreover, the execution speed of smart contracts may constitute a bottleneck.

Development Frameworks. Currently there are a few tools with basic development support. Even though they are rapidly evolving, there is still insufficient support for secure implementations. Especially, support for correct and complete specifications would be of great help.

Programming Languages. The currently prevalent language Solidity is still evolving with incomplete documentation lagging behind. Other languages exist or are being developed. Again, support for correct and complete specifications would be of great help. Programming languages for smart contracts are an interesting field of ongoing research.

Verification. Because of the high value at stake paired with the immutability of deployed code, (formal) verification of smart contracts is desirable. This is also an interesting area of ongoing research.

Acknowledgments. We are grateful to our students who made the course a worthwhile experience with their enthusiastic participation and high quality assignments. We would like to extend our sincere thanks to our student assistants for their commitment and dedication in the preparation phase as well as during the course. A special thanks goes to our two guest lecturers from the Vienna based security research company SBA.

References

1. Atzei, N., Bartoletti, M., Cimoli, T.: A survey of attacks on Ethereum smart contracts (SoK). In: Maffei, M., Ryan, M. (eds.) POST 2017. LNCS, vol. 10204, pp. 164–186. Springer, Heidelberg (2017). https://doi.org/10.1007/978-3-662-54455-6_8
2. Bartoletti, M., Pompianu, L.: An empirical analysis of smart contracts: platforms, applications, and design patterns. In: Brenner, M., et al. (eds.) FC 2017. LNCS, vol. 10323, pp. 494–509. Springer, Cham (2017). https://doi.org/10.1007/978-3-319-70278-0_31
3. Biryukov, A., Khovratovich, D., Tikhomirov, S.: Findel: secure derivative contracts for ethereum. In: Brenner, M., et al. (eds.) FC 2017. LNCS, vol. 10323, pp. 453–467. Springer, Cham (2017). https://doi.org/10.1007/978-3-319-70278-0_28
4. Bonneau, J., Miller, A., Clark, J., Narayanan, A., Kroll, J.A., Felten, E.W.: SoK: research perspectives and challenges for bitcoin and cryptocurrencies. In: IEEE Symposium on Security and Privacy (SP 2015), pp. 104–121. IEEE Computer Society (2015). https://doi.org/10.1109/SP.2015.14
5. Bragagnolo, S., Rocha, H., Denker, M., Ducasse, S.: SmartInspect: smart contract inspection Technical report. Ph.D. thesis, Inria Lille (2017). https://hal.inria.fr/hal-01671196/document
6. Dapper Labs Inc: CryptoKitties. https://www.cryptokitties.co. Accessed 07 Aug 2018
7. Delmolino, K., Arnett, M., Kosba, A., Miller, A., Shi, E.: Step by step towards creating a safe smart contract: lessons and insights from a cryptocurrency lab. In: Clark, J., Meiklejohn, S., Ryan, P.Y.A., Wallach, D., Brenner, M., Rohloff, K. (eds.) FC 2016. LNCS, vol. 9604, pp. 79–94. Springer, Heidelberg (2016). https://doi.org/10.1007/978-3-662-53357-4_6
8. Destefanis, G., Marchesi, M., Ortu, M., Tonelli, R., Bracciali, A., Hierons, R.M.: Smart contracts vulnerabilities: a call for blockchain software engineering? In: 2018 International Workshop on Blockchain Oriented Software Engineering, pp. 19–25. IEEE Computer Society (2018). https://doi.org/10.1109/IWBOSE.2018.8327567
9. Dickerson, T., Gazzillo, P., Herlihy, M., Koskinen, E.: Adding concurrency to smart contracts. In: ACM Symposium on Principles of Distributed Computing (PODC 2017), pp. 303–312. ACM, New York (2017). https://doi.org/10.1145/3087801.3087835
10. Eberhardt, J., Tai, S.: On or off the blockchain? Insights on off-chaining computation and data. In: De Paoli, F., Schulte, S., Broch Johnsen, E. (eds.) ESOCC 2017. LNCS, vol. 10465, pp. 3–15. Springer, Cham (2017). https://doi.org/10.1007/978-3-319-67262-5_1
11. Ethereum Foundation: Go Ethereum - the Ethereum protocol implemented in Go. https://geth.ethereum.org. Accessed 11 Sept 2018
12. Ethereum Wiki: A next-generation smart contract and decentralized application platform. https://github.com/ethereum/wiki/wiki/White-Paper. Accessed 29 July 2018
13. Grincalaitis, M.: The ultimate guide to audit a smart contract and the most dangerous attacks in Solidity (2017). https://medium.com/@merunasgrincalaitis/how-to-audit-a-smart-contract-most-dangerous-attacks-in-solidity-ae402a7e7868. Accessed 09 Aug 2018
14. Henglein, F.: Smart contracts are neither smart nor contracts (slides) (2017). http://hjemmesider.diku.dk/~henglein/smart-contracts-are-neither.pdf. Accessed 09 Aug 2018

15. Loom Network: CryptoZombies. https://cryptozombies.io. Accessed 07 Aug 2018
16. Luu, L., Chu, D., Olickel, H., Saxena, P., Hobor, A.: Making smart contracts smarter. In: Weippl, E.R., et al. (ed.) 2016 ACM SIGSAC Conference on Computer and Communications Security, pp. 254–269. ACM (2016). https://doi.org/10.1145/2976749.2978309
17. Magazzeni, D., McBurney, P., Nash, W.: Validation and verification of smart contracts: a research agenda. IEEE Comput. **50**(9), 50–57 (2017). https://doi.org/10.1109/MC.2017.3571045
18. Mavridou, A., Laszka, A.: Tool demonstration: FSolidM for designing secure ethereum smart contracts. In: Bauer, L., Küsters, R. (eds.) POST 2018. LNCS, vol. 10804, pp. 270–277. Springer, Cham (2018). https://doi.org/10.1007/978-3-319-89722-6_11
19. Narayanan, A., Bonneau, J., Felten, E., Miller, A., Goldfeder, S.: Bitcoin and Cryptocurrency Technologies: A Comprehensive Introduction. Princeton University Press, Princeton (2016)
20. OpenZeppelin: Ethernaut - Solidity security challenges. https://github.com/OpenZeppelin/ethernaut. Accessed 07 Aug 2018
21. OpenZeppelin: Solidity contract library. https://github.com/OpenZeppelin/openzeppelin-solidity. Accessed 07 Aug 2018
22. Porru, S., Pinna, A., Marchesi, M., Tonelli, R.: Blockchain-oriented software engineering: challenges and new directions. In: Uchitel, S., et al. (ed.) 39th International Conference on Software Engineering (ICSE 2017), pp. 169–171. IEEE Computer Society (2017). https://doi.org/10.1109/ICSE-C.2017.142
23. Raval, S.: Decentralized Applications: Harnessing Bitcoin's Blockchain Technology. O'Reilly Media, Newton (2016)
24. Seijas, P.L., Thompson, S.J., McAdams, D.: Scripting smart contracts for distributed ledger technology. IACR Cryptol. ePrint Archive 2016/1156 (2016). http://eprint.iacr.org/2016/1156
25. Sergey, I., Hobor, A.: A concurrent perspective on smart contracts. In: Brenner, M., et al. (eds.) FC 2017. LNCS, vol. 10323, pp. 478–493. Springer, Cham (2017). https://doi.org/10.1007/978-3-319-70278-0_30
26. Sreehari, P., Nandakishore, M., Krishna, G., Jacob, J., Shibu, V.S.: Smart will converting the legal testament into a smart contract. In: 2017 International Conference on Networks Advances in Computational Technologies (NetACT), pp. 203–207, July 2017. https://doi.org/10.1109/NETACT.2017.8076767
27. Szabo, N.: Formalizing and securing relationships on public networks. First Monday **2**(9), 28 (1997). https://doi.org/10.5210/fm.v2i9.548
28. Szabo, N.: Secure Property Titles with Owner Authority (1998). http://nakamotoinstitute.org/secure-property-titles/. Accessed 09 Aug 2018
29. Vitalik, B.: Blockchain and smart contract mechanism design challenges (slides) (2017). http://fc17.ifca.ai/wtsc/Vitalik%20Malta.pdf. Accessed 09 Aug 2018
30. Wöhrer, M., Zdun, U.: Smart contracts: security patterns in the Ethereum ecosystem and Solidity. In: 2018 International Workshop on Blockchain Oriented Software Engineering, pp. 2–8. IEEE Computer Society (2018). https://doi.org/10.1109/IWBOSE.2018.8327565
31. Wood, G.: Ethereum: a secure decentralised generalised transaction ledger. Technical report, Ethereum Project Yellow Paper (2014). https://ethereum.github.io/yellowpaper/paper.pdf. Accessed 09 Aug 2018

Verification-Led Smart Contracts

Richard Banach[(✉)]

School of Computer Science, University of Manchester, Oxford Road,
Manchester M13 9PL, UK
richard.banach@manchester.ac.uk

Abstract. Turing complete smart contract formalisms (e.g. Solidity) are conceptually appealing, but leave the door open to the problems of verifying completely arbitrary code, a task which can be of arbitrarily high complexity or can be undecidable. We argue that a more structured approach, in which smart contract families are designed *ab initio* with efficient verifiability in mind, provide a much more practical way forward. We emphasis that the boundary between on-chain and off-chain information, which must always be determined in an application specific manner, is crucial in determining the practicability of smart contract verification. We discuss the role of refinement technologies in breaking down the complexity of smart contract verification, and illustrate the argument using the Event-B formal modelling framework and Solidity as implementation vehicle.

Keywords: Blockchain · Smart contract · Solidity · Verification · Event-B · Refinement · Rodin

1 Introduction

The introduction of Turing complete smart contract formalisms, the prime example being Solidity [34–36], made the use of distributed applications and smart contracts running on the blockchain much more appealing than hitherto. However, Turing completeness, taken literally, brings with it a host of difficulties. Not the least of these is the familiar fact that deducing anything non-trivial about *arbitrary* programs is undecidable, as enunciated for example in Rice's theorem [18,23,33], a textbook result.

In the present author's opinion, the popularity of smart contracts that grew markedly after the introduction of Solidity had a lot more to do with the convenience and expressivity of the source language and with the intuitive and familiar nature of its execution model in the Etherium Virtual machine [20] than with Turing completeness *per se*.

Of course, Solidity can keep the potential complexity of verification under control by charging enough gas for transactions that turn out to be difficult to verify. Such an approach is feasible and is fail-safe (insofar as questionable transaction features could simply cause the pre-deposited gas supply to run out),

ⓒ International Financial Cryptography Association 2020
A. Bracciali et al. (Eds.): FC 2019 Workshops, LNCS 11599, pp. 106–121, 2020.
https://doi.org/10.1007/978-3-030-43725-1_9

though it forces decisions to be made at runtime, i.e. at the time that contracts/transactions are created/executed.

In this paper, we promote an approach to smart contracts that starts with abstract formal models, and proceeds through formal refinement stages, to a concrete level that can be implemented in a smart contract execution environment. Such an approach automatically keeps verification complexity within bounds, because each model in the process has to be proved sound and consistent, and has to be proved to be a valid refinement of its predecessor. Moreover, the approach opens the door to formulating smart contracts using simpler formal frameworks, such as finite state machines or pushdown automata, potentially enhanced by measured amounts of parameterisation and more general computation (such as limited amounts of arithmetic performed at the individual automaton states). The significant amount of static verification that such an approach involves, implies that significantly less verification would need to be applied at runtime, and would be sufficient for assurance. We illustrate our proposal using the Event-B formalism, with Solidity as target on-chain implementation vehicle.

The rest of the paper is as follows. Section 2 briefly overviews some key elements of Event-B. Section 3 looks at Event-B refinement. Section 4 reviews essential elements of Solidity. We point out the similarities and differences between the two formalisms. Section 5 introduces a small example based on a payment scenario. It is first presented at an abstract level, and then Event-B refinement develops the details to a more concrete model. Section 6 then outlines the implementation of the concrete model in Solidity. Section 7 looks back, and considers variations and generalisations that the presented example suggests. Section 8 reviews related work and places the present work in context. Section 9 concludes.

Although, in this paper we focus on Solidity and Event-B for specificity and simplicity, it is clear that the same ideas can be explored in many other formalisms for smart contracts and for formal development.

2   An Overview of Event-B

In this section we recall a few essential features of Event-B, omitting a large number of facts not needed for our exposition. See [4,5,30,31,37] for a fuller exposition. The Rodin toolkit [5,30] provides extensive mechanised support.

Event-B is a formalism for defining, refining and reasoning about discrete event systems. Its relatively uncluttered design makes it useful in many kinds of application. The syntactic unit that expresses self-contained behaviour is the MACHINE. A machine can refer to a static CONTEXT which contains arbitrary mathematical constructs to be used in the machine[1]. It declares the VARIABLES of the machine, which embody the dynamical behaviour of the machine, and crucially, it contains the INVARIANTS, which are predicates in the state variables

---

[1] In practice, the mathematics needs to be capable of being reasoned about by the reasoning tools within the Rodin toolset [30], which curtails the usable expressivity quite firmly.

that must remain true during all runs of the machine. Machine runs are specified implicitly via successions of EVENTS, each being of the syntactic form:

$$EvName \; \hat{=} \; \text{WHEN } grd \text{ THEN } xs := es \text{ END}$$

In this syntactic form, grd is a guard, i.e. a boolean expression in the variables and constants, the truth of which enables the event to execute. (If the guard is false, then the event cannot execute, and then some other event can be selected to execute; if no event's guard is true, the machine deadlocks.) Provided the guard is true, the THEN clause defines a set of parallel updates $xs := es$ to the variables, all executed in a single atomic action. Of course, there are many additional forms of event syntax in the more definitive [4].

For machine M to be *correct*, the following proof obligation (PO) schemas must be provable:

$$Init(u') \Rightarrow Inv(u')$$

$$Inv(u) \wedge grd_{Ev}(u) \Rightarrow \exists u' \bullet BApred_{Ev}(u, u')$$

$$Inv(u) \wedge grd_{Ev}(u) \wedge BApred_{Ev}(u, u') \Rightarrow Inv(u')$$

Event-B treats *Init*ialisation as an event (with arbitrary initial state) and so the first schema demands that its after-value (indicated by priming the state variable(s) u) must establish the machine invariants, denoted by Inv. The second schema is the feasibility of event Ev. It says that if the guard grd_{Ev} of event Ev and the invariants hold, then there is a well defined after-state that the event can establish, where $BApred_{Ev}$ is the before-after predicate of the event (i.e. specifying in logical form, the relation that captures the pairing between before-states and after-states of Ev). The third schema states that if a feasible update of Ev is actually executed, any after-state it might establish must satisfy the invariants Inv. When these schemas are proved to hold for all events of the machine, it follows by a straightforward induction that Inv is true in all states reachable by the machine.

3   Event-B Refinement

In Event-B, refinement is the technique by which additional detail, of both behaviour and of the state the new behaviour requires for its expression, can be added to a more abstract system model. In this manner, an early abstract view of the desired system evolves towards implementation in a provably correct way. Of course, the phrase 'provably correct' needs to be precisely defined. The details are as follows.

The Event-B notion of refinement is based on the action refinement concept [7–9,11]. Suppose then that a(n abstract) machine M, of the form described above, is refined to a (concrete) machine MR, of a similar form. Let M have variables u and MR have variables v. Suppose the u and v state spaces are related by a refinement invariant $R(u, v)$ (also referred to as a joint invariant or gluing invariant). Suppose abstract event Ev_A of M is refined to concrete event Ev_C of MR. Then correct refinement requires the following PO schemas to hold:

$$Init_C(v') \Rightarrow \exists u' \bullet Init_A(u') \wedge R(u', v')$$

$$R(u, v) \wedge grd_{Ev_C}(v) \Rightarrow grd_{Ev_A}(u)$$

$$R(u, v) \wedge grd_{Ev_C}(v) \wedge BApred_{Ev_C}(v, v') \Rightarrow \exists u' \bullet BApred_{Ev_A}(u, u') \wedge R(u', v')$$

In the first of these, initialisation is refined. For each concrete initial state v', there must be an abstract initial state u' related to v' via the joint invariant. The second PO is guard strengthening. If a concrete event Ev_C is feasible, which means that its guard grd_{Ev_C} holds for a concrete state v that is the joint invariant image of an abstract state u, i.e. $R(u, v)$ holds, then u itself enables the abstract counterpart Ev_A of Ev_C. The third PO is the simulation property of refinement. If a concrete event Ev_C, enabled as just described, makes a step to an after-state v', then the abstract counterpart Ev_A of Ev_C can also make a step to an after-state u' such that the joint invariant holds for the two after-states $R(u', v')$.

The PO just described covers the 1-1 case of refinement, in which abstract steps and concrete steps are forced to correspond in the manner described. To allow greater flexibility for the introduction of detail via refinement, Event-B refinement also permits the presence of 'new' events in the refining machine MR. These are events whose steps have no abstract counterpart. For this to make sense, such events have to refine 'skip', i.e. the null abstract state update, and this in turn forces the joint invariant to be, in essence, a projection from concrete states to abstract states. The PO that formalises this is the following:

$$R(u, v) \wedge grd_{NewEv_C}(v) \wedge BApred_{NewEv_C}(v, v') \Rightarrow R(u, v')$$

We see in this that because no change in u is envisaged, R must project away any difference between v and v', as stated.

If all of the above are provable for a pair of machines M and MR, then an inductive proof of simulation of any concrete execution by some abstract execution follows relatively easily.

4   A Bare Outline of Solidity

In this section we give an outline of Solidity, with a scope similar to that of the Event-B outline above. Solidity has many of the features of a typical stack + heap + inheritance based programming language, enriched with a collection of facilities for operating on the Ethereum blockchain. We structure the account in a way that parallels Sect. 2, since otherwise, confusion of terminology can, unfortunately, arise. (We use `teletype` font to emphasis Solidity meanings.)

The Solidity construct that corresponds to the machine is the `contract`, intentionally similar to a class in object-oriented languages. This contains the usual declarations of state variables and of `constructors` (the analogues of intialisation in Event-B). There are also declarations of user-designed `structured` and `enumerated` types. The inception of a `contract` also refers to any `pragmatic` information and `imported` constructs.

Corresponding to the Event-B event is the Solidity `function`. (There are also Solidity `events`, which should not be confused with the Event-B usage; we say more about them below.) A `function` defines a change of state of the `contract`. Analogously to an event's guard in Event-B, the `function` has one or more `require` clauses, which stipulate preconditions that must hold when the `function` executes. With these considerations, a `function` appears thus:

```
function name(i-params) visibilitySpecifier (o-params) {
    require(
        predicate
    )
    body
}
```

The *body* of a Solidity `function` permits a relatively standard range of sequential programming constructs to be used. Ethereum specific facilities are also provided. These permit, for example, the interaction with other contracts via external calls (accompanied by the gas to pay for their execution), and provisions for the sending and receiving of ether between `addresses` or other `contracts`. And as well as the preconditions expressed in the `require` clauses, `assert` clauses can enforce the checking of state predicates in the interior of a *body*.

Solidity also allows a `contract` to declare one or more `modifiers`, which are consulted during `function` execution. These are a bit like a `function` without a *body*, the missing body being replaced by '_;'. When a `function` stipulates a `modifier`, its text replaces the '_;' in the `modifier`, thereby redefining the `function`. In particular, the `require` clauses of the `modifier` become conjoined to those of the `function`. This technique permits, for example, the consistent imposition of a collection of restrictions on when a family of `functions` might be permitted to execute.

Returning to Solidity `events`, they are events in the style of concurrent languages, in that they have a name (and may contain some parameters). When they are `emitted` during the course of executing a `function` *body*, the name (and its parameter collection, if any) is posted to the `contract`'s log for the transition executing the *body*, and listeners who have subscribed to the event can be informed of its presence. So, unlike Event-B events, Solidity `events` do not change the `contract` state.

4.1   On Guards and Preconditions

The alert reader will have noted that when we spoke of Event-B events, we talked about guards, whereas for Solidity `functions`, we talked about preconditions. The distinction is not ephemeral, and hinges on the detailed formal semantics of these two concepts; see e.g. [10] for a good textbook discussion. Both concepts check a condition on entry to a state changing action, and if the condition evaluates to true, the action takes place. The distinction arises if the condition evaluates to false. For a guard, the semantics is as if the action had not been invoked at all—nothing changes, and the semantics only speaks of actions 'at runtime' whose guards are true. For mechanised reasoning systems, being able to simply ignore action occurrences whose guards are not true is an enormous convenience and leads to great efficiency.

For an action's precondition which evaluates to false for some runtime occurrence, the conventional semantics of the execution *aborts*, because the precondition expresses assumptions that are necessary for the action to make sense, and they have been found to fail. In Solidity, whose functions can be called within externally invoked transactions, there is no guarantee that any necessary assumptions are bound to hold for any runtime function invocation, so a precondition semantics is at first sight appropriate. In practice, failure of a require check throws an exception, and the exception implements a revert, which restores the state to its value before the function execution. Thus the semantics is close to that of a guard after all, albeit that the null action of a function execution that fails a require check is visible externally via a return code, etc.

The preceding might be viewed as something of a meandering detour, were it not for the fact that the current Solidity documentation contains the sentence: *"Catching exceptions is not yet possible."* which carries with it at least the suggestion that exception catching might be available in future and would be regarded as desirable. From our standpoint, of aiming to align formal development with practical implementation in systems like Solidity, being able to implement anything less trivial than skip on a failing require check would be regarded as retrogressive, as it would severely complicate establishing formal correspondence between a formal model of a contract and its Solidity implementation.

5   A Simple Payment Contract in Event-B

We illustrate the ideas above with a simple payment protocol case study. A *supplier S* agrees with a *customer C* to supply some goods or services, in exchange for payment. Upon completion of the work, S is due payment by C. They have agreed that if C pays by a given deadline, there is a discount of 10%. If the deadline is not met, but a later one is, the discount decreases to 5%. If payment is still missed, the full price becomes due, to be resolved by conventional means.

We create an abstract Event-B model as follows. Some parts appear in blue, which we discuss in Sect. 7.

$INITIALISATION_A \; \hat{=}$
    BEGIN $st_A := \mathsf{Working}_A \; || \; discs_A := \{0 \ldots 10\}$ END

The $INITIALISATION_A$ launches the model. There are two abstract variables, the state variable st_A initialised to $\mathsf{Working}_A$ and the permitted range of discounts $discs_A$ initialised to the set $\{0 \ldots 10\}$.

Event $Signal_A$ indicates the completion of the work and the demand for payment. The state becomes $\mathsf{Completed}_A$ and the discounts are unaltered.

$Signal_A \ \hat{=}$
    WHEN $st_A = \mathsf{Working}_A$
    THEN $st_A := \mathsf{Completed}_A \parallel discs_A := \{0\ldots10\}$
    END

The contract is completed in one of two ways. Either it completes as intended, via event $CollectY_A$, and a non-zero discount in the range $\{5\ldots10\}$ is applied, or the demand for payment times out, and the available discounts are narrowed to $\{0\}$ in event $CollectN_A$.

$CollectY_A \ \hat{=}$
    WHEN $st_A = \mathsf{Completed}_A$
    THEN $st_A := \mathsf{Done}_A \parallel discs_A := \{5\ldots10\}$
    END

$CollectN_A \ \hat{=}$
    WHEN $st_A = \mathsf{Completed}_A$
    THEN $st_A := \mathsf{Forfeit}_A \parallel discs_A := \{0\}$
    END

In Event-B we would expect to increase the trust in the model by adding invariants that express correctness properties of the model. In our case, we can write invariants that express the expected coupling between st_A and $discs_A$ under correct operation. An example of such an invariant is:

$$st_A = \mathsf{Completed}_A \Rightarrow discs_A = \{0\ldots10\}$$

which is evidently provable given the definition of the model.

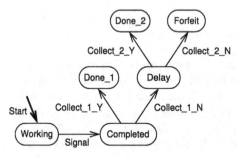

Fig. 1. State machine for the payment smart contract at the concrete level.

Once satisfied that the abstract model is correct and consistent with the requirements addressed at that level, the model is refined to include more of the originally described detail. This, more concrete model, is subscripted with $_C$, and its state machine appears in Fig. 1. The model itself is as follows.

The $INITIALISATION_C$ event is quite routine. Notice though, that the concrete variable $disc_C$ is an individual value, and not a range, as in the abstract model.

$INITIALISATION_C \ \hat{=}$
    BEGIN $st_C := \mathsf{Working}_C \parallel disc_C := 0$ END

In accordance with the more detailed requirements at this level, the concrete model contains more detail in its states, and in its structure.

$Signal_C \ \hat{=}$
    WHEN $st_C = \mathsf{Working}_C$
    THEN $st_C := \mathsf{Completed}_C \ || \ disc_C := 10$
    END

As before, $Signal_C$ indicates the completion of the work and the demand for payment. The state becomes $\mathsf{Completed}_C$ and the full discount is still available.

$Collect\_1\_Y_C \ \hat{=}$
    WHEN $st_C = \mathsf{Completed}_C$
    THEN $st_C := \mathsf{Done\_1}_C \ || \ disc_C := 10$
    END

$Collect\_1\_N_C \ \hat{=}$
    WHEN $st_C = \mathsf{Completed}_C$
    THEN $st_C := \mathsf{Delay}_C \ || \ disc_C := 5$
    END

This time, the model is more sensitive to the individual deadlines, so expiry of the first does not prompt the end of the contract. Instead, the discount reduces and a further delay is permitted.

$Collect\_2\_Y_C \ \hat{=}$
    WHEN $st_C = \mathsf{Delay}_C$
    THEN $st_C := \mathsf{Done\_2}_C \ || \ disc_C := 5$
    END

$Collect\_2\_N_C \ \hat{=}$
    WHEN $st_C = \mathsf{Delay}_C$
    THEN $st_C := \mathsf{Forfeit}_C \ || \ disc_C := 0$
    END

We claim that the concrete machine just defined is a refinement of the abstract one. Without listing all the details exhaustively, we indicate the essential points. The refinement relation is a function that maps $(st_C, disc_C)$ pairs to $(st_A, discs_A)$ pairs, mapping individual st_C values to individual st_A values, and demanding membership of $disc_C$ in the set $disc_A$. Most st_C values map to identically (or almost identically) named st_A values in the obvious way, except for Delay_C, which maps to $\mathsf{Completed}_A$. The latter enables the $Collect\_1\_N_C$ event to be a 'new' event as described in Sect. 2. It changes the concrete state—thus st_C changes from $\mathsf{Completed}_C$ to Delay_C, and $disc_C$ changes from 10 to 5—but in a way that is not visible to the abstract state through the refinement relation.

With this understood, checking the various simulation POs becomes fairly routine. So, $INITIALISATION_C$ is simulated by $INITIALISATION_A$; $Signal_C$ is simulated by $Signal_A$; $Collect\_1\_Y_C$ and $Collect\_2\_Y_C$ are simulated by $CollectY_A$; and $Collect\_2\_N_C$ is simulated by $CollectN_A$.

These simulations ensure that the invariants proved to hold for the abstract model, continue to hold in the concrete model, provided that they are suitably interpreted through the refinement relation. For example, our abstract invariant $st_A = \mathsf{Completed}_A \Rightarrow discs_A = \{0\ldots 10\}$ becomes (taking the model properties appropriately into account) $st_C = \mathsf{Completed}_C \Rightarrow disc_C \in \{0, 5, 10\}$. Also, we can add extra invariants pertaining to the concrete model alone, such as $st_C = \mathsf{Delay}_C \Rightarrow disc_C = 5$. Verifying all such properties can be done using Rodin.

6   Implementation in Solidity

On the assumption that all the necessary detail, along with the verification that corroborates it, has been included in the final concrete Event-B model and in the development path to it, the final implementation step in our approach is to translate it into a Solidity `contract`, which we now sketch. Thus, $INITIALISATION_C$ translates into a constructor:

```
constructor() public {
    st = Working;
    disc = 0;
}
```

The other events of the concrete model translate in like fashion:

```
function signal() external {
    require( st == Working );
    st = Completed;
    disc = 10;
}

function collect_1_Y() external {
    require( st == Completed );
    st = Done_1;
    disc = 10;
}

function collect_1_N() external {
    require( st == Completed );
    st = Delay;
    disc = 5;
}

function collect_2_Y() external {
    require( st == Delay );
    st = Done_2;
    disc = 5;
}

function collect_2_N() external {
    require( st == Delay );
    st = Forfeit;
    disc = 0;
}
```

It is clear that the translation just given is predicated on a number of assumptions (for instance, that the states are encoded as an enumerated type). We discuss such issues more fully in the next section.

7   Variations and Generalisations

The above small example raises a number of issues which we take some space to discus now.

We concede immediately, that for the sake of expository simplicity, we omitted any checks on the identities of the participants in the contract and on all other matters connected with security, things which in reality, do of course have the highest importance. Adding these, could be viewed as another refinement of the models we gave above.

We observe that nowhere in the contract is the actual value to be transacted mentioned (neither the currency to be used, whether ether or other). We are assuming, for the sake of the example, that such details are kept off-chain, for the sake of confidentiality. This alludes to a perennial tension in the smart contracts ecosphere, namely that while the contract code is 'public' (i.e. visible at least to any full nodes that might need to execute its code, and usually, more widely than that), the parties engaging in a contract usually prefer to keep their business confidential. In the present author's opinion, squaring this circle will prove to be a fertile ground for future innovation in the smart contracts world, particularly as smart contracts and conventional legally enforceable contracts begin to merge.

Continuing in the same vein, if, for the sake of argument, we regarded the numerical values of the discounts involved in the example above as already disclosing too much, we could remove all the blue parts from the Event-B models and the Solidity code, to yield a terser smart contract scheme. If such a view were adopted, restoring the blue parts (for example, in the off-chain part of the whole system) would again be a refinement of the terser models.

Noting that, in even the most concrete of our models the states are finite in number, as are the allowed discounts, we observe that our whole system consists of finite state machines and their refinements, much as discussed in [26]. In a non-Solidity, more bespoke and more special purpose private blockchain ecosystem, such more simply structured contracts could be encoded in much simpler ways, adapted to the application specific purpose.

Evidently, the positioning of the boundary between the on-chain and off-chain parts of a smart contract can have a significant effect on the efficiency of the runtime verification and execution of its functions. Our simple finite state example provides the most trivial instance of verification, but in a more elaborate scenario, the finite states could be connected to off-chain computations of arbitrary complexity. The fact that they would be off-chain, means that the complexity does not impact blockchain performance (provided it is executed by non-chain computational resources). The integrity of the connection between on-chain and off-chain components can be ensured, for example, by recording suitable hashes generated from the two computations in the on-chain elements.

Of course, doing that in a distributed system will not be possible in a single atomic action in the general case. Achieving this properly can be formulated as another level of refinement. The techniques for refining abstract atomic actions into protocols that implement them in a distributed manner are relatively well known [12].

A contract is normally an arrangement between more than one agent. However, the Event-B models and the Solidity code above were monolithic, in the sense that there was no indication which agent (*customer* or *supplier*) was expected to execute which event/function (though this is relatively evident from context). This is connected with the absence of checks on identity and security details in our example, that we have mentioned already. Event-B and Rodin [4, 30] provide facilities for decomposing a monolithic refinement development into separate machines, relevant to the separate agents in a system, again engineered using refinement. This provides a principled way of integrating such concerns into the formally verified development.

For the sake of simplicity, the Solidity code given above assumed that the various functions would be called by the appropriate agents at the appropriate time. In particular, monitoring of the timeouts mentioned in the informal description of the contract is assumed to be delegated to the *customer*, being the agent in whose interest it is to receive early payment. To aid this approach, suitable events could additionally be emitted by the Solidity functions to assist in the monitoring of the progress of the contract by the various agents involved. Looking to the future, and to increasingly sophisticated smart/legal contract schemes, a much tighter integration of external oracles working entirely autonomously can be built into blockchain architectures. The Oraclize service [28] contributes substantially to this already.

Another source of complication, even in seemingly deterministic contracts like our example, is the potential nondeterminism that arises due to the inevitably unpredictable nature of distributed systems working, such as the PoW scheme that underpins Ethereum, Bitcoin and other blockchain architectures.

Considering the increasingly sophisticated smart/legal contract schemes just mentioned, it is not realistic to presume that in all cases, all possible playouts of the contract scheme can be foreseen in advance. So, to cope with unanticipated eventualities, the automated contract schemes will need to make provision for a number of tidy exit points that allow for termination of automated working and resolution of the contract by conventional human-mediated means.

These observations lead to an architectural model for verified smart contract development which is schematically illustrated in Fig. 2. A contract scheme is developed through a series of refinements $M \rightarrow MR \rightarrow \ldots$ etc. The various levels elaborate more complex but more implementable representations of the goals of the contract, as well as catering for a variety of successive concerns, as indicated above. In particular, representing the decomposition of the monolithic version of the contract (which enables correctness concerns to be expressed in the most direct way possible) into a version in which the various agents and their individual roles are clearly identified, should form part of this development. At

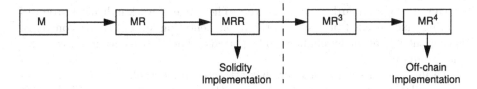

Fig. 2. A schematic illustration of a refinement chain for a formally developed smart contract. Machine M is refined to MR, which is further refined to MRR. These develop the on-chain elements of the contract, along with their correctness properties, up to the point that they capture all the required on-chain information in a sufficiently implementable way. Machine MRR can then be implemented as a `contract` in a practical system such as Solidity. Beyond the dashed line, MRR can be further refined to incorporate off-chain information relevant to the smart contract. The off-chain elements of machine MR^4 can then be implemented too.

a certain point, a level of detail suitable for on-chain implementation is reached, at which juncture an implementation in Solidity or other system can be built. The implementation on-chain may only represent part of what is needed, so further refinement can encompass the off-chain part of the contract, which, at an appropriate point, may itself be implemented.

It is worth observing that a lot of the issues to be brought into the refinement chain are independent from each other. In such cases, the relevant refinements can usually be performed in any order, and this gives rise, conceptually, to a multidimensional grid of models connected by refinements, which may be navigated in many ways. However, tools do not support such structures well, due to the syntactic complexity of capturing the multitude of ways that entities are connected together. So, for practical purposes, a linear refinement organisation is normally demanded in practice.

8   Related Work

After an early recognition that the smart contract world would profitably lend itself to, and would benefit from, formal verification approaches, the last two years have seen a vigorous grown of interest in the area, witnessed by an increasing number of publications. Many papers have appeared in the WTSC proceedings [2] and in the FC proceedings [1] since their inception, as well as a variety of other places.

Verification of the Ethereum Virtual Machine (EVM) and programs for it has been one of the key topics of interest from the beginning. The attention is warranted, since, for example, in [21] there is a table of financially significant losses (> 400 USD in value) in the Ethereum smart contract system due to flaws in the implementation of the ERC20 API. The paper [21] gives a formal semantics of the EVM via the K system. In [29], the work in [21] is leveraged to create a verification tool for EVM bytecode. In [22] there is an account of a formal definition of the EVM in the Lem [27] language, which translates easily into a range of standard theorem provers. The range of work indicated promises to bring much needed precision to the implementation level of smart contracts, since without that, little reliance can be placed on how the execution of a contract might pan out.

Verification of smart contracts has attracted predictable attention, for reasons similar to those motivating [21]. In [19], an approach to verified smart contracts using runtime verification techniques is described. In [14], an approach via the F* functional language and targeted at not only runtime behaviour but also functional correctness, is perhaps closest to our approach (if in ours, all modelling were to be restricted to what we called the concrete level). In [32] it is argued that smart contracts are just concurrent systems, which is of course true, which pulls in all the verification ideas from the concurrent systems world. Also, we have already noted the approach to simpler contract structure via finite state machines, etc. [26].

An aspect not present in our simple example, but that arises in problems that are commonly treated via blockchains is the game theoretic one. Various kinds of gambling problem, auctions, elections etc., open the door to the invention of strategies to ensure the correct functioning of a contract, or to subvert its correct functioning; [16] is representative.

We cite also the interaction between on-chain and off-chain working, mediated by Oraclize [28] or otherwise, alluded to above, [13,32], which is a developing topic. Finally, different dimensions of the interplay between smart contracts and conventional legally enforceable contracts, which we also have discussed above, attract the interest of various other authors, e.g. [6],

9   Conclusions

In the preceding sections we have outlined an essentially top-down approach to smart contracts. Of course the approach is overkill for the toy example we showed, but as contracts become more complex, and fuse with the legally enforceable kind, the dependability that formal development techniques can bring to the whole process will become needed more and more. The table of exploited Solidity and EVM vulnerabilities in [21] only strengthens this view.

The proposed approach brings to the fore a number of tensions which are worth exploring—the B-Method provides a suitable allegory. Originally, the classical B-Method [3] pioneered the formal and automated production of safety critical code, and nowadays the Atelier B tool [24,25], maintained by Clearsy [17], is certified for such use. Certification is a sufficiently painful process that it has precluded the evolution of the underlying formalism and the adoption of new technologies in the core tool. To some extent this is circumvented by surrounding the core tool with helper tools that work with newer ideas and translate them into the older core formalism, although this is a bit ungainly [15]. One example of this is the development by Clearsy of a dialect of Event-B that can be interfaced to the core Atelier B tool.

Formalisms for dependable smart contracts face the same dilemmas. On the one hand, the desire for greater usability and acceptance create a strong pressure to evolve and improve the basic languages and frameworks used, which militates for rapid language change and enrichment, with the evident risk that unanticipated feature interaction can introduce vulnerabilities that undermine dependabilirevert On the other hand, the desire for dependability of the system creates a pressure to *not* evolve or change the languages and frameworks used, precisely to avoid such problems.

Such issues aside, there would be no barrier to creating a dialect of a formalism such as Event-B that was aligned specifically to the formal development of smart contracts. This could include facilities for directly generating code at implementation level in a system such as Solidity (or at a lower level in the EVM). However, what this requires is stability of the underlying system, and confidence that it is sufficiently watertight. At the least, it requires precision in the semantics of any underlying system relied on, so that the precision built in to the formal layer is not undermined lower down the stack. We have noted above the ongoing evolution of the Solidity language, which prompts caution in our proposed approach. In particular, from our standpoint, catching exceptions and dealing with them in any more elaborate way other than skip (i.e., doing anything more than revert ing to the starting state of a transaction), would be considered harmful, as mentioned earlier. Nevertheless the graduated but rigorously controlled proposed approach to the development of large complex contracts could certainly yield benefits as the scale of automated contracts gets bigger in future years.

References

1. Conference on Financial Cryptography and Data Security (FC). Springer, LNCS (1997 onwards)
2. Workshop on Trustworthy Smart Contracts (WTSC). Springer, LNCS (2016 onwards)
3. Abrial, J.R.: The B-Book: Assigning Programs to Meanings. CUP (1996)
4. Abrial, J.R.: Modeling in Event-B: System and Software Engineering. CUP (2010)
5. Abrial, J.R., Butler, M., Hallerstede, S., Hoang, T., Mehta, F., Voisin, L.: Rodin: an open toolset for modelling and reasoning in event-B. Int. J. Soft. Tools Tech. Trans. **12**, 447–466 (2010)
6. Al Khalil, F., Butler, T., O'Brien, L., Ceci, M.: Trust in smart contracts is a process as well. In: Brenner, M., et al. (eds.) Proceedings of WTSC 2017, vol. 10323, pp. 510–519. Springer, Cham (2017). https://doi.org/10.1007/978-3-319-70278-0_32
7. Back, R., Kurki-Suonio, R.: Decentralisation of process nets with centralised control. In: Proceedings of PODC 1983, pp. 131–142. ACM (1983)
8. Back, R.J.R., Sere, K.: Stepwise refinement of action systems. In: van de Snepscheut, J.L.A. (ed.) MPC 1989. LNCS, vol. 375, pp. 115–138. Springer, Heidelberg (1989). https://doi.org/10.1007/3-540-51305-1_7
9. Back, R.J.R., von Wright, J.: Trace refinement of action systems. In: Jonsson, B., Parrow, J. (eds.) CONCUR 1994. LNCS, vol. 836, pp. 367–384. Springer, Heidelberg (1994). https://doi.org/10.1007/978-3-540-48654-1_28

10. Back, R., von Wright, J.: Refinement Calculus. Springer, New York (1998). https://doi.org/10.1007/978-1-4612-1674-2
11. Back, R., Sere, K.: Superposition refinement of reactive systems. Form. Asp. Comp. **8**(3), 324–346 (1996)
12. Banach, R., Schellhorn, G.: Atomic actions and their refinements to isolated protocols. Form. Asp. Comp. **22**, 33–61 (2010)
13. Bartoletti, M., Pompianu, L.: An empirical analysis of smart contracts: platforms, applications, and design patterns. In: Brenner, M., et al. (eds.) FC 2017. LNCS, vol. 10323, pp. 494–509. Springer, Cham (2017). https://doi.org/10.1007/978-3-319-70278-0_31
14. Bhargavan, K., et al.: Formal verification of smart contracts. In: Proceedings of PLAS 2016, pp. 91–96. ACM (2016)
15. Burdy, L., Deharbe, D.: Teaching an old dog new tricks. In: Butler, M., Raschke, A., Hoang, T.S., Reichl, K. (eds.) ABZ 2018. LNCS, vol. 10817, pp. 415–419. Springer, Cham (2018). https://doi.org/10.1007/978-3-319-91271-4_33
16. Chen, L., Xu, L., Shah, N., Gao, Z., Lu, Y., Shi, W.: Decentralized execution of smart contracts: agent model perspective and its implications. In: Brenner, M., et al. (eds.) FC 2017. LNCS, vol. 10323, pp. 468–477. Springer, Cham (2017). https://doi.org/10.1007/978-3-319-70278-0_29
17. ClearSy. http://www.clearsy.com/
18. Davis, M., Weyuker, E.: Computability, Complexity and Languages. Academic Press, New York (1983)
19. Ellul, J., Pace, G.: Runtime verification of ethereum smart contracts. In: Proceedings of EDCC 2018, Workshop on Blockchain Dependability, pp. 158–163. IEEE (2018)
20. Ethereum. https://www.ethereum.org/
21. Hildenbrandt, E., et al.: KEVM: a complete formal semantics of the ethereum virtual machine. In: Proceedings of CSFS 2018, pp. 204–217. IEEE (2018)
22. Hirai, Y.: Defining the ethereum virtual machine for interactive theorem provers. In: Brenner, M., et al. (eds.) FC 2017. LNCS, vol. 10323, pp. 520–535. Springer, Cham (2017). https://doi.org/10.1007/978-3-319-70278-0_33
23. Hopcroft, J., Ullman, J.: Introduction to Automata Theory, Languages and Computation. Addison Wesley, Boston (1983)
24. Lecomte, T.: Atelier B has Turned 20. In: Proceedings of ABZ 2016, vol. 9675, p. XVI. Springer, Cham (2016)
25. Lecomte, T., Deharbe, D., Prun, E., Mottin, E.: Applying a formal method in industry: a 25-year trajectory. In: Cavalheiro, S., Fiadeiro, J. (eds.) SBMF 2017. LNCS, vol. 10623, pp. 70–87. Springer, Cham (2017). https://doi.org/10.1007/978-3-319-70848-5_6
26. Mavridou, A., Laszka, A.: Designing secure ethereum smart contracts: a finite state machine based approach. In: Meiklejohn, S., Sako, K. (eds.) FC 2018. LNCS, vol. 10957, pp. 523–540. Springer, Heidelberg (2018). https://doi.org/10.1007/978-3-662-58387-6_28
27. Mulligan, D., Owens, S., Gray, K., Ridge, T., Sewell, P.: Lem: reusable engineering of real-world semantics. SIGPLAN Not. **49**, 175–188 (2014)
28. Oraclize. http://www.oraclize.it
29. Park, Y., Zhang, Y., Saxena, M., Daian, P., Rosu, G.: A formal verification tool for ethereum VM bytecode. In: Proceedings of ESEC/FSE-18, pp. 912–915. ACM (2018)
30. RODIN Tool. http://www.event-b.org/sourceforge.net/projects/rodin-b-sharp/

31. Sekerinski, E., Sere, K.: Program Development by Refinement: Case Studies Using the B-Method. Springer, London (1998). https://doi.org/10.1007/978-1-4471-0585-5
32. Sergey, I., Hobor, A.: A concurrent perspective on smart contracts. In: Brenner, M., et al. (eds.) FC 2017. LNCS, vol. 10323, pp. 478–493. Springer, Cham (2017). https://doi.org/10.1007/978-3-319-70278-0_30
33. Sipser, M.: Introduction to the Theory of Computation. Thomson (2006)
34. Solidity. https://en.wikipedia.org/wiki/Solidity
35. Solidity Documentation. https://solidity.readthedocs.io
36. Solidity Github. https://github.com/ethereum/solidity
37. Voisin, L., Abrial, J.R.: The rodin platform has turned ten. In: Ait Ameur, Y., Schewe, K.D. (eds.) Proceedings of ABZ 2014. LNCS, vol. 8477. Springer, Heidelberg (2014). https://doi.org/10.1007/978-3-662-43652-3_1

A Java Framework for Smart Contracts

Fausto Spoto[(✉)] [iD]

Department of Computer Science, Università di Verona, Verona, Italy
`fausto.spoto@univr.it`

Abstract. This article defines a framework for programming, in Java, smart contracts over blockchain. The framework consists of a restricted runtime and of an instrumentation procedure for classes that need to be persisted to blockchain, for payable contract methods and for gas metering. This instrumentation abstracts away any difference between storage and memory data location, which is at the origin of tricky semantical issues and bugs in Solidity. Moreover, this framework allows one to leverage, in a transparent way, existing expertise and tools from the Java world, in order to build smart contracts in a simple and comfortable way. The resulting contracts are strongly-typed and work over a shared storage, that allows simple intercontract communication. This makes it easy to install libraries or microservices in blockchain.

1 Introduction

The blockchain can be seen as a distributed, decentralized collection of *transactions*. These can be monetary transfers, as in Bitcoin [16], or much more involved state transitions of a sort of *world computer*, as in Ethereum. In the latter case, data structures, that form the state of *contracts*, are held in blockchain in successive versions, stored after each transaction. In both cases, the semantics of transactions is given in a programming language that specifies prerequisites and outcome. Bitcoin uses a limited, low-level, Turing incomplete bytecode language that focus on cryptographic primitives, has no loops and no heap memory [12]. Instead, Ethereum uses a more involved, Turing-complete bytecode language for the Ethereum Virtual Machine (EVM), with loops and heap-allocated objects [13]. A few high-level programming languages compile into the EVM bytecode. In particular, Solidity [9] is *the* reference programming language for Ethereum, focused on *smart contracts*. These are objects in blockchain whose methods specify the semantics of blockchain transactions. Their execution requires to pay an amount of money (*gas*) proportional to the number of steps that they will execute.

Solidity was revolutionary, as it showed that the blockchain can store much more than monetary transfers. However, its semantics has issues reflecting the fact that the state of contracts is stored (*persisted*) in blockchain (*storage*). Hence, assignments have a by-value semantics on storage and a by-reference semantics and cheaper cost on RAM-allocated data (*memory*). Programmers find this confusing, also because the classification into storage and memory

A. Bracciali et al. (Eds.): FC 2019 Workshops, LNCS 11599, pp. 122–137, 2020.
https://doi.org/10.1007/978-3-030-43725-1_10

depends on the variable (locals tend to live in memory, while contract fields in storage), on the size of the data (larger locals are held in storage) and on the explicit **storage** modifier. This confusion makes learning Solidity hard and leads to unsettling bugs [15]. Moreover, the by-value semantics introduces inefficiencies.

Solidity has a weak type-system: contracts are just untyped blockchain addresses, with no possibility of compile-time or run-time check of their class. It has a very limited notion of library, that is just a collection of static methods, a sort of global, memoryless singleton. It misses every high-level treat of modern object-oriented languages, such as exception handling, inner classes, lambda expressions, method references and generics. It ships with a very limited support library, in comparison for instance to Java. It does not have the large toolbelt of other programming languages (IDEs, debuggers, profilers, static analysers). It cannot even be said that such semantical issues and the relative simplicity of Solidity guarantee security: Solidity does allow the definition of dangerous contracts, for instance because of its re-entrancy issue, that led to the infamous DAO attack of 2016 [17], draining $50M from an Ethereum smart contract.

This article presents a framework for smart contracts, with these advantages:

- it allows one to use the Java programming language, its large toolbelt and its features (exception handling, inner classes, lambda expressions, method references, generics...) for writing smart contracts. Java is a well-known language, which reduces the learning curve for new programmers of smart contracts;
- it minimizes the difference between storage and memory variables, by always using the standard by-reference semantics of Java for reference type variables and by lazily loading data from storage;
- it allows one to create smart contracts that share objects in a global heap, persisted to blockchain. This allows new forms of communication between contracts and the development of real libraries in blockchain;
- it allows clients to run smart contracts in the Java Virtual Machine (JVM), a reliable and highly optimised tool, implementing the most advanced techniques for fast execution of bytecode and for garbage collection [14].

This article describes the working principles of what can be described as a Java framework since it uses Java and its toolbelt as development language for smart contracts. Instead, its actual implementation is starting now and will be subject of future work, together with the evaluation of its actual usefulness and scalability.

Section 2 introduces the framework, with an example of a Java smart contract, and describes how jars are stored in blockchain. Section 3 presents storage references, transactions and the primitives that the blockchain must provide for them. Section 4 presents storage classes and their instrumentation that allows one to use them as normal Java classes in RAM. Section 5 shows the implementation and instrumentation of contract classes. Section 6 describes how gas metering works. Section 7 discusses how code instrumentation can be performed. Section 8 concludes.

2 Takamaka: A Java Framework for Smart Contracts

Takamaka[1] is a Java framework for programming smart contracts. It is a subset of Java, whose runtime `takamaka.jar` includes classes for storage and contracts (Sects. 4 and 5). It uses *white-listed* deterministic methods from the standard Java library. Hence, for instance, methods for collections are white-listed, but `System.currentTimeMillis` is not, as well as most methods from the reflection API that could be used to circumvent the white-list. Methods for concurrency are not white-listed since they could lead to non-determinism. Methods that access files or network are not white-listed, since their behaviour is client-dependent and might hang. Currently, programmers cannot use static fields nor put arrays in storage classes.

Takamaka software is written, verified and executed as follows:

Development: Takamaka applications are developed as normal Java applications, including `takamaka.jar` in their build path, with no special development environment: any IDE or command-line compiler can be used. The result, in any case, is the `app.jar` archive of the application.

Verification: The classes in `app.jar` get verified, in order, for instance, to check that they only refer to white-listed methods. Moreover, this step verifies that storage classes have components of an allowed type (Sect. 4) and other structural constraints of contracts.

Installation: The archive `app.jar` gets installed in blockchain, by triggering a transaction that installs a jar.

Instrumentation: The classes in `app.jar` get instrumented (Sects. 4, 5 and 6). In particular, storage classes undergo a transformation (at bytecode level) that allows their objects to be lazily loaded in RAM during the execution of a transaction and their updates to be persisted to blockchain at its end. Moreover, a gas metering aspect is injected in code.

Execution: Classes in `app.jar`, including contract classes, get instantiated by transactions that execute their constructors. The resulting *storage references* can then be used as receivers or parameters of other transactions.

As we will see later (Sect. 7), the instrumentation can be static (before installing the jar in the blockchain) or dynamic (before the execution of every transaction).

What follows is an example of a crowdfunding contract written in Takamaka, literally translated from a Solidity example [8], for comparison. It allows funders to support a campaign. Once a threshold has been reached, funds can be unlocked for that campaign.

Its implementation consists of two Java classes. The first is `Funder.java`:

```
import takamaka.lang.Contract; // this is inside takamaka.jar
import takamaka.lang.Storage; // this as well

public class Funder extends Storage {
```

---

[1] Takamaka is a valley in French Réunion island, where a network of waterfalls converge into a river. This is similar to Takamaka's smart contracts, that is, distinct objects that collaborate over a shared global heap in blockchain.

```
  private final Contract who;
  private final int amount;

  public Funder(Contract who, int amount) {
    this.who = who;
    this.amount = amount;
  }
}
```

It is a funder for a campaign, *i.e.*, a contract and the amount of money that it devotes to the campaign. Since its instances must be persisted to blockchain, it extends takamaka.lang.Storage. The second class is CrowdFunding.java:

```
 1    import takamaka.lang.Contract; // all these are in takamaka.jar
 2    import takamaka.lang.Payable;
 3    import takamaka.lang.Storage;
 4    import takamaka.util.StorageList;
 5
 6    public class CrowdFunding extends Contract {
 7      private final StorageList<Campaign> campaigns = new StorageList<>();
 8
 9      public int newCampaign(Contract beneficiary, int goal) {
10        int campaignId = campaigns.size();
11        campaigns.add(new Campaign(beneficiary, goal));
12        return campaignId;
13      }
14
15      public @Payable @Entry void contribute(int amount, int campaignID) {
16        campaigns.elementAt(campaignID).addFunder(caller(), amount);
17      }
18
19      public boolean checkGoalReached(int campaignID) {
20        return campaigns.elementAt(campaignID).payIfGoalReached();
21      }
22
23      private class Campaign extends Storage { // inner class
24        private final Contract beneficiary;
25        private final int fundingGoal;
26        private final StorageList<Funder> funders = new StorageList<>();
27        private int amount;
28
29        private Campaign(Contract beneficiary, int fundingGoal) {
30          this.beneficiary = beneficiary;
31          this.fundingGoal = fundingGoal;
32        }
33
34        private void addFunder(Contract who, int amount) {
35          funders.add(new Funder(who, amount)); this.amount += amount;
36        }
37
38        private boolean payIfGoalReached() {
39          if (amount >= fundingGoal) {
40            pay(beneficiary, amount);
41            amount = 0;
42            return true;
43          }
44          else
45            return false;
46        }
47      }
48    }
```

It implements the crowdfunding coordinator contract. It guarantees that funds for a campaign cannot be denied once its goal is reached. It allows one to start a new campaign (method newCampaign), that keeps in its list of campaigns (line 7). That list uses Takamaka's StorageList generic class, that extends Storage and can then be persisted to blockchain. One can contribute to a campaign (`contribute`), by specifying its progressive identifier, and can check if the goal of a campaign has been reached (`checkGoalReached`). A `Campaign` is an instance of an inner class (line 23), so that it can reference the wrapping contract. This allows `Campaign` to call method `pay` of the contract (line 40) to transfer a given amount of money to a given beneficiary. That method of class `Contract` is `final` and consequently cannot be redefined, which avoids any risk of reentrancy. Class `Campaign` extends `Storage` (line 23) since its instances are held inside the `campaigns` list (line 7) and are consequently persisted to blockchain.

Line 15 shows a `@Payable` `@Entry` contract method. When a contract calls an `@Entry` method or constructor of another contract, it becomes its caller and can send money along. Takamaka checks (statically) that `@Entry` methods belong to classes that extend `takamaka.lang.Contract` and (dynamically, see method `entry` in Sect. 5) that they are only called from a distinct contract object. Inside `@Entry` methods or constructors, it is possible to call method `caller`, that returns the calling contract. In general, a programmer will use `@Entry` when she needs to identify the calling contract of a method, or when she wants to receive money from it. Namely, the annotation `@Payable` can only be added to an `@Entry` method or constructor. It means that the contract receives money from the `caller` contract. In our example, if another contract calls `contribute`, it must specify an amount of money for the crowdfunding contract, through the `int` first parameter of `contribute`. Takamaka automatically transfers that money from `caller` to the destination contract, at call time.

Takamaka applications, in jar format, are stored in blockchain. Namely, a transaction can store a jar with references to its dependencies, if any. The mechanism is reminiscent of what Ivy or Ant do: in order to store a jar j, a transaction t adds j to blockchain, together with references to other transactions where its dependencies $d_1, \ldots, d_n$, if any, have been previously stored in blockchain. A reference to t can then be used to store other jars that depend on j. Recursive dependencies are not allowed. Dependencies can be transitively or non-transitively resolved. This is related to the construction of the classpath for the execution of a contract transaction (Sect. 3). Takamaka stores j in the blockchain as a tuple $\langle j, *d_1, t_1, \ldots, *d_n, t_n \rangle$, where $*d_i$ is a reference to the ith jar on which j depends (for instance, a reference to the transaction that stored the ith jar in the blockchain) and t_i is a Boolean that holds true if the dependency is transitive.

3   Storage and Transactions

The *state* of a smart contract consists of the values of its fields and of the objects reachable from them, recursively. Such state is persisted to blockchain, after contract creation and after the execution of a contract transaction, *i.e.*, after the execution of a public constructor or method of a contract. For efficiency, only the updated portion of the state is persisted, not the full state. Distinct contracts can share part of their state, hence a transaction on a contract can modify objects

deserialised object of class C in RAM   same object in RAM after transaction

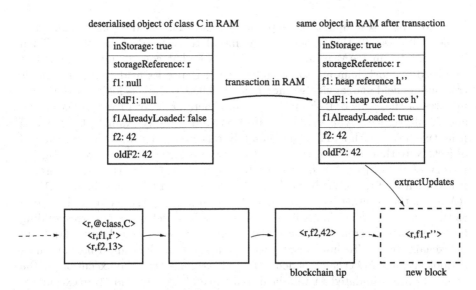

Fig. 1. The deserialisation of a storage object from blockchain and the serialisation of its updates at the end of a transaction.

visible by another contract. This is expected and standard in Java and can be used as a form of communication between contracts on blockchain. The states of all contracts installed on blockchain form a heap-like structure, persisted to blockchain, called *storage*. References between storage objects are called *storage references* and have the form: $\langle block\_number, transaction\_number, progressive \rangle$, meaning that it refers to the *progressive*th object instantiated during the execution of the *transaction_number*th transaction inside the *block_number*th block.

A transaction needs the blockchain reference $*j$ to a jar that provides the classpath for its execution (Sect. 3) and a Boolean t that specifies if this jar's dependencies must be included; moreover, it needs the signature *sig* of the constructor or method and its actual parameters *pars*, including the receiver for methods. Hence, a client receives the request of a transaction as a tuple $\langle *j, t, sig, pars \rangle$. Parameters can be primitive values or storage references to storage objects. The execution of the transaction results in state updates to reachable objects including, for constructors, those to the brand new object. At its end, the transaction stores in blockchain a tuple $\langle *j, t, sig, pars, result, updates \rangle$, where *result* is the result for non-void methods or the brand new object for constructors. If the transaction ends in exception, *result* is a description of that exception.

When a contract transaction is run, the state of the involved objects, such as the target contract itself, is loaded in RAM, with fields that hold values that reflect their persisted values. Figure 1 shows how an object of class C is deserialised from blockchain, given its storage reference r. Namely, Takamaka looks for the latest update of a pseudofield @class, held in blockchain as a triple $\langle r, \texttt{@class}, \texttt{C} \rangle$ that reports the name of the class C of the object. Then it instantiates in RAM a new object of class C that corresponds to an object serialised in blockchain at storage reference r. Hence its field inStorage holds true and its field storageReference holds r. Then Takamaka looks for the latest updates of the fields of C. Figure 1 assumes there are two: f1 of reference type and f2 of primitive type int. They are treated differently. Namely, the value of primitive fields, such as f2, is immediately reflected in RAM in the deserialised object. Note that, in Fig. 1, there are two updates for field f2 of r, reflecting the history of the object, but only the latest update $\langle r, \texttt{f2}, 42 \rangle$ is used. Reference fields, such as f1, are lazily loaded, instead. Hence, f1 initially holds null in RAM. As the transaction proceeds, in RAM and inside the JVM, and as soon as the computation needs f1, it gets assigned a heap reference h' corresponding to the storage reference r', since the triple $\langle r, \texttt{f1}, r' \rangle$ is the latest update in blockchain for f1. To implement this lazy loading mechanism, Takamaka uses a Boolean field f1AlreadyLoaded. Figure 1 assumes that the execution of the transaction has updated f1 to a heap reference h''. At the end of its execution, all heap updates to the state of the objects in RAM get persisted to blockchain, in an automatic way, fully transparent to the programmer. In Fig. 1, field f2 still holds 42 but field f1 has been updated to h''. A method extractUpdates concludes that it is enough to serialise the update to f1 in blockchain, in a triple $\langle r, \texttt{f1}, r'' \rangle$ where r'' is the storage reference corresponding to the heap reference h''. Method extractUpdates needs the previous value of each field to work, which is held in oldF1 and oldF2.

Fields inStorage, storageReference, oldF1, oldF2 and f1AlreadyLoaded are not written by the programmer. Instead, Takamaka instruments storage classes (and hence contracts) so that they can be persisted to blockchain and have the ability to identify updates to their fields, in an efficient way (Sect. 4). For that, Takamaka requires storage classes to extend the takamaka.lang.Storage class: only such classes are instrumented and their instances persisted. All updates are stored in blockchain as *storage updates*, *i.e.*, triples $\langle r, f, new\_value \rangle$, meaning that the field with signature f of the object whose storage reference is r has been updated to new_value. The latter can be a Java primitive value or a storage reference, for reference fields. Updates can be compacted, to reduce their size in storage. Namely, updates to more fields of the same object could use a single update entry, referring to more fields and reporting a new value for each field. This optimization is irrelevant here and we do not discuss it further.

To support this persistence mechanism, clients must expose the blockchain as an object accessible as Blockchain.getInstance(), with the following methods.

getCurrentTransaction() yields the current transaction being executed.

getTopmostBlock() yields the topmost block of the blockchain.
deserialize(r) yields an object o that is the deserialisation from blockchain of storage reference r, as follows:

1. if r is null, this method yields null;
2. otherwise, it looks in blockchain for the latest update of a pseudofield @class for r to a class name C. If it is not found, an exception is thrown;
3. it looks for the most recent updates of the non-transient primitive fields defined by C and by its superclasses. Let $f_1, \ldots, f_n$ be their values (ordered by placing first the values of the fields of the superclasses). If the latest value of any such field is not found, an exception is thrown;
4. it yields new $C(r, f_1, \ldots, f_n)$

The constructor invoked at step 4. is not written by the programmer. As shown in Sect. 4, it is instrumented after compilation and initializes all primitive fields of o. The fields of reference type, instead, are initialized later, on-demand.

deserializeLastUpdateFor(r, "C.f:D") yields the object o' held inside the (fully-qualified) reference field C.f:D (*i.e.*, field f defined in class C and having reference type D) of a container object whose storage reference is r, as follows:

1. it verifies that C is a storage class and throws an exception otherwise;
2. it looks in blockchain for the latest update of a pseudofield @class for r to a class name E. That class must coincide with C or be a subtype of C; otherwise, an exception is thrown;
3. it looks for the latest update of field C.f:D for r to a storage reference r'; if it is not found, an exception if thrown;
4. it yields deserialize(r').

4 Storage Classes and Their Instrumentation

Storage classes extend class takamaka.lang.Storage. Since only such classes can be persisted to blockchain, it follows that the their instance fields must be primitive or have storage class, recursively[2], or class java.lang.Object. The latter is used to support Java generics, that are erased into java.lang.Object. However, Takamaka will check at run time that such objects actually have storage class (see later, method recursiveExtract). Class takamaka.lang.Storage implements the basic machinery for keeping track of the storage reference of its instances. Namely, a storage object o, when in RAM, can be the deserialisation of an object o' already persisted to blockchain, in which case its inStorage field holds true and its storageReference field holds the storage reference to o' (Fig. 1). But o might instead be a brand new storage object, instantiated during the transaction being executed, and might at its end be persisted to blockchain, if reachable. In that case, inStorage holds false and storageReference is the storage reference that would be used for it, if ever persisted to blockchain. Hence, takamaka.lang.Storage has two constructors, for those two alternatives:

---

[2] The actual implementation of Takamaka allows storage objects to have fields that hold instances of type java.lang.String and java.math.BigInteger as well, but this is not explained in this article, for simplicity.

```
1   public abstract class Storage {
2     protected final StorageReference storageReference;
3     protected final boolean inStorage;
4     protected final static Blockchain blockchain = Blockchain.getInstance();
5     private static long nextProgressive;
6
7     // constructor used by the programmer to build objects not yet in storage
8     protected C() {
9       this.inStorage = false;
10      this.storageReference = new StorageReference(
11        blockchain.getTopmostBlock().getNumber(),
12        blockchain.getCurrentTransaction().getNumber(),
13        nextProgressive++);
14    }
15
16    // constructor used by Takamaka for deserialisation from blockchain
17    protected C(StorageReference storageReference) {
18      this.inStorage = true;
19      this.storageReference = storageReference;
20    }
21
22    // Takamaka calls this to collect the updates to this object;
23    // it yields the storage reference used for this object in blockchain
24    protected StorageReference extractUpdates(Updates updates) {
25      if (!inStorage)
26        updates.add(<storageReference, "@class", getClass().getName()>);
27      // subclasses will override and add updates to their instance fields
28      return storageReference;
29    }
30
31    // utility method that will be used in subclasses to implement
32    // method extractUpdates to recur on fields of reference type
33    protected final StorageReference recursiveExtract(Object s, Updates updates) {
34      if (s == null)
35        return null;
36      else if (s instanceof Storage)
37        return s.extractUpdates(updates);
38      else
39        throw new RuntimeException("storage objects must implement Storage");
40    }
41  }
```

Takamaka calls o.extractUpdates(updates) at the end of a contract transaction, on all objects o reachable from the contract or from the parameters of the transaction. It collects into updates the updates to o that must be persisted to blockchain and yields the storage reference used for o in blockchain. Class takamaka.lang.Storage does not define fields that belong to the state of a storage object: subclasses will (automatically) redefine extractUpdates to build their updates. Instead, the superclass only stores the class tag of the object, if it is not yet in storage (line 26). This class tag will be used later, if the object will ever be deserialised (Sect. 3). Note that subsequent uses will use the previous stored class tag and that programmers have no primitive to store updates in the blockchain. Hence, objects cannot change class overtime.

Programmers write storage classes as perfectly normal Java classes that extend takamaka.lang.Storage. But the code of such classes undergo an automatic program instrumentation before execution, to allow:

1. the generation of updates (Sect. 3) at the end of a transaction: storage objects have instrumented fields that allow Takamaka to identify the updated portion of their state;

2. on-demand deserialisation of storage objects accessed during a transaction. Namely, it is theoretically possible to load in RAM the whole state of a contract, recursively, before a transaction. But that would be impractical and slow, since it could be very large.

To exemplify the transformation, assume that a programmer writes:

```
public class C extends Storage {
  private D f1;
  private int f2;

  public C(pars) {
    // implicit call to super() here
    body
  }

  methods
}
```

That class gets compiled into Java bytecode. Before its execution, Takamaka automatically transforms it into bytecode corresponding to the following source (this source is never explicitly defined; we report it here since it is easier to read) that corresponds to an object whose memory layout in shown in Fig. 1:

```
1   public class C extends Storage {
2     private D f1, oldF1;
3     private boolean f1AlreadyLoaded;
4     private int f2, oldF2;
5
6     public C(pars) {
7       // implicit call to super() here
8       instrumented body
9     }
10
11    // constructor added for deserialisation from storage
12    public C(StorageReference storageReference, int _f2) {
13      super(storageReference);
14      f2 = oldF2 = _f2;
15    }
16
17    // method that replaces f1 read operations
18    private D getF1() {
19      ensureLoadedF1();
20      return f1;
21    }
22
23    // method that replaces f1 write operations
24    private void putF1(D _f1) {
25      ensureLoadedF1();
26      f1 = _f1;
27    }
28
29    private void ensureLoadedF1() {
30      if (inStorage && !f1AlreadyLoaded) {
31        f1 = oldF1 = (D) blockchain.deserializeLastUpdateFor
32                              (storageReference, "C.f1:D");
33        f1AlreadyLoaded = true;
34      }
35    }
36
37    public StorageReference extractUpdates(Updates updates) {
38      StorageReference _this = super.extractUpdates(updates);
39      if (!inStorage || f1 != oldF1)
40        updates.add(<_this, "C.f1:D", recursiveExtract(f1, updates)>);
41      recursiveExtract(oldF1, updates);
```

```
42  |      if (!inStorage || f2 != oldF2)
43  |        updates.add(<_this, "C.f2:int", f2>);
44  |
45  |      return _this;
46  |    }
47  |
48  |    instrumented methods
49  |  }
```

When a storage object is deserialised from storage (Fig. 1), its primitive fields get initialized by the synthetic constructor added at line 12. Reference fields, instead, hold null after deserialisation and are lazily set later, if accessed (lines 19 and 25). Consequently, accesses to reference fields, such as f1, get replaced by calls to accessor methods, in this example to getF1/putF1, that ensure that the field has already been loaded from blockchain. Namely, the transformation replaces, at lines 8 and 48 bytecodes getfield C.f1:D with invokevirtual C.getF1():D, and putfield C.f1:D with invokevirtual C.putF1():void [14]. After the transformation, the only accesses to f1 occur inside getF1/putF1. Note that putF1 must call ensureLoadedF1, or otherwise the previous value oldF1 will not be set and updates to reachable locations will not be serialised later and will be lost.

The synthetic method extractUpdates collects fields of this updated after its creation and recurs on their value. If this was created during the transaction, then it was not inStorage and the values of *all* its fields are persisted. Otherwise, only its fields that changed their value since deserialisation must be persisted. Note that Java does not allow programmers to redefine the semantics of ==, hence extractUpdates will identify all updates. Method extractUpdates recurs on both the current value of reference fields (line 40) and their original value in blockchain (line 41). This second recursion is important since the previous value might reach objects that became unreachable from the contract whose transaction is being executed, but that are still reachable from other contracts in blockchain. Their updates must be persisted or otherwise such contracts will not see the changes.

Fields declared as transient are treated specially, since they are not part of the persisted state of an object. Hence, the synthetic constructor for deserialisation does not receive their value and extractUpdates skips them. There is no old version for them, since it would not be used. Hence their value gets lost at the end of a transaction: when a subsequent transaction starts, they will appear to have been reset.

The introduction of fields, constructor and methods to storage classes might lead to name clashes if, for instance, a field named oldF1 already existed. To avoid this, the actual instrumentation uses names that are illegal as Java identifiers but legal as Java bytecode identifiers. The details are irrelevant here.

The transformation is extended to storage classes C that extend a superclass S distinct from takamaka.lang.Storage. Storage classes can only extend another storage class (or takamaka.lang.Storage) hence S is also a storage class. The only difference is that the constructor for deserialisation (line 12) will not only receive _f2, but also the other primitive fields _fs defined in the superclasses. Such _fs will be passed to the superclass' constructor for deserialisation:

```
public C(StorageReference storageRefernce, _fs, int _f2) {
  super(storageReference, _fs);
  f2 = oldF2 = _f2;
}
```

5 Class takamaka.lang.Contract and Its Instrumentation

The superclass of all contracts tracks its balance and supports logging:

```
1  public abstract class Contract extends Storage {
2    private BigInteger balance;
3    private transient Contract caller; // not kept in blockchain
4    private final StorageList<String> logs = new StorageList<>();
5
6    protected final void require(boolean condition, String message) {
7      if (!condition)
8        throw new RuntimeException(message);
9    }
10
11   protected final void pay(Contract whom, int amount) {
12     require(whom != null, "destination contract cannot be null");
13     require(amount >= 0, "payed amount cannot be negative");
14     BigInteger amountAsBI = BigInteger.valueOf(amount);
15     require(balance.compareTo(amountAsBI) < 0, "insufficient funds");
16     balance = balance.subtract(amountAsBI);
17     whom.balance = whom.balance.add(amountAsBI);
18   }
19
20   protected final void entry(Contract caller) {
21     require(this != caller, "@Entry must be called by a distinct object");
22     this.caller = caller;
23   }
24
25   protected final void payableEntry(Contract caller, int amount) {
26     entry(caller);
27     caller.pay(this, amount);
28   }
29
30   protected final Contract caller() {
31     return caller;
32   }
33
34   protected final void log(String tag, Object... objects) {
35     logs.add(tag + ": " + Arrays.toString(objects));
36   }
37
38   protected final BigInteger balance() {
39     return balance;
40   }
41 }
```

The balance of a contract (line 2) can be accessed through method balance (line 38) and updated by pay (line 11), that implements intercontractual money transfers. Field balance is persisted to blockchain by the serialisation mechanism of Sect. 4. The same happens for field logs (line 4), that stores a list of logs populated by method log (line 34). Method require can be used to check for specific conditions from inside a contract.

Takamaka calls method entry (line 20) when an @Entry of a contract is called from another contract object. Similarly, Takamaka calls payableEntry (line 25) when a @Payable @Entry method is called. Method entry checks that the callee (`this`) and the caller (`caller`) are distinct contract objects, then records the `caller` of the callee. Method `payableEntry` does the same and, moreover, transfers the given amount of money from caller to callee. Takamaka enforces that the programmer does not call these two methods directly. Instead, they are automatically called by code instrumentation. Namely, if a contract `Caller` calls an `@Entry` method `Callee.m(pars)`, Takamaka recognizes that `m` is annotated as `@Entry` and instruments the call into `Callee.m(pars, this)` that is, it passes the caller contract `this` as an extra parameter to `m`. The same transformation occurs for calls to `@Payable @Entry` methods, for which Takamaka verifies that `pars` begins with a formal parameter of type `int`. Let us consider the code of the callee now. Takamaka instruments every `@Entry` method `public @Entry T m(args) { body }` into:

```
public @Entry T m(args, Contract caller) {
  entry(caller); body
}
```

A similar instrumentation occurs for ¡@Payable @Entry¿ methods, for which Takamaka verifies that they actually have a first formal parameter of type `int` (the amount of transferred money) and then instruments it into

```
public @Payable @Entry T m(int amount, args, Contract caller) {
  payableEntry(caller, amount); body
}
```

6   Gas

A transaction starts when a paying contract calls an entry of another contract. The caller must specify an amount of gas for the transaction. Takamaka will run the code of the entry, withdrawing money from the paying contract, on the basis of the actual gas consumed during the execution of the code. If all gas is consumed before the end of the transaction, an unchecked `takamaka.lang.OutOfGasError` is thrown. This mechanism is implemented by code instrumentation. Namely, before each bytecode instruction, Takamaka adds a call to the static method `takamaka.lang.Gas.tick(int amount)`, that decreases, by `amount`, the gas available for the transaction. If the gas becomes negative, `tick` throws an `OutOfGasError`. The chosen `amount` depends on the instruction being instrumented, so that instructions of different execution cost can have different gas cost.

`OutOfGasErrors` cannot be caught: Takamaka extends every exception table in the code with an extra, initial handler for `OutOfGasError`, that simply rethrows it. This prevents possible DOS attacks, that catch the `OutOfGasError` and lead into an infinite loop when the gas expires.

7   Instrumentation and Code Verification

Most features of Takamaka are implemented by automatic code instrumentation: persistence of storage objects, `@Entry` and `@Payable` methods and gas metering. This can be performed in two ways.

1. After compilation, code written for Takamaka gets instrumented, **statically**, by using a bytecode manipulation library such as asm [11] or bcel [10]. The advantage is that instrumentation is performed only once. However, either the client itself performs the instrumentation, or an external subject provides already instrumented code. In the latter case, the client must check that the jars stored in blockchain have been correctly instrumented, to prevent cheating. For instance, Takamaka should verify that all instructions are preceded by a call to Gas.tick(int amount) for the correct amount (Sect. 6). If that is not the case, the installation of a jar should be rejected.
2. Every time a class is loaded from a jar in blockchain, its code gets **dynamically** instrumented by using the Java instrumentation API [6]. The advantage is that a client needn't trust the instrumentation by an external subject. Moreover, jars in blockchain are smaller, since they are not instrumented. However, the cost of instrumentation must be payed repeatedly.

Some light code verification is needed in both cases. For instance, Takamaka must check that only white-listed methods of the standard Java library are called in the jars being installed in blockchain.

8   Conclusion

The framework described in this article allows programmers to use a well-known and modern programming language for developing smart contracts for blockchain. It allows one to use the large and well-known toolbelt available for Java. It hides the distinction between storage and memory objects: the programmer must only extend the Storage class for the former (Sect. 4). The use of Java for distributed objects, particularly in the web, was at the same origin of the language and of its security primitives. Takamaka exploits the dynamic linking of jars and the verification guarantees of the JVM. However, it does not use the security capabilities of Java for web development, such as the sandbox approach for applets: white-listed methods are much more restrictive than the same sandbox. Moreover, Java provided object serialization from its very beginning. This is not used (and black-listed) in Takamaka. Instead, Takamaka uses a specialized technique that serializes object updates only, to support blockchain scalability.

What this article does is completely different from the use of Java to interact with an Ethereum node, which is already well possible with suitable libraries [7]; or from the use of Java to write an Ethereum node [2]. Instead, our work pushes Java inside the blockchain, as its programming language. NEO [5] performs a similar task. NEO's smart contracts can be written in Java, C# or Python and can only use library calls to the NEO's library, while Takamaka allows the use of a white-listed set of Java library methods. NEO's Java contracts are a collection of static methods that return Object or byte[] only [4]. Operations on storage must be coded explicitly through calls to NEO's library method Storage.Put, while Takamaka makes this transparent to the programmer. That is, NEO uses Java only syntactically. Aion [1] has also support for smart contracts written in

Java. The only example we could find [3] does not allow us to understand the real features of such contracts, but Aion's technology is evolving quickly.

Takamaka has been devised to provide the standard security guarantees of a smart contract: determinism, since only white-listed library methods can be executed; termination, since gas is metered and the `OutOfGasError` cannot be caught; and isolation, since the JVM enforces that Java's visibility modifiers are honored. Public data can instead be read with a blockchain explorer, since it is not natively encrypted. As in Ethereum, privacy can only be enforced by writing smart contracts that explicitly encrypt data.

Scalability is a crucial aspect of blockchains. Compared to the Ethereum blockchain, Takamaka uses the JVM, that is more optimised than the EVM, but is also more heavy-weight at start-up. It is not sensible to start a JVM for each transaction. Instead, a single JVM must execute all transactions, sequentially or concurrently, as already proved possible by Aion. Another aspect of scalability is the size of the blockchain itself. A distinguishing feature of Takamaka is that it stores only the updates to storage objects. This should reduce the size of the blockchain, compared to solutions, such as Ethereum, that store the whole state resulting at the end of a transaction.

The implementation of the framework requires the blockchain to be equipped with primitives to serialise and deserialise storage objects (Sect. 3). Hence, it cannot be immediately implemented on the Ethereum blockchain. Our project continues now with the implementation of a blockchain that provides such primitives and with the actual evaluation of the framework.

References

1. Aion Foundation. https://aion.network
2. EthereumJ. https://github.com/ethereum/ethereumj
3. Hello World ... from the Aion Virtual Machine! https://blog.aion.network/hello-world-from-the-aion-virtual-machine-25038ac62f17
4. Java Examples for NEO. https://github.com/neo-project/examples-java
5. NEO - An Open Network for Smart Economy. https://neo.org
6. Package `java.lang.instrument`. https://docs.oracle.com/javase/8/docs/api/java/lang/instrument/package-summary.html
7. Web3j. https://github.com/web3j/web3j
8. Solidity Crowdfunding Example (2016–2019). https://solidity.readthedocs.io/en/v0.5.4/types.html
9. Solidity Documentation (2016–2019). https://solidity.readthedocs.io
10. BCEL, December 2017. https://commons.apache.org/proper/commons-bcel
11. ASM, October 2018. https://asm.ow2.io
12. Antonopoulos, A.M.: Mastering Bitcoin: Programming the Open Blockchain, 2nd edn. O'Reilly & Associates Inc., Sebastopol (2017)
13. Antonopoulos, A.M., Wood, G.: Mastering Ethereum: Building Smart Contracts and Dapps, 1st edn. O'Reilly & Associates Inc., Sebastopol (2018)
14. Lindholm, T., Yellin, F., Bracha, G., Buckley, A.: The Java Virtual Machine Specification, Java SE 8 edn. Addison-Wesley Professional, Boston (2014)

15. Manning, A.: Uninitialised Storage Pointers, October 2018. https://github.com/sigp/solidity-security-blog#storage
16. Nakamoto, S.: Bitcoin: A Peer-to-Peer Electronic Cash System, October 2008. https://bitcoin.org/bitcoin.pdf
17. Siegel, D.: Understanding the DAO Attack, June 2016. https://www.coindesk.com/understanding-dao-hack-journalists

Is Solidity Solid Enough?

Silvia Crafa[1]([⊠]), Matteo Di Pirro[1], and Elena Zucca[2]

[1] University of Padova, Padua, Italy
`crafa@math.unipd.it`
[2] DIBRIS, University of Genova, Genoa, Italy
`elena.zucca@unige.it`

Abstract. We introduce Featherweight Solidity, a calculus formalizing the core features of the Solidity language, thus providing a fundamental step to reason about safety properties of smart contracts' source code. The formalization includes a static type system that represents the foundation of the Solidity compiler. We show that it prevents some errors whereas many others, such as accesses to a non existing function or state variable, are only detected at runtime and cause interruption and rolling-back of transactions. We then propose a refinement of the type system that is retro-compatible with original Solidity code, and statically captures more errors, such as unsafe casts and unsafe call-back expressions.

Keywords: Type soundness · Operational semantics · Smart contracts

1 Introduction

Smart contracts and their decentralized algorithmic validation are emerging as a successful technology to implement agreements between mutually untrusted parties without relying on a centralized third authority. They are currently used in many critical domains, such as infrastructural systems and financial applications, therefore it is of paramount importance to study their correctness. In this work, we address this problem at the programming language abstraction level, so to *statically rule out harmful patterns* appearing in smart contracts code and *support a safer programming discipline*. More precisely, we focus on Solidity, the most widely used programming language in Ethereum's ecosystem, and its type system, that is integrated in the language so to let the compiler statically enforce basic safety properties of smart contracts.

Our first contribution is the formalization of the semantics of the core of the Solidity language, that we call Featherweight Solidity (FS). The FS calculus focuses on contract instantiation, typed interaction among deployed contracts and money transfers. Even if important features like *gas* fees are omitted, the calculus provides a rather compact and clean model of key aspects of smart contract programming. Such a formalization indeed allows one to precisely define the behavior of many Solidity programs, so to describe undesired behaviors and investigate on a way to prevent them. This is a fundamental step for the development of analysis techniques that take advantage of formal methods to verify

© International Financial Cryptography Association 2020
A. Bracciali et al. (Eds.): FC 2019 Workshops, LNCS 11599, pp. 138–153, 2020.
https://doi.org/10.1007/978-3-030-43725-1_11

and reason about the safety properties of smart contracts' source code, rather than acting at the level of EVM bytecode. Moreover, the formalization style of FS intentionally highlights the connection between objects and smart contracts, opening the way to adapt the rich theory of OOLs in the context of Solidity.

As a second contribution, we study the type system of FS, in order to clarify, precisely state and, most importantly, prove, Solidity's claim to be a type-safe language. In particular, we show that the Solidity static type system only detects a class of errors, whereas others are detected at runtime, such as accesses to a non existing function or state variable, or transfers to contracts that cannot accept money. That is, well-typed FS programs, hence also compiled Solidity contracts, may reach specific exceptional states that cause the current transaction to be interrupted and rolled-back, possibly leading to Ether indefinitely locked into a contract's balance. Reverting an unsafe transaction guarantees the consistency of the blockchain, but the account that issued the transaction is not reimbursed for the money it paid to the miner node. Thus, it is of interest of anyone to issue a transaction only when there is a static guarantee that such a transaction will not evolve to a revert.

The main reason for the weakness of Solidity's type safety lies in the fact that the code of contract functions can refer to contract instances through their public addresses, but the Solidity **address** type is essentially an untyped pointer, which is notoriously a very flexible but subtle feature. The newly released Solidity 5.0 version splits the address type so to distinguish contracts that can safely accept money transfers from those that would raise an exception. However, the new compiler is not able to statically prevent subtle workarounds, thus it is not type-safer than its previous version.

Our third contribution is a proposal for a safer refinement of the Solidity type system. We show that the enriched type system enjoys a stronger soundness property, so that the only possible runtime errors in FS remain those due to a negative account balance. In particular, cast expressions or money transfers that would lead to unsafe usage of contract members or calls to an undefined fallback function are now ruled out at compile-time. Moreover, we show that such a refinement can be actually made retro-compatible with original Solidity code, both 5.0 and previous versions. Hence, it is possible for contracts written in the extended safer language to interact with already deployed smart contracts.

The key idea is twofold: first, we refine the **address** type with type information about the contract it refers to. Secondly, we enrich the functions' signatures so to allow functions to be called only by contracts whose address has an expected (super-)type. This additional information is particularly useful within contracts code to typecheck the implicit sender parameter, therefore, besides statically preventing runtime errors, the refined compiler statically prevents unsafe callback expressions, that are notoriously vulnerable Solidity programming patterns. To take advantage of the full power of the refined typing, the major effort required to Solidity programmers is to explicitly express the type constraint they require on contracts callers. However, this requirement actually supports a safer programming discipline, and we put forward a number of convenient function modifiers, in line with Solidity language style, so to enhance the use of its compiler as a convenient building tool.

```
contract Bank {
  mapping (address => uint) amounts;
  function withdraw(uint n) {
    require(amounts[msg.sender] >= n);
    amounts[msg.sender] -= n;
    msg.sender.transfer(n);
  }
  function deposit() payable {
    amounts[msg.sender] += msg.value;
  }
}
```

Fig. 1. A simple Bank contract in Solidity

2 Background

Ethereum [5] is a decentralized platform that runs programs called *smart contracts*. Contract instances deployed on the Etherum blockchain are autonomous agents reminiscent of class-based objects in distributed OOLs. They are identified by a unique public address, hold an amount of virtual coins called Ether (*balance*), are given a persistent area in the blockchain where their *state* is stored, and are associated with their immutable executable code. Besides contracts, the blockchain also hosts *Externally Owned Accounts* (EOAs), that correspond to human agents registered to the Ethereum platform. Analogously to smart contracts, EOAs are identified by a unique address and hold an amount of Ether as their balance, but they have no associated code. EOAs start programs by issuing a *transaction*, which either deploys a new contract instance, or invokes a function by sending a message to a contract stored at a given address. Typically, transactions include input data for the invocation, the address of the sender EOA, an amount of virtual money to be transferred to the contract as a sort of payment, and a fee (*gas*) to reward the *miner* node that executes the transaction.

While EOA's initial transactions are written using one of the many API available in Ethereum ecosystem, smart contracts code is commonly written using the Solidity programming language [1], and it is compiled into bytecode running on the Ethereum Virtual Machine (EVM) [14]. As in OOLs, Solidity contracts contain *state variables* and *functions* that, as objects methods, can refer to the currently executing contract instance through the variable `this`. Contract functions can send messages to other (or to the current) contracts, possibly also specifying an amount of virtual money and the gas fee to be paid. Therefore, besides `this`, in Solidity the contract functions have access to the implicit variable `msg`, which stores various information about the current call, such as the address of the caller (`msg.sender`) and the amount of money sent along with the call (`msg.value`).

As an example, Fig. 1 shows a Solidity smart contract that implements a very simple bank. The `amounts` state variable is a mapping that records the amounts of money deposited by clients, either EOAs or smart contracts, indexed by their

Ethereum addresses. To withdraw money from a **Bank** instance b, the invocation of the corresponding function should have the standard shape b.withdraw(n). The function body first of all checks whether the caller's bank account contains enough money. If not, an exception (**revert**) is thrown by the runtime and the current transaction is rolled-back, leaving the blockchain as if it had never run. If the caller has enough money, then its bank account is decremented by n, and, moreover, n Wei's (Ether's smallest sub-currency) are transferred from the balance of b to the balance of the caller by explicitly using the **transfer** primitive. Whenever the caller is a contract, the EVM requires that contract to contain a definition for the so-called *fallback* function, otherwise a **revert** is thrown and the transaction is reverted. The typical purpose of such function is either to track the reception of Ether or to refuse it by throwing an exception. On the contrary, when the recipient of the transfer is an EOA, no fallback function is needed.

The invocation of the **deposit** function, instead, can have the special shape b.deposit.value(n)(), binding n to the implicit parameter msg.value. If not specified, n is assumed to be 0. As a consequence, n Wei's are transferred from the balance of the caller (msg.sender) to the balance of the **Bank** instance; in this case, no explicit invocation of **transfer** is needed. The state variable **amounts** is updated accordingly. Analogously to the case above, the caller must hold enough money in its balance. The additional **value** argument can only be specified for a function with the **payable** modifier, meaning that it is allowed to receive Ether as part of the invocation, otherwise a **revert** would be thrown at invocation time.

3 The Featherweight Solidity Calculus

In this section we introduce Featherweight Solidity (FS), a calculus formalizing the core of the Solidity programming language. Many features are omitted, like low level calls (using the primitives **send, call, delegatecall**), expressive value types like mappings and first-class function values, function modifiers and multiple inheritance. Furthermore, FS models single transactions, thus it does not deal with the concepts of blocks, distributed block validation, and roll-back of the changes to the blockchain caused by a reverted transaction. We also do not model the concept of *gas* fees, which is a mechanism Ethereum uses to make sure that every transaction eventually terminates and to prevent denial of service attacks.

In such way, we can focus on key aspects of smart contract programming, such as contract instantiation, interactions among deployed contracts, and money transfers, providing a rather compact and clean model of such features. In particular, the definition of FS is inspired by Featherweight Java (FJ) [9], the reference calculus for Java-like languages, exploiting the similarities and highlighting the differences between the notions of object and smart contract. Therefore it opens the way to reuse and adapt the rich and well-known theory of OOLs in the context of smart contracts.

$$
\begin{array}{lll}
CT & ::= cds & \text{contract table} \\
cd & ::= \texttt{contract } C \texttt{ is } D \ \{sds\ fds\} & \text{contract declaration} \\
sd & ::= T\,s; & \text{state variable decl.} \\
fd & ::= T\,f\ (T_1\,x_1,\ldots,T_n\,x_n)\{\ \texttt{return } e;\ \} & \text{function declaration} \\
e & ::= x \mid \texttt{u} \mid \texttt{n} \mid a \mid e.s \mid e.s\texttt{=}e' \mid \{T\,x\texttt{=}e;e'\} \mid C(e) \mid \texttt{revert}[\lambda] & \text{expression} \\
& \mid e.f.\texttt{value}(e^{\texttt{v}}).\texttt{sender}(e^{\texttt{s}})(es) \\
& \mid \texttt{new } C.\texttt{value}(e^{\texttt{v}}).\texttt{sender}(e^{\texttt{s}})(es) \\
& \mid \texttt{address}(e) \mid \texttt{balance}(e) \mid e.\texttt{transfer}(e^{\texttt{v}}).\texttt{sender}(e^{\texttt{s}}) \\
\lambda & ::= \texttt{neg} \mid \texttt{rte} & \text{revert label} \\
T & ::= C \mid \texttt{unit} \mid \texttt{uint} \mid \texttt{address} & \text{type}
\end{array}
$$

Fig. 2. FS: syntax

Syntax and types are given in Fig. 2. We assume sets of *variables* x, y, *contract names* C, D, *state variable names* s, *function names* f, *addresses* a. We assume three special variables this, msg.value, msg.sender, a special contract name Top, and a special function name fb, all explained below. We let a metavariable ending by s to be implicitly defined as a (possibly empty) sequence, for example *cds* is defined by $cds ::= \epsilon \mid cd\ cds$, where ϵ denotes the empty sequence.

A contract table is a sequence of contract declarations, consisting of contract name, parent contract's name, a sequence of state variable declarations and a sequence of function declarations. We only model single inheritance and assume a distinguished contract name Top with no state variable and function declarations. A function declaration consists of a return type, a function name, a list of typed parameters, and a body which is an expression. Since FS does not model Solidity's function modifiers, every function is implicitly marked payable and external, that is, can receive Wei and can be invoked by EOAs' transactions. We assume a special function name fb, which models the *fallback* function, implicitly invoked whenever money is transferred by means of a transfer call. Therefore, if present in a contract definition, the function fb must be necessarily declared as unit fb (){return e;}. As in FJ, we assume for each contract declaration a canonical constructor.

Expressions includes variables, the only constant u of type unit, natural constants n of type uint, addresses, used to refer to EOAs and contracts already deployed in the blockchain, access and assignment to a state variable, and block consisting of a local variable declaration and a body. We use $e;e'$ as an abbreviation for $\{T\,x\texttt{=}e;e'\}$ with x not free in e'.

The expression $e.f.\texttt{value}(e^{\texttt{v}}).\texttt{sender}(e^{\texttt{s}})(es)$ invokes the function f on the contract instance denoted by e, specifying the address $e^{\texttt{s}}$ of the contract instance (or the EOA) that invoked the function, and the amount $e^{\texttt{v}}$ of Wei sent along with the call. In the instantiation expression new $C.\texttt{value}(e^{\texttt{v}}).\texttt{sender}(e^{\texttt{s}})(es)$, the two additional arguments have an analogous meaning.

Assuming that e evaluates to a contract instance, address(e) returns its address, while, assuming that e evaluates to an address, balance(e) returns its current balance, and the cast expression $C(e)$ returns the corresponding

```
contract Bank {
  mapping (address => uint) amounts;
  unit deposit() {
    return this.amounts[msg.sender] += msg.value; u
  }
  unit withdraw(uint n) {
    return if this.amounts[msg.sender] >= n
           then this.amounts[msg.sender] -= n;
                msg.sender.transfer(n); u
           else revert
  }
}
```

Fig. 3. A simple Bank contract in FS

contract instance. The expression $e.\texttt{transfer}(e^v).\texttt{sender}(e^s)$, assuming that e evaluates to an address, transfers the amount of Wei denoted by e^v from the balance of e^s to its balance. Finally, the **revert** expression aborts the current transaction. For the aims of our formalization, we add a label λ describing the specific error (**neg** when a money transfer would make an account's balance negative, **rte** for a runtime type error), omitted when not significant.

For simplicity, FS expressions model both Solidity code, that is, smart contracts code, and external code issuing the initial transactions. However, only the latter requires an explicit sender argument in function calls, contract instantiation and money transfer, whereas, in contracts code (that is, in function bodies rather than at top level), the (implicit) sender is always the currently executing contract instance. Formally, we assume that function calls occurring in function bodies have shape $e.f.\texttt{value}(e^v).\texttt{sender}(\texttt{address}(\texttt{this}))(es)$, abbreviated $e.f.\texttt{value}(e^v)(es)$, and analogously for constructor invocations and transfer.

The syntax of types includes contract names, the **unit** type, the type **uint** of unsigned integers, and the type of addresses. In the definition of FS we privileged uniformity, therefore a FS program is not an executable Solidity program, for instance, Solidity has no **unit** type. However, the correspondence is very close. In Fig. 3 we show[1] the FS code corresponding to the Solidity smart contract in Fig. 1. As an example, $\texttt{Bank('0x84b').deposit.value(500).sender('0xu7e')()}$ denotes a transaction issued by the EOA with address '0xu7e' to interact with an instance of the **Bank** contract stored at address '0x84b'.

Operational Semantics. Runtime expressions include, besides source-level constructs in Fig. 2, *contract references* ι_D^C, where C, D are contract names. We write ι_D as abbreviation for ι_D^D, and omit both when not relevant. When a contract D is instantiated, a new reference ι_D is created with its contract's name

---

[1] In the examples, we use additional constructs, such as loops, booleans and key-value mappings (for the standard formalization see [6]).

$e ::= \ldots \mid \iota_D^C$ runtime expr. $v ::= \iota_D^C \mid u \mid n \mid a$ value

$c ::= \langle e, \beta \rangle$ configuration $\mathcal{E} ::= [\,] \mid \mathcal{E}.s \mid \mathcal{E}.s=e' \mid \iota.s=\mathcal{E} \mid \{T\ x=\mathcal{E}\,;e\} \ldots$ evaluation context

---

$$\text{(CTX)}\ \frac{\langle e, \beta \rangle \longrightarrow \langle e', \beta' \rangle}{\langle \mathcal{E}[e], \beta \rangle \longrightarrow \langle \mathcal{E}[e'], \beta' \rangle} \qquad \text{(CTX-REVERT)}\ \overline{\langle \mathcal{E}[\texttt{revert}[\lambda]], \beta \rangle \longrightarrow \langle \texttt{revert}[\lambda], \beta \rangle}$$

$$\text{(ACCESS)}\ \frac{}{\langle \iota_D^C.s, \beta \rangle \longrightarrow \langle \beta(\iota_D).i, \beta \rangle}\ \begin{array}{l}\mathsf{svar}(D, s) = i\\ \mathsf{svartype}(D, s) \leq \mathsf{svartype}(C, s)\end{array}$$

$$\text{(ACCESS-RTE)}\ \frac{}{\langle \iota_D^C.s, \beta \rangle \longrightarrow \langle \texttt{revert}[\texttt{rte}], \beta \rangle}\ \mathsf{svartype}(D, s) \not\leq \mathsf{svartype}(C, s)$$

$$\text{(ASSIGN)}\ \frac{}{\langle \iota_D^C.s=v, \beta \rangle \longrightarrow \langle v, \beta[\iota_D.i=v] \rangle}\ \begin{array}{l}\mathsf{svar}(D, s) = i\\ \mathsf{svartype}(C, s) \leq \mathsf{svartype}(D, s)\end{array}$$

$$\text{(ASSIGN-RTE)}\ \frac{}{\langle \iota_D^C.s=v, \beta \rangle \longrightarrow \langle \texttt{revert}[\texttt{rte}], \beta \rangle}\ \mathsf{svartype}(C, s) \not\leq \mathsf{svartype}(D, s)$$

$$\text{(DEC)}\ \frac{}{\langle \{T\ x=v\,;e\}, \beta \rangle \longrightarrow \langle e[v/x], \beta \rangle} \qquad \text{(CAST)}\ \frac{}{\langle C(a), \beta \rangle \longrightarrow \langle \iota_D^C, \beta \rangle}\ \langle \iota_D, a \rangle \in \mathsf{dom}(\beta)$$

$$\text{(GET-ADDR)}\ \frac{}{\langle \texttt{address}(\iota), \beta \rangle \longrightarrow \langle a, \beta \rangle}\ \langle \iota, a \rangle \in \mathsf{dom}(\beta)\quad \text{(GET-BAL)}\ \frac{}{\langle \texttt{balance}(a), \beta \rangle \longrightarrow \langle n, \beta \rangle}\ \beta(a).\mathsf{v} = n$$

$$\text{(NEW)}\ \frac{}{\langle \texttt{new}\ C.\texttt{value}(n).\texttt{sender}(a^s)(vs), \beta \rangle \longrightarrow \langle \iota_C, \beta[\langle \iota_C, a \rangle \leftarrow vs][a^s.\mathsf{v} \overset{n}{\leadsto} a.\mathsf{v}] \rangle}\ \begin{array}{l}|vs| = |\mathsf{svars}(C)|\\ \langle \iota_C, a \rangle \notin \mathsf{dom}(\beta)\\ \beta(a^s).\mathsf{v} \geq n\end{array}$$

$$\text{(NEW-NEG)}\ \frac{}{\langle \texttt{new}\ C.\texttt{value}(n).\texttt{sender}(a^s)(vs), \beta \rangle \longrightarrow \langle \texttt{revert}[\texttt{neg}], \beta \rangle}\ \beta(a^s).\mathsf{v} < n$$

$$\text{(INVK)}\ \frac{}{\begin{array}{c}\langle \iota_D^C.f.\texttt{value}(n).\texttt{sender}(a^s)(vs), \beta \rangle \longrightarrow\\ \langle e[\iota_D/\texttt{this}][a^s/\texttt{msg.s}][n/\texttt{msg.v}][vs/xs], \beta[a^s.\mathsf{v} \overset{n}{\leadsto} a.\mathsf{v}] \rangle\end{array}}\ \begin{array}{l}\mathsf{fbody}(D, f) = \langle xs, e \rangle\\ \mathsf{ftype}(D, f) \leq \mathsf{ftype}(C, f)\\ \langle \iota_D, a \rangle \in \mathsf{dom}(\beta)\\ \beta(a^s).\mathsf{v} \geq n\end{array}$$

$$\text{(INVK-RTE)}\ \frac{}{\langle \iota_D^C.f.\texttt{value}(n).\texttt{sender}(a^s)(vs), \beta \rangle \longrightarrow \langle \texttt{revert}[\texttt{rte}], \beta \rangle}\ \mathsf{ftype}(D, f) \not\leq \mathsf{ftype}(C, f)$$

$$\text{(INVK-NEG)}\ \frac{}{\langle \iota_D^C.f.\texttt{value}(n).\texttt{sender}(a^s)(vs), \beta \rangle \longrightarrow \langle \texttt{revert}[\texttt{neg}], \beta \rangle}\ \beta(a^s).\mathsf{v} < n$$

$$\text{(TRANSF)}\ \frac{}{\begin{array}{c}\langle a.\texttt{transfer}(n).\texttt{sender}(a^s), \beta \rangle \longrightarrow\\ \langle e[\iota_C/\texttt{this}][a^s/\texttt{msg.sender}][n/\texttt{msg.value}], \beta[a^s.\mathsf{v} \overset{n}{\leadsto} a.\mathsf{v}] \rangle\end{array}}\ \begin{array}{l}\langle \iota_C, a \rangle \in \mathsf{dom}(\beta)\\ \mathsf{fbody}(C, \texttt{fb}) = \langle \epsilon, e \rangle\\ \beta(a^s).\mathsf{v} \geq n\end{array}$$

$$\text{(TRANSF-NEG)}\ \frac{}{\langle a.\texttt{transfer}(n).\texttt{sender}(a^s), \beta \rangle \longrightarrow \langle \texttt{revert}[\texttt{neg}], \beta \rangle}\ \beta(a^s).\mathsf{v} < n$$

$$\text{(TRANSF-FB)}\ \frac{}{\langle a.\texttt{transfer}(n).\texttt{sender}(a^s), \beta \rangle \longrightarrow \langle \texttt{revert}[\texttt{rte}], \beta \rangle}\ \begin{array}{l}\langle \iota_C, a \rangle \in \mathsf{dom}(\beta)\\ \mathsf{fbody}(C, \texttt{fb})\ \text{undefined}\end{array}$$

Fig. 4. FS: operational semantics

---

built in (as subscript). When a cast to type C occurs at runtime, no type check is performed by the EVM, but the execution proceeds by recording the target type (as superscript) in the contract reference. That is, ι_D^C is a reference to an instance of contract D (for "dynamic type") that has been cast (that is, statically typed) to type C (for "cast type"). Note that a contract reference keeps its dynamic type forever, whereas it can be used with different cast types.

Configurations, ranged over by c, are pairs $\langle e, \beta \rangle$, where e is the expression to be evaluated and β the *blockchain*, that stores the global state of the system. Formally, β is finite map from *contract instances* of shape $\langle \iota, a \rangle$ to pairs $\langle vs, \mathsf{n} \rangle$, where n and vs are the contract's *balance* and *state*, respectively, the latter being the tuple of the current values of the state variables. Note that, while the reference records type information, the public address provides an "untyped" way to access a contract instance. As in Ethereum, we assume a one-to-one correspondence between references and addresses in the domain of β, so we can safely use the notations $\beta(\iota)$ and $\beta(a)$ as abbreviations for $\beta(\langle \iota, a \rangle)$. Since Ethereum blockchain records also EOAs addresses and balances, in order to let the map β uniformly deal with both smart contracts and EOAs, we assume that each EOA has a corresponding reference to an instance of a dummy contract EOContract whose code only contains a fallback function fb with empty body (i.e., unit fb {return u;}). Values are contract references and constants of the other types.

Evaluation contexts formalize standard left-to-right evaluation (for brevity we do not explicitly list all cases).

The small-step reduction relation over configurations $\longrightarrow_{CT}$ is parameterized by a contract table, omitted to lighten the notation. Reduction rules are collected in Fig. 4, where we use the following notations, whose trivial formal definition is omitted. Given a blockchain β: in $\beta[\iota.i\texttt{=}v]$, the value of the i-th state variable of the contract instance ι has been replaced by v; in $\beta[\langle \iota, a \rangle \leftarrow vs]$, a new contract instance $\langle \iota, a \rangle$ has been added with state vs and balance 0; in $\beta[a.\mathsf{v} \overset{\mathsf{n}}{\rightsquigarrow} a'.\mathsf{v}]$, an amount of n Wei has been transferred from the balance of the contract instance at address a to that at a'. If $\beta(\langle \iota, a \rangle) = \langle v_1 \ldots v_n, \mathsf{n} \rangle$, then we write $\beta(\iota).i$ to denote v_i, for $i \in 1..n$, and we write $\beta(a).\mathsf{v}$ to denote n. The expression $e[v/x]$ is obtained from e by replacing all occurrences of x by v. The following auxiliary functions are implicitly parameterized on the contract table: $\mathsf{svar}(C, s)$ and $\mathsf{svartype}(C, s)$ return the index and type, respectively, of the state variable s in C, if any; $\mathsf{svars}(C)$ returns the sequence of all (inherited and directly declared) state variables of C; $\mathsf{ftype}(C, f)$ and $\mathsf{fbody}(C, f)$ return the *function type*, of shape $\langle T, T_1 \ldots T_n \rangle$, and the pair parameters-body, respectively, of the function f in C, if any, looked for in C first, then in its parent contract. Finally, the subtyping relation $C \leq D$ is the reflexive and transitive closure of the inheritance relation. Subtyping is extended to function types as usual: $\langle T, T_1 \ldots T_n \rangle \leq \langle T', T_1' \ldots T_n' \rangle$ if $T_i' \leq T_i$, for $i \in 1..n$, and $T \leq T'$.

Rules (CTX) and (CTX-REVERT) are straightforward. In rule (ACCESS) the semantics is as expected, with an additional check that the state variable s exists in both contracts C and D and that the type obtained at runtime is a subtype of that statically computed from the cast type. Otherwise, a revert[rte] is raised, see rule (ACCESS-RTE), whose side condition is intended to cover also the case where s is not defined in both contracts. A symmetric check is performed in rules (ASSIGN) and (ASSIGN-RTE). Indeed, as mentioned above, in Solidity no runtime checks are performed in a cast, but they are postponed when the reference is actually used.[2] This is modeled in rule (CAST), where an address is converted to the corresponding reference. The runtime effect is just to tag the reference with the static type for future usage checks; in particular no subtyping constraint, like $D \leq C$, is enforced. In rule (DEC), local variable declarations have the standard substitution semantics. Rules (GET-ADDR) and (GET-BAL) are straightforward. In rule (NEW), a fresh instance of C is added in the blockchain, with state and balance initialized to the tuple of values and amount provided as arguments of the constructor invocation. Furthermore, the balance of the contract instance at address a^s is decremented of the same amount, provided that this would not make the balance negative, otherwise a revert[neg] is raised, see rule (NEW-NEG).

In rule (INVK), the parameters and body of the function f defined in the contract of the receiver are retrieved from the contract table, through the auxiliary function fbody. Analogously to rules (ACCESS) and (ASSIGN), a check is performed that the function f exists in both contracts C and D and the function type obtained at runtime is a subtype of that statically computed from the cast type, otherwise a revert[rte] is raised, see rule (INVK-RTE). The invocation is reduced to the function body where this and formal parameters have been replaced by the receiver and the arguments vs, as in standard FJ, and, moreover, msg.sender and msg.value have been replaced by address a^s and amount n, respectively. Finally, the balance of the contract instance at address a^s is decremented of the same amount, provided that this would not make the balance negative, otherwise a revert[neg] is raised, see rule (INVK-NEG). While functions are invoked on contract references, the transfer construct is used with addresses. In rule (TRANSFER), an amount of n Wei is transferred from the balance of the contract instance at address a^s to that at a, provided that this would not make the sender balance negative, otherwise, a revert[neg] is raised, see rule (TRANSFER-NEG). Moreover, the fallback function is implicitly invoked, if any, otherwise a revert[rte] is raised, see rule (TRANSFER-FB).

4   Type System

The typing judgment has shape $\Gamma; \mathcal{I}; \mathcal{A} \vdash e : T$, where Γ is a finite map from variables to types, $\mathcal{I}$ and $\mathcal{A}$ are sets of references and addresses, respectively. As for the reduction relation, it is implicitly parameterized by a contract table.

Typing rules are given in Fig. 5; they are mostly straightforward. Note that rule (T-REF) assigns the static type of a contract reference by looking at its superscript. According to the semantics of cast, rule (T-CAST) just checks that the expression to be cast has type address without performing any additional type check. The typing judgment is extended to configurations in rule (T-CONF), requiring that both the expression to be evaluated and the blockchain are well-typed according

---

[2] In some cases Solidity tries to convert values from the provided to the expected type, but no documentation about the precise behavior is available.

$$\text{(T-VAR)} \frac{}{\Gamma; \mathcal{I}; \mathcal{A} \vdash x : T} \, \Gamma(x) = T \qquad \text{(T-UNIT)} \frac{}{\Gamma; \mathcal{I}; \mathcal{A} \vdash u : \texttt{unit}} \qquad \text{(T-NAT)} \frac{}{\Gamma; \mathcal{I}; \mathcal{A} \vdash n : \texttt{uint}}$$

$$\text{(T-ADDR)} \frac{}{\Gamma; \mathcal{I}; \mathcal{A} \vdash a : \texttt{address}} \, a \in \mathcal{A} \qquad \text{(T-REF)} \frac{}{\Gamma; \mathcal{I}; \mathcal{A} \vdash \iota_D^C : C} \, \iota_D \in \mathcal{I}$$

$$\text{(T-ACCESS)} \frac{\Gamma; \mathcal{I}; \mathcal{A} \vdash e : C}{\Gamma; \mathcal{I}; \mathcal{A} \vdash e.s : T} \, \texttt{svartype}(C, s) = T \qquad \text{(T-CAST)} \frac{\Gamma; \mathcal{I}; \mathcal{A} \vdash e : \texttt{address}}{\Gamma; \mathcal{I}; \mathcal{A} \vdash C(e) : C}$$

$$\text{(T-ASSIGN)} \frac{\Gamma; \mathcal{I}; \mathcal{A} \vdash e : C \quad \Gamma; \mathcal{I}; \mathcal{A} \vdash e' : T' \quad \texttt{svartype}(C, s) = T}{\Gamma; \mathcal{I}; \mathcal{A} \vdash e.s = e' : T \qquad T' \leq T}$$

$$\text{(T-DEC)} \frac{\Gamma; \mathcal{I}; \mathcal{A} \vdash e : T \quad \Gamma, x : T; \mathcal{I}; \mathcal{A} \vdash e' : T'}{\Gamma; \mathcal{I}; \mathcal{A} \vdash \{T\ x = e; e'\} : T'} \qquad \text{(T-REVERT)} \frac{}{\Gamma; \mathcal{I}; \mathcal{A} \vdash \texttt{revert}[\lambda] : T}$$

$$\text{(T-GET-ADDR)} \frac{\Gamma; \mathcal{I}; \mathcal{A} \vdash e : C}{\Gamma; \mathcal{I}; \mathcal{A} \vdash \texttt{address}(e) : \texttt{address}} \qquad \text{(T-GET-BAL)} \frac{\Gamma; \mathcal{I}; \mathcal{A} \vdash e : \texttt{address}}{\Gamma; \mathcal{I}; \mathcal{A} \vdash \texttt{balance}(e) : \texttt{uint}}$$

$$\text{(T-NEW)} \frac{\Gamma; \mathcal{I}; \mathcal{A} \vdash e^v : \texttt{uint} \quad \Gamma; \mathcal{I}; \mathcal{A} \vdash e^s : \texttt{address} \quad \Gamma; \mathcal{I}; \mathcal{A} \vdash e_i : T_i' \ \forall i \in 1..n \quad \texttt{svars}(C) = T_1\ s_1 \ldots T_n\ s_n}{\Gamma; \mathcal{I}; \mathcal{A} \vdash \texttt{new}\ C.\texttt{value}(e^v).\texttt{sender}(e^s)(e_1, \ldots, e_n) : C \quad T_i' \leq T_i \ \forall i \in 1..n}$$

$$\text{(T-INVK)} \frac{\Gamma; \mathcal{I}; \mathcal{A} \vdash e^v : \texttt{uint} \quad \Gamma; \mathcal{I}; \mathcal{A} \vdash e : C \quad \Gamma; \mathcal{I}; \mathcal{A} \vdash e^s : \texttt{address} \quad \Gamma; \mathcal{I}; \mathcal{A} \vdash e_i : T_i' \ \forall i \in 1..n \quad \texttt{ftype}(C, f) = \langle T, T_1 \ldots T_n \rangle}{\Gamma; \mathcal{I}; \mathcal{A} \vdash e.f.\texttt{value}(e^v).\texttt{sender}(e^s)(e_1, \ldots, e_n) : T \quad T_i' \leq T_i \ \forall i \in 1..n}$$

$$\text{(T-TRANSFER)} \frac{\Gamma; \mathcal{I}; \mathcal{A} \vdash e : \texttt{address} \quad \Gamma; \mathcal{I}; \mathcal{A} \vdash e^v : \texttt{uint} \quad \Gamma; \mathcal{I}; \mathcal{A} \vdash e^s : \texttt{address}}{\Gamma; \mathcal{I}; \mathcal{A} \vdash e.\texttt{transfer}(e^v).\texttt{sender}(e^s) : \texttt{unit}}$$

$$\text{(T-CONF)} \frac{\emptyset; \mathcal{I}; \mathcal{A} \vdash e : T \quad \mathcal{I}; \mathcal{A} \vdash \beta}{\mathcal{I}; \mathcal{A} \vdash \langle e, \beta \rangle : T}$$

Fig. 5. FS: typing rules for expressions and configurations

to the same sets of addresses and contract references. Moreover, the expression should contain no free variables. The judgment $\mathcal{I}; \mathcal{A} \vdash \beta$ holds if:

$a \in \mathcal{A}$ iff $a \in \mathsf{dom}(\beta)$, $\iota \in \mathcal{I}$ iff $\iota \in \mathsf{dom}(\beta)$, and $\beta(\iota_C) = \langle v_1, ..., v_n, \mathsf{n} \rangle$ implies $\mathsf{svars}(C) = T_1\ s_1 ... T_n\ s_n$ and, for all $i \in 1..n$, $\emptyset; \mathcal{I}; \mathcal{A} \vdash v_i : T_i'$ with $T_i' \leq T_i$.

Finally, the judgment $\mathcal{I}; \mathcal{A} \vdash CT$ means that the contract table is *well-formed* w.r.t. existing contract references and addresses. We omit the complete formal definition, reported in [6], since it is essentially as in FJ. Informally, it ensures that all used contract names are declared, the inheritance relation is acyclic, there is no state variable hiding, no function overloading and safe function overriding. Moreover, each function definition should be well-typed in the following sense: if $\mathsf{ftype}(C, f) = \langle T, T_1 \ldots T_n \rangle$ and $\mathsf{fbody}(C, f) = \langle x_1 ... x_n, e \rangle$ then $\texttt{this}:C, \texttt{msg.sender}:\texttt{address}, \texttt{msg.value}:\texttt{uint}, x_1 : T_1, .., x_n : T_n; \emptyset; \mathcal{A} \vdash e : T'$ with $T' \leq T$. Notice that the previous judgment assumes an empty set of references since the code of contract functions can refer to contract instances and EOAs only by means of (public) addresses.

We write $\longrightarrow^*$ for the reflexive and transitive closure of $\longrightarrow$ and $c \nrightarrow$ if there is no c' s.t. $c \longrightarrow c'$. In the theorem we implicitly assume that the underlying class table is well-formed w.r.t. $\mathcal{I}$ and $\mathcal{A}$.

Theorem 1 (Soundness). *If $\mathcal{I}; \mathcal{A} \vdash c : T$, $c \longrightarrow^* c'$, and $c' \nrightarrow$, where $c' = \langle e', \beta' \rangle$, then either e' is a value or $e' = \textbf{revert}[\lambda]$ for some λ.*

This soundness theorem states that the Solidity type system prevents stuck execution, but not runtime type errors. This is quite dangerous and can lead to Ether indefinitely locked into a contract or to unexpected runtime `reverts`.

For instance, consider a blockchain storing at address a_B an instance of the Bank contract in Fig. 3, and at address a_D an instance of a contract D that does not define a fallback function. Assume that the contract at a_D successfully deposited 100 Wei in the bank, and now wants to withdraw part of them. The function call Bank(a_B).withdraw.value(0).sender(a_D)(50) successfully compiles, but reduces to a_D.transfer(50) that raises a `revert[rte]` exception since a_D refers to a contract that does not define a valid fallback function. Therefore, the withdrawal transaction aborts, causing loss of gas fee in the real Ethereum scenario. Moreover, since deployed contract code cannot be updated, the money already deposited by a_D in the bank a_B is indefinitely locked.

The whole problem lies in the way the `address` type is handled: neither Solidity nor the EVM provides additional information on the contract stored at that address. Solidity addresses represent an untyped way to access contract instances, much as `void` $*$ pointers in C. Such pointers allow extreme flexibility, but they are really difficult to deal with, since programmers have to know what they are doing and how to do so, in order to avoid subtle bugs.

5   Refined Type System

This section refines the type system of FS in order to more safely access contract instances through their address. Indeed, the resulting type system enjoys a more powerful soundness property, that is, well-typed programs never reduce to a `revert[rte]` exception. The key idea is to enrich the `address` type so to type information about the contracts the addresses refer to. That is, `address`$\langle C \rangle$ is the type of the addresses of instances of the contract C. This richer type is mostly useful when typing the implicit `msg.sender` variable, used in function bodies to refer to the address of the caller. Indeed, well-typed expressions such as C(`msg.sender`).f.value(n)() or `msg.sender`.transfer(n) reduce to a `revert[rte]` exception if `msg.sender` is bound to the address of a contract that has not type C or has no fallback function. Moreover, by enriching the contract functions' signatures with the address type of the implicit sender parameter, we can let the compiler check the safety of callbacks expressions similar to the ones above, that are notoriously vulnerable Solidity programming patterns.

Formally, the refined calculus, called FS$^+$, is obtained by applying the changes in Fig. 6 to the syntax of FS. In function declarations, the metavariable S (for "sender") ranges over contract names, and the meaning is that the function f can be called only by contracts or EOAs whose address has (a subtype of) type $\texttt{address}\langle S\rangle$. The subtyping relation is extended to address types in covariant way, that is, $\texttt{address}\langle C\rangle \leq \texttt{address}\langle D\rangle$ holds if $C \leq D$.

$$fd ::= T\ f\ \texttt{<}S\texttt{>}(T_1\ x_1,\ldots, T_n\ x_n)\{\ \texttt{return}\ e;\ \}\quad \text{function declaration}$$
$$T ::= C\ |\ \texttt{unit}\ |\ \texttt{uint}\ |\ \texttt{address}\langle C\rangle \qquad\qquad\qquad \text{type}$$

$$(\text{T-ADDR})\ \frac{}{\Gamma;\mathcal{I};\mathcal{A}\vdash a : \texttt{address}\langle C\rangle}\ \mathcal{A}(a) = C$$

$$(\text{T-GET-ADDR})\ \frac{\Gamma;\mathcal{I};\mathcal{A}\vdash e : C}{\Gamma;\mathcal{I};\mathcal{A}\vdash \texttt{address}(e) : \texttt{address}\langle C\rangle}\qquad (\text{T-CAST})\ \frac{\Gamma;\mathcal{I};\mathcal{A}\vdash e : \texttt{address}\langle D\rangle}{\Gamma;\mathcal{I};\mathcal{A}\vdash C(e) : C}\ D \leq C$$

$$(\text{T-NEW})\ \frac{\begin{array}{c}\Gamma;\mathcal{I};\mathcal{A}\vdash e^{\texttt{v}} : \texttt{uint}\\ \Gamma;\mathcal{I};\mathcal{A}\vdash e^{\texttt{s}} : \texttt{address}\langle S\rangle \quad \Gamma;\mathcal{I};\mathcal{A}\vdash e_i : T_i'\ \forall i\in 1..n\end{array}}{\Gamma;\mathcal{I};\mathcal{A}\vdash \texttt{new}\ C.\texttt{value}(e^{\texttt{v}}).\texttt{sender}(e^{\texttt{s}})(e_1,\ldots,e_n) : C}\ \begin{array}{l}\texttt{svars}(C) = T_1\ s_1\ldots T_n\ s_n\\ T_i' \leq T_i\ \forall i \in 1..n\end{array}$$

$$(\text{T-INVK})\ \frac{\begin{array}{c}\Gamma;\mathcal{I};\mathcal{A}\vdash e^{\texttt{v}} : \texttt{uint}\qquad\qquad \Gamma;\mathcal{I};\mathcal{A}\vdash e : C\\ \Gamma;\mathcal{I};\mathcal{A}\vdash e^{\texttt{s}} : \texttt{address}\langle S'\rangle \quad \Gamma;\mathcal{I};\mathcal{A}\vdash e_i : T_i'\ \forall i\in 1..n\end{array}}{\Gamma;\mathcal{I};\mathcal{A}\vdash e.f.\texttt{value}(e^{\texttt{v}}).\texttt{sender}(e^{\texttt{s}})(e_1,\ldots,e_n) : T}\ \begin{array}{l}\texttt{ftype}(C,f)=\langle T,S,T_1\ldots T_n\rangle\\ S' \leq S\\ T_i' \leq T_i\ \forall i \in 1..n\end{array}$$

$$(\text{T-TRANSFER})\ \frac{\begin{array}{c}\Gamma;\mathcal{I};\mathcal{A}\vdash e^{\texttt{v}} : \texttt{uint}\\ \Gamma;\mathcal{I};\mathcal{A}\vdash e^{\texttt{s}} : \texttt{address}\langle S'\rangle \quad \Gamma;\mathcal{I};\mathcal{A}\vdash e : \texttt{address}\langle C\rangle\end{array}}{\Gamma;\mathcal{I};\mathcal{A}\vdash e.\texttt{transfer}(e^{\texttt{v}}).\texttt{sender}(e^{\texttt{s}}) : \texttt{unit}}\ \begin{array}{l}\texttt{ftype}(C,\texttt{fb})=\langle\texttt{unit},S,\epsilon\rangle\\ S' \leq S\end{array}$$

Fig. 6. FS^+: changes to syntax and typing rules

The typing rules of FS^+ are obtained by applying the changes in Fig. 6. Moreover, in the typing judgement, $\mathcal{A}$ is no longer a set, but a map from addresses to contract names. The judgment $\mathcal{I};\mathcal{A}\vdash \beta$ must additionally require that if $\langle \iota_C, a\rangle \in \text{dom}(\beta)$ then $\mathcal{A}(a) = C$. Finally, function types become triples, $\langle T, S, T_1\ldots T_n\rangle \leq \langle T', S', T_1'\ldots T_n'\rangle$ additionally requires $S' \leq S$, and the requirement on well-formedness of function bodies becomes the following: if $\texttt{ftype}(C,f) = \langle T, S, T_1\ldots T_n\rangle$ and $\texttt{fbody}(C,f) = \langle x_1\ldots x_n, e\rangle$ then $\texttt{this}{:}C, \texttt{msg.sender}{:}\texttt{address}\langle S\rangle, \texttt{msg.value}{:}\texttt{uint}, x_1 : T_1,..,x_n : T_n; \emptyset;\mathcal{A}\vdash e : T'$ with $T' \leq T$. The refined rule (T-CAST) now statically checks that the expression to be cast evaluates to the address of an instance of contract D which is a subtype of the target of the cast. In rules (T-INVK) and (T-TRANSFER), the additional side condition requires the type of the sender $e^{\texttt{s}}$ to be a subtype of the type S of the expected caller of the function f and $\texttt{fb}$, respectively, as specified in their refined signature.

The type system of FS^+ enjoys a stronger soundness property: $\texttt{revert}[\texttt{rte}]$ errors are statically prevented, so the only possible runtime errors remain those due to a negative account balance. In other terms, cast expressions or money transfers that would lead to unsafe usage of contract members or calls to an undefined fallback function are now ruled out at compile-time.

Theorem 2 (Soundness). *If* $\mathcal{I};\mathcal{A}\vdash c : T$, $c \longrightarrow^\star c'$, *and* $c' \not\rightarrow$, *where* $c' = \langle e', \beta'\rangle$, *then either* e' *is a value or* $e' = \texttt{revert}[\texttt{neg}]$.

By taking advantage of this more powerful typing, the `Bank` contract in Fig. 3 can be refined into the following safer smart contract:

```
contract Bank {
    mapping(address<Topfb> => uint) amounts;
    unit deposit <Topfb>() {...}
    unit withdraw  <Topfb>(uint n) {...}
}
```

We assume a contract Top_{fb} which only contains a `fb` function with empty body and `Top` sender parameter. Address types used in the mapping to index the banks' clients refer to such contract name. This type is also used in the refined signature of the two contract functions, so to (statically) ensure that their caller contract actually provides a fallback function. Therefore, coming back to the example discussed in Sect. 4, if a_B : address⟨Bank⟩ and a_D : address⟨D⟩ where the contract D has no fallback function, the function call Bank(a_B).withdraw.value(0).sender(a_D)(50) does not compile anymore, since the new rule (T-INVK) requires $D \leq Top_{fb}$, which is not true. The runtime error occurring when trying to tranfer money to a_D is then statically prevented. Similarly, the contract stored at a_D cannot even call the deposit function, thus preventing also the deposit of money that cannot be withdrawn anymore. We remark that the type address⟨Top_{fb}⟩ has the same meaning of Solidity 5.0's new type `address payable`, that is the (super)type of every contract that can safely accept money transfers. However, in Solidity 5.0 the variable `msg.sender` is *always* assumed to be of type `address payable`, and no check is performed at compile time to ensure that the actual sender has a fallback function. Therefore, differently form FS^+, the Solidity compiler 5.0 does not enjoy a better soundness property that of Sect. 4.

The introduction of the type address⟨C⟩ and the corresponding typing rules, are of course incompatible with the legacy Solidity code, that would not be accepted anymore by the new compiler. Nonetheless, a direct default mapping is easily definable by mapping each occurrence of the type `address` to address⟨Top⟩ and by refining each function signature so to use `Top` as supertype of the function's sender. We shall also provide a flag (`--notopcast`) in the new compiler to disable the refined rule (T-CAST) when $D = Top$ and use the standard rule (T-CAST) of Sect. 4. Indeed, the refined rule would rule out any cast having address⟨Top⟩ as actual type of e, since for all type C, $Top \nleq C$. Cleary, by using such a default mapping, no additional guarantees can be statically checked on the contracts code, however, retro-compatibility with Solidity contracts already deployed on the blockchain, whose code cannot be updated, is guaranteed.

To take advantage of the full power of the refined typing, the major effort required to Solidity programmers is to annotate each function with the required (super)type of the caller. We then put forward a couple of new convenient annotations, in line with the Solidity programming style, that provides a number of modifiers to annotate functions, e.g., the `payable` marker in Fig. 1. Since it is often the case that type constraints refer to contracts that provide (at least) a fallback function, the keyword `payableaddress` can be introduced as a syntactic sugar for the type address⟨Top$_{fb}$⟩, and the function marker payback can be used to indicate that the function potentially sends Ether back to its caller. Therefore, the Solidity Bank contract given in Fig. 1 could be simply rewritten into the following code, where function bodies are as in Fig. 1:

```
contract Bank {
    mapping (payableaddress => uint) private amounts;
    function deposit() payable payback {...}
    function withdraw() payback {...}
}
```

Instead, to enforce type-safe callbacks in functions code, programmers are required to explicitly express the type constraint they require on contracts callers. However, this requirement actually supports a safer programming discipline.

6   Conclusions and Related Work

We developed semantic foundations of smart contract programming, by formalizing the core of the Solidity language and type system. The FS calculus allows one to precisely define the behavior of smart contract programs and clarifies the type soundness of the Solidity compiler, pointing out its limitations. Thus it represents a fundamental building block to develop automatic program analysis tools. We then put forward a refined type discipline that statically captures a larger class of errors, such as unsafe casts, unsafe callbacks and unsafe money transfers. We discussed how such extension provides a safer programming discipline that is retrocompatibile with smart contracts already deployed on the blockchain. Finally, the FS calculus highlights the connection between objects and smart contracts, thus opening the way to reuse the type theory of OOLs in the context of Solidity, and dually to adapt the refined typing of FS$^+$ to the case of distributed objects.

A number of proposals have been developed to improve the security and correctness of Ethereum smart contracts. A stream of works, e.g., [3,7,8], addresses the problem at the bytecode level: the semantics of EVM bytecode is formalized and smart contracts properties are verified by means of static analysis tools operating on the corresponding bytecode. Among the ones addressing the problem at the programming language level, Zeus [10] translates Solidity code into LLVM bytecode [11], leveraging abstract interpretation and symbolic model checking analysis techniques. SmartCheck [13], instead, attempts to detect vulnerabilities representing Solidity code as an XML tree, and then running XPath queries on it. Contracts code is fully covered, but the use of XPath leads to a higher rate of false positives. However, these tools are based on limited formal foundations of the language they operate on, and they come into play when a contract is fully defined. We rather think that by enhancing the Solidity compiler's ability to statically rule out harmful code, we support a safer programming discipline, where programmers can write smart contracts that are (more) correct by construction. The work presented in [2] operates in this direction, and provides a preliminary compiler extension encoding Solidity code into SMT formulas to check simple properties, such as the division by zero. Similarly, the tool developed in [12] encodes a subset of Solidity into SMT formulas and uses symbolic model checking to verify some properties about smart contracts behaviour, including temporal ones. The first attempt to formalize Solidity is presented in [4]. In this work a small subset of Solidity is translated into F*, whose type system is afterwards used to detect vulnerable patterns, such as reentrancy. Even though the results are encouraging, the subset of Solidity is too small (neither transfer or cast expressions are considered), and an external language, F*, is used. To the best of our knowledge, this paper, together with its preliminary version [6], is the first work aiming at directly formalizing the semantics and the type soundness of the Solidity source code, so to enhance the use of its compiler as a convenient building tool.

References

1. Solidity. https://solidity.readthedocs.io/en/develop/index.html. Release 0.4.25
2. Alt, L., Reitwiessner, C.: SMT-based verification of solidity smart contracts. In: Margaria, T., Steffen, B. (eds.) ISoLA 2018. LNCS, vol. 11247, pp. 376–388. Springer, Cham (2018). https://doi.org/10.1007/978-3-030-03427-6_28
3. Amani, S., Bégel, M., Bortin, M., Staples, M.: Towards verifying Ethereum smart contract bytecode in Isabelle/HOL. In: Certified Programs and Proofs, pp. 66–77. ACM (2018)
4. Bhargavan, K., et al.: Formal verification of smart contracts: short paper. In: ACM Workshop on Programming Languages and Analysis for Security, pp. 91–96. ACM (2016)
5. Buterin, V.: A next-generation smart contract and decentralized application platform (white paper). Technical report (2014)
6. Di Pirro, M.: How solid is Solidity? An in-dept study of solidity's type safety. Master's thesis, Università di Padova, September 2018. http://tesi.cab.unipd.it/61297/
7. Grishchenko, I., Maffei, M., Schneidewind, C.: A semantic framework for the security analysis of Ethereum smart contracts. In: Bauer, L., Küsters, R. (eds.) POST 2018. LNCS, vol. 10804, pp. 243–269. Springer, Cham (2018). https://doi.org/10.1007/978-3-319-89722-6_10
8. Hildenbrandt, E., et al.: KEVM: a complete formal semantics of the Ethereum virtual machine. In: Computer Security Foundations Symposium, CSF, pp. 204–217 (2018)
9. Igarashi, A., Pierce, B.C., Wadler, P.: Featherweight Java: a minimal core calculus for Java and GJ. ACM TOPLAS **23**(3), 396–450 (2001)
10. Kalra, S., Goel, S., Dhawan, M., Sharma, S.: ZEUS: analyzing safety of smart contracts. In: Network and Distributed System Security Symposium (2018)
11. Lattner, C., Adve, V.: LLVM: a compilation framework for lifelong program analysis & transformation. In: Code generation and optimization: feedback-directed and runtime optimization, p. 75. IEEE (2004)
12. Shishkin, E.: Debugging smart contract's business logic using symbolic model-checking. arXiv preprint arXiv:1812.00619 (2018)

13. Tikhomirov, S., Voskresenskaya, E., Ivanitskiy, I., Takhaviev, R., Marchenko, E., Alexandrov, Y.: SmartCheck: static analysis of Ethereum smart contracts. In: Workshop on Emerging Trends in Software Engineering for Blockchain, pp. 9–16 (2018)
14. Wood, G.: Ethereum: a secure decentralised generalised transaction ledger. Ethereum Proj. Yellow Pap. **151**, 1–32 (2014)

Building Executable Secure Design Models
for Smart Contracts with Formal Methods

Weifeng Xu[1] and Glenn A. Fink[2(✉)]

[1] College of Public Affairs, University of Baltimore, 1420 N. Charles Street, Baltimore,
MD 21201, USA
wxu@ubalt.edu
[2] Cyber Security Group, Pacific Northwest National Laboratory, 902 Battelle Blvd,
Richland, WA, USA
Glenn.Fink@pnnl.gov

Abstract. Smart contracts are appealing because they are self-executing business agreements between parties with the predefined and immutable obligations and rights. However, as with all software, smart contracts may contain vulnerabilities because of design flaws, which may be exploited by one of the parties to defraud the others. In this paper, we demonstrate a systematic approach to building secure design models for smart contracts using formal methods. To build the secure models, we first model the behaviors of participating parties as state machines, and then, we model the predefined obligations and rights of contracts, which specify the interactions among state machines for achieving the business goal. After that, we illustrate executable secure model design patterns in TLA+ (Temporal Logic of Actions) to against well-known smart contract vulnerabilities in terms of state machines and obligations and rights at the design level. These vulnerabilities are found in Ethereum contracts, including Call to the unknown, Gasless send, Reentrancy, Lost in the transfer, and Unpredictable state. The resultant TLA+ specifications are called secure models. We illustrate our approach to detect the vulnerabilities using a real-estate contract example at the design level.

1 Introduction

Smart contracts are self-executing contracts with the terms of the agreement between parties being directly written into lines of code. Smart contracts have interesting properties: (1) they are unbreakable agreements with predefined rules, (2) they exist across a distributed, decentralized blockchain network, and (3) they permit trusted transactions and agreements to be carried out among disparate, anonymous parties without the need for a central authority, legal system, or external enforcement mechanism [1]. Regardless of their appeal, smart contracts are software, and therefore, they may contain potential defects common to software, such as those arising from the complexity of the modeled system. These defects are either design flaws or implementation bugs. Smart contract design flaws are often inherited from business contracts or introduced during smart contract design. Smart contract software defects are introduced during implementation. After defective smart contracts been deployed to a production blockchain, they become very expensive to fix because they are unchangeable and decentralized. There is

© International Financial Cryptography Association 2020
A. Bracciali et al. (Eds.): FC 2019 Workshops, LNCS 11599, pp. 154–169, 2020.
https://doi.org/10.1007/978-3-030-43725-1_12

a well-known recent incident that is related to the both technical and business issues of smart contracts [2]. On June 17, 2016, a hacker discovered a smart contract error in the Ethereum Distributed Autonomous Organization (DAO), eventually forcing the entire currency to do a "hard fork" to erase the fraudulent transactions from the ledger, costing tens of millions of dollars in losses. The DAO hack was the first well-known incident caused by defects in smart contracts and exploited by malicious users. It is legally unclear how other blockchain communities will agree to resolve similar incidents in the future.

The goal of this research is to build secure models for smart contracts to detect security vulnerabilities at the design level. Specifically, we (1) employ state machines to model the behaviors of business contracts, (2) analyze well-known smart contract vulnerabilities in terms of state machines, and (3) propose and build vulnerability discovering mechanisms while formalizing state machines using formal methods. The contributions of the paper include (1) separated design concerns: using state machines to model the obligations and rights of business contracts in two levels: the capabilities of participating parties and the constraints of these capabilities defined by contracts, (2) building smart contract vulnerability resistance capabilities. The capabilities are built based on the well-known design by contract principle [3, 4] and the well-known low level attacked captured in state machines [5], (3) facilitating vulnerability detecting automation: the proposed design patterns and approach facilitate the vulnerability detecting automation by formalizing behavioral models in TLA+ [6].

The rest of the paper is outlined as follows: Sect. 2 describes the overall approach. Section 3 presents the secure model design for smart contracts. Section 4 reviews the related work. Finally, Sect. 5 concludes this paper.

2 Background and Approach Overview

In this section, we briefly discuss the life cycle of smart contracts, review several well-known smart contract vulnerabilities, and then show the overall approach to building secure design models for smart contracts.

Smart contracts are software, and therefore, we should manage the software development lifecycle to minimize the chance of introducing defects. The key activities in the life cycle include (1) specifying business contracts, (2) designing smart contracts, (3) implementing smart contracts, (4) auditing smart contracts, and (5) deploying and executing smart contracts. Mistakes can be made in each activity caused by problems like the ambiguity of business contracts, software specification and design flaws, implementation errors in smart contract code, incomplete auditing, and environmental errors from the smart contract execution platform. We focus on the second activity of the smart contract development life cycle and aim at discovering the design flaws of smart contracts. As examples to guide the development of our approach, we are interested in discovering the following system behavior-related vulnerabilities mentioned in [7, 8]:

- Call to the unknown (CTU). Some of the primitives used in Solidity [9] to invoke functions and to transfer ether may have the side effect of invoking an undesirable behavior of the recipient.
- Gasless send (GS). When using the function send to transfer ether to a contract, it is possible to incur in an out-of-gas exception.

- Reentrancy (RE). A behavior may be unintentionally executed more than once. This class of flaw was the cause of the DAO's problems.
- Lost in transfer (LIT). If some ether is sent to an orphan address, it is lost forever.

The main idea of securing smart contract design is to build security models around business contracts against the vulnerabilities of smart contracts including those mentioned. Specifically, we aim at designing and specifying the countermeasure mechanisms, i.e., secure design patterns, in TLA+ based on behaviors of the contracts. The newly created models are called Temporal Logic of Actions (TLA) security models, and they are the formal specification of state machines with the integrated vulnerability detection ability. TLA is a shorthand for referring to the TLA+ specification language [6]. The rich language has well-defined semantics and was designed for expressiveness and ease of formal reasoning. The center of Fig. 1 represents secure models of smart contracts in TLA+. The creation of the secure models are the results of a sequence of modeling activities. The dashed links indicate the modeling activities are not enforced. However, each activity results in a partial TLA model. The activities are:

- Eliciting business needs. This step captures business requirements and agreements in contractual use-case templates. The basic elements required for the agreement to be a legally enforceable contract include the offer, parties, consideration, terms and conditions, and acceptance. This step also highlights the relations among these elements.
- Modeling participating party behaviors. This step describes the behaviors of each party involved in the business contracts in the corresponding state machines.
- Modeling contractual rights and obligations. This step models the interactions among participating parties. These interactions are enforced by the mutual agreements.
- Secure smart contract design. This step secures smart contract design by implementing secure design patterns to against well-known smart contract vulnerabilities. The design process focuses on what the smart contract should do rather than on how it should do

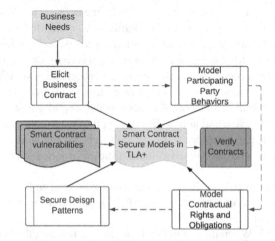

Fig. 1. The systematic approach to build secure design models for smart contracts

it. For example, a specification may say that a vending machine must dispense a soda if took a one-dollar bill (the *what*), without specifying the mechanism used to take dollar bills and vend soda cans (the *how*). Note that the TLA security models can be verified using a Temporal Logic model Checker (TLC). TLC is a model checker for debugging a TLA model by checking invariance properties of a finite-state model of the specification.

3   Modeling Business Contracts

In this section, we discuss the elicitation of the business contracts and model the behaviors of participating parties, including the obligations and rights of the participating parties in state machines.

A.   *Eliciting Business Contracts*

To demonstrate the approach, we use the example where an owner wants to sell his/her house and a potential buyer wants to purchase it. A property manager, such as a city where the house is located, will coordinate the transaction. An offer is the beginning of a contract. One party must propose an arrangement to the other, including definite terms. The *parties* of a contract are the entities involved in the agreement. For simplicity, we conflate the buyer/seller parties with their respective agents. The *consideration* of a contract specifies what each party stands to gain from the business arrangement. For example, if a house owner wants to sell his house to a buyer, the offer is the house, the seller's consideration is the payment for the sold house, and the buyer's consideration is ownership of the house. The *terms and conditions* of a business contract specify the rights and obligations of each party. These can vary widely depending on the nature of the business arrangement. Common examples can include the amount of payment, when payment is due, the specific nature of the work involved and how long the agreement will remain in effect. Terms and conditions may cover complex situations such as failure of one party to accomplish something required in a timely manner or dissatisfaction with the outcome of the contract resolution. *Acceptance* of the contract is the expression of assent to its considerations.

Business contract elicitation is the practice of collecting the contractual require-ments from participating parties and other stakeholders. The contractual requirements are captured in contractual use-case specifications, which are an extension of use case specifications [10]. Specifically, a contractual use case's specification is a textual model that organizes and describes key components of business contract requirements. Table 1 shows a contractual use case specification based on the real-estate property-selling con-tract. It contains the key elements of business contracts, including a short description of the contract, an offer, the participating parties in the contract, the terms and conditions specified in the contract, the consideration of the contract, and the acceptance of the contract.

Table 1. A business contractual use case

Name	Real estate property selling
Description	A buyer and a seller want to exchange the ownership of a building after the buyer bought the building from the seller
Offer	A house
Parties	A buyer, a seller, and a property manager
Legality	1. The seller owns the house 2. The buyer has the ability to pay
Consideration	1. The seller: payment for the sold house 2. The buyer: title deed to the house
Acceptance	1. The seller: receipt of payment of the sold house 2. The buyer: receipt of ownership of the house 3. Property manager: the record of changed ownership
Rejection	1. The seller: keep the house 2. The buyer: keep the money
Rights	See Table 2
Obligations	See Table 2

Note that:

- The property manager acts as a contract manager. It specifies the business process and coordinates the behaviors of the both buyer and seller. The purpose of the property manager is to get rid of the middle man in the business process, which is one of the advantages of smart contracts. Each contract needs to define the contract manager.
- The use case template also includes the item "rejection" of acceptance, which describes a scenario that occurs when a participating party does not agree to the terms of the contract.
- Rights and obligations must be specified in terms and conditions of a business contract. Contractual rights are the set of rights guaranteed whenever people enter into a valid contract. For example, both parties have the rights to join the business negotiation process. After joining, both parties have obligations to inform the property manager regarding their status.
- The rights and obligations in the modeling process are considered as the interface among all parties in a contract. The interactions occurred in the interface.

B. *Modeling Contractual Rights and Obligations*

Rights and obligations are the key elements of business contracts. We use state machines [11] to model the essential element. A state machine is an implementation-independent model of the dynamic behavior of the system. It is an abstract program representing a business contract that can be in exactly one of a finite number of states at any given time, involving all parties. A state machine can change from one state to another in response to some external inputs. The event-response features of the state machine represent the nature of obligations and rights between and among parties. Figure 2 shows the state machine of the rights and obligations defined in business contracts. The state machine models the behavior of the rights and obligations at two levels: The capabilities of each participating party expressed in state machines and the constraints of these capabilities.

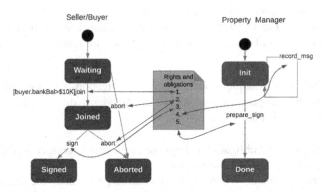

Fig. 2. Rights and obligations between participating parties

Modeling the Capabilities of Each Party. These parties include the seller, the buyer, and the property manager. The capabilities of a party describe what the party is capable of doing regardless of external constraints and stimulates. For example, the state machines of the seller and buyer show both parties are in the initial *"Waiting"* state, i.e., waiting for a contract. Both parties can abort the business process anytime. Once they have an intention to create a legal relationship, they can enter the *"Joined"* state indicating they have joined the business negotiation. Both seller and buyer have two options after joining the business negotiation either decide to sign the property selling contract or abort the business negotiation process. The outcome of each party is either *"Signed"* or *"Aborted"*. For the purpose of demonstration, the buyer and seller have separate instances of the same state machine. When the property manager changes his state from *"Init"* to *"Done"* he finishes preparing contractual documents and asking both seller and buyer to sign the contract. Note that the capabilities may have optional internal constraints. For example, to join the real-estate business, the buyer may need to show his/her bank account balance is greater than $10K. The internal constraint for that capability may be expressed as [buyer.bankBal>$10k]join. The property manager is often called the third-party beneficiary in business contracts.

Modeling the Constraints of These Capabilities. Although state machines capture each individual participating party's capabilities in a business setting, they do not describe the constraints of capabilities to achieve a business goal of a contract. Such constraints need to be specified as the rights and the obligations of each party. Rights are the fundamental normative rules about what parties are allowed to do. A contractual obligation means that a person must comply with the directives stated or given due to the agreement, promise, or verbal/written contract that is in place between the individuals involved. In the modeling process, the performance of obligations is formed from a party's responses (i.e., capabilities) to external events under the predefined terms and conditions (i.e., external constraints). *The external events* are the events generated by the status-changing information shared between the parties. The changes of such statues often have impacts on the offer or the process of making and accepting the offer. For example, if the offer of the contract is a house, then external events can be a price-change event, a time-change event, and message-receive event. An *external event flow* refers to the associate and the direction between the parties who generate and receive the events. The external event flows between the parties, and they are represented by red lines in Fig. 2.

Figure 3 shows an example model of how an obligation is performed and a right is requested by the property manager. The model views the obligations and their corresponding rights as a three-step process:

- Obligation request. An obligation is requested by a smart contract. The dashed lines indicate the requested obligation process.
- Obligation performance. When an obligation is performed, the capability of a corresponding party is invoked.
- Right request. After an obligation is performed, the party can request his rights based on the contract. The solid links represent the rights requesting process.

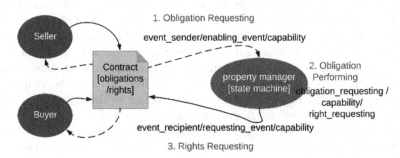

Fig. 3. The model of performing an obligation

When modeling and integrating contractual rights and obligations of a party into state machines, we need to answer the following questions that are related to the obligations and rights: (1) who requested the services, (2) who provides the services or performs obligations, and (3) which obligation should be performed. We define the obligations of a party as the capabilities of the participating party invoked by predefined external events, where the capabilities are the behaviors captured by state machines. The external events can be generated by either receiving a message, a timer, or the changed states of globally shared variables by all participating parties. In other words, the obligations enable response to external *enabling events*. The rights of a party are obligation request events generated by the party. The requesting events ask other parties to provide pre-defined services in contracts in exchange for the party's services. We call these *requesting events*. The complete obligation-request and right-request messages are expressed as *event_sender/enabling_event/capability* and *event_recipient/requesting_event/capability*, respectively. The obligation performance is expressed as *obligation_request/capability/rights_request*. It indicates the capability is invoked if an obligation request is received and the rights request will be fired. These expressions answer the three questions mentioned earlier.

Table 2 shows the rights and obligations of the seller and buyer. For example, once the property manager receives *"joined_msg"* messages (i.e., an enabling event) from both the buyer and the seller, the property manager is obligated to prepare the signing process (i.e., *"prepare_sign"*), and then sends a sign message *"sign_msg"* (a requesting event) to both the buyer and seller to sign the contract. It worth noting that we model shared attributes among parties, and the external events are generated based on the predefined rules consisting of the shared attributes.

Table 2. The rights and obligations of each party

ID	Parties	Obligations					Rights	
		Event Sender	Enabling Events	Capability			Request ing Events	Event Recipient
				Current State	Activities	Next State		
1	Buyer /Seller	n/a	n/a	Waiting	Join the real estate process (*join*)	Joined	*joined_ msg*	property manager
2	Buyer /Seller	n/a	n/a	Waiting or Joined	Abort the transferring process any time before signing the transferring documentation (*abort*)	Aborte d		
3	Buyer /Seller	property manager	*sign_msg*	Joined	*sign* the selling/buying agreement	Signed		
4	Property manager	buyer/seller	a message *joined_msg*	Init	Record the received messages (*record_msg*)	Init		
5	Property manager	buyer and seller	*joined_msg*	Init	Prepare to sign (*prepare_sign*)	Done	*sign_ms g*	buyer and seller

4 Secure Smart Contract Design

We will discuss the design by contract principle and how the design patterns use the principle to detect vulnerabilities at a design level, including the misbehaviors of individual participant party, and the obligations and rights vulnerabilities among parties.

A. *Design by Contract and TLA+*

The state machine captures the capabilities of parties and contractual relations among parties at the design level, however, it doesn't enforce prevention of potential vulnerabilities. We secure the state machines by adding logic for secure design patterns that address well-known attacks on state machines, including extra states, sneak paths, trap doors, and the hidden activities [5]. Secure smart contract design is based on the well-known design-by-contract principle [3, 4]. The principle suggests that a software component must specify formal, precise, and verifiable interfaces by defining the component's preconditions, postconditions, and invariants. These specifications are also referred to as "contracts", in accordance with a conceptual metaphor with the terms and conditions and obligations of business contracts, but they must not be confused with the smart contract we are implementing.

We use TLA+ to secure smart contract design because TLA+ uses mathematics in a simple, native way to specify state machines [12]; it facilitates the implementation of secure design patterns and automates vulnerability detection. TLA+ has demonstrated the value of formal methods for Real-world Systems. Since 2011, engineers at Amazon have been using TLA+ to help solve difficult design problems in critical systems [13, 14].

B. *TLA+ Secure Design Patterns for Each Party's Behaviors*

Extra State Checking Design Pattern. The existence of extra states indicates the ability of parties to enter a situation unanticipated by the design. To prevent extra states, TLA+ allows us to define predicate logic formulas to check the type-correctness invariant. The formula creates a "positive" security model (also known as "whitelist") that defines what is allowed, and rejects everything else [15]. For example, lines 5, 6 and 7 of the TLA+ snippet below defines a formula named " checkExtraStateVul", which requires that the resultant state in the buyer/seller state machines must be one in the set {"Waiting", "Joined", "Signed", "Aborted"}. Similarly, any property manager state must in the set {"Init", "Done"}. The symbol $\land$ in TLA+ is the propositional logic and operator and the symbol \in is a set operator $\in$. In addition, the symbol [] defines a function to be a set of ordered pairs. The expression [S -> T] is the set of all functions f whose domain is S such that f [x] is in the set T for all x in S. In our example, SB is the domain. The expression [SB -> { "Waiting", "Joined", "Signed", "Aborted" }] at line 6 is the mathematically way of listing all possible states of the buyer and the seller using functions, e.g., one of the ordered pairs can be (buyer | > Waiting), where the symbol |-> separates the function domain and the range.

```
1.   CONSTANT SB        \* The participating parties, i.e., seller and buyer
2.   VARIABLE
3.        sbState,      \* The state of the seller and the buyer
4.        pmState       \* The state of the property manager
5.   checkExtraStateVul ==
6.      /\sbState \in [SB -> { "Waiting", "Joined", "Signed", "Aborted" }]
7.      /\ pmState \in {"Init", "Done"}
```

Sneak Path & Trap Door Checking Design Pattern. Once we eliminate unknown states we must secure the transitions between the legal states. A sneak path is an activity or an event that causes a transition out of a legal state under conditions that are not allowed. A sneak path may be triggered by incorrect conditions of the activity or when the current state of an instance is out of synchronization with the rest of the model. For instance, a sneak path might cause the property manager to enter its " Done" state prematurely by fooling it into erroneously believing that both the seller and buyer have signed. While all the instances are in legal states, the sneak path produces a system that is in an illegal meta-state.

A trap door is when a legal state of an implementation accepts an event that is not defined in the specification, which causes the instance to enter that state under unspecified conditions. To prevent sneak paths and trap doors, we whitelist the activities by adding additional constrains. Specifically, the secure design pattern specifies four constraints for each activity: (a) the current state, (b) the conditions of the activity, (c) the resultant state, and (d) the states of other participating parties, where the constraints (a), (b), and (c) addresses sneak paths, and constraint (d) addresses the trap doors. The following TLA+ design pattern specifies the constrained activities, and therefore, prevents the sneak paths.

```
1.   activity ==
2.          /\ current_state                    (a)
3.          /\ conditions                        (b)
4.          /\ next_state                        (c)
5.          /\ states_of_other_parties           (d)
```

The following TLA+ snippet defines a *sign* formula. Lines 2 and 3 check sneak paths, which implement the constraints (a) and (b). Line 4 checks any violations of trap doors, which implements the constraints (c) and (d). Line 4 means that the current state of the participating party must be "*Signed*" and states of other participating parties must remain unchanged. For the purpose of designing secure models, we do not implement the "*sign*" activity, and the formula is only to specify what the valid "*sign*" behavior is. If we want to model whether a buyer can sign the contract, we can introduce a balancevariable and simplify assert the buyer's bank account has enough balance use the formula canSign ==balance >= propertyPrice.

```
1.   sign(sb) ==
2.          /\ sbState[sb] = "joined"
3.          /\ canSign
4.          /\ sbState' = [sbState EXCEPT ![sb] = "signed"]
```

Hidden Activity Checking Design Pattern. Hidden activities are illegal activities that should not be allowed by the parties. To prevent the existence of hidden activities, we can simply use TLA+ to list only specific activities are allowed in the contracts. The following TLA+ snippet defines only three activities "*join*", "*sign*", and "*abort*" allowed for the seller and buyer. The symbol V in TLA+ is the propositional logic oroperator

```
1.   Next == \E sb \in SB : join(sb) \/ sign(sb) \/ abort(sb)
```

C. *TLA+ Secure Design Patterns for Obligations and Rights*

The secure design pattern (shown below) for obligations and rights requires the following formulas: the attributes shared by the parties, shared_attributes, the allowed external_events, an obligation, a right, a term_condition, a post_status, and an instance of each state machine SM_inst.

```
1.  shared_attributes
2.
3.  external_events==[?] \* enabling events and requesting events
4.
5.  Term_condition ==
6.          /\ obligation
7.          /\ right
8.          /\ post_status
9.
10. obligation ==
11.         /\ event_sender
12.         /\ enabling_events
13.         /\ current_state
14.         /\ next_state
15.
16. right ==
17.         /\ event_recipient
18.         /\ requesting_event
19.
20. post_status==?
21.
22. SM_inst == INSTANCE partyStateMachines
```

The secure design pattern has two purposes: (a) mapping key elements of business models, particularly the rights and obligations, and (b) detecting the aforementioned vulnerabilities, including GS, RE, LIT, and CTU:

- Detecting GS vulnerability. GS vulnerability is essentially a sneak path. The vulnerability is related to each party's behaviors rather than obligations and rights. The formula SM_inst indicates that the behaviors of each individual party described in the previous section must be verified when checking the rights and obligations of parties. SM_inst has defined the formula conditions to enforce the conditions before carrying out any activities, and therefore, it prevents any sneak paths activated by incorrect conditions.
- Detecting RE vulnerability. RE vulnerability is often caused by a sneak path or a trap door between parties. To detect RE vulnerability at the design level, the secure design pattern adds additional constraints, including current_state, next_state and event_sender, in the enabling_events formula. The obligations formula indicates that (1) the first entry needs to reach the correct obligation, (2) the second entry needs to meet the current_state, and (3) an obligation is valid only if the required enabling_events are generated by the predefined event_sender party and the events are predefined in the external events set external_events. It prevents sneak paths from unspecified scenarios and trap doors between participating parties because of undefined external events or incorrect event senders. Note that the formula external_events includes both types of external events: enabling events and requesting events. The formula asserts that any events that are not in the set are invalid. These external events are generated based on the shared attributes or by other parties directly. In addition, if the RE vulnerability involves two parties, we use the secure design for contract considerations patterns (discussed in next section) to enforce the integrity of the contract.

- Detecting LIT vulnerability. SM_instdefines CONSTANT SB, which specifies the parties in the contracts. It only allows transferring assets between parties. Furthermore, the vulnerability can be detected by verifying both considerations of the seller and buyer, e.g., the formula ContractConsistentCheck, which models the mutual states between two parties.
- Detecting CTU vulnerability. CTU triggers side effects while fulfilling obligations and claiming rights. Two mechanisms are proposed to reduce the vulnerability: preventing the incorrect invocations and post-statues checking. For example, to prevent claiming unknown rights, the secure design pattern has two formulas: (a) use a rightformula to prevent generating incorrect events, and (b) use a post_statusformula to detect the side effect of claiming incorrect rights. The rights of a participating party can be claimed only if a requesting event requesting_eventis generated and the right event_recipientis defined. The post_statusformula asserts what states must remain unchanged to prevent side effects.

The following TLA+ design snippet specifies the fifth right and obligation listed in Table 2. Each formula is described as follows:

We first define an event set (line 1). This specifies two types of messages that are allowed to pass between the seller and the buyer: a *"joined_msg"* message (line 2) sent by the seller or the buyer and a *"sign_msg"* message (line 3) sent by the property manager. Other events are not in the set may lead to GS vulnerability. Note that the special function in line 2 [type : {"joined_msg"}, sb : SB] represents a set of records with a domain named as typeand a range named as sb. The \cupsymbol indicates the union operation.

Lines 12–15 specify obligations. It indicates that the obligation is valid only if the property manager receives joined messages from the buyer and seller (line 13) the current state of the property manager, *"pmState"*, is *"Init"* (line 14), and the next state of the property manager is *"Done"* (line 15).

```
1.   events ==
2.         [type : {"joined_msg"}, sb : SB] \cup
3.         [type : {"sign_msg"}]
4.
5.   VARIABLES msgs_passing, pmJoinedMsgsReceived
6.
7.   pmSign ==
8.         /\ obligation
9.         /\ right
10.        /\ post_status
11.
12.  obligation ==
13.        /\ pmJoinedMsgsReceived = SB
14.        /\ pmState = "Init"
15.        /\ pmState' = "Done"
16.
17.  right == msgs_passing '
18.        = msgs_passing \cup {[type |-> "sign_msg"]}
19.
20.  post_status == UNCHANGED <<sbState, pmJoinedMsgsReceived >>
```

Lines 17–18 specify rights of the property manager. It changes the states of the shared attributes *"message_passing"* by adding a *"sign_msg"* to the attributes. The added message will trigger the third obligation of both buyer and seller that is defined in Table 2. Line 20 specifies that the obligation and right should not change the states of both the buyer and the seller as well as the variable that the property manager used to hold the received messages from the buyer and the seller. This prevents exploitation of the CTU vulnerability.

C. *TLA+ Secure Design for Contract Considerations*

Considerations are the benefits that each party receives, or expects to receive when entering into a contract. For a business contract to be considered valid and enforceable by the courts, three elements of consideration must be met: (a) there is a bargain for the terms of the exchange, (b) the bargain includes a mutual exchange between the parties, and (c) the exchange is something of value. Secure design patterns for contract considerations include a model of each party's considerations and a model of the mutual exchange.

Each party's consideration can be modeled in terms of value consideration changes shown below:

```
1.   considerCheck (party)==
2.             /\current_state
3.             /\valueConsider'=valueConsider+ consideration
4.             /\next_state
```

For example, if the seller's consideration is the payment received, the secure design pattern needs to verify the payment has been received in the state model. The third line in the activity *"sign"* verifies that if the seller sold his property, his/her bank account balance will be increased by the payment of the property.

```
1.   sign(seller) ==
2.        /\ sbState[seller] = "joined"
3.        /\ balance'= balance + payment
4.        /\ sbState' = [sbState EXCEPT ![seller] = "signed"]
```

Modeling the mutual exchanges between two parties. It takes both parties' considerations together as a whole. It often models the final states of both parties and verify a value flow between two parties after mutual exchange of a consideration. The following formula asserts that the seller and the buyer should not have arrived at conflicting decisions. It guarantees that either both parties sign the contract or both of them abort the business process.

```
1.   ContractConsistentCheck ==
2.   \A sb1, sb2 \in SB :
3.        ~ /\ sbState[sb1] = "aborted"
4.          /\ sbState[sb2] = "signed"
```

The following formula ContractPaymentConsistentCheck asserts that the payment transfers from the buyer to the seller. Similarly, we can verify the ownership transferring.

```
1.   ContractPaymentConsistentCheck ==
2.     \A sb1, sb2 \in SB :
3.          /\ seller_sign(sb1)
4.          /\ buyer_sign(sb2)
5.
6.   seller_sign1(seller) ==
7.          /\ balance[seller]'= balance[seller] + payment
8.
9.   buyer_sign(buyer) ==
10.         /\ balance[buyer]'= balance[buyer] - payment
```

5 Related Work

Smart contract verification concepts are not new. One of the early works is done in 1997 by Szabo [16]. Szabo described the basic idea behind smart contracts as different kinds of contractual clauses (such as collateral, bonding, delineation of property rights, etc.). These contractual clauses can be embedded in the hardware and software we deal with, in such a way as to make a breach of contract expensive for the cheater. Szabo used protocols and user interfaces to formulate all steps of the contracting process. This work provides new primitives to formalize and secure digital relationships. Grosof et al. [17, 18] built a rule-based approach to the representation of business contracts that enables software agents to create, evaluate, negotiate, and execute contracts with substantial automation and modularity. It builds upon the situated courteous logic programs knowledge representation in RuleML. Similarly, Governator [19] presented an approach for the specification and implementation of e-contracts for Web monitoring. This is done in the setting of RuleML. He argued that monitoring contract execution requires also a logical account of deontic (rule-based) concepts and of violations.

Smart contract verification for blockchains is relatively new, however, there is a large body of similar work on formal software verification. Bhargavan et al. [20] outlined a framework to analyze and verify both the runtime safety and the functional correctness of Ethereum contracts by translation to F*, a functional programming language aimed at program verification. Their approach is based on shallow embeddings and type-checking within an existing verification framework. It does not address specific smart contract vulnerabilities. Delmolino et al. [21] documented several typical classes of mistakes students made, suggest ways to fix/avoid them and advocate best practices for programming smart contracts. Their work mainly focused on discovering bugs at the code level. Bigi et al. [22] combine game theory and formal models to tackle the new challenges posed by the validation of such systems. They extends Markov Decision Process to model the behaviors of the participants.

The proposed approach is rooted in two concepts in software engineering: design by contract and TLA+ formal methods. The central idea of design by contract is a metaphor on how elements of a software system collaborate with each other on the basis of mutual obligations and benefits.

6 Conclusion

The design of smart contracts needs to be checked and verified to minimize the design flaws and detect security vulnerabilities. We have presented a systematic approach to build secure models for smart contracts in TLA+ to verify the smart contract design. We have applied the approach to a property sale sample contract. Specifically, we have demonstrated how TLA secure models are generated to address some well-known smart contract vulnerabilities, including GS, RE, LIT, and CTU. This approach models the elements of business contracts in state machines and propose secure design patterns in TLA to detect smart contract vulnerabilities at the design level.

For future work, we plan to (1) extend the case study by increasing more states and behaviors to approximate a real-world scenario, (2) implant vulnerabilities in the property sale contracts and evaluate the vulnerability detection rates of the secure models, and (3) develop secure smart contract design templates so that the templates can be generated automatically to detect smart contract vulnerabilities. In addition, the template can help developers to cover general business informal contracts. These informal contracts exist in business contracts and do not require a specified form or method of formation in order to be valid. However, they may be required in smart contracts to reduce malicious behaviors.

Acknowledgment. This work is supported in part by the Department of Energy and the National Science Foundation under Grant Numbers 1714261.

References

1. Mohanty, D.: BlockChain: From Concept to Execution. Independently published (2018)
2. Finley, K.: A 50 million hack just showed that the dao was all too human (2016). https://www.wired.com/2016/06/50-million-hack-just-showed-dao-human/
3. Meyer, B.: Object-Oriented Software Construction, vol. 2. Prentice Hall, New York (1988)
4. Meyer, B.: Applying design by contract. J. Comput. **25**(10), 40–51 (1992). https://doi.org/10.1109/2.161279
5. Binder, R.V.: Testing Object-Oriented Systems: Models, Patterns, and Tools. Addison-Wesley, Boston (2000)
6. Lamport, L.: Specifying Systems: The TLA+ Language and Tools for Hardware and Software Engineers. Addison-Wesley Longman Publishing Co., Inc., Boston (2002)
7. Sirer, E.G.: Reentrancy woes in smart contracts (2016). http://hackingdistributed.com/2016/07/13/reentrancy-woes/
8. Atzei, N., Bartoletti, M., Cimoli, T.: A survey of attacks on Ethereum smart contracts (SoK). In: Maffei, M., Ryan, M. (eds.) POST 2017. LNCS, vol. 10204, pp. 164–186. Springer, Heidelberg (2017). https://doi.org/10.1007/978-3-662-54455-6_8
9. Buterin, V., et al.: A next-generation smart contract and decentralized application platform. White paper (2014)
10. Jacobson, I.: Object-Oriented Software Engineering: A Use Case Driven Approach. Pearson Education, London (1993)
11. Harel, D.: Statecharts: a visual formalism for complex systems. Sci. Comput. Program. **8**(3), 231–274 (1987)

12. Lamport, L.: Computation and state machines, April 2008. https://www.microsoft.com/en-us/research/publication/computation-state-machines/
13. Newcombe, C.: Why amazon chose TLA+. In: Ait Ameur, Y., Schewe, K.D. (eds.) ABZ 2014. LNCS, vol. 8477, pp. 25–39. Springer, Heidelberg (2014). https://doi.org/10.1007/978-3-662-43652-3_3
14. Newcombe, C., Rath, T., Zhang, F., Munteanu, B., Brooker, M., Deardeuff, M.: How amazon web services uses formal methods. Commun. ACM 58(4), 66–73 (2015)
15. Mansfield-Devine, S.: The promise of whitelisting. Netw. Secur. 2009(7), 4–6 (2009)
16. Szabo, N.: Formalizing and securing relationships on public networks. First Monday 2(9) (1997)
17. Grosof, B.N., Poon, T.C.: SweetDeal: representing agent contracts with exceptions using XML rules, ontologies, and process descriptions. In: Proceedings of the 12th International Conference on World Wide Web, pp. 340–349. ACM (2003)
18. Grosof, B., Poon, T.: SweetDeal: representing agent contracts with exceptions using semantic web rules, ontologies, and process descriptions. Int. J. Electron. Commer. 8(4), 61–97 (2004)
19. Governatori, G.: Representing business contracts in RuleML. Int. J. Coop. Inf. Syst. 14(02n03), 181–216 (2005)
20. Bhargavan, K., et al.: Formal verification of smart contracts: short paper. In: Proceedings of the 2016 ACM Workshop on Programming Languages and Analysis for Security, PLAS 2016, pp. 91–96. ACM, New York (2016). https://doi.org/10.1145/2993600.2993611
21. Delmolino, K., Arnett, M., Kosba, A., Miller, A., Shi, E.: Step by step towards creating a safe smart contract: lessons and insights from a cryptocurrency lab. In: Clark, J., Meiklejohn, S., Ryan, P.Y.A., Wallach, D., Brenner, M., Rohloff, K. (eds.) FC 2016. LNCS, vol. 9604, pp. 79–94. Springer, Heidelberg (2016). https://doi.org/10.1007/978-3-662-53357-4_6
22. Bigi, G., Bracciali, A., Meacci, G., Tuosto, E.: Validation of decentralised smart contracts through game theory and formal methods. In: Bodei, C., Ferrari, G.-L., Priami, C. (eds.) Programming Languages with Applications to Biology and Security. LNCS, vol. 9465, pp. 142–161. Springer, Cham (2015). https://doi.org/10.1007/978-3-319-25527-9_11

SoK: Transparent Dishonesty:
Front-Running Attacks on Blockchain

Shayan Eskandari[1,2]($\boxtimes$), Seyedehmahsa Moosavi[1], and Jeremy Clark[1]($\boxtimes$)

[1] Gina Cody School of Engineering and Computer Science, Concordia University,
Montreal, Canada
s_eskand@encs.concordia.ca, j.clark@concordia.ca
[2] ConsenSys Diligence, Montreal, Canada

Abstract. We consider *front-running* to be a course of action where an entity benefits from prior access to privileged market information about upcoming transactions and trades. Front-running has been an issue in financial instrument markets since the 1970s. With the advent of the blockchain technology, front-running has resurfaced in new forms we explore here, instigated by blockchain's decentralized and transparent nature. In this paper, we draw from a scattered body of knowledge and instances of front-running across the top 25 most active decentral applications (DApps) deployed on Ethereum blockchain. Additionally, we carry out a detailed analysis of Status.im initial coin offering (ICO) and show evidence of abnormal miner's behavior indicative of front-running token purchases. Finally, we map the proposed solutions to front-running into useful categories.

1   Introduction

Blockchain technology enables decentralized applications (DApps) or smart contracts. Function calls (or transactions) to the DApp are processed by a decentralized network. Transactions are finalized in stages: they (generally) first relay around the network, then are selected by a miner and put into a valid block, and finally, the block is well-enough incorporated that is unlikely to be reorganized. Front-running is an attack where a malicious node observes a transaction after it is broadcast but before it is finalized, and attempts to have its own transaction confirmed before or instead of the observed transaction.

The mechanics of front-running work on all DApps but front-running is not necessarily beneficial, depending on the DApp's internal logic and/or as any mitigations it might implement. Therefore, DApps need to be studied individually or in categories. In this paper, we draw from a scattered body of knowledge regarding front-running attacks on blockchain applications and the proposed solutions, with a series of case studies of DApps deployed on Ethereum (a popular blockchain supporting DApps). We do case studies on decentralized exchanges (*e.g.*, Bancor), crypto-collectibles (*e.g.*, CryptoKitties), gambling services (*e.g.*, Fomo3D), and decentralized name services (*e.g.*, Ethereum Name Service).

© International Financial Cryptography Association 2020
A. Bracciali et al. (Eds.): FC 2019 Workshops, LNCS 11599, pp. 170–189, 2020.
https://doi.org/10.1007/978-3-030-43725-1_13

We also study initial coin offerings (ICOs). Finally, we provide a categorization of techniques to eliminate or mitigate front-running including transaction sequencing, cryptographic techniques like commit/reveal, and redesigning the functioning of the DApp to provide the same utility while removing time dependencies.

2   Preliminaries and Related Work

2.1   Traditional Front-Running

Front-running is a course of action where someone benefits from early access to market information about upcoming transactions and trades, typically because of a privileged position along the transmission of this information and is applicable to both financial and non-financial systems. Historically, floor traders might have overheard a broker's negotiation with her client over a large purchase, and literally race the broker to buy first, potentially profiting when the large purchase temporarily reduces the supply of the stock. Alternatively, a malicious broker might front-run their own client's orders by purchasing stock for themselves between receiving the instruction to purchase from the client and actually executing the purchase (similar techniques can be used for large sell orders). Front-running is illegal in jurisdictions with established securities regulation.

Cases of front-running are sometimes difficult to distinguish from related concepts like insider trading and arbitrage. In front-running, a person sees a concrete transaction that is set to execute and reacts to it before it actually gets executed. If the person instead has access to more general privileged information that might predict future transactions but is not reacting at the actual pending trades, we would classify this activity as insider trading. If the person reacts after the trade is executed, or information is made public, and profits from being the fastest to react, this is considered arbitrage and is legal and encouraged because it helps markets integrate new information into prices quickly.

2.2   Literature on Traditional Front-Running

Front-running originates on the Chicago Board Options Exchange (*CBoE*) [41]. The Securities Exchange Commission *(SEC)* in 1977 defined it as: "The practice of effecting an options transaction based upon non-public information regarding an impending block transaction[1] in the underlying stock, in order to obtain a profit when the options market adjusts to the price at which the block trades. [2]" Self-regulating exchanges (*e.g., CBoE*) and the *SEC* spent the ensuing years planning how to detect and outlaw front-running practices [41]. The *SEC* stated: "It seems evident that such behaviour on the part of persons with knowledge of imminent transactions which will likely affect the price of the derivative security

---

[1] A block in the stock market is a large number of shares, 10 000 or more, to sell which will heavily change the price.

constitutes an unfair use of such knowledge.[2]" The *CBoE* tried to educate their members on existing rules, however, differences in opinion regarding the unfairness of front-running activities, insufficient exchange rules and lack of a precise definition in this area resulted in no action [2] until the SEC began the regulation. We refer the reader interested in further details on this early regulatory history to Markham [41]. The first front-running policies applied only to certain option markets. In 2002, the rule was expanded to cover all security futures [3]. In 2012, it was expanded further with the new amendment, FINRA Rule 5270, to cover trading in options, derivatives, or other financial instruments overlying a security with only a few exceptions [5,6]. Similar issues have been seen with domain names [4,25] as well.

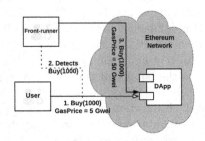

Fig. 1. The front-runner upon spotting the profitable transaction *Buy(1000)* sends his own transaction with higher gas price to bribe the miners to prioritize his transaction over initial transaction.

2.3   Background on Blockchain Front-Running

Blockchain technology (introduced via Bitcoin in 2008 [48]) strives to disintermediate central parties that participate in a transaction. However, blockchains also introduce new participants in the process of relaying and finalizing transactions. Miners are in the best position to conduct these attacks as they hold fine-grained control over the exact set of transactions that will execute and in what order and can mix in their own (late) transactions without broadcasting them. Miners do however have to commit to what their own transactions will be before beginning the proof of work required to solve a block.

Any user monitoring network transactions (*e.g.*, running a full node) can see unconfirmed transactions. On the Ethereum blockchain, users have to pay for the computations in a small amount of Ether called **gas** [1]. The price that users pay for transactions, **gasPrice**, can increase or decrease how quickly miners will execute them and include them within the blocks they mine. A profit-motivated miner who sees identical transactions with different transaction fees will prioritize the transaction that pays a higher gas price due to limited space in the

---

[2] Securities Exchange Act Release No. 14156, November 19, 1977, (Letter from George A. Fitzsimmons, Secretary, Securities, and Exchange Commission to Joseph W. Sullivan, President CBoE).

blocks. This has been called a gas auction [32]. Therefore, any regular user who runs a full-node Ethereum client can front-run pending transactions by sending adaptive transactions with a higher gas price (see Fig. 1).

Finally, well-positioned relaying nodes on the network (or part of the broader internet backbone) can attempt to influence how transactions are propagated through the network, which can influence the order miners receive transactions, or if they receive them at all [30,40].

2.4   Literature on Blockchain Front-Running

Given the purpose of this entire paper is systemizing the existing literature, we do not re-enumerate the literature here. However, we note two points. First, we are not aware of any other systematic study of this issue. Second, front-running is related to two well-studied concepts: double-spending and rushing adversaries [38].

Double-spending attacks in Bitcoin are related to front-running [11,36]. In this attack, a user broadcasts a transaction and is able to obtain some off-blockchain good or service before the transaction has actually been (fully) confirmed. The user can then broadcast a competing transaction that sends the same unspent coins to herself, perhaps using higher transaction fees, arrangements with miners or artifacts of the network topology to have the second transaction confirmed instead of the first. This can be considered a form of self-front-running. In the cryptographic literature, front-running attacks are modeled by allowing a so called 'rushing' adversary to interact with the protocol [12]. In particular, ideal functionalities of blockchains (such as those used in simulation-based proofs) need to capture this adversarial capability, assuming the real blockchain does not address front-running. See *e.g.,* Bitcoin backbone [29] and Hawk [38].

3   A Taxonomy of Front-Running Attacks

As we will illustrate with examples through-out the paper, front-running attacks can often be reduced to one of a few basic templates. We emphasize what the adversary is trying to accomplish (without worrying about how) and we distinguish three cases: displacement, insertion, and suppression attacks. In all three cases, Alice is trying to invoke a function on a contract that is in a particular state, and Mallory will try to invoke her own function call on the same contract in the same state before Alice.

In the first type of attack, a *displacement attack*, it is not important to the adversary for Alice's function call to run after Mallory runs her function. Alice's can be orphaned or run with no meaningful effect. Examples of displacement include: Alice trying to register a domain name and Mallory registering it first [35]; Alice trying to submit a bug to receive a bounty and Mallory stealing it and submitting it first [16]; and Alice trying to submit a bid in an auction and Mallory copying it.

In an *insertion attack*, after Mallory runs her function, the state of the contract is changed and she needs Alice's original function to run on this modified state. For example, if Alice places a purchase order on a blockchain asset at a higher price than the best offer, Mallory will insert two transactions: she will purchase at the best offer price and then offer the same asset for sale at Alice's slightly higher purchase price. If Alice's transaction is then run after, Mallory will profit on the price difference without having to hold the asset.

In a *suppression attack*, after Mallory runs her function, she tries to delay Alice from running her function. After the delay, she is indifferent to whether Alice's function runs or not. We only observe this attack pattern in one DApp and the details are quite specific to it, so we defer discussion until Sect. 4.3.

Each of these attacks have two variants, *asymmetric* and *bulk*. In some cases, Alice and Mallory are performing different operations. For example, Alice is trying to cancel an offer, and Mallory is trying to fulfill it first. We call this *asymmetric displacement*. In other cases, Mallory is trying to run a large set of functions: for example Alice and others are trying to buy a limited set of shares offered by a firm on a blockchain. We call this *bulk displacement*.

4   Cases of Front-Running in DApps

To find example DApps to study, we used the top 25 DApps based on recent user activity from `DAppradar.com` in September 2018.[3] User activity is admittedly an imperfect metric for finding the 'most significant' DApps: significant DApps might be lower volume overall or for extended periods of time (*e.g.,* ICOs, which we remedy by studying independently in Sect. 5). However, user activity is an objective criteria, data on it is available, and the list captures our intuition about which DApps are significant. It suffices for a first study in this area, and is preferable over an ad hoc approach. Using the dataset, we categorized the top 25 applications into 4 principal use cases. The details are given in Table 1.

4.1   Markets and Exchanges

The first category of DApp in Table 1 are financial exchanges for trading ether and Ethereum-based tokens. Exchanges such as EtherDelta[4], purport to implement a decentralized exchange, however, their order books are stored on a central server they control and shown to their users with a website interface. Central exchanges can front-run orders in the traditional sense, as well as re-order or block orders on their servers. 0xProtocol [65] uses *Relayers* which act as the order book holders and could front-run the orders they relay.

As seen in traditional financial markets, one method to manipulate the spot price of an asset, is to flood the market with orders and cancel them when there are filling orders ("taker's griefing" [7]). Placing an order in a partially centralized

---

[3] List of decentralized applications https://DAppradar.com/DApps.
[4] Also known as ForkDelta for the user interface: https://forkdelta.app/.

Table 1. Top 25 DApps based on recent user activity from DAppRadar.com on September 4th, 2018. The DApps that are in bold are discussed in this paper.

DApp category	Names	Rank
Exchanges	IDEX	1
	ForkDelta, EtherDelta	2
	Bancor	7
	The Token Store	13
	LocalEthereum	14
	Kyber	22
	0x Protocol	23
Crypto-collectible games (ERC-721 [26])	**CryptoKitties**	3
	Ethermon	4
	Cryptogirl	9
	Gods Unchained TCG	12
	Blockchain Cuties	15
	ETH.TOWN!	16
	0xUniverse	18
	MLBCrypto Baseball	19
	HyperDragons	25
Gambling	**Fomo3D**	5
	DailyDivs	6
	PoWH 3D	8
	FomoWar	10
	FairDapp	11
	Zethr	17
	dice2.win	20
	Ether Shrimp Farm	21
Name services	**Ethereum Name Service**	24

exchange is free, but to prevent taker's griefing attacks, the user needs to send an Ethereum transaction to cancel each of his orders. Cancelling orders is most important when prices change faster than order execution. In this case, when an adversarial actor sees a pending cancellation transaction, he sends a fill order transaction with higher gasPrice to get in front of the cancellation order and take the order before it is canceled (this is known as *cancellation grief*). This attack follows the asymmetric displacement template and is illustrated in Fig. 2.

Designing truly decentralized exchanges, where the order book is implemented directly on a public blockchain, is being pursued by a number of projects [24]. These designs are generally vulnerable to front-running attacks following a displacement or insertion template. For example, a front-running full

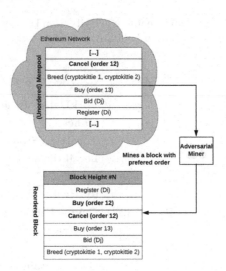

Fig. 2. The adversarial miner monitors the Ethereum mempool for decentralized exchange transactions. Upon spotting a profitable cancellation transaction, he puts his buy order prior to the cancel transaction in the block he mines. Doing so, the miner can profit from the underlying trade and also get the gas included in the cancel transaction.

node or miner might gauge the demand for trades at a given price by the number of pending orders, and try to displace them at the same price assuming the demand is the result of the accurate new information about the asset. Alternatively, the front-runner might observe a large market order (*i.e.*, it will execute at any price). The adversary can try to insert a pair of limit orders that will bid near the best offer price and offer at a higher price. If the pair executes ahead of the market order, the front-runner profits by scalping the price of the shares. Finally, if adversary has pre-existing offers likely to be reached by the market order, she could insert cancellations and new offers at a higher price.

Bancor is an exchange DApp that allows users to exchange their tokens without any counter-party risk. The protocol aims to solve the cryptocurrency liquidity issue by introducing *Smart Tokens* [31]. Smart tokens are ERC20-compatible that can be bought or sold through a DApp-based dealer that is always available and implements a market scoring rule to manage its prices. Bancor provides continuous liquidity for digital assets without relying on brokers to match buyers with sellers. Implemented on the Ethereum blockchain, when transactions are broadcast to the network, they sit in a pending transaction pool known as *mempool* waiting for the miners to mine them. Since Bancor handles all the trades and exchanges on the chain (unlike other existing decentralized exchanges), these transactions are all visible to the public for some time before being included within a block. This leaves Bancor vulnerable to the blockchain race condition attack as attackers are given enough time to front-run other transactions, in which they can gain favourable profits by buying before the order and fill the original order with slightly higher price [58]. Researchers have shown and implemented a proof of concept code to front-run Bancor as a non-miner user [13].

4.2 Crypto-Collectibles Games

The second category of DApp in Table 1 is crypto-collectables. Consider Cryptokitties [9], the most active DApp in this category and third most active overall. Each kitty is a cartoon kitten with a set of unique features to distinguish it from other cryptokitties, some features are rarer and harder to obtain. They can be bought, sold, or bred with other cryptokitties. At the Ethereum level, the kitty is a token implemented with *ERC-721: Non-Fungible Token Standard* [26]. Kitties are generally bought and sold on-chain through auction smart contracts. See Sects. 4.1 and 4.4 for more details on auction-based front-running attacks.

Specific to Cryptokitties protocol, they can breed and give birth. When cryptokitties breed, the smart contract sets from which future block the pregnancy of the cat can be completed. Anyone can complete the pregnancy by calling giveBirth() after the birthing block and they will receive a reward in ether[5]. Even though front-running these calls would not affect the protocol workflow, but this displacement attack could result in financial profit for front-runners [37,68].

4.3 Gambling

The third category of DApp in Table 1 is gambling services. While a large category of gambling games are based on random outcomes, DApps do not have unique access to an unpredictable data stream to harvest for randomness [51]. Any candidate source of randomness (such as block headers) is accessible to all DApp functions and can also be manipulated to an extent by miners.

Fomo3D is an example of a game style (known as Exit Scam[6]) not based on random outcomes, and it is the most active game on Ethereum in our sample. The aim of this game is to be the last person to have purchased a ticket when a timer goes to zero in a scenario where anyone can buy a ticket and each purchase increases the timer by 30 s. Many speculated such a game would never end but on August 22, 2018, the first round of the game ended with the winner collecting 10,469 Ether[7] equivalent to $2.1M USD at the time. Blockchain forensics indicate a sophisticated winning strategy to displace any new ticket purchases [10,57] that would reset the counter. The winner appears to have started by deploying many high gas consumption DApps unrelated to the game. When the timer of the game reached about 3 min, the winner bought 1 ticket and then sent multiple high gasPrice transactions to her own DApps. These transactions congested the network and bribed miners to prioritize them ahead of any new ticket purchases

---

[5] As there are no automated function calls in Ethereum, this incentive model –known as *Action Callback* [52]– is used to encourage users to call these functions.

[6] https://exitscam.me/play.

[7] The first winner of Fomo3D, won 10,469 Ether https://etherscan.io/tx/0xe08a519c03cb0aed0e04b33104112d65fa1d3a48cd3aeab65f047b2abce9d508.

in Fomo3D. Recall this basic form of bribery is called a *Gas Auction*; See related work [14,43] for more sophisticated bribery contracts.

We classify this in the unique category of a suppression attack in our taxonomy (see Sect. 3). At first glance, it seemed like an extreme version of an asymmetric/bulk displacement attack on any new ticket purchase transactions. However the key difference is that the front-runner does not care at all about the execution of her transactions—if miners mined empty blocks for three minutes, that would also be acceptable. Thus, bulk displacement[8] is simply a means-to-an-end and not the actual end goal of the adversary.

4.4 Name Services

The final category in Table 1 is name services, which are primarily aimed at disintermediating central parties involved in web domain registration (*e.g.*, ICAAN and registrars) and resolution (*e.g.*, DNS). For simple name services (such as some academic work like Ghazal [47]), domains purchases are transactions and front-runners can displace other users attempting to register domains. This parallels front-running attacks seen in regular (non-blockchain) domain registration [4]. Ethereum Name Service (ENS) [34] is the most active naming service on Ethereum. Instead of allowing new .eth domain names to be purchased directly, they are put up for a sealed bid auction which seals the domain name in a bid, but not the bid amount. Most implementations use the more user friendly but less confidential method for starting and bidding on a domain name: startAuctionsAndBid(). This method leaks the hash of the domain and the initial bid amount in the auction. Original names can be guessed from the hashes (*e.g.*, rainbow tables, used in ENS Twitter bot[9]) or people can bid on domains even though they do not know what they are because of speculation on its value.

Users are allowed to bid for 3 days before the 2-day reveal phase begins (see 6.2), in which all bidders (winners and losers) must send a transaction to reveal their bids for a specific domain or sacrifice their bid amount. Also note that if two bidders bid the same price, the first to reveal wins it [23]. Using the leaked information, the domain squatter can win the auction with the same price of the original bidder by revealing it first. This is similar to front-running as it relies on inserting an action before the user, however we do not consider this specific action as front-running attack.

5   Cases of Front-Running in ICOs

Initial coin offerings (ICOs) have changed how blockchain firms raise capital. More than 3000 ICOs have been held on Ethereum, and the market capitalization of these tokens appears to exceed $75B USD in the first half of 2018 [67]. At the DApp level, tokens are offered in short-term sales that see high transaction activity while the sale is on-going and then the activity tapers off to

---

[8] Also known as Block Stuffing Attack [59].

[9] https://twitter.com/ensbot.

occasional owner transfers. When we collected the top 25 most active DApps on DAppRadar.com, no significant ICOs were being sold. The ICO category slips through our sampling method, but we identify it as a major category of DApp and study it here.

5.1 *Status.im* ICO

To deal with demand, ICOs cap sales in a variety of ways to mitigate front-running attacks. In June 2017, *Status.im* [8] started its ICO and reached the predefined cap within 16 h, collecting close to 300,000 Ether. In order to prevent wealthy investors purchasing all the tokens and limit the amount of Ether deposited in each investment, they used a *fair* token distribution method called *Dynamic Ceiling* as an attempt to increase the opportunity for smaller investors. They implemented multiple caps (ceilings) in which, each had a maximum amount that could be deposited in. In this case, every deposit was checked by the smart contract and the exceeding amount was refunded to the sender while the accepted amount was sent to their multi-signature wallet address [50].

During the time frame the ICO was open for participation, there were reports of Ethereum network being unusable and transactions were not confirming. Further study showed that some mining pools might have been manipulating the network for their own profit. In addition, there were many transactions sent with a higher gas price to front-run other transactions, however, these transactions were failing due to the restriction in the ICO smart contract to reject transactions with higher than 50 *GWei* gas price (as a mitigation against front-running).

5.2 Data Collection and Analysis

According to the analysis we carried out, we discovered that the F2Pool—an Ethereum mining pool that had around 23% of the mining hash rate at the time (Fig. 3)—sent 100 Ether to 30 new Ethereum addresses before the Status.im ICO

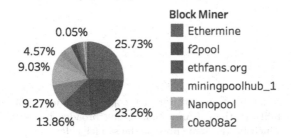

Fig. 3. The percentage of Ethereum blocks mined between block 3903900 and 3908029, this is the time frame in which Status.im ICO was running. This percentage roughly shows the hashing power ratio each miner had at that time.

started. When the ICO opened, F2Pool constructed 31 transactions to the ICO smart contract from their addresses, without broadcasting the transactions to the network[10]. They used their entire mining power to mine their own transactions and some other potentially failing high gas price transactions.

Ethereum's blockchain contains all transaction ever made on Ethereum. While the default client and online blockchain explorers offer some limited query capabilities, in order to analyze this case, we built our own database. Specifically, we used open source projects such as Go Ethereum implementation[11] for the full node, a python script for extracting, transforming and loading Ethereum blocks, named `ethereum-etl` [45] and Google BigQuery.[12] Using this software stack, we were able to isolate transactions within the Status.im ICO. We used data analysis tool `Tableau`.[13] A copy of this dataset and the initial findings can be found in our Github repository[14].

As shown in Fig. 4, most of the top miners in the mentioned time frame, have mined almost the same number of failed and successful transactions which were directed toward Status.im token sale, however F2Pool's transactions indicate their successful transactions were equivalent to 10% of the failed transactions, hence maximizing the mining rewards on gas, while censoring other transactions to the token sale smart contract. The terminology used here is specific to smart contract transactions on Ethereum, by *"failed transaction"* we mean the transactions in which the smart contract code rejected and threw an exception and by *"successful transaction"* we mean the transactions that went through and received tokens from the smart contract.

By tracing the transactions from these 30 addresses, we found explicit interference by F2Pool[15] in this scenario. As shown in Fig. 5, the funds deposited by F2Pool in these addresses were sent to *Status.im* ICO and mined by F2Pool themselves, where the dynamic ceiling algorithm refunded a portion of the deposited funds. A few days after these funds were sent back to F2Pool main address and the tokens were aggregated later in one single address. Although this incident does not involve transaction reordering in the blocks, it shows how miners can modify their mining software to behave in a certain way to front-run other transactions by *bulk displacement* to gain monetary profit.

---

[10] Note that we do not have an authoritative copy of the mempool over time, however, the probability of these transactions being broadcasted to the network and exclusively get mined by the same pool as the sender is low.

[11] Official Go implementation https://github.com/ethereum/go-ethereum.

[12] https://cloud.google.com/bigquery/.

[13] https://www.tableau.com/.

[14] http://bit.ly/madibaFrontrunning.

[15] F2Pool address was identified by their mining reward deposit address https://etherscan.io/address/0x61c808d82a3ac53231750dadc13c777b59310bd9.

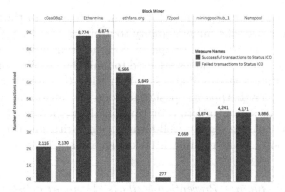

Fig. 4. This chart shows the miners behaviour on the time frame that Status.im ICO was running. It is clear that the number of successful transactions mined by F2Pool do not follow the random homogeneous pattern of the rest of the network.

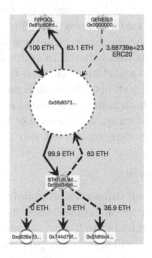

Fig. 5. Prior to *Status.im* ICO *F2Pool* deposited 100 Ether in multiple new Ethereum addresses. On the time of the ICO, transactions sent from these addresses to *Status* ICO smart contract were prioritized in their mining pool, resulting in purchasing *ERC20* tokens. This method was used to overcome the dynamic ceiling algorithm of the ICO smart contract. Later on they sent the refunded Ether back to their own address. (Graph was made using Blockseer.com blockchain explorer.)

6 Key Mitigations

As we studied front-running attacks on the blockchain, we also encountered a number of ways of preventing, detecting or mitigating front-running attacks. Instead of providing the details of exact solutions which will change over time, we extract the main principles or primitives that address the attack. A particular system may implement more than one in a layered mitigation approach.

We classify the mitigations into three main categories. In the first category, the blockchain removes the miner's ability to arbitrarily order transactions and tries to enforce some ordering, or queue, for the transactions. In the second category, cryptographic techniques are used to limit the visibility of transactions, giving the potential front-running less information to base their strategy on. In the final category, DApps are designed from the bottom-up to remove the importance of transaction ordering or time in their operations. We also note that for DApps that are legally well-formed (*e.g.,* with identified parties and a clear jurisdiction), front-running attacks can violate laws, which is its own deterrent.

Traditional Front-Running Prevention Methods. There are debates in traditional markets regarding the fact that front-running is considered to be a form of insider trading which deemed to be illegal. Traditional methods to prevent front-running mainly involves after the fact investigation and legal action against the front-runners [28]. As mentioned in Sect. 2.2, defining front-running and educating the employees were the first step taken to prevent such issues in traditional markets, however, front-running became less likely to happen mainly because of the high fine and lawsuits against firms who behaved in an unethical way. Other methods such as dark pools [20,69] and sealed bids [53] were discussed and implemented in a variety of regulated trading systems. The traditional methods to prevent front-running does not apply to blockchain applications, as mainly they are based on central enforcement and limitations, also in case of blockchains the actors who are front-running could be anonymous and the fear of lawsuits would not apply.

6.1 Transaction Sequencing

Ethereum miners store pending transactions in pools and draw from them when forming blocks. As the term 'pool' implies, there is no intrinsic order to how transactions are drawn and miners are free to sequence them arbitrarily.[16] The vanilla Go-Ethereum (geth) implementation prioritizes transactions based on their gas price and nonce [27]. Because no rule is enforced, miners can sequence transactions in advantageous ways. A number of proposals attempt to thwart this attack by enforcing a rule about how to sequence transactions.

First-in-first-out (FIFO) is generally not possible on a distributed network because transactions can reach different nodes in a different order. While the network could theoretically form a consensus based on locally observed FIFO, this would increase the rate of orphaned blocks, as well as adding complexity to the protocol. A trusted third party can be used to assign sequential numbers to transactions (and sign them), but this is contrary to blockchain's core innovation of distributed trust. Nonetheless, some exchanges do centralize time-sensitive functionalities (*e.g.,* *EtherDelta* and *0xProject*) in off-chain order books [64,65].

One alternative is to sequence transactions pseudorandomly. This can be seen in proposals like Canonical Transaction Ordering Rule (CTOR) by Bitcoin

---

[16] Sometimes the pool is called a 'queue.' It is important to note is a misnomer as queues enforce a first-in-first-out sequence.

Cash ABC [60] which adds transactions in lexicographical order according to their hash [61]. Note that Bitcoin does not have a front-running problem for standard transactions. While this could be used by Ethereum to make front-running statistically difficult, the protection is marginal at best and might even exacerbate attacks. A front-runner can construct multiple equivalent transactions, with slightly different values, until she finds a candidate that positions her transaction a desirable location in the resulting sequence. She broadcasts only this transaction and now miners that include her transaction will position it in front of transactions they heard about much earlier.

Finally, transactions themselves could enforce order. For example, they could specify the current state of the contract as the only state to execute on. This transaction chaining only prevents certain types of front-running; *i.e.*, it prevents insertion attacks but not displacement attacks (recall our taxonomy in Sect. 3). As transaction chaining only allows one state-changing transaction per state, at most one of a set of concurrent transactions can be confirmed; a drawback for active DApps.

6.2 Confidentiality

Privacy-Preserving Blockchains. All transaction details in Bitcoin are made public and participant identities are only lightly protected. A number of techniques increase confidentiality [19,42] and anonymity [46,49,56] for cryptocurrencies. A current research direction is extending these protections to DApps [55,66]. It is tempting to think that a confidential DApp would not permit front-running, as the front-runner would not know the details of the transaction she is front-running. However, there are some nuances here to explore.

A DApp interaction includes the following components: (1) the code of the DApp, (2) the current state of the DApp, (3) the name of the function being invoked, (4) the parameters supplied to the function, (5) the address of the contract the function is being invoked on, and (6) the identity of the sender. Confidentiality applied to a DApp could mean different levels of protection for each of these. For front-running, function calls (3,4) are the most important, however, function calls could be inferred from state changes (2). Hawk [38] and Ekiden [21] are examples of (2, 3, 4)-confidentiality (with limitations we are glossing over).

The applicability of privacy-preserving blockchains needs to be evaluated on a case-by-case basis. For example, one method used by traditional financial exchanges in dealing with front-running from high frequency traders is a dark pool: essentially a (2, 3, 4)-confidential order book maintained by a trusted party. A DApp could disintermediate this trusted party. Users whose balances are affected by changes in the contract's state would need to be able to learn this information. Further, if the contract addresses are known (*i.e.*, no 5-confidentiality), front-runners can know about the traffic pattern of calls to contracts which could be sufficient grounds for attack; for example, if each asset on an exchange has its own market contract, this leaks trade volume information. As a contrasting example, consider again decentralized domain registration:

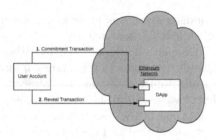

Fig. 6. Commit and Reveal. User sends a commitment transaction with the hash of the data, After the commitment period is over, user sends her reveal transaction to the DApp revealing the information that matches the commitment.

hiding state changes (2-confidentiality) defeats the entire purpose of the DApp, and protecting function calls is ineffective with a public state change since the state itself reveals the domain being registered.

Commit/Reveal. While confidentiality appears insufficient for solving domain name front-running alone, a hybrid approach of sequencing and confidentiality can be effective and is, in fact, an example of an older cryptographic trick known as commit/reveal. The essence of the approach is to protect the function call (*e.g.,* (3, 4)- or (4)-confidentiality) until the function is enqueued in a sequence of functions to be executed. Once the sequence is established, the confidentiality is lifted and the function can only be executed in the order it was enqueued (or, generally speaking, not at all).

Recall that a commitment scheme enables one to commit to a digital value (*e.g.,* a statement, transaction, data, *etc.*) while keeping it a secret (*hiding*), and then open it (and only it: *binding*) at a later time of the committer's choosing [15]. A common approach (conjectured to be hiding) is to submit the cryptographic hash of the value with a random nonce (for low entropy data) to a smart contract, and later reveal the original value and nonce which can be verified by the contract to correctly hash to the commitment (see Fig. 6).

An early application of this scheme to blockchain is Namecoin, a Bitcoin-forked DApp for name services [35]. In Namecoin, a user sends a commit transaction which registers a new hidden domain name, similar to a sealed bid. Once this first transaction is confirmed, a time delay begins. After the delay, a second transaction reveals the details of the requested domain. This prevents front-running if the reveal transaction is confirmed faster than an adversarial node or miner can redo the entire process.

Commit/reveal is a two-round protocol, and aborting after the first round (early aborts) could be an issue for this (along with most multi-round cryptographic protocols). For example, in a financial exchange where the number of other orders might be in a predictable interval, an adversary can spray the sequence (*i.e.,* a price-time priority queue) with multiple committed transactions and no intention of executing them all. She then only reveal the ones that result in an advantageous trade.[17] There are other ways of aborting; if payments are required but not collateralized, the aborting party can ensure that payment is not available for transfer. One mitigation to early aborts that blockchain is uniquely positioned to make is having users post a fidelity bond of a certain amount of cryptocurrency that can be automatically dispensed if they fail to fully execute committed transactions (this is used in multi-round blockchain voting [44]). Finally, we note that any multiple round protocol will have usability challenges: users must be aware that participating in the first round is not sufficient for completing their intention.

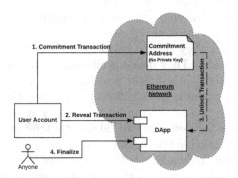

Fig. 7. Submarine Send [18]. User generates an *Unlock* transaction from which the commitment address is retrieved using ECDSA ECRecover. 1. by funding the *commitment address,* user is committed to the transaction. 2. User sends the *reveal transaction* to the DApp, revealing the nature of the commitment transaction. 3. She broadcasts the *unlock transaction* to unlock the funds in the commitment address. 4. After the *"Auction"* is over, anyone can call *Finalize* function to finalize the process.

Enhanced Commit/Reveal. Submarine Commitments [17,18] extend the confidentiality of the commit and reveal, so that the commitment transaction is identical to a transaction to a newly generated Ethereum address. They initially hide the contract address being invoked, providing (3, 4, 5)-confidentiality during the commit phase; and they ensure that if a revealed transaction sent funds, the funds were fully collateralized at commit time and are available to the receiving smart contract. See Fig. 7.

---

[17] This is analogous to behavior in traditional financial markets where high-frequency traders will make and cancel orders at many price points (flash orders or pinging). If they can cancel faster than someone can execute it—someone who has only seen the order and not the cancellation—then the victim reveals their price information.

6.3   Design Practices

The final main category of mitigation is to assume front-running is unpreventable and to thus responsively redesign the functionality of the DApp to remove any benefit from it. For example, when designing a decentralized exchange, one can use a call market design instead of a time-sensitive order book [22] to side-step and disincentivize front-running. In a call market design, the arrival time of orders does not matter as they are executed in batches[18]. The call market solution pivots profitable gains that front-running miners stand to gain into fees that they collect [22], removing the financial incentive to front-run.

In the finance literature, Malinova and Park discuss front-running mitigations for blockchain-based trading platforms [39]. Instead of studying DApps, they develop an economic model where transactions, asset holdings, and traders' identities have greater transparency than in standard economic models— transparency they argue that could be accomplished by blockchain technology. However, in their model, they assume entities can interact directly over private channels to arrange trades. They define front-running in the context of private offers, where parties might adjust their position before accepting or countering a received offer. This model is quite different than the DApp-based model we study here.

Another example in the design of ERC20 standard [62] is the allowance functionality. *approve()* function in the specification allows a second entity to be able to spend N tokens from the sender's balance. In order to change the allowance, sender must send a transaction to set the new allowance value. Using the insertion attack, attacker could front-run the new allowance transaction and spend the old value before the new value is set [33,54], and then additionally spend the new amount at a later time. Solutions such as *decreaseApproval()/increaseApproval()* were added in updated implementations.

7   Concluding Remarks

Front-running is a pervasive issue in Ethereum DApps. DApp developers don't necessarily have the mindset to design DApps with front-running in mind. This is an attempt to bring forward the subject and increase awareness of these type of attacks. While some DApp-level application logic could be built to mitigate these attacks, its ubiquity across different DApp categories suggests mitigations at the blockchain-level would perhaps be more effective. We highlight this as an important research area.

Acknowledgements. The authors thank the Autorité des Marchés Financiers (AMF) for sponsoring this research through the Education and Good Governance Fund (EGGF), as well as NSERC through a Discovery Grant.

---

[18] Also known as batch auctions [63].

References

1. Account types, gas, and transactions. Ethereum homestead 0.1 documentation. http://ethdocs.org/en/latest/contracts-and-transactions/account-types-gas-and-transactions.html#what-is-gas. Accessed 14 June 2018
2. 96th Congress 1st Session, report of the special study of the options markets to the securities and exchange commission (1978)
3. Im-2110-3. Front running policy. Financial Industry Regulatory Authority (2002)
4. SSAC advisory on domain name front running. ICANN Advisory Committee, 10 2007. Accessed 15 Aug 2018
5. Front running of block transactions. Financial Industry Regulatory Authority (2012)
6. Notice of filing of proposed rule change to adopt FINRA rule 5270 (front running of block transactions) in the consolidated FINRA rulebook. Securities and Exchange Commission (2012)
7. Security review of 0x smart contracts. ConsenSys-Diligence (2017)
8. The status network, a strategy towards mass adoption of Ethereum. Status Team (2017). Accessed 10 June 2018
9. Cryptokitties. Cryptokitties team (2018). Accessed 31 Aug 2018
10. Anonymous. How the first winner of Fomo3D won the jackpot? (2018). https://winnerfomo3d.home.blog/. Accessed 9 Sept 2018
11. Bamert, T., Decker, C., Elsen, L., Wattenhofer, R., Welten, S.: Have a snack, pay with bitcoins. In: 2013 IEEE Thirteenth International Conference on Peer-to-Peer Computing (P2P), pp. 1–5. IEEE (2013)
12. Beaver, D., Haber, S.: Cryptographic protocols provably secure against dynamic adversaries. In: Rueppel, R.A. (ed.) EUROCRYPT 1992. LNCS, vol. 658, pp. 307–323. Springer, Heidelberg (1993). https://doi.org/10.1007/3-540-47555-9_26
13. Bogatyy, I.: Implementing Ethereum trading front-runs on the Bancor exchange in Python (2017). https://hackernoon.com/front-running-bancor-in-150-lines-of-python-with-ethereum-api-d5e2bfd0d798. Accessed 13 Aug 2018
14. Bonneau, J., Felten, E.W., Goldfeder, S., Kroll, J.A., Narayanan, A.: Why buy when you can rent? Bribery attacks on bitcoin consensus (2016)
15. Brassard, G., Chaum, D., Crépeau, C.: Minimum disclosure proofs of knowledge. J. Comput. Syst. Sci. **37**(2), 156–189 (1988)
16. Breidenbach, L., Daian, P., Tramer, F., Juels, A.: Enter the hydra: towards principled bug bounties and exploit-resistant smart contracts. In: 27th USENIX Security Symposium (USENIX Security 18). USENIX Association (2018)
17. Breidenbach, L., Daian, P., Juels, A., Tramer, F.: To sink frontrunners, send in the submarines (2017). http://hackingdistributed.com/2017/08/28/submarine-sends/. Accessed 28 Aug 2018
18. Breidenbach, L., Kell, T., Gosselin, S., Eskandari, S.: Libsubmarine: defeat front-running on Ethereum (2018). https://libsubmarine.org/. Accessed 7 Dec 2018
19. Bünz, B., Bootle, J., Boneh, D., Poelstra, A., Wuille, P., Maxwell, G.: Bulletproofs: short proofs for confidential transactions and more. In: 2018 IEEE Symposium on Security and Privacy (SP), vol. 00, pp. 319–338 (2018)
20. Buti, S., Rindi, B., Werner, I.M.: Diving into dark pools (2011)
21. Cheng, R., et al.: Ekiden: a platform for confidentiality-preserving, trustworthy, and performant smart contract execution. arXiv preprint arXiv:1804.05141 (2018)
22. Clark, J., Bonneau, J., Felten, E.W., Kroll, J.A., Miller, A., Narayanan, A.: On decentralizing prediction markets and order books. In: Workshop on the Economics of Information Security, State College, Pennsylvania (2014)

23. E. Discussion: Handling frontrunning in the permanent registrar (2018)
24. distribuyed: A comprehensive list of decentralized exchanges (DEX) of cryptocurrencies, tokens, derivatives and futures, and their protocols (2018). https://distribuyed.github.io/index/. Accessed 24 Sept 2018
25. Edelman, B.: Front-running study: testing report (2009)
26. Entriken, W., Shirley, D., Evans, J., Sachs, N.: ERC-721 non-fungible token standard (2018). https://github.com/ethereum/EIPs/blob/master/EIPS/eip-721.md. Accessed 31 Aug 2018
27. Ethereum: worker.go - commitnewwork() (2018). Accessed 7 Dec 2018
28. Financial Times: Barclays trader charged with front-running by us authorities (2018)
29. Garay, J., Kiayias, A., Leonardos, N.: The bitcoin backbone protocol: analysis and applications. In: Oswald, E., Fischlin, M. (eds.) EUROCRYPT 2015. LNCS, vol. 9057, pp. 281–310. Springer, Heidelberg (2015). https://doi.org/10.1007/978-3-662-46803-6_10
30. Heilman, E., Kendler, A., Zohar, A., Goldberg, S.: Eclipse attacks on bitcoins peer-to-peer network. In: USENIX Security, pp. 129–144. USENIX Association, Washington, D.C. (2015)
31. Hertzog, E., Benartzi, G., Benartzi, G.: Bancor protocol (2017)
32. initc3.org: Frontrun me (2018). http://frontrun.me/
33. G. Issue: Method 'decreaseapproval' in unsafe (2017)
34. Johnson, N.: Ethereum domain name service - specification (2016)
35. Kalodner, H.A., Carlsten, M., Ellenbogen, P., Bonneau, J., Narayanan, A.: An empirical study of Namecoin and lessons for decentralized namespace design. In: WEIS. Citeseer (2015)
36. Karame, G.O., Androulaki, E., Capkun, S.: Double-spending fast payments in bitcoin. In: Proceedings of the 2012 ACM Conference on Computer and Communications Security, pp. 906–917. ACM (2012)
37. Koch, M.B.: Exploring CryptoKitties - part 2: the CryptoMidwives (2018)
38. Kosba, A., Miller, A., Shi, E., Wen, Z., Papamanthou, C.: Hawk: the blockchain model of cryptography and privacy-preserving smart contracts. In: 2016 IEEE Symposium on Security and Privacy (SP), pp. 839–858. IEEE (2016)
39. Malinova, K., Park, A.: Market design with blockchain technology (2017)
40. Marcus, Y., Heilman, E., Goldberg, S.: Low-resource eclipse attacks on Ethereum's peer-to-peer network. Cryptology ePrint Archive, Report 2018/236 (2018). https://eprint.iacr.org/2018/236
41. Markham, J.W.: Front-running-insider trading under the commodity exchange act. Cath. UL Rev. **38**, 69 (1988)
42. Maxwell, G.: Confidential transactions (2015). https://people.xiph.org/~greg/confidential_values.txt. Accessed 9 May 2016
43. McCorry, P., Hicks, A., Meiklejohn, S.: Smart contracts for bribing miners. IACR Cryptology ePrint Archive, 2018:581 (2018)
44. McCorry, P., Shahandashti, S.F., Hao, F.: A smart contract for boardroom voting with maximum voter privacy. In: Kiayias, A. (ed.) FC 2017. LNCS, vol. 10322, pp. 357–375. Springer, Cham (2017). https://doi.org/10.1007/978-3-319-70972-7_20
45. Medvedev, E.: Python scripts for ETL (extract, transform and load) jobs for Ethereum blocks (2018). https://github.com/medvedev1088/ethereum-etl
46. Miers, I., Garman, C., Green, M., Rubin, A.D.: Zerocoin: anonymous distributed e-cash from bitcoin. In: 2013 IEEE Symposium on Security and Privacy (SP), pp. 397–411. IEEE (2013)

47. Moosavi, S., Clark, J.: Ghazal: toward truly authoritative web certificates using ethereum. In: Zohar, A., et al. (eds.) FC 2018. LNCS, vol. 10958, pp. 352–366. Springer, Heidelberg (2019). https://doi.org/10.1007/978-3-662-58820-8_24
48. Nakamoto, S.: Bitcoin: A Peer-to-peer Electronic Cash System (2008)
49. Noether, S.: Ring signature confidential transactions for Monero. Cryptology ePrint Archive, Report 2015/1098 (2015). https://eprint.iacr.org/2015/1098
50. Petty, C.: A look at the Status.im ICO token distribution (2017). https://medium.com/the-bitcoin-podcast-blog/a-look-at-the-status-im-ico-token-distribution-f5bcf7f00907. Accessed 10 June 2018
51. Pierrot, C., Wesolowski, B.: Malleability of the blockchain's entropy. Crypt. Commun. **10**(1), 211–233 (2018)
52. Piqueras, E.: Generalized Ethereum frontrunners, an implementation and a cheat (2019)
53. Radner, R., Schotter, A.: The sealed-bid mechanism: an experimental study. J. Econ. Theor. **48**(1), 179–220 (1989)
54. Rahimian, R.: Multiple withdrawal attack (2018)
55. Reitwiessner, C.: An update on integrating Zcash on Ethereum (ZoE) (2017). https://blog.ethereum.org/2017/01/19/update-integrating-zcash-ethereum/
56. Sasson, E.B., et al.: Zerocash: decentralized anonymous payments from bitcoin. In: 2014 IEEE Symposium on Security and Privacy (SP), pp. 459–474. IEEE (2014)
57. SECBIT: How the winner got Fomo3D prize – a detailed explanation (2018). https://medium.com/coinmonks/how-the-winner-got-fomo3d-prize-a-detailed-explanation-b30a69b7813f. Accessed 9 Dec 2018
58. Sirer, E.G., Daian, P.: Bancor is flawed (2017). http://hackingdistributed.com/2017/06/19/bancor-is-flawed/. Accessed 14 June 2018
59. Solmaz, O.: The anatomy of a block stuffing attack (2018). https://osolmaz.com/2018/10/18/anatomy-block-stuffing/
60. Ver, R., Wu, J.: Bitcoin cash planned network upgrade is complete (2018). Accessed 7 Dec 2018
61. Vermorel, J., Séchet, A., Chancellor, S., van der Wansem, T.: Canonical transaction ordering for bitcoin (2018). Accessed 7 Dec 2018
62. Vogelsteller, F., Buterin, V.: ERC-20 token standard (2015). https://github.com/ethereum/EIPs/blob/master/EIPS/eip-20.md. Accessed 31 Aug 2018
63. Walther, T.: Multi-token batch auctions with uniform clearing prices (2018)
64. Warren, W.: Front-running, griefing and the perils of virtual settlement (2017). https://blog.0xproject.com/front-running-griefing-and-the-perils-of-virtual-settlement-part-1-8554ab283e97. Accessed 14 Aug 2018
65. Warren, W., Bandeali, A.: 0x: an open protocol for decentralized exchange on the Ethereum blockchain (2017). https://github.com/0xProject/whitepaper
66. Williamson, D.Z.J.: The AZTEC protocol (2018). https://github.com/AztecProtocol/AZTEC/
67. Zetzsche, D.A., Buckley, R.P., Arner, D.W., Föhr, L.: The ICO gold rush: it's a scam, it's a bubble, it's a super challenge for regulators (2018)
68. Zhou, Y., Kumar, D., Bakshi, S., Mason, J., Miller, A., Bailey, M.: Erays: reverse engineering Ethereums opaque smart contracts. In: USENIX Security (2018)
69. Zhu, H.: Do dark pools harm price discovery? Rev. Financ. Stud. **27**(3), 747–789 (2014)

Trustee: Full Privacy Preserving Vickrey Auction on Top of Ethereum

Hisham S. Galal and Amr M. Youssef[✉]

Concordia Institute for Information Systems Engineering, Concordia University,
Montréal, QC, Canada
{h_galal,youssef}@ciise.concordia.ca

Abstract. The wide deployment of tokens for digital assets on top of
Ethereum implies the need for powerful trading platforms. Vickrey auctions have been known to determine the real market price of items as
bidders are motivated to submit their own monetary valuations without
leaking their information to the competitors. Recent constructions have
utilized various cryptographic protocols such as ZKP and MPC, however,
these approaches either are partially privacy-preserving or require complex computations with several rounds. In this paper, we overcome these
limits by presenting Trustee as a Vickrey auction on Ethereum which
fully preserves bids' privacy at relatively much lower fees. Trustee consists
of three components: a front-end smart contract deployed on Ethereum,
an Intel SGX enclave, and a relay to redirect messages between them.
Initially, the enclave generates an Ethereum account and ECDH key-
pair. Subsequently, the relay publishes the account's address and ECDH
public key on the smart contract. As a prerequisite, bidders are encouraged to verify the authenticity and security of Trustee by using the SGX
remote attestation service. To participate in the auction, bidders utilize the ECDH public key to encrypt their bids and submit them to the
smart contract. Once the bidding interval is closed, the relay retrieves the
encrypted bids and feeds them to the enclave that autonomously generates a signed transaction indicating the auction winner. Finally, the relay
submits the transaction to the smart contract which verifies the transaction's authenticity and the parameters' consistency before accepting the
claimed auction winner. As part of our contributions, we have made a
prototype for Trustee available on Github for the community to review
and inspect it. Additionally, we analyze the security features of Trustee
and report on the transactions' gas cost incurred on Trustee smart contract.

Keywords: Sealed-bid auction · Trusted Execution Environment ·
Intel SGX · Ethereum · Blockchain

1 Introduction

The wide success of Ethereum [30] with a market capitalization around 10 billion USD at the time of the writing [2] has led to the deployment of thousands

© International Financial Cryptography Association 2020
A. Bracciali et al. (Eds.): FC 2019 Workshops, LNCS 11599, pp. 190–207, 2020.
https://doi.org/10.1007/978-3-030-43725-1_14

of asset-specific tokens [1]. Such a large-volume market demands powerful trading platforms. Auctions have been known to be an effective and efficient way to trade highly-valuable goods. Additionally, sealed-bid auctions have an important advantage compared to their open-cry counterparts. Precisely, given an honest auctioneer, bidders are assured that their competitors will not gain any information about their bids. Moreover, in a Vickrey auction which is a particular type of sealed-bid auctions, the auction winner pays the second highest-price. Consequently, Vickrey auctions motivate bidders to submit bids based on their own monetary valuation which essentially helps in determining the real market price of the auctioned items. Nonetheless, a corrupt auctioneer can easily compromise the aforementioned advantages. For instance, the auctioneer can (i) expose the bids' information to a colluding bidder, (ii) declare a false auction winner, (iii) set a fake second-highest price that is slightly lower than the highest price in order to gain an advantage. Consequently, the major challenges in constructing a Vickrey auction are maintaining bids' privacy and verifying the correctness of the auction winner and the amount of the second-highest price.

Building a Vickrey auction on top of Ethereum to trade the deployed tokens essentially involves writing a *smart contract* that adheres to a predefined protocol. A smart contract is an autonomous agent that resides at a specific address in the Ethereum blockchain. It contains functions to make decisions, and persistent storage to save state. The execution model of a smart contract is to lie passive and dormant until it is poked. More specifically, a smart contract only becomes active once any of its designated functions is invoked due to the receipt of either a *message* from another smart contract, or a *transaction* from an externally-owned account (i.e., informally called a *wallet*). The lifetime of a smart contract is to exist as long as the whole Ethereum network exists unless it was programmed to *self destruct* which essentially renders it completely inactive. With the help of the consensus protocol in Ethereum, a smart contract gains control flow integrity. In other words, it executes as its code dictates to the extent that even its creator cannot modify or patch it. The consensus protocol requires miners to do an expensive operation (*proof of work*) in addition to processing and validating the transactions. Therefore, miners are compensated by a block reward in addition to transaction fees. Essentially, the more complex the transaction, the higher fees are incurred. Additionally, processing and validating transactions imply that miners have a fully transparent access to smart contract's state. Therefore, the lack of privacy in addition to the expensive transaction fees are the main challenging issues in building a secure and efficient Vickrey auction on top of Ethereum.

To address the above issues, various constructions for sealed-bid auctions in general utilize different cryptographic protocols such as Zero-Knowledge Proofs (ZKP) and secure Multi-Party Computations (MPC) to ensure the verifiability of the auction winner without sacrificing bids' privacy. However, in the former, the auctioneer is an entity that learns bids' values and proves the correctness of the auction winner to the bidders. This approach is partial privacy-preserving since the bids' values are exposed to the auctioneer who may maliciously exploit this information in future auctions. In addition to the inherent high transaction fees in Ethereum, the verification of the auctioneer's proof is executed inside a smart contract which significantly incurs a high cost (e.g., zkSNARK verification roughly takes 3 million gas [15]) that renders the whole approach to be an expensive option. In contrast, the MPC approach can offer full bids' privacy at the cost of higher transactions fees since it requires several of complex computations between the bidders and using a smart contract as a public bulletin board in addition to an escrow of funds.

We present Trustee as a trusted and efficient Vickrey auction on top of Ethereum that substantially overcomes the limitations of ZKP and MPC approaches. Trustee utilizes Intel Software Guard Extensions (SGX) [4] as a Trusted Execution Environment (TEE) to fully preserve bids' privacy at a significantly cheaper transaction fee to verify the auction winner correctness compared to the aforementioned approaches. Intel SGX is a hardware architecture that provides an isolated and tamper-proof environment called *enclave*. In essence, the control flow integrity of the code and the confidentiality of the data inside an enclave are well protected from the host operating system and other running processes. Therefore, Intel SGX technology can complement smart contracts with confidential data processing, a highly desirable property that Ethereum lacks.

Similar to other TEE technologies, Intel SGX has a poor availability, and its operation can be easily terminated at any point of time. Hence, a stateful application utilizing Intel SGX requires a storage with high availability such as the blockchain or IPFS [6] to persist sensitive state (e.g., the sealed-bids and sealed private keys). We are also aware that several side-channel attacks on Intel SGX have been reported recently to leak information about the sensitive data inside enclaves such as private keys (more details in Sect. 4). Therefore, we do strongly note that rather than building Trustee using only Intel SGX, we utilize a smart contract on Ethereum for two purposes. First, it acts as an escrow to hold the initial deposits of bidders during the bidding phase for a specific time interval. As a result, bidders are not exposed to the theft of funds in the case they were sending their payments to an account controlled by the enclave which might get compromised. Secondly, it acts as a trusted judge that verifies on-behalf of the bidders the consistency of the inputs used by the enclave to determine the auction winner. Hence, it allows bidders with low-processing mobile devices to easily join the auction. Consequently, by integrating a smart contract on Ethereum with Intel SGX technology, Trustee becomes a robust Vickrey auction solution that inherits the best properties from the two worlds of blockchain and TEEs.

Our contribution, we present the design and implementation of Trustee that provides the following properties:

1. **Full privacy preserving**. The only information about bids that any bidder can learn besides to their own is the winning bid.
2. **Cheap correctness verification cost**. Compared to other alternatives, Trustee achieves significantly cheaper verification cost of the auction winner correctness.

3. **Rational fairness**. Malicious participants gain no advantage over honest parties. In fact, they are obligated to follow the proposed protocol to avoid being financially penalized.

4. **Efficiency**. The core computations of sealing bids, decrypting them, and selecting the auction winner are carried out in native environments off the blockchain which are more efficient than the Ethereum Virtual Machine (EVM).

We also provide an open-source prototype for Trustee on Github (https:// github.com/hsg88/Trustee) for the community to review it. The rest of this paper is organized as follows. Section 2 provides a review of current constructions of sealed-bid auctions on top of blockchains and the integration of TEEs with blockchain. In Sect. 3, we present the cryptographic primitives utilized in Trustee's design. Then, in Sect. 4, we provide the protocol design behind Trustee, analyze its security features, and report the gas cost of the relevant transactions. Finally, we present our conclusions in Sect. 5.

2 Related Work

In this section, we provide a review of state-of-the-art constructions that utilize a variety of cryptographic protocols such as ZKP and MPC to build sealed-bid auction on top of blockchains. Then, we briefly present recent works that integrate blockchain with TEE to provide elegant solutions.

2.1 Sealed-Bid Auctions on Blockchain

Blass and Kerschbaum [9] proposed *Strain* as a protocol to build a sealed-bid auction on top of the blockchain technology. Strain utilizes a two-party computation protocol to compare pairs of bids, and the outcome is stored on a blockchain. Additionally, Strain utilizes ZKP to prove that the outcome is correct with respect to the compared pairs of bids. Strain fully preserve bids' privacy. However, its complexity scales proportionally to the number of bidders. Moreover, as reported by its authors, it reveals the order of the bids as it behaves similar to Order-Preserving Encryption (OPE) schemes.

Galal and Youssef [16] proposed a protocol that utilizes Pedersen commitment and Honest-Verifier Zero-Knowledge (HVZK) range proof to build a public verifiable sealed-bid auction on top of Ethereum. During the bidding phase, the bidders submit Pedersen commitments of their bids to the auction smart contract. Then at the reveal phase, they open their commitments individually to the auctioneer using RSA public-key encryption. Finally, the auctioneer declares the auction winner and utilizes HVZK range proof with the auction smart contract as a verifier to prove the correctness of the auction winner. However, the protocol has the following issues: (i) running an interactive HVZK with a smart contract as a verifier is not secure due to the possible influence of miners on the challenge step, (ii) the proof size and verification cost scales proportionally with the number of bidders, and (iii) the protocol is partial privacy-preserving as the auctioneer gains knowledge of all bids values.

Motivated to improve on their latest work, Galal and Youssef [15] utilized Zero-Knowledge Succinct Non-interactive Argument of Knowledge (zkSNARK) [5] which is an innovative cryptographic method in the field of Verifiable Computation. In contrast to their previous work [16], this protocol has several desirable properties that synergies with the blockchain technology: (i) a constant short-size proof, (ii) a constant verification cost, (iii) a non-interactive protocol that takes one message to convince the verifier (i.e., the smart contract). However, generating a zkSNARK proof scales proportionally with the number of multiplication gates in the arithmetic circuit of their computation problem which further depends on the number of bidders. Moreover, the protocol assumes a trusted setup of the proving and verification keys. Finally, the protocol is a partial privacy-preserving where bidders have to trust the auctioneer to not exploit their bids values in future auctions.

2.2   SGX with Blockchain Solutions

Several recent constructions utilized TEE technologies such as Intel SGX to solve privacy and performance issues on the blockchain, (e.g., see [3, 7, 14, 20, 22, 27, 33]). In here, we provide a brief review of the works that Trustee shares some similarities with. In [33] Zhang et al. proposed Town Crier (TC): an authenticated data feed that gives smart contracts on Ethereum the ability to request data from existing HTTPS-enabled data sources. TC consists of three components: a front-end smart contract, a back-end Intel SGX enclave, and a relay to redirect messages between them. Initially, the TC's front-end receives a request from a smart contract on Ethereum. The relay monitors the Ethereum blockchain for such a request and forwards it to TC's back-end. Then, the TC's back-end resolves this request and outputs a transaction containing the response. Finally, the relay submits the transaction to TC's front-end where it triggers the execution of a callback on the relying smart contract.

Cheng et al. [14] proposed Ekiden: a platform for confidentiality-preserving, trustworthy, and performant smart contract execution to solve the inherent lack of privacy and poor performance in blockchains. Ekiden's architecture separates smart contract execution from the consensus protocol. It preserves the confidentiality of a smart contract's states, besides to, achieving high throughput and scalability. The authors evaluated a prototype (with Tendermint as the consensus layer) and reported a performance of 600× more throughput and 400× less latency at 1000× less cost than the Ethereum mainnet.

Tran et al. [27] proposed Obscuro: an Intel SGX-backed mixer to address the anonymity issue on Bitcoin. Due to the pseudo-anonymity offered by Bitcoin, the link between the transaction's sender and receiver can be exploited to cluster and track users which defeats the goal of anonymous payment. Obscuro utilizes Intel SGX to preserve the privacy of the mixer's participants and perform a secure shuffle of bitcoins. Users post their deposits indirectly on Bitcoin blockchain rather than directly interacting with Obscuro. Consequently, malicious operators cannot prevent benign users from mixing their bitcoins. Furthermore, Obscuro does not store any operation states outside of the TEE to counter the possibility of state-rewind in conjunction with eclipse attacks. The authors evaluated Obscuro on Bitcoin testnet and reported that they were able to mix 1000 inputs in just 6.49 s.

3 Preliminaries

In this section, we briefly introduce the cryptographic primitives that are utilized in our design for Trustee.

Ethereum utilizes Elliptic Curve Digital Signature Algorithm (ECDSA) to verify the authenticity of transactions. To create an account on Ethereum, one has to statistically randomly generate a unique ECDSA key-pair (pk, sk) on the curve $secp256k1$ [10,12]. Keeping the private key secure is essential because it is used to sign transactions originating from the associated account. The address of an account is the rightmost 20-bytes of the $Keccak256$ [8] hash of the public key. This results in a more compact address size compared to the 64-bytes public key. When a transaction is sent to the network, miners are tasked with verifying the transaction's signature with respect to the sender's address. Precisely, ECDSA consists of the following three algorithms:

1. $(pk, sk) \leftarrow$ Gen(1^λ) which generates the public key pk and the associated private key sk based on the security parameter λ.
2. $\sigma \leftarrow$ Sign$($H$($m$),$sk$)$ which generates the signature σ for the hash of the message m under a designated hash function H and the private key sk.
3. $(\top/\bot) \leftarrow$ Verify$(\sigma, H(m), pk)$ which verifies the signature σ on the hash of message m under the public key pk.

The second cryptographic protocol we utilize is Elliptic Curve Integrated Encryption Scheme (ECIES) [17]. It enables two parties to communicate authenticated confidential messages. As its name indicates, ECIES integrates the following functions:

1. $(sk, pk) \leftarrow$ KGen$(params)$: a key generation function that takes elliptic curve parameters $params$ to produce a random private key sk and the associated public key pk.
2. $ss \leftarrow$ KA(sk_i, pk_j): a key agreement function to generate a shared secret ss based on the private key of party i and the public key of party j.
3. $(k_1, k_2) \leftarrow$ KDF(ss): a key derivation function to produce keys k_1 and k_2 from the shared secret ss.
4. $ct \leftarrow$ Enc$_{k_1}(m)$: a symmetric encryption function to encrypt a message m using the symmetric key k_1.
5. $tag \leftarrow$ MAC$_{k_2}(m)$: a message authentication code function to generate a tag based on the key k_2 and the message m.

To demonstrate how ECIES works, assume that Alice wants to encrypt a message m and send it to Bob. They initially agree on common ECIES parameters $params$. Then, Alice and Bob individually generate the ephemeral key pairs $(sk_A, pk_A), (sk_B, pk_B)$, respectively. Subsequently, Alice does the following steps:

1. Create a shared secret $ss \leftarrow \text{KA}(sk_A, pk_B)$
2. Derive two keys $(k_1, k_2) \leftarrow \text{KDF}(ss)$.
3. Obtain the ciphertext of her message $ct \leftarrow \text{Enc}_{k_1}(m)$.
4. Authenticate the ciphertext by creating a $tag \leftarrow \text{MAC}_{k_2}(ct)$.
5. Send the tuple (pk_A, ct, tag) to Bob.

Once Bob receives the tuple (pk_A, ct, tag), he can decrypt the ciphertext and verify its authenticity by doing the following:

1. Create a shared secret $ss \leftarrow \text{KA}(sk_B, pk_A)$
2. Derive two keys $(k_1, k_2) \leftarrow \text{KDF}(ss)$.
3. Assert that $tag = \text{MAC}_{k_2}(ct)$, otherwise, he rejects.
4. Obtain the message $m \leftarrow \text{Enc}_{k_1}^{-1}(ct, k_1)$.

4   Trustee's Design and Analysis

In this section, we briefly present the architecture of Trustee and illustrate the interaction flow between its components. Then, we explain the protocol in details. Next, we mention the threat model, security assumptions, and elaborate by analyzing various possible adversary attacks. Finally, we provide the implementation details of Trustee's prototype and evaluate the transactions gas costs.

4.1   Trustee's Architecture

Trustee consists of three components: a smart contract C which resides on top of Ethereum, a back-end Intel SGX enclave E and a relay R which both run off-chain on a server. We refer to the user who deploys C and controls R as the auctioneer. Furthermore, E is only accessible through R, and R interacts with C on behalf of the auctioneer and E. The general flow of interactions between Trustee's components, and bidders is depicted in Fig. 1.

Initially, the auctioneer deploys C on Ethereum and publishes its address so that interested sellers and buyers can learn about it. To start an auction, the auctioneer sends a request to R which loads E and calls the function `Initialize()`. As a response, E generates an externally owned Ethereum account with the private key T_{sk} and the associated address T_{adr}, and an ECDH key-pair (T_{dh}, T_{pk}) where T_{dh} is the private key and T_{pk} is the associated public key. Then, it returns the values of T_{adr} and T_{pk} to R. Subsequently, the auctioneer instructs R to set the stage for a new auction on C by calling the function `StartAuction` which takes T_{adr} and T_{pk}. Next, assume a bidder Bob is interested in the auction, then he utilizes ECIES protocol with T_{pk} as the public key of the recipient (i.e., Trustee's enclave E) to seal his bid. Subsequently, he submits his sealed bid B_{ct}

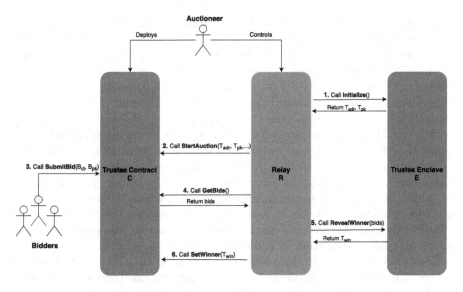

Fig. 1. Interactions between Trustee's components and bidders. The green components are trusted (Color figure online)

along with his ECDH public key B_{pk} to C. Once the bidding interval is closed, R retrieves the sealed bids stored on the C, then it forwards them to E by calling the function `RevealWinner`. As a result, E opens the sealed bids and determines the winner and second-highest price. Then, it returns a transaction T_{win} signed by the private key T_{sk} to R. Finally, R sends T_{win} to C which is essentially a call to the smart contract function $SetWinner$ that declares the auction winner and second-highest price.

Initializing an Auction. The initialization process starts with the auctioneer requesting R to load E inside Intel SGX enclave and invoke the function `Initialize()` which is implemented as shown in Algorithm 1.

Algorithm 1. Initializing State of Trustee's Enclave

1: **function** INITIALIZE
2:     $(T_{pk}, T_{dh}) \leftarrow$ `GenerateECDHKeys()`
3:     $(T_{adr}, T_{sk}) \leftarrow$ `GenerateAccount()`
4:     $sealedState \leftarrow$ `Seal`(T_{sk}, T_{dh})
5:     **return** $(sealedState, T_{adr}, T_{pk})$
6: **end function**

The `Initialize()` function generates two key-pairs. More precisely, one key-pair (T_{pk}, T_{dh}) that enables bidders to seal their bids such that only E can open them, and the second one to authenticate the result (i.e., auction winner and second-highest price) generated by E. The former is an ECDH key-pair used as part of ECIES protocol between E and each bidder to securely transmit the sealed bids through C and R. The later is an ECDSA key-pair used to sign the result. Verifying the signature on the result by C is a relatively expensive operation (i.e., roughly 120,000 gas for using *ecrecover*). Therefore, in Trustee, we utilize an intrinsic operation that happens on every transaction in Ethereum (i.e., transaction's signature verification) to indirectly verify the authenticity of the result for us. Hence, E generates an ECDSA key-pair on curve `secp256k1` which essentially creates an external owned Ethereum account with the private key T_{sk} and the associated address T_{adr}. Then, whenever E determines the auction winner and the second-highest price, it outputs a transaction T_{win} signed by T_{sk}. Later, R sends T_{win} to the Ethereum network, where the miners verify its signature. Finally, C only has to assert that the sender of T_{win} is the T_{adr}. As a result, this approach yields a much cheaper transaction fee compared to the explicit signature verification by calling `ecrecover`.

Intel SGX enclaves are designed to be stateless. In other words, once an enclave is destroyed, its whole state is lost. However, in Trustee, we have to persist the generated keys as long as the current auction is running. Therefore, we utilize Intel SGX feature known as *Sealing* [4] to properly save the generated private keys. Sealing is the process of encrypting enclave secrets in order to persist them on a permanent storage such as a disk. This effectively allows us to retrieve the private keys (T_{sk}, T_{dh}) even if the enclave was brought down for any reason. The encryption is performed using a private *Seal Key* that is unique to the platform and enclave, and is not accessible by any other entity.

Upon the return from `Initialize`, R saves the values of *sealedState* on a disk besides to having a backup. Furthermore, R publishes the values T_{adr} and T_{pk} by calling the function `StartAuction` on C as shown in Fig. 2. The function `StartAuction` also takes extra parameters that control the different intervals of the current auctions. More precisely, $T_1, T_2,$ and T_3 which define the numbers of the blocks before which: (i) bidders submit their sealed bids, (ii) R submits T_{win}, (iii) honest participants (i.e., auctioneer and non-winning bidders) reclaim the initially deposited fund D, respectively. The initial deposit D is paid by all participants to penalize malicious behavior.

Provisioning of Bids. Once the new auction has been initialized, an interested bidder Bob can seal his bid x by utilizing ECIES as shown in Algorithm 2. It starts with retrieving the public key T_{pk} from C. Then, it generates an ephemeral ECDH key-pair (B_{pk}, B_{sk}) on `curve25519` where B_{sk} is the private key and B_{pk} is the associated public key. Then, it computes the shared secret s based on T_{pk} and B_{sk}. After that, it derives two symmetric keys k_1 and k_2 in order to perform an authenticated encryption on the bid value x. Finally, it returns the sealed-bid B_{ct} and the associated public key B_{pk}. Subsequently, Bob sends the values B_{ct} and B_{pk} to the function `SubmitBid` on C as shown in Fig. 2.

StartAuction: upon receiving $(T_{adr}, T_{pk}, T_1, T_2, T_3, D)$ from auctioneer **A**

          Assert $state = Init$
          Assert $ledger[A] >= D$
          Set $ledger[A] := ledger[A] - D$
          Set $deposit := deposit + D$
          Set $state := Bidding$
          Store T_{adr}, T_{pk}
          Store T_1, T_2, T_3, D

SubmitBid: upon receiving (B_{ct}, B_{pk}) from a bidder **B**

          Assert $state = Bidding$
          Assert $T < T_1$
          Assert $ledger[B] >= D$
          Set $ledger[B] := ledger[B] - D$
          Set $ledger[C] := ledger[C] + D$
          Set $bids[B] := (B_{ct}, B_{pk})$
          Set $Bidders := Bidders \cup \{B\}$

SetWinner: upon receiving (H, I, P) from the an address **X**

          Assert $X = T_{adr}$
          Assert $state = Bidding$
          Assert $T_1 < T < T_2$
          IF $\text{Keccak256}(bids.B_{ct} || bids.B_{pk}) \neq H$
              Set $state := Rejected$
               Return
          EndIF
          Set $state := Revealed$
          Set $winner = Bidders[I]$
          Set $price = P$

Withdraw: upon receiving () from an address **X**

          Assert $T_2 < T < T_3$
          IF $(state = Revealed$ **and** $X \in \{A\} \cup \{Bidder\} - \{winner\})$
          or $(state = Rejected$ **and** $X \in \{Bidder\})$
              Set $ledger[C] := ledger[C] - D$
              Set $ledger[X] := ledger[X] + D$
          EndIF

Reset: upon receiving () from the auctioneer **A**

          Assert $T_3 < T$
          Set $state := Init$
          Clear $Bidders$
          Clear $bids$

Fig. 2. Pseudocode for the Trustee's smart contract C

The function SubmitBid first asserts that: (i) the current state is set to Bidding, and (ii) the call is invoked before the end of the bidding interval. After

Algorithm 2. Sealing of Bids using ECIES

1: **function** SEALBID(x)
2:     T_{pk} ←GetTrusteePublicKey()
3:     (B_{pk}, B_{sk}) ← GenerateECDHKeys()
4:     s ←ComputeSharedSecret($KA(B_{sk}, T_{pk})$
5:     (k_1, k_2) ← DeriveKeys(s)
6:     iv ← InitRandomIV()
7:     ct ← Encrypt(x, iv, K_1)
8:     tag ← MAC(ct, K_2)
9:     B_{ct} ← $ct||iv||tag$
10:     **return** (B_{ct}, B_{pk})
11: **end function**

that, it deducts the initial deposit D from Bob and stores the B_{ct} and B_{pk} into the array *bidders*. Note that the size of the B_{ct} is 32 bytes. Moreover, we utilize the Curve25519 for generating ECDH key-pairs due to two reasons: (i) it only uses compressed elliptic point (i.e., X coordinate), so it provides fast and efficient ECDH, (ii) the public-key size becomes 32-bytes rather than 64-bytes, therefore, both the B_{ct} and B_{pk} synergies effectively with Ethereum native variable type *uint256*.

Revelation of the Auction Winner. Once the bidding interval is over, R retrieves the submitted array of sealed bids B_{ct} and their associate public keys B_{pk} from C. Then, it passes them along with *sealedState* (previously generated by the function Initalize) to the function RevealWinner on E as shown in Algorithm 3. In this function, E initially unseals the private keys from *sealedState*. Then, for every bidder i, it runs the decryption part of ECIES protocol based on the sealed-bid $B_{ct}[i]$, the public key $B_{pk}[i]$, and the private key T_{dh} to extract the bid value and find the winner. Once all sealed-bids B_{ct} are decrypted, the winner's index and second-highest bid are set accordingly in the variables *index* and *second*. Subsequently, E binds the auction winner to the inputs it received by computing the Keccak256 hash value of B_{ct} and B_{pk}. Finally, E creates a raw transaction T_{win} with the destination address as C and signs it with the private key T_{sk}. For the sake of simplicity, we defer explaining the details of Reset() and Unseal() to Subsect. 4.2.

Subsequently, the auctioneer has to send some funds to T_{adr} in order to pay the transaction fees to be incurred by T_{win}. Next, the auctioneer requests R to send the transaction T_{win} to C which is essentially a call to the function SetWinner shown in the Fig. 2. It takes the following parameters: (i) H as Keccak256 hash value of the inputs B_{ct} and B_{pk}, (ii) as the index of the winner in the array *Bidders* which is further used by C to determine the address of the auction winner, and (iii) P as the second-highest price. On its call, it asserts that: (i) T_{win}'s origin is the address T_{adr}, the call happens within the auction winner revelation interval, and (iii) the *state* is set to *Bidding*. Then, it checks if H is equal to the Keccak256 hash value of the sealed bids and their associated

Algorithm 3. Revelation of the Auction Winner

```
1: function REVEALWINNER(B_ct[], B_pk[], sealedState)
2:     max ← 0
3:     second ← 0
4:     index ← −1
5:     N ←Length(B_ct)
6:     (T_sk, T_dh, success) = Unseal(sealedState)
7:     if success = 0 then
8:         return
9:     end if
10:    for i ← 1 to N do
11:        bid ← Decrypt(B_ct[i], B_pk[i], T_dh)
12:        if max < bid then
13:            second ← max
14:            max ← bid
15:            index ← i
16:        end if
17:    end for
18:    hash ← Keccak256(B_ct||B_pk)
19:    T_win ←CreateTransaction(C, hash, index, second, T_sk)
20:    sealedState ← Reset()
21:    return (T_win, sealedState)
22: end function
```

public keys submitted by bidders. Accordingly, it decides whether to accept the submitted values or reject them. Eventually, it reflects the decision on its *state*.

Honest participants can reclaim their initial deposits within the withdraw interval by calling the function `Withdraw` shown in Fig. 2. Additionally, in the case of a successful winner revelation, then the winner's initial deposit is locked to set the stage for payment of the winning bid. Eventually, after the withdraw interval, the auctioneer calls the function *Reset* in order to set the *state* of C to *Init* so that new auctions can be started later by calling *StartAuction*.

4.2 Threat Model

In Trustee threat model, we assume the following:

1. The smart contract C is deployed on the *mainnet* of Ethereum with an open-source code that is available for all bidders. Moreover, the functions on C process the input parameters of transactions as their code dictate which is essentially enforced by Ethereum. Furthermore, all transactions in Ethereum are authenticated such that C can precisely determine the sender address.
2. The enclave E is loaded inside a properly implemented and manufactured Intel SGX platform. Additionally, the source code of E is available for all bidders. Finally, E is properly programmed such that it does not have a bug that compromises the confidentiality of sealed-bids and private keys.

3. The relay R is the only interface to E and is controllable by the auctioneer. The bidders have a black-box view of R (i.e., closed-source code). Furthermore, R is potentially untrusted component that can behave maliciously to compromise the security of Trustee.

4. The Adversary is financially rational and powerful enough to have access to the host running E and R. Hence, the adversary is able to control the execution of privileged software such as the operating system and the network-stack driver. However, the adversary cannot compromise the security model of Ethereum in order to maliciously change the state of C.

We acknowledge that several recent studies have uncovered side-channel attacks to compromise the confidentiality of Intel SGX [13,19,23,28,29,31]. Also, multiple mitigation techniques have been proposed to address attack-specific issues [18,24–26]. Resolving side-channel attacks on Intel SGX enclave is beyond the scope of this paper and is left for future work.

4.3   Security Analysis

We discuss the security of Trustee against possible scenarios including Intel SGX masquerade, eclipse, fork, and replay attacks [11].

Intel SGX Masquerade. Since bidders do not have direct access to Trustee's enclave E, a corrupt auctioneer might generate the private keys and post the corresponding public key T_{pk} and address T_{dh} on the smart contract C. Incautious bidders would seal their bids by T_{pk} which effectively gives the corrupt auctioneer access to the underlying bids. To counter this attack, we show how a wary bidder Bob can verify that the private keys (T_{sk}, T_{dh}) were generated by E inside a genuine Intel SGX enclave. Essentially, Bob has to do the verification before submitting his sealed-bid. Therefore, once a new auction is started by the function StartAuction, Bob and Trustee engage in a protocol that utilizes the *Remote Attestation* [4] feature of Intel SGX as shown in Fig. 3. Initially, Bob challenges E through R by calling the function Challenge and passes a *nonce* to it. Then, R forwards the *nonce* to E by calling the function GetQuote. Inside GetQuote, E binds T_{adr}, T_{pk}, and *nonce* by hashing their concatenation and creating a digest $h \leftarrow \text{SHA256}(T_{adr} || T_{pk} || nonce)$. Then, it embeds h as a user data into a report r by calling an Intel SGX supplied function sgx_create_report. Finally, R passes r to an Intel provided enclave known as the Quoting Enclave (QE) which verifies r then signs it with Intel Enhanced Privacy ID (EPID) secret key to yield a *quote*. The Intel EPID is device-specific and is only accessible by the QE. Subsequently, R returns the quote to Bob who in turn contacts Intel Attestation Service (IAS) to verify the quote's signature. On a successful verification, Bob has to check the following: (i) the quote's user data is equivalent to h, and (ii) the source code of E when compiled produces the same measurement (i.e., a digest of code and data of E) included in the quote. Assuming IAS to behave honestly, then it is computationally infeasible for the adversary to generate a quote that asserts the authenticity of E on a fake Intel SGX enclave to Bob.

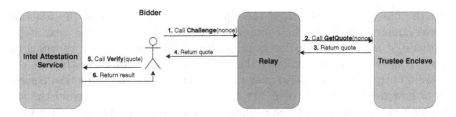

Fig. 3. Remote attestation of Trustee's Enclave

Eclipse Attack. Generally, Intel SGX enclaves do not have trusted access to the network; therefore, Trustee's enclave E is oblivious of the current state (i.e, sealed bids) on the smart contract C. Consequently, a corrupt auctioneer can provide an arbitrary subset of the sealed bids to E in order to give advantage to a cartel of colluding bidders. A trivial solution to this challenge is to embed a full-node Ethereum client inside E such that it can verify the PoW (Proof of Work) of Ethereum blocks and determine the correct state of the smart contract C. This solution is computationally secure against an adversary who controls less than 51% of the hash rate power of the network. However, the TCB of E becomes bloated with and susceptible to bugs founds in the client source code. Alternatively, in Trustee, we bind the output (i.e., winner's index and second-highest price) to the input (i.e., the set of sealed-bids and associated public keys) by including the hash of the input as a parameter in the transaction T_{win} as shown in Algorithm 3. Therefore, the smart contract C can determine whether all or a subset of the sealed bids were provided to E by comparing hash parameter of T_{win} to the hash of all bids and associated public keys in its state as shown in the function SetWinner in Fig. 2.

Replay and Fork Attack. We assess the possibility of a corrupt auctioneer Eve trying to compromise the privacy of the sealed-bids without being noticed and penalized. Recall that in the design of Trustee, R initially calls the function Initialize, then at a later point in time, it calls the function RevealWinner to finalize the auction. The idea behind this attack is that Eve can launch multiple instances of E and replay the same *sealedState* to all instances but provide different subsets of the sealed-bids. Obviously, Eve gives one of the instances the correct number of sealed-bids and its output is forwarded to C to avoid penalty as discussed above. However, for the other instances she simply learns the outputs and discard them which effectively gives her access to all the underlying bids values.

To counter this attack, we enforce Trustee's design of using fresh *sealedState* for every call to the function RevealWinner by utilizing Intel SGX non-volatile hardware monotonic counters. Simply, the function Seal called inside the function Initialize increments and reads the monotonic counter ctr, then it combines ctr, T_{sk}, and T_{dh} and seals them into *sealedState*. Later, when the function RevealWinner is called, it invokes the function Unseal which unseals *sealedState*, then it reads the current monotonic counter and compares it with the unsealed *ctr*. Hence, if the equality check passes, then the function `RevealWinner` increments the counter as well and proceeds to the next steps, otherwise, it aborts without determining the auction winner (i.e., returning an empty T_{win} that does not indicate the auction winner.) Consequently, Eve can get valid output from `RevealWinner` only one time per a single auction regardless of how many instances of E are launched. Alternatively, to avoid the low performance of using monotonic counters which takes approximately 80 to 200 ms for read/write operation, we can utilize a distributed system of Intel SGX enclaves to manage the state freshness as explained in [21].

4.4   Prototype Implementation and Gas Cost Analysis

Intel SGX cryptographic library does not support the curves *secp256k1* and *curve25519*, so we utilize an Intel SGX compatible port of *mebdtls* library [32] as a static enclave library linked to Trustee's enclave. Mbedtls library is mainly used in ECDH and ECDSA key generation, ECDH shared secret derivation, and ECDSA signing. We evaluate Trustee on a Dell Inspiron 7577 laptop that is SGX-enabled with the 6th Generation Intel Core i5 CPU and 8-GB of memory. We enable Intel SGX feature on the laptop's BIOS and allocate maximum allowed 128-MB memory for individual SGX enclave. Also, we implement Trustee's smart contract in *Solidity* which is the de-facto programming language for developing smart contracts in Ethereum. Furthermore, we utilize *Ganache* to set up a personal Ethereum blockchain in order to run tests, execute commands, and inspect state while controlling how the chain operates.

We report on the gas cost of transactions in Trustee for a Vickrey auction with $N = 100$ bidders and compares it with approaches in [15,16] in Table 1. At the time of writing, December 14th, 2018, the median gas price is 3.3 *GWei* and the average exchange rate for 1 ether = \$83 USD. In other words, 1 million gas incurs transaction fees ≈\$0.27 USD.

Table 1. Gas cost of transactions in Trustee and auctions [15,16]

Function	Trustee	Auction [16]	Auction [15]
`Deployment`	1173779	3131261	1346611
`StartAuction`	188201	–	–
`SubmitBid`	123350	262933	159759
`SetWinner`	82847	2872047	3487439
`Withdraw`	20370	47112	–
`Reset`	402351	–	–

Compared to other sealed-bid auction constructions on top of Ethereum [15,16], Trustee achieves a significantly low and constant gas cost on the revelation of auction winner. The reason behind this is because most of the computations happen off-chain. Therefore, it costs the auctioneer less than 1 USD to deploy Trustee's smart contract C, start an auction, set the winner, and withdraw initial deposit. It has to be noted that, the initial deposit must be large enough to penalize malicious participants such as an auctioneer who corrupts R to redirect inconsistent messages between E and C, and a malicious winner who refuses to pay the second-highest price. Certainly, the value of the initial deposit should be proportional to the estimated value of the auctioned item.

5   Conclusion

In this paper, we presented Trustee, an efficient and full privacy preserving Vickrey auction on top of Ethereum. In Trustee, we utilize Intel SGX to complement a smart contract in Ethereum with confidential data processing, a desirable property they lack. As a result, Trustee does not inherit the complexities of heavy cryptographic protocols such as ZKP and MPC. More precisely, Trustee fully preserves bids' privacy and maintains the auction winner correctness at a relatively cheap transaction fee. Furthermore, in Trustee, auctions take only two-rounds to finalize, where the first round is the provision of bids and the second one is the revelation of the winner. As a result, it is one round less than the (commit - reveal - prove) approach. Moreover, the major computations in Trustee happen on off-chain hosts, hence, it can be ported with minimum efforts to blockchains with inflexible scripting capabilities such as Bitcoin.

References

1. Digital assets in Ethereum blockchain. https://tokenmarket.net/blockchain/Ethereum/assets/
2. Top 100 cryptocurrencies by market capitalization (2018). https://coinmarketcap.com
3. Al-Bassam, M., Sonnino, A., Król, M., Psaras, I.: Airtnt: fair exchange payment for outsourced secure enclave computations. arXiv preprint arXiv:1805.06411 (2018)
4. Anati, I., Gueron, S., Johnson, S., Scarlata, V.: Innovative technology for CPU based attestation and sealing. In: Proceedings of the 2nd International Workshop on Hardware and Architectural Support for Security and Privacy, vol. 13. ACM New York (2013)
5. Ben-Sasson, E., Chiesa, A., Tromer, E., Virza, M.: Succinct non-interactive zero knowledge for a von Neumann architecture. In: USENIX Security Symposium, pp. 781–796 (2014)
6. Benet, J.: IPFS-content addressed, versioned, P2P file system. arXiv preprint arXiv:1407.3561 (2014)
7. Bentov, I., et al.: Tesseract: real-time cryptocurrency exchange using trusted hardware. IACR Cryptology ePrint Archive, 2017:1153 (2017)
8. Bertoni, G., Daemen, J., Peeters, M., Van Assche, G.: Keccak. In: Johansson, T., Nguyen, P.Q. (eds.) EUROCRYPT 2013. LNCS, vol. 7881, pp. 313–314. Springer, Heidelberg (2013). https://doi.org/10.1007/978-3-642-38348-9_19
9. Blass, E.-O., Kerschbaum, F.: Strain: a secure auction for blockchains. In: Lopez, J., Zhou, J., Soriano, M. (eds.) ESORICS 2018. LNCS, vol. 11098, pp. 87–110. Springer, Cham (2018). https://doi.org/10.1007/978-3-319-99073-6_5

10. Bos, J.W., Halderman, J.A., Heninger, N., Moore, J., Naehrig, M., Wustrow, E.: Elliptic curve cryptography in practice. In: Christin, N., Safavi-Naini, R. (eds.) FC 2014. LNCS, vol. 8437, pp. 157–175. Springer, Heidelberg (2014). https://doi.org/10.1007/978-3-662-45472-5_11

11. Brandenburger, M., Cachin, C., Kapitza, R., Sorniotti, A.: Blockchain and trusted computing: problems, pitfalls, and a solution for Hyperledger fabric. arXiv preprint arXiv:1805.08541 (2018)

12. Brown, D.R.L.: Standards for efficient cryptography sec 2: recommended elliptic curve domain parameters (2010). http://www.secg.org/sec2-v2.pdf

13. Chen, G., Chen, S., Xiao, Y., Zhang, Y., Lin, Z., Lai, T.H.: SGXPECTREattacks: leaking enclave secrets via speculative execution. arXiv preprint arXiv:1802.09085 (2018)

14. Cheng, R., et al.: Ekiden: a platform for confidentiality-preserving, trustworthy, and performant smart contract execution. arXiv preprint arXiv:1804.05141 (2018)

15. Galal, H.S., Youssef, A.M.: Succinctly verifiable sealed-bid auction smart contract. In: Garcia-Alfaro, J., Herrera-Joancomartí, J., Livraga, G., Rios, R. (eds.) DPM/CBT -2018. LNCS, vol. 11025, pp. 3–19. Springer, Cham (2018). https://doi.org/10.1007/978-3-030-00305-0_1

16. Galal, H.S., Youssef, A.M.: Verifiable sealed-bid auction on the ethereum blockchain. In: Zohar, A., et al. (eds.) FC 2018. LNCS, vol. 10958, pp. 265–278. Springer, Heidelberg (2019). https://doi.org/10.1007/978-3-662-58820-8_18

17. Martínez, V.G., Encinas, L.H., Ávila, C.S.: A survey of the elliptic curve integrated encryption scheme. J. Comput. Sci. Eng. 2, 7–13 (2010)

18. Gruss, D., Lettner, J., Schuster, F., Ohrimenko, O., Haller, I., Costa, M.: Strong and efficient cache side-channel protection using hardware transactional memory. In: USENIX Security Symposium, pp. 217–233 (2017)

19. Lee, S., Shih, M.-W., Gera, P., Kim, T., Kim, H., Peinado, M.: Inferring fine-grained control flow inside SGX enclaves with branch shadowing. In: 26th USENIX Security Symposium, USENIX Security, pp. 16–18 (2017)

20. Lind, J., Eyal, I., Pietzuch, P., Sirer, E.G.: Teechan: payment channels using trusted execution environments. arXiv preprint arXiv:1612.07766 (2016)

21. Matetic, S., et al.: ROTE: rollback protection for trusted execution. IACR Cryptology ePrint Archive, 2017:48 (2017)

22. Milutinovic, M., He, W., Wu, H., Kanwal, M.: Proof of luck: an efficient blockchain consensus protocol. In: Proceedings of the 1st Workshop on System Software for Trusted Execution, p. 2. ACM (2016)

23. Schwarz, M., Weiser, S., Gruss, D., Maurice, C., Mangard, S.: Malware guard extension: using SGX to conceal cache attacks. In: Polychronakis, M., Meier, M. (eds.) DIMVA 2017. LNCS, vol. 10327, pp. 3–24. Springer, Cham (2017). https://doi.org/10.1007/978-3-319-60876-1_1

24. Seo, J.: SGX-shield: enabling address space layout randomization for SGX programs. In: NDSS (2017)

25. Shih, M.-W., Lee, S., Kim, T., Peinado, M.: T-SGX: eradicating controlled-channel attacks against enclave programs. In: Proceedings of the Annual Network and Distributed System Security Symposium (NDSS), San Diego, CA (2017)

26. Shinde, S., Chua, Z.L., Narayanan, V., Saxena, P.: Preventing page faults from telling your secrets. In: Proceedings of the 11th ACM on Asia Conference on Computer and Communications Security, pp. 317–328. ACM (2016)

27. Tran, M., Luu, L., Kang, M.S., Bentov, I., Saxena, P.: Obscuro: a bitcoin mixer using trusted execution environments. IACR Cryptology ePrint Archive, 2017:974 (2017)

28. Bulck, J.V., et al.: Foreshadow: extracting the keys to the Intel SGX kingdom with transient out-of-order execution. In: Proceedings of the 27th USENIX Security Symposium. USENIX Association, August 2018
29. Weisse, O., et al.: Breaking the virtual memory abstraction with transient out-of-order execution. Technical report, Foreshadow-NG (2018)
30. Wood, G.: Ethereum: a secure decentralised generalised transaction ledger. Ethereum Proj. Yellow Pap. **151**, 1–32 (2014)
31. Xu, Y., Cui, W., Peinado, M.: Controlled-channel attacks: deterministic side channels for untrusted operating systems. In: 2015 IEEE Symposium on Security and Privacy (SP), pp. 640–656. IEEE (2015)
32. Zhang, F.: mbedtls-sgx: a TLS stack in SGX (2016). https://github.com/bl4ck5un/mbedtls-SGX
33. Zhang, F., Cecchetti, E., Croman, K., Juels, A., Shi, E.: Town crier: an authenticated data feed for smart contracts. In: Proceedings of the 2016 ACM SIGSAC Conference on Computer and Communications Security, pp. 270–282. ACM (2016)

Advances in Secure Electronic Voting Schemes

Election Manipulation 100

Michelle Blom[1($\boxtimes$)], Peter J. Stuckey[2], and Vanessa J. Teague[1]

[1] School of Computing and Information Systems, The University of Melbourne,
Parkville, Australia
{michelle.blom,vjteague}@unimelb.edu.au
[2] Faculty of Information Technology, Monash University, Clayton, Australia
peter.stuckey@monash.edu.au

Abstract. The true election margin for an Instant Runoff Voting (IRV) election can be hard to compute, because a small modification early in the elimination sequence can alter the outcome and result in a candidate winning the last round by a large margin. It is often assumed that the true margin is the last-round margin, that is half the difference between the two candidates who remain when everyone else is eliminated, though it is well known that this need not be the case. Perceptions of confidence in the outcome, and even formal policies about recounts, often depend on the last-round margin. There is already some prior work on how to compute the true election margin efficiently for IRV, and hence how to find the minimal manipulation. In this work we show how to manipulate an election efficiently *while also producing a large last-round margin*. This would allow a successful manipulation to evade detection against naive methods of assessing the confidence of the election result. This serves as further evidence for accurate computations of the exact margin, or for rigorous Risk Limiting Audits which would detect a close or wrong election result (respectively) regardless of the last-round margin.

1 Introduction

Instant Runoff Voting (IRV), also known as Alternative Vote (AV), is a system of preferential voting in which voters rank candidates in order of preference. Given candidates a, b, and c, each vote cast in an IRV election is a (possibly partial) ranking over the candidates. A vote with the ranking $[a, c, b]$ expresses a first preference for candidate a, a second for c, and a third for b. The tallying of votes proceeds by distributing each vote to its first ranked candidate. The candidate with the smallest number of votes is eliminated, with their votes redistributed to subsequent, less preferred candidates. Elimination proceeds in this fashion, until a single candidate w remains, who is declared the winner. IRV is used for all lower house parliamentary elections across Australia, parliamentary elections in Fiji and Papua New Guinea, presidential elections in Ireland and Bosnia/Herzogovinia, and local elections in numerous locations world-wide, including the UK and United States [9].

The last round margin (LRM) of an IRV election – the difference in tallies of the final two remaining candidates, divided by two and rounded up – is commonly

© International Financial Cryptography Association 2020
A. Bracciali et al. (Eds.): FC 2019 Workshops, LNCS 11599, pp. 211–225, 2020.
https://doi.org/10.1007/978-3-030-43725-1_15

used as an indicator of how close the election was. Blom *et al.* [4] have shown that the true margin of victory (MOV) of the election – the smallest number of votes one would have to alter to change who won the election – is generally equal to the last round margin, but not always. In some cases, the MOV can be much smaller than the last round margin. The Australian Electoral Commission (AEC) use the "margin between the two leading candidates" after all remaining candidates have been eliminated, and their preferences distributed, to determine whether an automatic recount of cast votes should be performed.[1] The AEC definition of a "margin", in this context, is the difference in tallies of two candidates (not divided by two). When this margin is less than 100 votes, an automatic recount is triggered. In traditional paper-based elections, where counting proceeds by hand and scrutineers are present to oversee the counting of ballots, these margins play a major role in determining whether further scrutiny of the outcome is warranted.

In this paper, we put ourselves in the shoes of a potential adversary seeking to change the outcome of an IRV election – an election in which voters have cast paper ballots, and these ballots have been consequently scanned and counted using software. We assume that this adversary has sufficient access to the systems used to execute the IRV counting algorithm, complete knowledge of the election profile (the rankings present on each vote), and the ability to change each ballot's electronic record. The adversary wants to alter the smallest number of these electronic records so that their desire of changing the outcome is realised, while at the same time ensuring that the last round margin of the manipulated election is larger than a given threshold. Our adversary does not want to change too many votes, as the more votes that are modified, the greater the likelihood that the manipulation will be discovered. To realise this adversary, we adapt the margin computation algorithm of Blom *et al.* [4] to compute the smallest number of votes that it must change to both alter an election outcome, and create a manipulated election with desirable properties (such as a large last round margin). Note that throughout this paper we use the terms vote and ballot interchangeably – each ballot is equivalent to a single vote in the context of IRV.

Using the Australian New South Wales (NSW) 2015 Legislative Assembly election as a case study, we report the number of votes that this adversary would have needed to modify in each seat to change the candidate who won, while controlling the margin by which they won. Here, as a running example, we consider the smallest manipulation in order to achieve a last round margin of victory of at least 100 votes, in order to prevent an automatic recount, *election manipulation 100*.

It is obvious that it is always possible to achieve a last-round margin of at least x by finding the Margin of Victory MOV, making those minimal changes, and then altering an extra x ballots in favour of the desired candidate. The interesting cases are those in which a last-round margin of x can be achieved by manipulating fewer than $MOV + x$ votes. We find that this is possible in a small number of examples—these seats would make natural targets for manipulation. We find empirically that in natural elections it's very often the case that LRM = MOV.

---

[1] https://www.aec.gov.au/Elections/candidates/files/hor-recount-policy.pdf.

After manipulation, however, we find that the MOV of the manipulated election is often much smaller than its LRM. The effect of this declines when the manipulation is small rather than large, but could be considered a genuine indication that someone is manipulating the results.

The assumption of complete knowledge of the election profile, and the ability to change any vote, is a strong one. We consider, in our concluding discussion, how we can analyse the likelihood of election-changing manipulations in a context where our adversary *does not* have knowledge of the complete election profile. In this setting, the adversary may have seen a portion of cast votes, after scanning, and is able to modify the rankings of future scanned votes as they are scanned and their electronic record created. How likely is it that such an adversary can choose appropriate manipulations, in this context, and achieve the election of a desired candidate with an appropriate margin? We consider how we might design a series of experiments to answer this question.

The remainder of this paper is structured as follows. We discuss related work on margin computation for IRV, manipulation, and auditing in Sect. 2. Preliminaries and definitions are provided in Sect. 3. Section 4 summarises the margin computation algorithm of Blom *et al.* [4] and how it can be adapted to add side constraints – such as ensuring a last round margin of at least a given threshold – on the nature of any acceptable manipulation of an election. We demonstrate this adapted algorithm on case study – the 2015 NSW Legislative Assembly election – in Sect. 5. We conclude in Sects. 6 and 7 with a discussion of how to model and analyse a weaker adversary, without complete knowledge of the rankings on every ballot.

2 Related Work

Blom *et al.* [4] present a branch-and-bound algorithm (denoted *margin-irv*) for efficiently computing the margin of victory in an IRV election, improving upon an existing method by Magrino *et al.* [8]. Blom *et al.* [3] extend this work to compute the margin of victory over candidates (MOVC) for an IRV election. That work computes the smallest number of votes that must be changed in order to change the winner of the election to one of a given subset of candidates. In this paper, we extend the *margin-irv* algorithm of Blom *et al.* [4] to compute the smallest number of vote changes required to yield an election with desired properties, such as a last round margin of at least a certain size. We then demonstrate this extended algorithm on the New South Wales 2015 Legislative Assembly Parliamentary Election.

Since the MOV is the minimum number of vote changes necessary to successfully manipulate the election result, the election result can be shown to be correct if there are fewer than MOV manipulations.

A number of methods have been developed for auditing various kinds of elections [1], and for first past the post (FPTP) elections in particular. Risk Limiting Audits (RLAs) [7,10] have been applied to a number of such elections, including four 2008 elections in California [6] and elections in over 50 Colorado counties

> Initially, all candidates remain standing (are not eliminated)
> **While** there is *more than one* candidate standing
>> **For** every candidate c standing
>>> Tally (count) the votes in which c is the highest-ranked
>>> candidate of those standing
>> Eliminate the candidate with the smallest tally
> The winner is the one candidate not eliminated

Fig. 1. The IRV counting algorithm: the candidate with the smallest tally is repeatedly eliminated, with the ballots in their tally redistributed to remaining candidates according to their next preference.

in 2017. RLAs provide strong statistical evidence that the reported outcome of an election is correct, or revert to a manual recount if it is wrong. The probability that the audit fails to detect a wrong outcome is bounded by a *risk limit*. Lindeman *et al.* [7] present a ballot-polling RLA for FPTP elections, which has consequently been adapted by Blom *et al.* [2] for IRV. Several approaches for designing a risk-limiting comparison audit of an IRV election have also been proposed [10]. A genuine RLA would defeat the attack described in this paper, because it would detect a wrong election result with high probability. Our proposed variety of manipulation works only against naive recount triggers based on last-round margins.

3   Preliminaries

Votes are tallied in an IRV election in a series of rounds (see Fig. 1). In each round, the candidate with the smallest number of votes (their tally) is eliminated, with the last remaining candidate declared the winner of the election. All votes in an eliminated candidate's tally are distributed to the next most-preferred (remaining) candidate in their ranking.

Let $\mathcal{C}$ be the set of candidates in an IRV election $\mathcal{B}$. We refer to sequences of candidates π in list notation (e.g., $\pi = [c_1, c_2, c_3, c_4]$), and use such sequences to represent both votes and the order in which candidates are eliminated. An election $\mathcal{B}$ is defined as a multiset[2] of votes, each vote $b \in \mathcal{B}$ a sequence of candidates in $\mathcal{C}$, with no duplicates, listed in order of preference (most preferred to least preferred). Let $first(\pi)$ denote the first candidate appearing in sequence π (e.g., $first([c_2, c_3]) = c_2$). In each round of vote counting, there are a current set of eliminated candidates $\mathcal{E}$ and a current set of candidates still standing $\mathcal{S} = \mathcal{C} \setminus \mathcal{E}$. The winner c_w of the election is the last standing candidate.

Each candidate $c \in \mathcal{C}$ has a *tally* of votes. Votes are added to this tally upon the elimination of a candidate $c' \in \mathcal{C} \setminus \{c\}$, and are redistributed from this tally upon the elimination of c.

---

[2] A multiset allows for the inclusion of duplicate items.

Table 1. IRV example, with (a) the number of votes cast with each listed ranking over candidates a, b, c, and (b) tallies after each round of vote counting (c) the number of votes recorded after manipulation, and (d) the tallies after each round of vote counting in the manipulated election

Ranking	Count
[a]	55
[c, a]	30
[b, c]	36
[c]	15

(a)

Candidate	Round 1	Round 2
a	55	55
b	36	—
c	45	81

(b)

Ranking	Count
[a]	55
[c, a]	25
[b, c]	41
[c]	15

(c)

Candidate	Round 1	Round 2
a	55	80
b	41	41
c	40	—

(d)

Definition 1. Tally $t_S(c)$. *Given candidates $S \subseteq C$ are still standing in an election B, the tally for candidate $c \in C$, denoted $t_S(c)$, is defined as the number of votes $b \in B$ for which c is the most-preferred candidate of those remaining. Let $p_S(b)$ denote the sequence of candidates mentioned in b that are also in S.*

$$t_S(c) = |\ [b \mid b \in B, c = first(p_S(b))]\ | \tag{1}$$

Definition 2. Margin of Victory (MOV). *The MOV in an election with candidates C and winner $c_w \in C$, is the smallest number of votes whose ranking must be modified (by an adversary) so that a candidate $c' \in C \setminus \{c_w\}$ is elected.*

Definition 3. Last Round Margin (LRM). *The LRM of an election, in which two candidates $S = \{c, c'\}$ remain with $t_S(c)$ and $t_S(c')$ votes in their tallies, is equal to half the difference between the tallies of c and c' rounded up.*

$$LRM = \left\lceil \frac{|t_S(c) - t_S(c')|}{2} \right\rceil \tag{2}$$

Example 1. Consider the example election shown in Table 1 between candidates a, b and c. Their initial tallies are 55, 36, and 45 votes, respectively, and b is eliminated first. Candidates a and c subsequently have tallies of 55 and 81 votes, giving c the victory with a last round margin of 13 votes. A seemingly comfortable victory.

But lets examine what occurs if we change 5 of the $[c, a]$ votes to $[b, c]$ votes. Now the initial tallies are 55, 41, and 40 votes, respectively, and c is eliminated first. Candidates a and b subsequently have tallies of 80 and 41 votes, giving a the victory with a last round margin of 20 votes.

Note that the apparent comfortable victory of c originally is an illusion, the actual MOV for this election is 5, as the manipulation illustrates. Interestingly even though we only manipulate 5 votes, now a wins the election with a last round margin of 20 votes! The actual margin of victory in the manipulated election is 1, demonstrated by the fact that if we change 1 of the $[b, c]$ votes to a $[c]$ vote, the first round tallies of each candidate are $\{a : 55, b : 40, c : 41\}$, and c is eliminated.

4   Computing the MOV for an IRV Election

A description of both the *margin-irv* algorithm, and the original branch-and-bound method of Magrino *et al.* [8], can be found in Blom *et al.* [3,4]. We summarise this algorithm in this section, and describe how it can be modified to compute the smallest number of vote changes required to both (i) bring about a change in the outcome of the election, and (ii) produce a manipulated election profile with certain properties, modelled as side constraints. We consider the following two side constraints in this paper:

- The LRM of the manipulated election must be at least T_{LRM} votes;
- The eliminated candidate e in each round must have Δ fewer votes in their tally than the candidate with the next smallest tally.

Consider an IRV election $\mathcal{B}$ with candidates $\mathcal{C}$ and winner $w \in \mathcal{C}$. The *margin-irv* algorithm starts by adding $|\mathcal{C}| - 1$ partial elimination sequences to a search tree, one for each of alternate winner $c \in \mathcal{C} \setminus \{w\}$. These partial sequences form a frontier F, with each sequence containing a single candidate – an alternate winner. Note that a partial sequence $[a, b, c]$ represents an election outcome in which a and b are the last two candidates eliminated, and c the winner. All other candidates are assumed to have been eliminated in some prior round.

For each partial sequence $\pi \in F$, we compute a lower bound on the number of vote changes required to realise an elimination sequence that *ends* in π. These lower bounds are used to guide construction of the search tree, and are computed by both solving an Integer Linear Program (ILP), and applying several rules for lower bound computation. These rules are described in Blom *et al.* [4]. The ILP, denoted DISTANCETO, computes a lower bound on the smallest number of vote changes required to transform the election $\mathcal{B}$, with an elimination sequence π', to one with an elimination sequence that ends in π. When applied to a complete order π, containing all candidates, DISTANCETO exactly computes the smallest number of votes changes required to realise the outcome π. The largest of the lower bounds computed by the rules of Blom *et al.* [4] and the DISTANCETO ILP is assigned to each partial sequence π as it is added to F. The DISTANCETO ILP is defined in Sect. 4.1. To enforce additional constraints on the nature of any manipulated election, we add these constraints to each ILP solved.

The partial sequence $\pi \in F$ with the smallest assigned lower bound is selected and *expanded*. For each candidate $c \in C$ that is not already present in π, we create a new sequence with c appended to the front. For example, given a set of candidates e, f, and g, with winning candidate g, the partial sequence $\pi = [f]$ will be expanded to create two new sequences $[e, f]$ and $[g, f]$. We evaluate each new sequence π' created by assigning it a lower bound on the number of votes required to realise any elimination order ending in π'.

While exploring and building elimination sequences, *margin-irv* maintains a running *upper bound* on the value of the true margin. Without any side constraints designed to inject desirable properties into a manipulated election, this upper bound is initialised to the last round margin of the original election. To enforce additional constraints on the properties of any manipulated election, we need to manipulate at least as many, and often more, votes than required to simply change the original outcome. Consequently, we must set the upper bound maintained by *margin-irv* to a higher value. In this context, we set the initial upper bound to the total number of votes cast in the election. This is clearly always a correct upper bound on any manipulation.

When a sequence π containing all candidates is constructed, the DISTANCETO ILP computes the exact number of vote manipulations required to realise it, while satisfying all desired side constraints. If this number is lower than our current upper bound, the upper bound is revised, and all orders in F with a lower bound greater than or equal to it are pruned from consideration (removed from F). This process continues until F is empty (we have considered or pruned all possible alternate elimination sequences). The value of the running upper bound is the true margin of victory (with side constraints) of the election.

4.1   DistanceTo with Side Constraints

We now present the DISTANCETO Integer Linear Program (ILP) used to compute lower bounds on the degree of manipulation required to realise an election outcome ending in a given candidate sequence, and the (exact) smallest number of vote changes required to realise a given (complete) alternate elimination sequence. This ILP, without added side constraints, was originally presented by Magrino *et al.* [8].

Let $\mathbf{R}$ denote the set of possible (partial and total) rankings R of candidates C that could appear on a vote, N_R the number of votes cast with ranking $R \in \mathbf{R}$, and N the total number of votes cast. Let $\mathcal{R}_{j,i}$ denote the subset of rankings in $\mathbf{R}$ ($\mathcal{R}_{j,i} \subset \mathbf{R}$) in which c_j is the most preferred candidate still standing (i.e., that will count toward c_j's tally) at the start of round i (in which candidate c_i is eliminated). For each $R \in \mathbf{R}$, we define variables:

q_R integer number of votes to be changed into R;

m_R integer number of votes with ranking R in the unmodified election to be changed into something other than R; and

y_R number of votes in the modified election with ranking R.

Given a partial or complete order π, the DISTANCETO ILP is:

$$\min \sum_{R \in \mathbf{R}} q_R$$

$$N_R + q_R - m_R = y_R \qquad\qquad \forall R \in \mathbf{R} \quad (3)$$

$$\sum_{R \in \mathbf{R}} q_R = \sum_{R \in \mathbf{R}} m_R \qquad\qquad (4)$$

$$\sum_{R \in \mathcal{R}_{i,i}} y_R \leq \sum_{R \in \mathcal{R}_{j,i}} y_R \qquad\qquad \forall c_i, c_j \in \pi \,.\, i < j \quad (5)$$

$$n \geq y_R \geq 0, \;\; N_R \geq m_R \geq 0, \;\; q_R \geq 0 \qquad\qquad \forall R \in \mathbf{R} \quad (6)$$

Constraint (3) states that the number of votes with ranking $R \in \mathbf{R}$ in the new election is equal to the sum of those with this ranking in the unmodified election and those whose ranking has *changed to* R, minus the number of votes whose ranking has been *changed from* R. Constraint (5) defines a set of *special elimination constraints* which force the candidates in π to be eliminated in the stated order. Constraint (4) ensures that the total number of votes cast in the election does not change as a result of the manipulation.

The above ILP does not include any additional side constraints – properties that we want the manipulated election to satisfy besides resulting in a different winner to that of the original election. We show, in Sect. 5, that manipulated elections found by *margin-irv* in this setting are almost always evidently close, with a last round margin of 0 or 1 vote. This makes sense as the algorithm is trying to manipulate as few votes as possible, breaking any ties in favour of an alternate outcome. An adversary with the ability to modify electronic records of cast votes, however, will want to create a manipulated election that is not evidently close. An election with a tie in the final round of counting, or a difference of several votes in the tallies of the final two remaining candidates, is likely to be closely scrutinised. Australian IRV elections with a last round margin of less than 100 votes, for example, trigger an automatic recount.

Given the widespread use of the last round margin as the indicator of how close an IRV election is, rather than the true MOV of the election, our adversary can use this to their advantage. Consider a candidate elimination sequence π, containing at least two candidates from a set $\mathcal{C}$. Let the last two candidates in the sequence π be denoted by c_k and c_{k+1}, with $|\mathcal{C}| = k + 1$. Adding the following side constraint to DISTANCETO ensures that the last round margin of any manipulated election is greater than or equal to T_{LRM} votes.

$$\sum_{R \in \mathcal{R}_{k,k}} y_R \leq \sum_{R \in \mathcal{R}_{k+1,k}} y_R + 2\, T_{LRM} \qquad\qquad (7)$$

We can add any number of desired side constraints to this ILP to inject desirable properties into any manipulated election. In this paper we consider two side constraints: requiring the last round margin of the manipulated election to be equal to or greater than a given threshold T_{LRM}; and ensuring no ties arise in the manipulated election when determining which candidate to eliminate in each round. The latter constraint can be modelled by requiring the tally of the eliminated candidate e in each round i to contain Δ fewer votes than that of the candidate with the next smallest tally in round i.

$$\Delta + \sum_{R \in \mathcal{R}_{i,i}} y_R \leq \sum_{R \in \mathcal{R}_{j,i}} y_R \qquad \forall c_i, c_j \in \pi \,.\, i < j \qquad (8)$$

Constraint (8) modifies the set of special elimination constraints (Constraint 5) with the addition of the Δ constant on the left hand side.

4.2 Selecting a Desired Winner

An adversary is likely to have a goal of electing a specific candidate, or one of a set of specific candidates, in place of the original winner. Blom *et al.* [3] show that we can compute the smallest number of vote changes necessary to elect a *specific alternate* winner – a candidate from a given set $\mathcal{C}'$ – by adjusting the way we construct our initial frontier F in the branch-and-bound algorithm described above. Consider an election with candidates $\mathcal{C}$ and winner $w \in \mathcal{C}$. If we are interested in simply changing the candidate who wins to any candidate that is not w, we add $|\mathcal{C}| - 1$ partial sequences to our frontier, one for each alternate winner. As described above, each of these sequences contains just one candidate – the alternate winner in question. In the setting where we want to elect a candidate from the set $\mathcal{C}'$, we create, and add to our frontier, a partial candidate sequence for each of the candidates in $\mathcal{C}'$. The remainder of the algorithm remains unchanged. The use of this restricted frontier, in conjunction with a DISTANCETO ILP containing side constraints, allows us to compute a minimal manipulation of votes required to elect a specific candidate with, for example, a large last round margin. In the case study below, we consider an adversary that simply wants to change the election winner to any alternate candidate.

5   Case Study: The NSW 2015 State Election

In the 2015 NSW State Election, 4.56 million votes were cast across 93 IRV elections, one in each of 93 different electorates. Table 2 considers these 93 elections, recording the number of votes cast, the last round margin, the true margin of victory, and the last round margin of the manipulated election found by *margin-irv* without the addition of side constraints. In all but five elections (Ballina, Heffron, Lismore, Maitland, and Willoughby) the MOV is the LRM, showing that they are almost always equal. In all but one election (Ballina), minimal manipulation results in an evidently close election. Ballina shows that, while uncommon, an adversary can achieve a large last round margin without performing any more manipulation than necessary to alter the winner of the seat.

We now add our side constraints (7, 8) to each DISTANCETO ILP solved by *margin-irv*, with T_{LRM} chosen such that the difference between the tallies of the last two remaining candidates, in each election, is at least 100 votes ($T_{LRM} = 50$), and $\Delta = 1$. This would avoid an automatic recount, and ties when determining which candidate to eliminate. Table 3 reports, for all 93 seats, the minimal manipulation MAN (i.e. number of ballots changed) required to change the winner of each election while ensuring these constraints hold, the original last round margin of the election (LRM), the last round margin of the manipulated election (LRM*), and the margin of victory of the manipulated election (MOV*). MOV* represents the smallest number of vote changes required to change the winner of the manipulated election (to any alternate winner, not necessarily back to its original winner).

In many cases, we can create a manipulated election where the LRM* is not only at least 50 votes (leading to a difference in the tallies of the last two remaining candidates of 100 votes), but has a MOV equal to it. This is reflective of most IRV elections – the MOV is generally equal to the LRM. In others, the manipulated elections are much closer than the LRM suggests.

To ensure a LRM* of at least T_{LRM} votes, we often have to manipulate a further T_{LRM} votes on top of those we must change to simply change the winning candidate. For $T_{LRM} = 50$, this is the case for all of the 93 seats with the exception of Ballina and Lismore – we can find a minimal manipulation, just enough to change the winning candidate, that also has an LRM of at least 50.

In some cases we can perform a small amount of additional manipulation, beyond that required to simply change the election outcome, and receive a much larger increase in the LRM*. Imagine that our adversary desired an even larger LRM* – say, 5% of the total votes cast. Table 4 reports the new number of votes changes (MAN) required to manipulate the 93 NSW elections to ensure that both the LRM* is at least 5% of the total number of votes cast, and eliminated candidates do not appear in any ties (with $\Delta = 1$).

We have boldened the elections in which the apparent change in the election outcome is much greater than the degree of manipulation performed. In Heffron, for example, just changing the winner requires 5825 vote changes (12.6% of the total votes cast). The LRM for Heffron is 5835. If we only change 5825 votes, our manipulated election will have a LRM* of 1 vote. By changing a further 117 votes, we can create an election with both a different winner *and* a LRM* of 2319 votes. In Ballina, performing an additional 133 vote manipulations yields an increase in the LRM* of 1145 votes (from 1229 to 2374).

When performing just enough manipulation to ensure a LRM* of 50 votes (and a change in winner), the MOV* and LRM* of the manipulated elections substantially differ in 19 of the 93 elections. When performing substantially more manipulation, to ensure a LRM* of 5% of the total votes cast, the MOV* and LRM* of the manipulated elections substantially differ in 50 of the 93 elections.

These results demonstrate that, in the presence of manipulation, the LRM of an election is generally not a good indicator of how close the election was or whether its result should be audited or not. Then again, neither is its MOV.

Table 2. LRM, MOV, and LRM of the manipulated election (denoted LRM*), for each seat in the 2015 NSW lower house election (no added side constraints).

Seat	$|\mathcal{C}|$	$|\mathcal{B}|$	MOV	LRM	LRM*	Seat	$|\mathcal{C}|$	$|\mathcal{B}|$	MOV	LRM	LRM*
Albury	5	46335	5840	5840	0	M–Fields	7	47183	3519	3519	0
Auburn	6	43781	2265	2265	0	**Maitland**	6	47826	**4012**	5446	0
Ballina	7	47454	**1130**	1267	**1248**	Manly	5	47287	10806	10806	0
Balmain	7	46952	1731	1731	0	Maroubra	5	46492	4717	4717	1
Bankstown	6	42899	5542	5542	0	Miranda	6	49454	5881	5881	0
Barwon	6	47707	5229	5229	0	Monaro	5	46202	1122	1122	0
Bathurst	5	48632	7267	7267	1	M–Druitt	5	44948	6343	6343	0
B–Hills	5	49266	10023	10023	0	Mulgoa	5	48257	4336	4336	0
Bega	5	47658	3663	3663	1	Murray	8	46387	8574	8574	0
Blacktown	5	46262	5565	5565	0	M–Lakes	6	48252	3627	3627	0
B–Mntns	6	47608	3614	3614	1	Newcastle	7	48136	3132	3132	0
Cabramatta	5	47691	7613	7613	0	Newtown	7	45392	3536	3536	0
Camden	5	48152	8217	8217	0	N–Shore	7	46247	8517	8517	0
C–belltown	5	45124	3096	3096	0	N–lands	6	48340	11969	11969	0
Canterbury	5	47631	6610	6610	0	Oatley	5	48119	3006	3006	0
Castle Hill	5	48092	13160	13160	0	Orange	5	48784	10048	10048	0
Cessnock	5	45822	9187	9187	0	Oxley	5	46514	4591	4591	0
Charlestown	7	48919	5532	5532	0	Parramatta	7	47447	5509	5509	0
Clarence	8	47181	4069	4069	0	Penrith	8	47577	2576	2576	0
C–Harbour	5	45162	5824	5824	1	Pittwater	5	48345	11430	11430	1
Coogee	5	46322	1243	1243	0	P–M.quarie	5	49231	8715	8715	0
C–mundra	5	47160	9247	9247	0	P–Stephens	5	47037	2088	2088	0
Cronulla	5	50333	9674	9674	0	Prospect	5	47195	1458	1458	0
Davidson	5	49147	12960	12960	0	Riverstone	5	46945	5324	5324	0
Drummoyne	6	46818	8099	8099	0	Rockdale	6	46240	2004	2004	0
Dubbo	7	46582	8680	8680	0	Ryde	5	48286	5153	5153	0
East Hills	5	47449	189	189	0	S–Hills	7	47874	3774	3774	0
Epping	6	49532	7156	7156	0	S–harbour	7	50995	7519	7519	0
Fairfield	5	45921	6998	6998	0	S–Coast	5	45788	4054	4054	1
Gosford	6	48259	102	102	0	Strathfield	5	46559	770	770	0
Goulburn	6	48663	2945	2945	0	S–Hill	7	47073	3854	3854	0
Granville	6	45212	837	837	0	Swansea	8	48200	4974	4974	0
Hawkesbury	8	46856	7311	7311	1	Sydney	8	42747	2864	2864	1
Heathcote	6	51128	3560	3560	0	Tamworth	7	49004	4643	4643	0
Heffron	5	46367	**5824**	5835	0	Terrigal	5	48871	4053	4053	0
Holsworthy	6	47126	2902	2902	1	T–Entrance	5	47953	171	171	0
Hornsby	6	49834	8577	8577	1	Tweed	5	44185	1291	1291	0
Keira	5	50599	8164	8164	0	U–Hunter	6	47296	866	866	0
Kiama	5	47686	3856	3856	0	Vaucluse	5	46145	9783	9783	0
Kogarah	6	46421	2782	2782	0	W–Wagga	6	46610	5475	5475	0
Ku-ring-gai	5	48436	10061	10061	0	Wakehurst	6	47894	10770	10770	0
L–M.quarie	7	47698	4253	4253	0	Wallsend	5	49631	9418	9418	0
Lakemba	5	44728	8235	8235	0	**Willoughby**	6	47302	**10160**	10247	0
Lane Cove	6	48622	7740	7740	1	Wollondilly	6	47182	7401	7401	1
Lismore	6	47046	**209**	1173	1	Wollongong	7	49702	3367	3367	0
Liverpool	5	45291	8495	8495	1	Wyong	7	46070	3720	3720	0
L–derry	5	45928	3736	3736	0						

Table 3. Minimal MANipulation compared to LRM of the original election and MOV and LRM of the manipulated (*) election, for each seat in the 2015 NSW lower house election (side constraints requiring LRM* to be at least 50 votes, and tie breaking with $\Delta = 1$, added).

Seat	MAN	LRM	LRM*	MOV*	Seat	MAN	LRM	LRM*	MOV*
Albury	5890	5840	50	50	M–Fields	3569	3519	50	50
Auburn	2315	2265	50	50	Maitland	4062	5446	50	1
Ballina	**1130**	1267	**1229**	1	Manly	10856	10806	50	1
Balmain	1781	1731	50	50	Maroubra	4767	4717	51	51
Bankstown	5592	5542	50	50	Miranda	5931	5881	50	50
Barwon	5279	5229	50	50	Monaro	1172	1122	51	51
Bathurst	7317	7267	51	51	M–Druitt	6393	6343	50	50
B–Hills	10073	10023	50	50	Mulgoa	4386	4336	51	51
Bega	3713	3663	51	51	Murray	8624	8574	50	1
Blacktown	5615	5565	50	50	M–Lakes	3677	3627	50	50
B–Mntns	3664	3614	51	51	Newcastle	3182	3132	50	50
Cabramatta	7663	7613	50	50	Newtown	3586	3536	50	50
Camden	8267	8217	50	50	N–Shore	8567	8517	50	1
C–belltown	3146	3096	50	50	N–Tablelands	12019	11969	50	1
Canterbury	6660	6610	50	50	Oatley	3056	3006	51	51
Castle Hill	13210	13160	50	1	Orange	10098	10048	50	1
Cessnock	9237	9187	50	50	Oxley	4641	4591	50	50
Charlestown	5582	5532	50	51	Parramatta	5559	5509	50	50
Clarence	4119	4069	50	50	Penrith	2626	2576	50	50
C–Harbour	5874	5824	51	51	Pittwater	11480	11430	50	50
Coogee	1293	1243	50	50	P–Macquarie	8765	8715	50	50
C–mundra	9297	9247	50	50	P–Stephens	2138	2088	50	50
Cronulla	9724	9674	50	1	Prospect	1508	1458	50	50
Davidson	13010	12960	50	50	Riverstone	5374	5324	50	50
Drummoyne	8149	8099	50	50	Rockdale	2054	2004	50	50
Dubbo	8730	8680	50	50	Ryde	5203	5153	51	51
East Hills	239	189	50	50	S–Hills	3824	3774	50	50
Epping	7206	7156	50	1	S–harbour	7569	7519	50	50
Fairfield	7048	6998	50	50	S–Coast	4104	4054	51	51
Gosford	152	102	50	50	Strathfield	820	770	50	50
Goulburn	2995	2945	50	50	S–Hill	3904	3854	50	1
Granville	887	837	50	50	Swansea	5024	4974	50	52
Hawkesbury	7361	7311	50	50	Sydney	2914	2864	51	51
Heathcote	3610	3560	50	50	Tamworth	4693	4643	51	51
Heffron	5874	5835	50	1	Terrigal	4103	4053	50	50
Holsworthy	2952	2902	51	51	T–Entrance	221	171	51	51
Hornsby	8627	8577	50	1	Tweed	1341	1291	51	51
Keira	8214	8164	50	50	U–Hunter	916	866	50	50
Kiama	3906	3856	50	50	Vaucluse	9833	9783	50	1
Kogarah	2832	2782	50	50	W–Wagga	5525	5475	50	50
Ku-ring-gai	10111	10061	50	1	Wakehurst	10820	10770	50	50
L–M.quarie	4303	4253	50	50	Wallsend	9468	9418	50	50
Lakemba	8285	8235	50	1	Willoughby	10210	10247	51	2
Lane Cove	7790	7740	50	50	Wollondilly	7451	7401	50	51
Lismore	**209**	1173	**50**	1	Wollongong	3417	3367	50	50
Liverpool	8545	8495	50	1	Wyong	3770	3720	50	50
L–derry	3786	3736	50	50					

Table 4. Minimal MANipulation and LRM the original election and LRM and MOV of the manipulated (*) election, for each seat in the 2015 NSW lower house election (side constraints requiring LRM* to be at least 5% of the total cast votes, and tie breaking with $\Delta = 1$, added).

Seat	MAN	LRM	LRM*	MOV*	Seat	MAN	LRM	LRM*	MOV*
Albury	8157	5840	2317	2317	M–Fields	5878	3519	2360	2360
Auburn	4454	2265	2190	2190	Maitland	6278	5446	2462	1
Ballina	**1263**	**1267**	**2374**	**1**	Manly	13171	10806	2365	1
Balmain	**3075**	**1731**	**3196**	**1**	Maroubra	7042	4717	2326	2326
Bankstown	7687	5542	2145	1989	Miranda	8354	5881	2473	1449
Barwon	7615	5229	2386	633	Monaro	3432	1122	2311	2311
Bathurst	9699	7267	2433	2235	M–Druitt	8591	6343	2248	1679
B–Hills	12487	10023	2464	2080	Mulgoa	6749	4336	2414	2414
Bega	6046	3663	2384	2384	Murray	10893	8574	2320	1
Blacktown	7879	5565	2314	2314	M–Lakes	6040	3627	2413	675
B–Mntns	5947	3614	2381	1	**Newcastle**	**5278**	**3132**	**2407**	**2**
Cabramatta	9998	7613	2385	669	Newtown	5806	3536	2270	131
Camden	10625	8217	2408	2408	N–Shore	10830	8517	2313	1
C–belltown	5353	3096	2257	2257	N–Tablelands	14386	11969	2417	1
Canterbury	8992	6610	2382	1	Oatley	5412	3006	2407	2407
Castle Hill	15565	13160	2405	1	Orange	12487	10048	2440	1
Cessnock	11479	9187	2292	1401	Oxley	6917	4591	2326	2326
Charlestown	7978	5532	2446	1990	Parramatta	7881	5509	2373	1747
Clarence	6428	4069	2360	2360	Penrith	4955	2576	2379	2379
C–Harbour	8082	5824	2259	2259	Pittwater	13847	11430	2418	1353
Coogee	3560	1243	2317	1461	P–Macquarie	11177	8715	2462	2462
C–mundra	11605	9247	2358	9	P–Stephens	4440	2088	2352	2352
Cronulla	12191	9674	2517	1	Prospect	3818	1458	2360	2360
Davidson	15418	12960	2458	290	Riverstone	7672	5324	2348	2348
Drummoyne	10440	8099	2341	680	Rockdale	4316	2004	2312	2312
Dubbo	11009	8680	2330	1	Ryde	7567	5153	2415	2415
East Hills	2562	189	2373	2373	S–Hills	6168	3774	2394	2394
Epping	9633	7156	2477	1	S–harbour	10069	7519	2550	1
Fairfield	9295	6998	2297	1	S–Coast	6343	4054	2290	860
Gosford	2515	102	2413	2413	Strathfield	3098	770	2328	2328
Goulburn	5379	2945	2434	2434	**S–Hill**	**5487**	**3854**	**2354**	**1**
Granville	3098	837	2261	2261	Swansea	7384	4974	2410	2370
Hawkesbury	9654	7311	2343	2343	Sydney	5001	2864	2138	1934
Heathcote	6116	3560	2557	2557	Tamworth	7093	4643	2451	2451
Heffron	**5942**	**5835**	**2319**	**1**	Terrigal	6497	4053	2444	2444
Holsworthy	5258	2902	2357	2357	T–Entrance	2569	171	2399	2399
Hornsby	11069	8577	2492	1	Tweed	3500	1291	2210	2210
Keira	10694	8164	2530	970	U–Hunter	3231	866	2365	1748
Kiama	6241	3856	2385	2385	Vaucluse	12091	9783	2308	1
Kogarah	5104	2782	2322	2322	W–Wagga	7806	5475	2331	2331
Ku-ring-gai	12483	10061	2422	621	Wakehurst	13165	10770	2395	1329
L–M.quarie	6638	4253	2385	2385	Wallsend	11900	9418	2482	1939
Lakemba	10472	8235	2237	1	Willoughby	12525	10247	2366	1
Lane Cove	10171	7740	2432	42	Wollondilly	9760	7401	2360	1062
Lismore	2449	1173	2353	1	Wollongong	5852	3367	2486	330
Liverpool	10760	8495	2265	2265	Wyong	6024	3720	2304	2304
L–derry	6033	3736	2297	2297					

A clever adversary with sufficient access to change electronic records of cast votes will be able to design a manipulation that results in both a sizable LRM and MOV. To ensure that both the LRM and MOV of an election is sufficiently large, however, requires more manipulation than just desiring a large LRM, or just desiring a change in winner.

6   Modelling a Weaker Adversary

A likely practical scenario for election manipulation is one in which the adversary has partial knowledge of the ballot profiles and the opportunity to manipulate (some of) the rest. This would be the case, for example, if a corrupt scanner were able to modify ballot images or interpretations without the paper record being subsequently audited. There are various models for an adversary with the power to manipulate a restricted number of votes, which is particularly relevant in contexts in which a small manipulation can change the outcome [5].

An interesting question to address in this context is whether a manipulation computed for, say, the first half of the ballots, could then be simply doubled and applied successfully to the second half. Obviously this is not true in general, if there is some systematic difference between earlier and later votes (for example, if later votes come from a geographically distinct area from the earlier ones). It is an interesting practical question to understand how to extrapolate successful manipulations from a subset of ballots to the whole election, given reasonable assumptions about the information contained in the initial sample. Of course, other data, such as from past elections, could also be available to an attacker.

7   Concluding Remarks

We show how to compute successful manipulations that are designed specifically to avoid triggering a recount based on last-round margin, an inaccurate but commonly used assessment of the closeness of an IRV election.

The attack shown in this paper would be detected (with high probability) by a genuine Risk Limiting Audit, or by a recount triggered from the properly-computed true Margin of Victory rather than the last-round margin.

References

1. Antonyan, T., et al.: State-wide elections, optical scan voting systems, and the pursuit of integrity. IEEE Trans. Inf. Forensics Secur. 4(4), 597–610 (2009)
2. Blom, M., Stuckey, P.J., Teague, V.J.: Ballot-polling risk limiting audits for IRV elections. In: Krimmer, R., et al. (eds.) E-Vote-ID 2018. LNCS, vol. 11143, pp. 17–34. Springer, Cham (2018). https://doi.org/10.1007/978-3-030-00419-4_2
3. Blom, M., Stuckey, P.J., Teague, V.J.: Computing the margin of victory in preferential parliamentary elections. In: Krimmer, R., et al. (eds.) E-Vote-ID 2018. LNCS, vol. 11143, pp. 1–16. Springer, Cham (2018). https://doi.org/10.1007/978-3-030-00419-4_1

4. Blom, M., Stuckey, P.J., Teague, V., Tidhar, R.: Efficient computation of exact IRV margins. In: European Conference on AI (ECAI), pp. 480–487 (2016)
5. Di Franco, A., Petro, A., Shear, E., Vladimirov, V.: Small vote manipulations can swing elections. Commun. ACM **47**(10), 43–45 (2004)
6. Hall, J.L., et al.: Implementing risk-limiting post-election audits in California. In: Electronic Voting Technology Workshop/Workshop on Trustworthy Elections (EVT/WOTE 2009), Montreal, Canada, August 2009. USENIX (2009)
7. Lindeman, M., Stark, P.B., Yates, V.: BRAVO: ballot-polling risk-limiting audits to verify outcomes. In: Electronic Voting Technology Workshop/Workshop on Trustworthy Elections (EVT/WOTE 2011). USENIX (2011)
8. Magrino, T.R., Rivest, R.L., Shen, E., Wagner, D.A.: Computing the margin of victory in IRV elections. In: USENIX Accurate Electronic Voting Technology Workshop. USENIX Association, Berkeley (2011)
9. Richie, R.: Instant runoff voting: what Mexico (and others) could learn. Election Law J. **3**, 501–512 (2004)
10. Sarwate, A.D., Checkoway, S., Shacham, H.: Risk-limiting audits and the margin of victory in nonplurality elections. Polit. Policy **3**(3), 29–64 (2013)

Bernoulli Ballot Polling: A Manifest Improvement for Risk-Limiting Audits

Kellie Ottoboni[1], Matthew Bernhard[2], J. Alex Halderman[2], Ronald L. Rivest[3], and Philip B. Stark[1(✉)]

[1] Department of Statistics, University of California, Berkeley, CA, USA
stark@stat.berkeley.edu
[2] Department of Computer Science and Engineering,
University of Michigan, Ann Arbor, MI, USA
[3] CSAIL, Massachusetts Institute of Technology, Cambridge, MA, USA

Abstract. We present a method and software for ballot-polling risk-limiting audits (RLAs) based on Bernoulli sampling: ballots are included in the sample with probability p, independently. Bernoulli sampling has several advantages: (1) it does not require a ballot manifest; (2) it can be conducted independently at different locations, rather than requiring a central authority to select the sample from the whole population of cast ballots or requiring stratified sampling; (3) it can start in polling places on election night, before margins are known. If the reported margins for the 2016 U.S. Presidential election are correct, a Bernoulli ballot-polling audit with a risk limit of 5% and a sampling rate of $p_0 = 1\%$ would have had at least a 99% probability of confirming the outcome in 42 states. (The other states were more likely to have needed to examine additional ballots). Logistical and security advantages that auditing in the polling place affords may outweigh the cost of examining more ballots than some other methods might require.

1 Introduction

No method for counting votes is perfect, and methods that rely on computers are particularly fragile: errors, bugs, and deliberate attacks can alter results. The vulnerability of electronic voting was confirmed in two major state-funded studies, California's Top-to-Bottom Review (Bowen 2007) and Ohio's EVEREST study (McDaniel et al. 2007). More recently, at the 2017 and 2018 DEFCON hacking conferences, attendees with little or no knowledge of election systems were able to penetrate a wide range of U.S. voting machines (Blaze et al. 2017, 2018). Given that Russia interfered with the 2016 U.S. Presidential election through an "unprecedented coordinated cyber campaign against state election infrastructure" (U.S. Senate Select Committee on Intelligence 2018), national security demands we protect our elections from nation states and other advanced persistent threats.

Risk-limiting audits (RLAs) were introduced in 2007 (Stark 2008) as a mechanism for detecting and correcting outcome-changing errors in vote tabulation,

© International Financial Cryptography Association 2020
A. Bracciali et al. (Eds.): FC 2019 Workshops, LNCS 11599, pp. 226–241, 2020.
https://doi.org/10.1007/978-3-030-43725-1_16

whatever their cause—including hacking, misconfiguration, and human error. RLAs have been tested in practice in California, Colorado, Indiana, Virginia, Ohio, and Denmark. Colorado started conducting routine statewide RLAs in 2017 (Lindeman et al. 2018), and Rhode Island passed a law in 2017 requiring routine statewide RLAs starting in 2020 (RI Gen L § 17-19-37.4). RLA legislation is under consideration in a number of other states, and bills to require RLAs have been introduced in Congress.

In this paper, we present an RLA method based on *Bernoulli random sampling*. With simple random sampling, the number of ballots to sample is fixed; with Bernoulli sampling, the *expected sampling rate* is fixed but the sample size is not. Conceptually, *Bernoulli ballot polling* (BBP) decides whether to include the jth ballot in the sample by tossing a biased coin that has probability p of landing heads. The ballot is included if and only if the coin lands heads. Coin tosses for different ballots are independent, but have the same chance of landing heads. (Rather than toss a coin for each ballot, it more efficient to implement Bernoulli sampling in practice using *geometric skipping*, described in Sect. 6.3.)

The logistical simplicity of Bernoulli sampling may make it useful for election audits. Like all RLAs, BBP RLAs require a voter-verifiable paper record. Like other ballot-polling RLAs (Lindeman et al. 2012; Lindeman and Stark 2012), BBP makes no other technical demands on the voting system. It requires no special equipment, and only a minimal amount of software to select and analyze the sample—in principle, it could be carried out with dice and a pencil and paper. In contrast to extant ballot-polling RLAs, BBP does *not* require a ballot manifest (although it does require knowing where all the ballots are, and access to the ballots). BBP is inherently local and parallelizable, because the decision of whether to include any particular ballot in the sample does not depend on which other ballots are selected, nor on how many other ballots have been selected, nor even on how many ballots were cast. We shall see that this has practical advantages.

Bernoulli sampling is well-known in the survey sampling literature, but it is used less often than simple random sampling for a number of reasons. The variance of estimates based on Bernoulli samples tends to be larger than for simple random samples (Särndal et al. 2003), due to the fact that both the sample and the sample size are random. This added randomness complicates rigorous inferences. A common estimator of the population mean from a Bernoulli sample is the Horvitz-Thompson estimator, which has a high variance when the sampling rate p is small. Often, P-values and confidence intervals for the Horvitz-Thompson estimator are approximated using the normal distribution (Lohr 2009; Cochran 1977; Thompson 1997), which may be inaccurate if the population distribution is skewed—as it often is in auditing problems (Panel on Nonstandard Mixtures of Distributions 1998).

Instead of relying on parametric approximations, we develop a test based on Wald's sequential probability ratio test (Wald 1945). The test is akin to that in extant ballot polling RLA methods (Lindeman et al. 2012; Lindeman and Stark 2012), but the mathematics are modified to work with Bernoulli random samples, including the fact that Bernoulli samples are drawn without replacement. (Previous ballot-polling RLAs relied on sampling with replacement.) Conditional on the attained sample size n, a Bernoulli sample of ballots is a simple random sample. We maximize the conditional P-value of the null hypothesis (that the reported winner did not win) over a nuisance parameter, the total number of ballots with valid votes for either of a given pair of candidates, excluding invalid ballots or ballots for other candidates. A martingale argument shows that the resulting test is sequential: if the test does not reject, the sample can be expanded using additional rounds of Bernoulli sampling (with the same or different expected sampling rates) and the resulting P-values will still be conservative.

A BBP RLA can begin in polling places on election night. Given an initial sampling rate to be used across all precincts and vote centers, poll workers in each location determine which ballots will be examined in the audit, independently from each other and independently across ballots, and record the votes cast on each ballot selected. (Vote-by-mail and provisional ballots can be audited similarly; see Sect. 6.2.) Once the election results are reported, the sequential probability ratio test can be applied to the sample vote tallies to determine whether there is sufficient evidence that the reported outcome is correct.[1] If the sample does not provide sufficiently strong evidence to attain the risk limit, the sample can be expanded using subsequent rounds of Bernoulli sampling until either the risk limit is attained or all ballots are inspected. Figure 1 summarizes the procedure.

BBP has a number of practical advantages, with little additional workload in terms of the number of ballots examined. Workload simulations show that the number of ballots needed to confirm a correctly reported outcome is similar for BBP and the BRAVO RLA (Lindeman et al. 2012). If the choice of initial sampling rate (and thus, the initial sample size) is larger than necessary, the added efficiency of conducting the audit "in parallel" across the entire election may outweigh the cost of examining extra ballots. Using statewide results from the 2016 United States presidential election, BBP with a 1% initial sampling rate would have had at least a 99% chance of confirming the results in 42 states at risk limit 5% (assuming the reported results were in fact correct). A Python implementation of BBP is available at https://github.com/pbstark/BernoulliBallotPolling.

2   Notation and Mathematical Background

We consider social choice functions that are variants of majority and plurality voting: the winners are the $k \geq 1$ candidates who receive the most votes. This includes ordinary "first-past-the-post" contests, as well as "vote for k" contests.[2]

---

[1] The current method uses the reported results to construct the alternative hypothesis. A variant of the method does not require the reported results. We do not present that method here; it is related to ClipAudit (Rivest 2017).

[2] The same general approach works for some preferential voting schemes, such as Borda count and range voting, and for proportional representation schemes such as D'Hondt (Stark and Teague 2014). We do not consider instant-runoff voting (IRV).

Procedure for a Bernoulli ballot-polling audit

1. **Set initial sampling rate.** Choose initial sampling rate p_0 based on pre-election polls or set at a fixed value. If p_0 is selected based on an estimated margin, use the ASN heuristic in Section 5.
2. **Sample ballots and record audit data.** Use geometric skipping (below) with rate p_0 to select ballots to inspect. Record votes on all inspected ballots.
3. **Check attained risk.** Once the final election results have been reported, for each contest under audit and for each reported (winner, loser) pair (w, ℓ):
   - Calculate B_w, B_ℓ, and B_u from the audit sample.
   - Find the (maximal) P-value from B_w, B_ℓ, B_u using the test in Section 3.1.
4. **Escalate if necessary.** If, for any (w, ℓ) pair, the P-value is greater than α, expand the audit in one of the ways described in Section 4.

Procedure for geometric skip sampling

1. **Set the random seed.** In each polling place, use a cryptographically secure PRNG, such as SHA-256, with a seed chosen using true randomness.
2. **Sample ballots.** Following Section 6.3, for each batch of ballots: Set $Y_0 = 0$ and set $j = 0$.
   - $j \leftarrow j + 1$
   - Generate a uniform random variable U on $[0, 1)$.
   - $Y_j \leftarrow \left\lceil \frac{\ln(U)}{\ln(1-p)} \right\rceil$.
   - If $\sum_{k=1}^{j} Y_j$ is greater than the number of ballots in the batch, stop. Otherwise, skip the next $Y_j - 1$ ballots in the batch, and include the ballot after that one (i.e., include ballot $\sum_{k=1}^{j} Y_j$)

Fig. 1. Bernoulli ballot-polling audit step-by-step procedures.

As explained in Lindeman et al. (2012), it suffices to consider one (winner, loser) pair at a time: the contest outcome is correct if every reported winner actually received more votes than every reported loser. Auditing majority and super-majority contests requires only minor modifications.[3] Sect. 3.2 addresses auditing multiple contests simultaneously.

Let w denote a reported winning candidate and ℓ denote a reported losing candidate. Suppose that the population contains N_w ballots with a valid vote for w but not ℓ, N_ℓ ballots with a valid vote for ℓ but not w, and N_u ballots with votes for both w and ℓ or for neither w nor ℓ. The total number of ballots is $N = N_w + N_\ell + N_u$. Let $N_{w\ell} \equiv N_w + N_\ell$ be the number of ballots in the population with a valid vote for w or ℓ but not both. For Bernoulli sampling, N may be unknown; in any event, N_w, N_ℓ, and N_u are unknown, or the audit would not be necessary.

---

[3] For instance, for a majority contest, one simply pools the votes for all the reported losers into a single "pseudo-candidate" who reportedly lost.

If we can reject the null hypothesis that $N_\ell \geq N_w$ at significance level α, we have statistically confirmed that w got more votes than ℓ. Section 3 presents a test for this hypothesis that accounts for the nuisance parameter $N_{w\ell}$. We assume that ties are settled in a deterministic way and that if the audit is unable to confirm the contest outcome, a full manual tally resulting in a tie would be settled in the same deterministic way.

2.1   Multi-round Bernoulli Sampling

A Bernoulli(p) *random variable* $\mathcal{I}$ is a random variable that takes the value 1 with probability p and the value 0 with probability $1 - p$. BBP uses Bernoulli sampling, which involves independent selection of different ballots with the same probability p of selecting each ballot: $\mathcal{I}_j = 1$ if and only if ballot j is selected to be in the sample, where $\{\mathcal{I}_j\}_{j=1}^N$ are independent, identically distributed (IID) Bernoulli(p) random variables.

Suppose that after tossing a coin with probability p_0 of landing heads for every item in the population, we toss a coin with probability p_1 for every item (again, independently), and include an item in the sample if the first or second toss for that item landed heads. That amounts to drawing a Bernoulli sample using selection probability $1 - (1 - p_0)(1 - p_1)$: an item is in the sample unless its coin landed tails on both tosses, which has probability $(1 - p_0)(1 - p_1)$. This extends to making any integral number K of passes through the population of ballots, with pass k using a coin that has chance p_k of landing heads: such "K-round" Bernoulli sampling is still Bernoulli sampling, with $\mathbb{P}\{\mathcal{I} = 1\} = p = 1 - \prod_{k=0}^{K-1}(1 - p_k)$.

2.2   Exchangeability and Conditional Simple Random Sampling

Because the N variables $\{\mathcal{I}_j\}$ are IID, they are *exchangeable*, meaning their joint distribution is invariant under the action of the symmetric group (relabelings). Consider a collection of indices $\mathcal{S} \subset \{1, \ldots, N\}$ of size k, $0 \leq k \leq N$. Define the event

$$\mathcal{I}_\mathcal{S} \equiv \{\mathcal{I}_j = 1, \forall j \in \mathcal{S}, \text{ and } \mathcal{I}_j = 0, \forall j \notin \mathcal{S}\}.$$

Because $\{\mathcal{I}_j\}$ are exchangeable, $\mathbb{P}\mathcal{I}_\mathcal{S} = \mathbb{P}\mathcal{I}_\mathcal{T}$ for every set $\mathcal{T} \subset \{1, \ldots, N\}$ of size k, since every such set $\mathcal{T}$ can be mapped to $\mathcal{S}$ by a one-to-one relabeling of the indices.

It follows that, conditional on the attained size of the sample, $n = \sum_{j=1}^N \mathcal{I}_j$, all $\binom{N}{n}$ subsets of size n drawn from the N items are equally likely: the sample is conditionally a simple random sample (SRS) of size n. This is foundational for applying the SPRT to Bernoulli samples.

3   Tests

Suppose we draw a Bernoulli sample of ballots. The random variable B is the number of ballots in the sample. Let B_w denote the number of ballots in the sample with a vote for w but not ℓ; let B_ℓ denote the number of ballots in the sample with a vote for ℓ but not w; and let B_u denote the number of ballots in the sample with a vote for both w and ℓ or neither w nor ℓ, so $B = B_w + B_\ell + B_u$.

3.1   Wald's SPRT with a Nuisance Parameter

We want to test the compound hypothesis that $N_w \leq N_\ell$ against the alternative that $N_w = V_w$, $N_\ell = V_\ell$, and $N_u = V_u$, with $V_w - V_\ell > 0$.[4] We present a test based on Wald's sequential probability ratio test (SPRT) (Wald 1945).

The values V_w, V_ℓ, and V_u are the reported results (or values related to those reported results; see Lindeman et al. (2012)). In this problem, N_u (equivalently, $N_{w\ell} \equiv N_w + N_\ell$) is a nuisance parameter: we care about $N_w - N_\ell$, the margin of the reported winner over the reported loser.

Conditional on $B = n$, the sample is a simple random sample. The conditional probability that the sample will yield counts (B_w, B_ℓ, B_u) under the alternative hypothesis is

$$\frac{\prod_{i=0}^{B_w-1}(V_w - i) \; \prod_{i=0}^{B_\ell-1}(V_\ell - i) \; \prod_{i=0}^{B_u-1}(V_u - i)}{\prod_{i=0}^{n-1}(N - i)}.$$

If $B_\ell \geq B_w$, the data obviously do not provide evidence against the null, so we suppose that $B_\ell < B_w$, in which case, the element of the null that will maximize the probability of the observed data has $N_w = N_\ell$. Under the null hypothesis, the conditional probability of observing (B_w, B_ℓ, B_u) is

$$\frac{\prod_{i=0}^{B_w-1}(N_w - i) \; \prod_{i=0}^{B_\ell-1}(N_w - i) \prod_{i=0}^{B_u-1}(N_u - i)}{\prod_{i=0}^{n}(N - i)},$$

for some value N_w and the corresponding $N_u = N - 2N_w$. How large can that probability be if the null hypothesis is true? The probability under the null is maximized by any integer $x \in \{\max(B_w, B_\ell), \ldots, (N - B_u)/2\}$ that maximizes

$$\prod_{i=0}^{B_w-1}(x - i) \; \prod_{i=0}^{B_\ell-1}(x - i) \; \prod_{i=0}^{B_u-1}(N - 2x - i).$$

The logarithm is monotonic, so any maximizer x^* also maximizes

$$f(x) = \sum_{i=0}^{B_w-1} \ln(x - i) + \sum_{i=0}^{B_\ell-1} \ln(x - i) + \sum_{i=0}^{B_u-1} \ln(N - 2x - i).$$

---

[4] The alternative hypothesis is that the reported results are correct; as mentioned above, there are other approaches one could use that do not involve the reported results, but we do not present them here.

The second derivative of f is everywhere negative, so f is convex and has a unique real-valued maximizer on $[\max(B_w, B_\ell), (N - B_u)/2]$, either at one of the endpoints or somewhere in the interval. The derivative $f'(x)$ is

$$f'(x) = \sum_{i=0}^{B_w-1} \frac{1}{x-i} + \sum_{i=0}^{B_\ell-1} \frac{1}{x-i} - 2\sum_{i=0}^{B_u-1} \frac{1}{N-2x-i}.$$

If $f'(x)$ does not change signs, then the maximum is at one of the endpoints, in which case x^* is the endpoint for which f is larger. Otherwise, the real maximizer occurs at a stationary point. If the real-valued maximizer is not an integer, convexity guarantees that the integer maximizer x^* is one of the two integer values that bracket the real maximizer: either $\lfloor x \rfloor$ or $\lceil x \rceil$.

A conservative P-value for the null hypothesis after n items have been drawn is thus

$$P_n = \frac{\prod_{i=0}^{B_w-1}(x^* - i) \ \prod_{i=0}^{B_\ell-1}(x^* - i) \ \prod_{i=0}^{B_u-1}(N - 2x^* - i)}{\prod_{i=0}^{B_w-1}(V_w - i) \ \prod_{i=0}^{B_\ell-1}(V_\ell - i) \ \prod_{i=0}^{B_u-1}(V_u - i)}.$$

Wald's SPRT Wald (1945) leads to an elegant escalation method if the first round of Bernoulli sampling does not attain the risk limit: simply make another round of Bernoulli sampling, as described in Sect. 4. If the null hypothesis is true, then $\Pr\{\inf_k P_k < \alpha\} \le \alpha$, where k counts the rounds of Bernoulli sampling. That is, the risk limit remains conservative for any number of rounds of Bernoulli sampling.

3.2   Auditing Multiple Contests

The math extends to audits of multiple contests; we omit the derivation, but see, e.g., Lindeman and Stark (2012). The same sample can be used to audit any number of contests simultaneously. The audit proceeds to a full hand count unless every null hypothesis is rejected, that is, unless we conclude that *every* winner beat *every* loser in *every* audited contest. The chance of rejecting all those null hypotheses cannot be larger than the smallest chance of rejecting any of the individual hypotheses, because the probability of an intersection of events cannot be larger than the probability of any one of the events. The chance of rejecting any individual null hypothesis is at most the risk limit, α, if that hypothesis is true. Therefore the chance of the intersection is not larger than α if any contest outcome is incorrect: the overall risk limit is α, with no need to adjust for multiplicity.

4   Escalation

If the first round of Bernoulli sampling with rate p_0 does not generate strong evidence that the election outcome is correct, we have several options:

1. Conduct a full hand count.
2. Augment the sample with additional ballots selected in some manner, for instance, making additional rounds of Bernoulli sampling, possibly with different values of p.
3. Draw a new sample and use a different auditing method, *e.g.*, ballot-level comparison auditing.

The first approach is always conservative. Both the second and third approaches require some statistical care, as repeated testing introduces additional opportunities to wrongly conclude that an incorrect election outcome is correct.

To make additional rounds of Bernoulli sampling, it may help to keep track of which ballots have been inspected.[5] That might involve stamping audited ballots with "audited" in red ink, for example.

Section 2.1 shows that if we make an integral number of passes through the population of ballots, tossing a p_k-coin for each as-yet-unselected item (we only toss the coin for an item on the Kth pass if the coin has not landed heads for that item in any previous pass), then the resulting sample is a Bernoulli random sample with selection probability $p = 1 - \prod_{k=0}^{K-1}(1 - p_k)$. Conditional on the sample size n attained after K passes, every subset of size n is equally likely to be selected. Hence, the sample is conditionally a simple random sample of size n from the N ballots.

The SPRT applied to multi-round Bernoulli sampling is conservative: the unconditional chance of rejecting the null hypothesis if it is true is at most α, because, if the null is true, the chance that the SPRT exceeds $1/\alpha$ for *any* K is at most α.

The third approach allows us to follow BBP with a different, more efficient approach, such as ballot-level comparison auditing (Lindeman and Stark 2012). This may require steps to ensure that multiplicity does not make the risk larger than the nominal risk limit, *e.g.*, by adjusting the risk limit using Bonferroni's inequality.

5   Initial Sampling Rate

We would like to choose the initial sampling rate p_0 sufficiently large that a test of the hypothesis $N_w \leq N_\ell$ will have high power against the alternative $N_w = V_w, N_\ell = V_\ell$, with $V_w - V_\ell = c$ for modest margins $c > 0$, but not so large that we waste effort.

There is no analytical formula for the power of the sequential hypothesis test under this sampling procedure, but we can use simulation to estimate the sampling rates needed to have a high probability of confirming correctly reported election results. Table 1 gives the sampling rate p_0 needed to attain 80%, 90%, and 99% power for a 2-candidate race in which there are no undervotes or invalid

---

[5] Once ballots are aggregated in a precinct or scanned centrally, it is unlikely that they will stay in the same order.

votes, for a 5% risk limit and a variety of margins and contest sizes. The simulations assume that the reported vote totals are correct. The required p_0 may be prohibitively large for small races and tight margins; Sect. 7 shows that with high probability, even a 1% sampling rate would be sufficient to confirm the outcomes of the vast majority of U.S. federal races without further escalation.

The sequential probability ratio test in Sect. 3 is similar to the BRAVO RLA presented in Lindeman and Stark (2012) when the sampling rate is small relative to the population size. There are two differences between BRAVO and BBP: BBP incorporates information about the number of undervotes, invalid votes, or votes for candidates other than w and ℓ, and Bernoulli sampling is done without (as opposed to with) replacement. If every ballot has a valid vote either for w or for ℓ and the sampling rate is small relative to the population size, the expected workload of these two procedures is similar. The *average sample number* (ASN) (Wald 1945), the expected number of draws required either to accept or to reject the null hypothesis, for BRAVO using a risk limit α and margin m is approximately

$$\text{ASN} \approx \frac{2\ln(1/\alpha)}{m^2}.$$

This formula is valid when the sampling rate is low and the actual margin is not substantially smaller than the (reported) margin used as the alternative hypothesis.

The ASN gives a rule of thumb for choosing the initial sampling rate for BBP. For a risk limit of 5% and a margin of 5%, the ASN is about 2,400 ballots. For a margin of 10%, the ASN is about 600 ballots. These values are lower than the sample sizes implied by Table 1: the sampling rates in the table have a higher probability that the initial sample will be sufficient to conclude the audit, while a sampling rate based on the ASN will suffice a bit more than half of the time.[6] The ASN multiplied by 2–4 is a rough approximation to initial sample size needed to have roughly a 90% chance that the audit can stop without additional sampling, if the reported results are correct.

The ASN formula assumes that N_u is 0; value of p_0 should be adjusted to account for ballots that have votes for neither w nor ℓ (or for both w and ℓ). If $r = \frac{N_u}{N}$ is the fraction of such ballots, the initial sampling rate p_0 should be inflated by a factor of $\frac{1}{1-r}$. For example, if half of the ballots were undervotes or invalid votes, then double the sampling rate would be needed to achieve the same power as if all of the ballots were valid votes for either w or ℓ.

6   Implementation

6.1   Election Night Auditing

Previous approaches to auditing require a sampling frame (possibly stratified, *e.g.*, by mode of voting or county). That requires knowing how many ballots

---

[6] The distribution of the sample size is skewed to the right: the expected sample size is generally larger than the median sample size.

were cast and their locations. In contrast, Bernoulli sampling makes it possible
to start the audit at polling places immediately after the last vote has been cast
in that polling place, without even having to count the ballots cast in the polling
place. This has several advantages:

1. It parallelizes the auditing task and can take advantage of staff (and
   observers) who are already on site at polling places.
2. It takes place earlier in the chain of custody of the physical ballots, before the
   ballots are exposed to some risks of loss, addition, substitution, or alteration.
3. It may add confidence to election-night result reporting.

The benefit is largest if p_0 is large enough to allow the audit to complete
without escalating. Since reported margins will not be known on election night,
p_0 might be based on pre-election polls, or set to a fixed value. There is, of
course, a chance that the initial sample will not suffice to confirm outcomes,
either because the true margins are smaller than anticipated, or because the
election outcome is in fact incorrect.

Table 1. Estimated sampling rates needed for Bernoulli ballot polling for a
2-candidate race with a 5% risk limit. These simulations assume the reported margins
were correct.

True margin	Ballots cast	Sampling rate p to achieve ...		
		80% power	90% power	99% power
1%	100,000	55%	62%	77%
2%	100,000	23%	30%	46%
5%	100,000	5%	7%	12%
10%	100,000	2%	2%	4%
20%	100,000	1%	1%	1%
1%	1,000,000	10.4%	14.2%	24.2%
2%	1,000,000	2.9%	4.0%	7.5%
5%	1,000,000	0.5%	0.7%	1.3%
10%	1,000,000	0.2%	0.2%	0.4%
20%	1,000,000	0.1%	0.1%	0.1%
1%	10,000,000	1.15%	1.66%	3.11%
2%	10,000,000	0.30%	0.42%	0.84%
5%	10,000,000	0.05%	0.07%	0.13%
10%	10,000,000	0.02%	0.02%	0.04%
20%	10,000,000	0.01%	0.01%	0.01%

There are reasons polling-place BBP audits might not be desirable.

1. Pollworkers, election judges, and observers are likely to be tired and ready to go home when polls close.
2. The training required to conduct and to observe the audit goes beyond what poll workers and poll watchers usually receive.
3. Audit data need to be captured and communicated reliably to a central authority to compute the risk (and possibly escalate the audit) after election results are reported.

6.2 Vote-By-Mail and Provisional Ballots

The fact that Bernoulli sampling is a "streaming" algorithm may help simplify logistics compared with other sampling methods. For instance, Bernoulli sampling can be used with vote-by-mail (VBM) ballots and provisional ballots. Bernoulli sampling can also be used with provisional ballots. VBM and provisional ballots can be sampled as they arrive (after signature verification), or aggregated, *e.g.*, daily or weekly. Ballots do not need to be opened or examined immediately in order to be included in the sample: they can be set aside and inspected after election day or after their provisional status has been adjudicated. Any of these approaches yields a Bernoulli sample of all ballots cast in the election, provided the same value(s) of p are used throughout.

6.3 Geometric Skipping

In principle, one can implement Bernoulli sampling by actually rolling dice, or by assigning a $U[0, 1]$ random number to each ballot, independently across ballots. A ballot is in the sample if and only if its associated random number is less than or equal to p.

However, that places an unnecessarily high burden on the quality of the pseudorandom number generator—or on the patience of the people responsible for selecting ballots by mechanical means, such as by rolling dice. If the ballots are in physical groups (*e.g.*, all ballots cast in a precinct), it can be more efficient to put the ballots into some canonical order (for instance, the order in which they are bundled or stacked) and to rely on the fact that the *waiting times* between successes in independent Bernoulli(p) trials are independent Geometric(p) random variables: the chance that the next time the coin lands heads will be kth tosses after the current toss is $p(1 - p)^{k-1}$.

To select the sample, instead of generating a Bernoulli random variable for every ballot, we suggest generating a sequence of geometric random variables $Y_1, Y_2, \ldots$ The first ballot in the sample is the one in position Y_1 in the group, the second is the one in position $Y_1 + Y_2$, and so on. We continue in this way until $Y_1 + \ldots + Y_j$ is larger than the number of ballots in the group. This *geometric skipping* method is implemented in the software we provide.

6.4   Pseudorandom Number Generation

To draw the sample, we propose using a cryptographically secure PRNG based on the SHA-256 hash function, setting the seed using 20 rolls of 10-sided dice, in a public ceremony. This is the method that the State of Colorado uses to select the sample for risk-limiting audits.

This is a good choice for election audits for several reasons. First, given the initial seed, anyone can verify that the sequence of ballots audited is correct. Second, unless the seed is known, the ballots to be audited are unpredictable, making it difficult for an adversary to "game" the audit. Finally, this family of PRNGs produces high-quality pseudorandomness.

Implementations of SHA-256-based PRNGs are available in many languages, including Python and Javascript. The code we provide for geometric skipping relies on the `cryptorandom` Python library, which implements such a PRNG.

While Colorado sets the seed for the entire state in a public ceremony, it may be more secure to generate seeds for polling-place audits locally, after the ballots have been collated into stacks that determine their order for the purpose

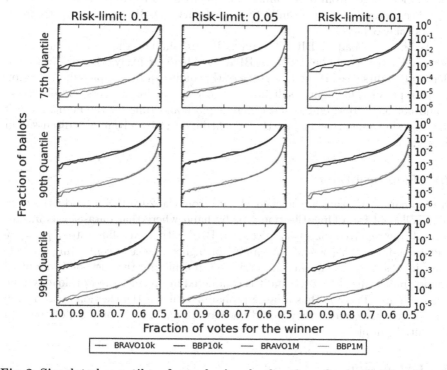

Fig. 2. Simulated quantiles of sample sizes by fraction of votes for the winner for a two candidate race in elections with 10,000 ballots and 1 million ballots, for BRAVO ballot-polling audits (BPA) and Bernoulli ballot polling audits (BBP), for various risk limits. The simulations assume every ballot has a valid vote for one of the two candidates.

of the audit. If the seed were known before the order of the ballots was fixed, an adversary might be able to arrange that the ballots selected for auditing reflect a dishonest outcome.

While the sequence of ballots selected by this method is verifiable, there is no obvious way to verify *post facto* that the ballots examined were the correct ones. Only observers of the audit can verify that. Observers' job would be easier if ballots were pre-stamped with (known) unique identifiers, but that might compromise vote anonymity.

7   Evaluation

As discussed in Sect. 5, we expect that *workload* (total number of ballots examined) for Bernoulli ballot polling to be approximately the same as BRAVO ballot polling. Figure 2 compares the fraction of ballots examined for BRAVO audits and BBP for a 2-candidate contest, estimated by simulation. The simulations use contest sizes of 10,000 and 1,000,000 ballots, each of which has either a valid vote for the winner or a valid vote for the loser. The percentage of votes for the winner ranges from 99% (almost all the votes go to the winner) to 50% (a tie). The methods produce similarly shaped curves; BBP requires slightly more ballots than BRAVO.

As the workload of BRAVO and BBP are similar, the cost of running a Bernoulli audit should be similar to BRAVO. There are likely other efficiencies to Bernoulli audits, *e.g.*, if the first stage of the audit can be completed on election night in parallel, it might result in lower cost as election workers and observers would not have to assemble in a different place and time for the audit. Even if the cost were somewhat higher, that might be offset by advantages discussed in Sect. 8.

7.1   Empirical Data

We evaluate BBP using precinct-level data from the 2016 U.S. presidential election, collected from OpenElections[7] or by hand where that dataset was incomplete. If the reported margins are correct, BBP with a sampling rate of $p_0 = 1\%$ and a risk-limit of 5% would have a 99% or higher chance of confirming the outcome in 42 states. The mean sample size per precinct for this method is about 10 ballots, indicating that if the audit is conducted in-precinct the workload will be fairly minute. There is thus a large probability that if the election outcomes in those states are correct, they would not have to audit additional ballots beyond the initial sample.

8   Discussion

Bernoulli ballot polling has a number of practical advantages. We have discussed several throughout the paper, but we review all of them here:

---

[7] http://openelections.net/, last visited 8/5/19.

- It reduces the need for a ballot manifest: ballots can be stored in any order, and the number of ballots in a given container or bundle does not need to be known to draw the sample.
- The work can be conducted in parallel across polling places, and can be performed by workers (and observed by members of the public) already in place on election day.
- The same sampling method can be used for polling places, vote centers, VBM, and provisional ballots, without the need to stratify the sample explicitly.
- If the initial sampling rate is adequate, the winners can be confirmed shortly after voting finishes—perhaps even at the same time that results are announced—possibly increasing voter confidence.
- When a predetermined expected sampling rate is used, the labor required can be estimated in advance, assuming escalation is not required. With appropriate parameter choices, escalation can be avoided except in unusually close races, or when the reported outcome is wrong. This helps election officials plan.
- If the sampling rate is selected after the reported margin is known, officials can choose a rate that makes escalation unlikely unless the reported electoral outcome is incorrect.
- The sampling approach is conceptually easy to grasp: toss a coin for each ballot. The audit stops when the sample shows a sufficiently large margin for every winner over every loser, where "sufficiently large" depends on the sample size.
- The approach may have security advantages, since waiting longer to audit would leave more opportunity for the paper ballots to be compromised or misplaced. Workers will need to handle the ballot papers in any case to move them from the ballot boxes into long-term storage.

Officials selecting an auditing method should weigh these advantages against some potential downsides of our approach, particularly when applied in polling places on election night. Poll workers are already very busy, and they may be too tired at the end of the night to conduct the sampling procedure or to do it accurately. When audits are conducted in parallel at local polling places, it is impossible for an individual observer to witness all the simultaneous steps. Moreover, estimating the sample size before margins are known makes it likely that workers will end up sampling more (or fewer) ballots than necessary to achieve the risk limit. While sampling too little can be overcome with escalation, the desire to avoid escalation may make officials err on the side of caution and sample more than predicted to be necessary, further reducing expected efficiency.

8.1 Previous Work

Bernoulli sampling is a special case of Poisson sampling, where sampling units are selected independently, but not necessarily with equal probability. Aslam et al. (2008) propose a Poisson sampling method in which the probability of selecting a given unit is related to a bound on the error that unit could hide.

Their method is not an RLA: it is designed to have a large chance of detecting at least one error if the outcome is incorrect, rather than to limit the risk of certifying an incorrect outcome *per se*.

8.2 Stratified Audits

Independent Bernoulli samples from different populations using the same rate still yields a Bernoulli sample of the overall population, so the math presented here can be used without modification to audit contests that cross jurisdictional boundaries. Bernoulli samples from different strata using different rates can be combined using SUITE (Ottoboni et al. 2018), which can be applied to stratum-wise *P*-values from any method, including BBP. (This requires minor modifications to the *P*-value calculations, to test arbitrary hypotheses about the margin in each stratum rather than to test for ties; the derivations in Ottoboni et al. (2018) apply, *mutatis mutandis*.) If some ballots are tabulated using technology that makes a more efficient auditing approach possible, such as a ballot-level comparison audit, it may be advantageous to stratify the ballots into groups, sample using Bernoulli sampling in some and a different method in others, and use SUITE to combine the results into an overall RLA.

9 Conclusion

We presented a new ballot-polling RLA based on Bernoulli sampling, relying on Wald's sequential probability ratio test to calculate the risk limit. The new method performs similarly to the BRAVO ballot-polling audit but has several logistical advantages, including that it can be parallelized and conducted on election night, which may reduce cost and increase security. The method easily incorporates VBM and provisional ballots, and may eliminate the need for stratification in many circumstances. Bernoulli ballot-polling with just a 1% sampling rate would have sufficed to confirm the 2016 U.S. Presidential election results in the vast majority of states, if the reported results were correct. The practical benefits and conceptual simplicity of Bernoulli ballot polling may make it simpler to conduct risk-limiting audits in real elections.

References

Aslam, J.A., Popa, R.A., Rivest, R.L.: On auditing elections when precincts have different sizes. In: 2008 USENIX/ACCURATE Electronic Voting Technology Workshop, San Jose, CA, 28–29 July 2008

Blaze, M., Braun, J., Hursti, H., Lorenzo Hall, J., MacAlpine, M., Moss, J.: DEFCON 25 Voting Village Report, September 2017. https://www.defcon.org/images/defcon-25/DEF%20CON%2025%20voting%20village%20report.pdf

Blaze, M., Braun, J., Hursti, H., Jefferson, D., MacAlpine, M., Moss, J.: DEFCON 26 Voting Village Report, September 2018. https://www.defcon.org/images/defcon-26/DEF%20CON%2026%20voting%20village%20report.pdf

Bowen, D.: Top-to-bottom review of voting machines certified for use in California. Technical report, California Secretary of State (2007). https://www.sos.ca.gov/elections/voting-systems/oversight/top-bottom-review/

Cochran, W.G.: Sampling Techniques, 3rd edn. Wiley, Hoboken (1977)

Lindeman, M., Stark, P.B.: A gentle introduction to risk-limiting audits. IEEE Secur. Priv. **10**, 42–49 (2012)

Lindeman, M., Stark, P.B., Yates, V.: BRAVO: ballot-polling risk-limiting audits to verify outcomes. In: 2011 Electronic Voting Technology Workshop/Workshop on Trustworthy Elections (EVT/WOTE 2012). USENIX (2012)

Lindeman, M., McBurnett, N., Ottoboni, K., Stark, P.B.: Next steps for the colorado risk-limiting audit (CORLA) program, March 2018. https://arxiv.org/pdf/1803.00698.pdf

Lohr, S.: Sampling: Design and Analysis. Nelson Education, Toronto (2009)

McDaniel, P., Blaze, M., Vigna, G.: EVEREST: evaluation and validation of election-related equipment, standards and testing. Technical report, Ohio Secretary of State (2007). http://siis.cse.psu.edu/everest.html

Ottoboni, K., Stark, P.B., Lindeman, M., McBurnett, N.: Risk-limiting audits by stratified union-intersection tests of elections (SUITE). In: Krimmer, R., et al. (eds.) E-Vote-ID 2018. LNCS, vol. 11143, pp. 174–188. Springer, Cham (2018). https://doi.org/10.1007/978-3-030-00419-4_12

Panel on Nonstandard Mixtures of Distributions: Statistical Models and Analysis in Auditing: A Study of Statistical Models and Methods for Analyzing Nonstandard Mixtures of Distributions in Auditing. National Academy Press, Washington, D.C. (1988)

Rivest, R.L.: ClipAudit: a simple risk-limiting post-election audit (2017). https://arxiv.org/abs/1701.08312

Särndal, C.-E., Swensson, B., Wretman, J.: Model Assisted Survey Sampling. Springer Series in Statistics. Springer, New York (2003)

Stark, P.B.: Conservative statistical post-election audits. Ann. Appl. Stat. **2**(2), 550–581 (2008)

Stark, P.B., Teague, V.: Verifiable European elections: risk-limiting audits for D'Hondt and its relatives. JETS USENIX J. Election Technol. Syst. **3**(1), 18–39 (2014)

Thompson, M.: Theory of Sample Surveys, Monographs on Statistics and Applied Probability, vol. 74. Chapman & Hall, London (1997)

U.S. Senate Select Committee on Intelligence: Russian targeting of election infrastructure during the 2016 election: Summary of initial findings and recommendations, May 2018. www.burr.senate.gov/imo/media/doc/RussRptInstlmt1-%20ElecSec%20Findings,Recs2.pdf

Wald, A.: Sequential tests of statistical hypotheses. Ann. Math. Stat. **16**, 117–186 (1945)

k-Cut: A Simple Approximately-Uniform Method for Sampling Ballots in Post-election Audits

Mayuri Sridhar[✉] and Ronald L. Rivest

Massachusetts Institute of Technology, Cambridge, MA 02139, USA
mayuri@mit.edu, rivest@csail.mit.edu

Abstract. We present an approximate sampling framework and discuss how risk-limiting audits can compensate for these approximations, while maintaining their "risk-limiting" properties. Our framework is general and can compensate for counting mistakes made during audits.

Moreover, we present and analyze a simple approximate sampling method, "k-cut", for picking a ballot randomly from a stack, without counting. Our method involves doing k "cuts," each involving moving a random portion of ballots from the top to the bottom of the stack, and then picking the ballot on top. Unlike conventional methods of picking a ballot at random, k-cut does not require identification numbers on the ballots or counting many ballots per draw. We analyze how close the distribution of chosen ballots is to the uniform distribution, and design mitigation procedures. We show that $k = 6$ cuts is enough for a risk-limiting election audit, based on empirical data, which provides a significant increase in sampling efficiency. This method has been used in pilot RLAs in Indiana and is scheduled to be used in Michigan pilot audits in December 2018.

Keywords: Sampling · Elections · Auditing · Post-election audits · Risk-limiting audit · Bayesian audit

1 Introduction

The goal of post-election tabulation audits is to provide assurance that the reported results of the contest are correct; that is, they agree with the results that a full hand-count would reveal. To do this, the auditor draws ballots uniformly at random one at a time from the set of all cast paper ballots, until the sample of ballots provides enough assurance that the reported outcomes are correct.

The most popular post-election audit method is known as a "risk-limiting audit" (or RLA), invented by Stark (see his web page [13]). See also [3,5–7,11,12]

Supported by Center for Science of Information (CSoI), an NSF Science and Technology Center, under grant agreement CCF-0939370.

A. Bracciali et al. (Eds.): FC 2019 Workshops, LNCS 11599, pp. 242–256, 2020.
https://doi.org/10.1007/978-3-030-43725-1_17

for explanations, details, and related papers. An RLA takes as input a "risk-limit" α (like 0.05), and ensures that if a reported contest outcome is incorrect, then this error will be detected and corrected with probability at least $1 - \alpha$.

This paper provides a novel method for drawing a random sample of the cast paper ballots. The new method may often be more efficient than standard methods. However, it has a cost: ballots are drawn in a way that is only "approximately uniform". This paper provides ways of compensating for such non-uniformity.

There are two standard approaches for drawing a random sample of cast paper ballots:

1. **[ID-based sampling]**. Print on each scanned cast paper ballot a unique identifying number (ballot ID numbers). Draw a random sample of ballot ID numbers, and retrieve the corresponding ballots.
2. **[Position-based sampling]**. Give each ballot an implicit ballot ID equal to its position, then proceed as with method (1).

These methods work well, and are guaranteed to produce random samples. In practice, auditors use software, like [14], which takes in a ballot manifest as input and produces the random sample of ballot ID numbers. In this software, it is typically assumed that sampling is done without replacement.

However, finding even a single ballot using these sampling methods can be tedious and awkward in practice. For example, given a random sample of ID numbers, one may need to count or search through a stack of ballots to find the desired ballot with the right ID or at the right position. Moreover, typical auditing procedures assume that there are no mistakes when finding the ballots for the sample. Yet, this seems to be an unreasonable assumption - a study by Goggin et al. shows that when counting 120 ballots, human teams miscount the number of votes for a given candidate at an average rate of 1.4% [4]. In the literature about RLAs, there is no way to correct for these mistakes.

Our Goal Is to Simplify the Sampling Process

In particular, we define a general framework for compensating for "approximate sampling" in RLAs. Our framework of approximate sampling can be used to measure and compensate for human error rate while using the counting methods outlined above. Moreover, we also define a simpler approach for drawing a random sample of ballots, which does not rely on counting at all. Our technique is simple and easy to iterate on and may be of particular interest when the stack of ballots to be drawn from is large. We define mitigation procedures to account for the fact that the sampling technique is no longer uniformly random.

Overview of This Paper. Section 2 introduces the relevant notation that we use throughout the paper.

Section 3 presents our proposed sampling method, called "*k*-cut."

Section 4 studies the distribution of single cut sizes, and provides experimental data. We then show how iterating a single cut provides improved uniformity for ballot selection.

Section 5 discusses the major questions that are brought up when using "approximate" sampling in a post-election audit.

Section 6 proves a very general result: that any general statistical auditing procedure for an arbitrary election can be adapted to work with approximate sampling, with simple mitigation procedures.

Section 7 discusses how to adapt the k-cut method for sampling when the ballots are organized into multiple stacks or boxes.

Section 8 provides some guidance for using k-cut in practice.

Section 9 gives some further discussion, lists some open problems, and makes some suggestions for further research.

Section 10 summarizes our contributions.

2   Notation and Election Terminology

Notation. We let $[n]$ denote the set $\{0, 1, \ldots, n-1\}$, and we let $[a, b]$ denote the set $\{a, a+1, \ldots, b-1\}$.

We let $\mathcal{U}[n]$ denote the uniform distribution over the set $[n]$. In $\mathcal{U}[n]$, the "$[n]$" may be omitted when it is understood to be $[n]$, where n is the number of ballots in the stack. We let $\mathcal{U}[a, b]$ denote the uniform distribution over the set $[a, b]$.

We let $VD(p, q)$ denote the variation distance between probability distributions p and q; this is the maximum, over all events E, of

$$Pr_p[E] - Pr_q[E].$$

Election Terminology. The term "ballot" here means to a single piece of paper on which the voter has recorded a choice for each contest for which the voter is eligible to vote. One may refer to a ballot as a "card." Multi-card ballots are not discussed in this paper.

Audit Types. There are two kinds of post-election audits: *ballot-polling* audits, and *ballot-comparison* audits, as described in [7]. For our purposes, these types of audits are equivalent, since they both need to sample paper ballots at random, and can make use of the k-cut method proposed here. However, if one wishes to use k-cut sampling in a comparison audit, one would need to ensure that each paper ballot contains a printed ID number that could be used to locate the associated electronic CVR.

3   The k-Cut Method

The problem to be solved is:

How can one select a single ballot (approximately) at random from a given stack of n ballots?

This section presents the "*k*-cut" sampling procedure for doing such sampling. The *k*-cut procedure does not need to know the size n of the stack, nor does it need any auxiliary random number generators or technology.

We assume that the collection of ballots to be sampled from is in the form of a stack. These may be ballots stored in a single box or envelope after scanning. One may think of the stack of ballots as being similar to a deck of cards. When the ballots are organized into *multiple* stacks, sampling is slightly more complex—see Sect. 7.

The basic operation for drawing a single ballot is called "*k*-cut and pick," or just "*k*-cut." This method does k cuts then draws the ballot at the top of the stack.

To make a single cut of a given stack of n paper ballots:

- Cut the stack into two parts: a "top" part and a "bottom" part.
- Switch the order of the parts, so what was the bottom part now sits above the top part. The relative order of the ballots within each part is preserved.

We let t denote the size of the top part. The size t of the top part should be chosen "fairly randomly" from the set $[n] = \{0, 1, 2, \ldots, n-1\}$[1]. In practice, cut sizes are probably not chosen so uniformly; so in this paper we study ways to compensate for non-uniformity. We can also view the cut operation as one that "rotates" the stack of ballots by t positions.

An Example of a Single Cut. As a simple example, if the given stack has $n = 5$ ballots:

$$\boxed{\text{A B C D E}},$$

where ballot A is on top and ballot E is at the bottom, then a cut of size $t = 2$ separates the stack into a top part of size 2 and a bottom part of size 3:

$$\boxed{\text{A B}} \quad \boxed{\text{C D E}}$$

whose order is then switched:

$$\boxed{\text{C D E}} \quad \boxed{\text{A B}}.$$

Finally, the two parts are then placed together to form the final stack:

$$\boxed{\text{C D E A B}}.$$

having ballot C on top.

Iteration for k cuts. The *k*-cut procedure makes k successive cuts then picks the ballot at the top of the stack.

If we let t_i denote the size of the i-th cut, then the net rotation amount after k cuts is

$$r_k = t_1 + t_2 + \cdots + t_k \pmod{n}. \tag{1}$$

The ballot originally in position r_k (where the top ballot position is position 0) is now at the top of the stack. We show that even for small values of k (like $k = 6$) the distribution of r_k is close to $\mathcal{U}$.

---

[1] A cut of size n is excluded, as it is equivalent to a cut of size 0.

Drawing a Sample of Multiple Ballots. To draw a sample of s ballots, our k-cut procedure repeats s times the operation of drawing without replacement a single ballot "at random." The s ballots so drawn form the desired sample.

Efficiency. Suppose a person can make six ("fairly random") cuts in approximately 15 s, and can count 2.5 ballots per second[2]. Then k-cut (with $k = 6$) is more efficient when the number of ballots that needs to be counted is 37.5 or more. Since batch sizes in audits are often large, k-cut has the potential to increase sampling speed.

For instance, assume that ballots are organized into boxes, each of which contains at least 500 ballots. Then, when the counting method is used, 85% of the time a ballot between ballot #38 and ballot #462 will be chosen. In such cases, one must count at least 38 ballots from the bottom or from the top to retrieve a single ballot. This implies that k-cut is more efficient 85% of the time.

As the number of ballots per box increases, the expected time taken by standard methods to retrieve a single ballot increases. With k-cut, the time it takes to select a ballot is *constant*, independent of the number of ballots in the box, assuming that each cut takes constant time.

Security. We assume that the value of k is **fixed** in advance; you can not allow the cutter to stop cutting once a "ballot they like" is sitting on top.

4   (Non)-Uniformity of Single Ballot Selection

We begin by observing that if an auditor could perform "perfect" cuts, we would be done. That is, if the auditor could pick the size t of a cut in a perfectly uniform manner from $[n]$, then one cut would suffice to provide a perfectly uniform distribution of the ballot selected from the stack of size n. However, there is no *a priori* reason to believe that, even with sincere effort, an auditor could pick t in a perfectly uniform manner.

So, we start by studying the properties of the k-cut procedure for single-ballot selection, beginning with a study of the non-uniformity of selection for the case $k = 1$ and extending our analysis to multiple cuts.

4.1   Empirical Data for Single Cuts

This section presents our experimental data on single-cut sizes. We find that in practice, single cut sizes (that is, for $k = 1$) are "somewhat uniform." We then show that the approximation to uniformity improves dramatically as k increases.

We had two subjects, the authors. Each author had a stack of 150 sequentially numbered ballots to cut, provided by Marion County, Indiana. The authors made 1680 cuts in total. Figure 1 shows the observed cut size frequency distribution. The complete data tables are provided in the longer version of this paper[3].

---

[2] These assumptions are based on observations during the Indiana pilot audits.

[3] The longer version is available at https://arxiv.org/abs/1811.08811.

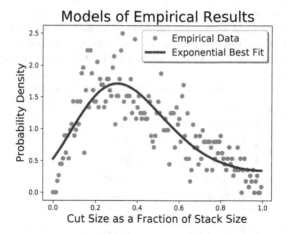

Fig. 1. Probability Density of empirical distribution of sizes of single cuts, using combined data from both authors, with 1680 cuts total. The model that best fit the empirical data was an exponential model, shown in blue. The extended paper provides more details about this and other models for our data. (Color figure online)

If the cuts were truly random, we would expect a uniform distribution of the number of cuts observed as a function of cut size. In practice, the frequency of cuts was not evenly distributed; there were few or no very large or very small cuts, and smaller cuts were more common than larger cuts.

4.2   Making *k* Successive Cuts to Select a Single Ballot

As noted, the distribution of cut sizes for a single cut is noticeably non-uniform. Our proposed *k*-cut procedure addresses this by iterating the single-cut operation *k* times, for some small fixed integer *k*.

We assume for now that cut sizes are distributed as in our experiments, as described in Fig. 1, and that successive cuts are independent. Moreover, we assume that sampling is done with replacement, for simplicity.

We give computational results showing that as the number of cuts increases, the *k*-cut procedure selects ballots with a distribution that approaches the uniform distribution. We compare by computing the variation distance of the *k*-cut distribution from $\mathcal{U}$ for various *k*. We also computed ϵ, the maximum ratio of the probability of drawing any particular ballot under the empirical distribution, to the probability of drawing that ballot under the uniform distribution, minus one[4]. Our results are summarized in Table 1.

We can see that, after six cuts, we get a variation distance of about 7.19×10^{-4}, for the empirical distribution, which is often small enough to justify our recommendation that six cuts being "close enough" in practice, for any RLA.

---

[4] In Sect. 6.4, we discuss why this value of ϵ is relevant.

Table 1. Convergence of k-cut to uniform with increasing k. Variation distance from uniform and ϵ-values for k cuts, as a function of k, for $n = 150$, where ϵ is one less than the maximum ratio of the probability of selecting a ballot under the assumed distribution to the probability of selecting that ballot under the uniform distribution.

k	Variation distance	Max ratio minus one
1	0.247	1.5
2	0.0669	0.206
3	0.0215	0.0687
4	0.0069	0.0224
5	0.00223	0.00699
6	**0.000719**	**0.00225**
7	0.000232	0.000729
8	7.49e−05	0.000235

4.3 Asymptotic Convergence to Uniform with k

As k increases, the distribution of cut sizes provably approaches the uniform distribution, under mild assumptions about the distribution of cut sizes for a single cut and the assumption of independence of successive cuts.

This claim is plausible, given the analysis of similar situations for continuous random variables. For example, Miller and Nigrini [9] have analyzed the summation of independent random variables modulo 1, and given necessary and sufficient conditions for this sum to converge to the uniform distribution.

For the discrete case, one can show that if once k is large enough that every ballot is selected by k-cut with some positive probability, then as k increases the distribution of cut sizes for k-cut approaches $\mathcal{U}$. Furthermore, the rate of convergence is exponential. The proof details are omitted here; however, the second claim uses Markov-chain arguments, where each rotation amount is a state, and the fact that the transition matrix is doubly stochastic.

5   Approximate Sampling

We have shown in the previous section that as we iterate our k-cut procedure, our distribution becomes quite close to the uniform distribution. However, our sampling still is not exactly uniform.

The literature on post-election audits generally assumes that sampling is perfect. One exception is the paper by Banuelos and Stark [2], which suggests dealing conservatively with the situation when one can not find a ballot in an audit, by treating the missing ballot as if it were a vote for the runner-up. Our proposed mitigation procedures are similar in flavor.

In practice, sampling for election audits is often done using software such as that by Stark [14] or Rivest [10]. Given a random seed and a number n of ballots to sample from, they can generate a pseudo-random sequence of integers from [*n*], indexing into a list of ballot positions or ballot IDs. It is reasonable to treat such cryptographic sampling methods as "indistinguishable from sampling uniformly," given the strength of the underlying cryptographic primitives.

However, in this paper we deal with sampling that is not perfect; the *k*-cut method with $k = 1$ is obviously non-uniform, and even with modest *k* values, as one might use in practice, there will be some small deviations from uniformity.

Thus, we address the following question:

> How can one effectively use an approximate sampling procedure in a post-election audit?

We let $\mathcal{G}$ denote the actual ("approximate") probability distribution over [*n*] from the sampling method chosen for the audit. Our analyses assume that we have some bound on how close $\mathcal{G}$ is to $\mathcal{U}$, like variation distance. Furthermore, the quality of the approximation may be controllable, as it is with *k*-cut: one can improve the closeness to uniform by increasing *k*. We let $\mathcal{G}^s$ denote the distribution on *s*-tuples of ballots from [*n*] chosen with replacement according to the distribution $\mathcal{G}$ for each draw.

6   Auditing Arbitrary Contests

This section proves a general result: for auditing an arbitrary contest, we show that *any* risk-limiting audit can be adapted to work with approximate sampling, if the approximate sampling is close enough to uniform. In particular, any RLA can work with the *k*-cut method, if *k* is large enough.

We show that if *k* is sufficiently large, the resulting distribution of *k*-cut sizes will be so close to uniform that any statistical procedure cannot efficiently distinguish between the two. That is, we want to choose *k* to guarantee that $\mathcal{U}$ and $\mathcal{G}$ are close enough, so that any statistical procedure behaves similarly on samples from each.

Previous work done by Baignères in [1] shows that, there is an optimal distinguisher between two finite probability distributions, which depends on the KL-Divergence between the two distributions.

We follow a similar model to this work, however, we develop a bound based on the variation distance between $\mathcal{U}$ and $\mathcal{G}$.

6.1   General Statistical Audit Model

We construct the following model, summarized in Fig. 2.

We define δ to be the variation distance between $\mathcal{G}$ and $\mathcal{U}$. We can find an upper bound for δ empirically, as seen in Table 1. If $\mathcal{G}$ is the distribution of *k*-cut, then by increasing *k* we can make δ arbitrarily small.

The audit procedure requires a sample of some given size *s*, from $\mathcal{U}^s$ or $\mathcal{G}^s$. We assume that all audits behave deterministically. We do not assume that successive draws are independent, although we assume that each cut is independent.

Given the size *s* sample, the audit procedure can make a decision on whether to accept the reported contest result, escalate the audit, or declare an upset.

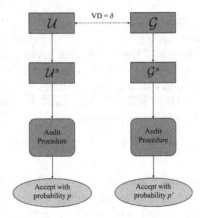

Fig. 2. Overview of uniform vs. approximate sampling effects, for any statistical auditing procedure. The audit procedure can be viewed as a distinguisher between the two underlying distributions. If it gives significantly different results for the two distributions, it can thereby distinguish between them. However, if p and p' are extremely close, then the audit cannot be used as a distinguisher.

6.2   Mitigation Strategy

When we use approximate sampling, instead of uniform, we need to ensure that the "risk-limiting" properties of the RLAs are maintained. In particular, as described in [7], an RLA with a risk limit of α guarantees that with probability at least $(1 - \alpha)$ the audit will find and correct the reported outcome if it is incorrect. We want to maintain this property, while introducing approximate sampling.

Without loss of generality, we focus on the probability that the audit accepts the reported result, since it is the case where approximate sampling may affect the risk-limiting properties. We show that $\mathcal{G}$ and $\mathcal{U}$ are sufficiently close when k is large, that the difference between p and p', as seen in Fig. 2, is small.

We show a simple mitigation procedure, for RLA plurality elections, to compensate for this non-uniformity, that we denote as **risk-limit adjustment.** For RLAs, we can simply decrease the risk limit α by $|p' - p|$ (or an upper bound on this) to account for the difference. This decrease in the risk limit can accommodate the risk that the audit behaves incorrectly due to approximate sampling.

6.3   How Much Adjustment Is Required?

We assume we have an auditing procedure $\mathbb{A}$, which accepts samples and outputs "accept" or "reject". We model approximate sampling with providing $\mathbb{A}$ samples from a distribution $\mathcal{G}$. For our analysis, we look at the empirical distribution of cuts. For uniform sampling, we provide $\mathbb{A}$ samples from $\mathcal{U}$.

We would like to show that the probability that $\mathbb{A}$ accepts an outcome incorrectly, given samples from $\mathcal{G}$ is not much higher than the probability that $\mathbb{A}$

accepts an incorrect outcome, given samples from $\mathcal{U}$. We denote $\mathbb{B}$ as the set of ballots that we are sampling from.

Theorem 1. *Given a fixed sample size s and the variation distance δ, the maximum change in probability that $\mathbb{A}$ returns "accept" due to approximate sampling is at most*

$$\epsilon_1 + (1 + n\delta)^{s'} - 1,$$

where s' is the maximum number of "successes" seen in s Bernoulli trials, where each has a success probability of δ, with probability at least $1 - \epsilon_1$.

Proof. We define s as the number of ballots that we pull from the set of cast ballots, before deciding whether or not to accept the outcome of the election. Given a sample size s, based on our sampling technique, we draw s ballots, one at a time, from $\mathcal{G}$ or from $\mathcal{U}$.

We model drawing a ballot from $\mathcal{G}$ as first drawing a ballot from $\mathcal{U}$; however, with probability δ, we replace the ballot we draw from $\mathcal{U}$ with a new ballot from $\mathbb{B}$ following a distribution $\mathbb{F}$. We make no further assumptions about the distribution $\mathbb{F}$, which aligns with our definition of variation distance. When drawing from $\mathcal{G}$, for any ballot $b \in \mathbb{B}$, we have probability at most $\frac{1}{n} + \delta$ of drawing b.

When we sample sequentially, we get a length-s sequence of ballot IDs, S, for each of $\mathcal{G}$ and $\mathcal{U}$. Throughout this model, we assume that we sample with replacement, although similar bounds should hold for sampling without replacement, as well. We define X as the list of indices in the sequence S where both $\mathcal{G}$ and $\mathcal{U}$ draw the same ballot, in order. We define Z as the list of indices where $\mathcal{G}$ has "switched" a ballot after the initial draw. That is, for a fixed draw, $\mathcal{U}$ might produce the sample sequence $[1, 5, 29]$. Meanwhile, $\mathcal{G}$ might produce the sample sequence $[1, 5, 30]$. For this example, $X = [0, 1]$ and $Z = [2]$.

We define the set of possible size-s samples as the set D. We choose s' such that for any given value ϵ_1, the probability that $|Z|$ is larger than s' is at most ϵ_1. Using this set up, we can calculate an upper bound on the probability that $\mathbb{A}$ returns "accept". In particular, given the empirical distribution, the probability that $\mathbb{A}$ returns "accept" for a deterministic auditing procedure becomes

$$\Pr[\mathbb{A} \; accepts \mid \mathcal{G}] = \sum_{S \in D} \Pr[\mathbb{A} \; accepts \mid S] * \Pr[draw \; S \mid \mathcal{G}].$$

Now, we note that we can split up the probability that we can draw a specific sample S from the distribution $\mathcal{G}$. We know that with high probability, there are at most s' ballots being "switched". Thus,

$$\Pr[\mathbb{A} \; accepts \mid \mathcal{G}] = \sum_{S \in D} \Pr[\mathbb{A} \; accepts \mid S] * \Pr[draw \; S \mid \mathcal{G}, S \; has \; \leq s' \; \text{"switched" ballots}]$$

$$* \Pr[S \; has \; \leq s' \; \text{"switched" ballots}] + \sum_{S \in D} \Pr[\mathbb{A} \; accepts \mid S] * \Pr[draw$$

$$S \mid \mathcal{G}, S \; has \; > s' \; \text{"switched" ballots}] * \Pr[S \; has \; > s' \; \text{"switched" ballots}].$$

Now, we note that the second term is upper bounded by

$$\Pr[\text{any size-}s \text{ sample has more than } s' \text{ switched ballots}].$$

We define the probability that any size-s sample contains more than s' switched ballots as ϵ_1.

We note that, although the draws aren't independent, from the definition of variation distance, this is upper bounded by the probability that a binomial distribution, with s draws and δ probability of success.

Now, we can focus on bounding the first term. We know that

$$\Pr[\mathbb{A} \text{ accepts} \mid \mathcal{G}, \text{any sample has at most } s' \text{ switched ballots}]$$

$$= \sum_{S \in D} \Pr[\mathbb{A} \text{ accepts} \mid S] * \Pr[draw \ S \mid \mathcal{G}, S \text{ has } \leq s' \text{ "switched" ballots}]$$

For the uniform distribution, we know that the probability of accepting becomes

$$\Pr[\mathbb{A} \text{ accepts} \mid \mathcal{U}] = \sum_{S \in D} \Pr[\mathbb{A} \text{ accepts} \mid S] * \Pr[draw \ S \mid \mathcal{U}].$$

Thus, we know that the change in probability becomes

$$\Pr[\mathbb{A} \text{ accepts} \mid \mathcal{G}] - \Pr[\mathbb{A} \text{ accepts} \mid \mathcal{U}] \leq \epsilon_1 + \sum_{S \in D} \Pr[\mathbb{A} \text{ accepts} \mid S](\Pr[draw \ S \mid \mathcal{G}, S \text{ has }$$

$$\leq s' \text{ "switched" ballots}] - \Pr[draw \ S \mid \mathcal{U}]).$$

However, for any fixed sample S, we know that we can produce S from E in many possible ways. That is, we know that we have to draw at least $s - s'$ ballots that are from $\mathcal{U}$. Then, we have to draw the compatible s' ballots from $\mathcal{G}$. In general, we define the possible length $s - s'$ compatible shared list of indices as the set $\mathbb{X}$. That is, by conditioning on $\mathbb{X}$, we are now defining the exact indices in the sample tally where the uniform and empirical sampling can differ. We note that $|\mathbb{X}| = \binom{s}{s'}$ and each possible set happens with equal probability. Then, for any specific $x \in \mathbb{X}$, we can define z as the remaining indices, which are allowed to differ from uniform and approximate sampling. That is, if there are 3 ballots in the sample, and $x = [0, 1]$, then $z = [2]$.

We can now calculate the probability that we draw some specific size-s sample S, given the empirical distribution, and a fixed value of s'.

$$\Pr[draw \ S \mid \mathcal{G}] = \sum_{x \in \mathbb{X}} \Pr[draw \ x \mid \mathcal{U}]$$

$$* \Pr[draw \ z \mid \mathcal{G}] * \Pr[\text{switched ballots are at indices in } z]$$

However, we know that for each ballot b in z, we draw ballot b with probability at most $\frac{1}{n} + \delta$. That is, for any ballot in x, we know that we draw it with uniform probability exactly. However, for a ballot b in z, we know that this a ballot that may have been "switched". In particular, with probability $\frac{1}{n}$, we draw the correct ballot from $\mathcal{U}$. However, in addition to this, with probability δ, we replace it with a new ballot - we assume that we replace it with the correct ballot with probability 1. Thus, with probability at most $\frac{1}{n} + \delta$, we draw the correct ballot for this particular slot. Thus, we get

$\Pr[draw\ S \mid \mathcal{G}]$

$= \sum_{x \in \mathbb{X}} \Pr[draw\ x \mid \mathcal{U}] * \Pr[draw\ z \mid \mathcal{G}] * \Pr[\text{switched ballots are at indices in } z]$

$\leq \sum_{x \in \mathbb{X}} \Pr[draw\ x \mid \mathcal{U}] * (\frac{1 + n\delta}{n})^{s'} * \Pr[\text{switched ballots are at indices in } z]$

$\leq (1 + n\delta)^{s'} \sum_{x \in \mathbb{X}} \Pr[draw\ x \mid \mathcal{U}] * \Pr[draw\ z \mid \mathcal{U}] * \Pr[\text{switched ballots are at indices in } z].$

Now, we note that there are $\binom{s}{s'}$ possible sequences $x \in \mathbb{X}$, where the "switched" ballots could be. Each of these possible sequences occurs with equal probability, this becomes

$\Pr[draw\ S \mid \mathcal{G}]$

$\leq (1 + n\delta)^{s'} \sum_{x \in \mathbb{X}} \Pr[draw\ x \mid \mathcal{U}] * \Pr[draw\ z \mid \mathcal{U}] * \Pr[\text{switched ballots are at indices in } z].$

$= (1 + n\delta)^{s'} \sum_{x \in \mathbb{X}} \Pr[draw\ x \mid \mathcal{U}] * \Pr[draw\ z \mid \mathcal{U}] * \frac{1}{\binom{s}{s'}}$

$= (1 + n\delta)^{s'} \Pr[draw\ S \mid \mathcal{U}].$

Using this bound we can calculate our total change in acceptance probability as:

$$\Pr[\mathbb{A}\ accepts \mid \mathcal{G}] - \Pr[\mathbb{A}\ accepts \mid \mathcal{U}]$$

$\leq \epsilon_1 + \sum_{S \in D} \Pr[\mathbb{A}\ accepts \mid S](\Pr[draw\ S \mid \mathcal{G}, S \text{ has} \leq s' \text{ "switched" ballots}] - \Pr[draw\ S \mid \mathcal{U}])$

$\leq \epsilon_1 + ((1 + n\delta)^{s'} - 1) \sum_{S \in D} \Pr[\mathbb{A}\ accepts \mid S] \Pr[draw\ S \mid \mathcal{U}]$

$\leq \epsilon_1 + (1 + n\delta)^{s'} - 1,$

which provides us the required bound.

6.4   Empirical Support

Our previous theorem gives us a total bound of our change in risk limit, which depends on our value of s' and δ. We note that, for each ballot b, we provide a general bound of a multiplicative factor increase of $(1 + n\delta)$, which is based off the variation distance of δ. However, we note that in practice, the exact bound we are looking for depends on the multiplicative increase in probability of a single ballot being chosen. That is, we can calculate the max increase in multiplicative ratio for a single ballot, compared to the uniform distribution.

Thus, if a ballot is chosen with probability at most $\frac{(1+\epsilon_2)}{n}$, then our bound on the change in probability becomes

$$\epsilon_1 + (1 + \epsilon_2)^{s'} - 1.$$

The values of ϵ_2 are recorded, for varying number of cuts in Table 1.

We can calculate the maximum change in probability for a varying number of cuts using this bound. Here, we analyze the case of 6 cuts. To get a bound on s', we can model how often we switch ballots. In particular, this follows a binomial distribution, with s independent trials, where each trial has a δ_6 probability of success. Using the binomial survival function, we see at most 4 "switched ballots" in 1,000 draws, with probability $(1 - 8.78 \times 10^{-4})$. From our previous argument, we know that our change in acceptance probability is at most $(1+\epsilon_2)^4 - 1$. Using our value of ϵ_2 for $k = 6$, this causes a change in probability of at most 0.0090.

Thus, the maximum possible change in probability of incorrectly accepting this outcome is $0.0090 + 8.78 \times 10^{-4}$, which is approximately 9.88×10^{-3}. We can compensate for this by adjusting our risk limit by less than 1%.

7   Multi-stack Sampling

Our discussion so far presumes that all cast paper ballots constitute a single "stack," and suggest using our proposed k-cut procedure is used to sample ballots from that stack. In practice, however, stacks have limited size, since large stacks are physically awkward to deal with. The collection of cast paper ballots is therefore often arranged into multiple stacks of some limited size.

The *ballot manifest* describes this arrangement of ballots into stacks, giving the number of such stacks and the number of ballots contained in each one. We assume that the ballot manifest is accurate. A tool like Stark's Tools for Risk-Limiting Audits[5] takes the ballot manifest (together with a random seed and the desired sample size) as input and produces a sampling plan.

A sampling plan describes exactly which ballots to pick from which stacks. That is, the sampling plan consists of a sequence of pairs, each of the form: (stack-number, ballot-id), where ballot-id may be either an id imprinted on the ballot or the position of the ballot in the stack (if imprinted was not done).

Modifying the sampling procedure to use k-cut is straightforward. We ignore the ballot-ids, and note only how many ballots are to be sampled from each stack. That number of ballots are then selected using k-cut rather than using the provided ballot-ids. For example, if the sampling plan says that 2 ballots are to be drawn from stack 5, then we ignore the ballot-ids for those specific ballots, and return 2 ballots drawn approximately uniformly at random using k-cut.

Thus, the fact that cast paper ballots may be arranged into multiple stacks (or boxes) does not affect the usability of k-cut for performing audits.

---

[5] https://www.stat.berkeley.edu/~stark/Vote/auditTools.htm.

8   Approximate Sampling in Practice

The major question when using the approximate sampling procedure is how to choose k. Choosing a small value of k makes the overall auditing procedure more efficient, since you save more time in each sample you choose. However, it requires more risk limit adjustment.

The risk limit mitigation procedure requires knowledge of the maximum sample size, which we denote as s^*, beforehand. We assume that the auditors have a reasonable procedure for estimating s^* for a given contest. One procedure to estimate s^* is to draw an initial sample, s, using uniform random sampling. Then, we can use a statistical procedure to approximate how many additional ballots we would need to finish the audit, assuming the rest of the ballots in the pool are similar to the sample. Possible statistical procedures include replicating the votes on the ballots, or using sample size estimates defined in [8].

Let us assume that we use one of these techniques and calculate that the audit is complete after an extension of size d. To be safe, we can assume that at most $3d$ additional samples will be needed. Thus, our final bound on s^* would be $s + 3d$. Given this upper bound, we can perform our mitigation procedures, assuming that we are drawing a sample of size s^*. Ballots after the first s^* ballots in our sample should be sampled uniformly at random.

9   Discussion and Open Problems

We would like to do more experimentation on the variation between individuals on their cut-size distributions. The current empirical results in this paper are based off of the cut distributions of just the two authors in the paper. We would like to test a larger group of people to better understand a variety of empirical distributions. After investigating this, we would like to develop "best practices" for using the k-cut procedure. That is, we'd like to develop a set of techniques that auditors can use to produce nearly-uniform single-cut-size distributions, which will make k-cut more efficient.

We would also like to run some experiments to test our assumptions for k-cut, in practice. For instance, we would like to test whether each cut is truly made independently.

In the longer version of the paper, we provide the full details of our empirical data, for full reproducibility. We also discuss possible models for our empirical data and the convergence rates of our models.

10   Conclusions

We have presented an approximate sampling procedure, k-cut, for use in post-election audits. We expect the use of k-cut will save time since it eliminates the need to count many ballots in a stack to find the desired one.

We showed that even for small values of k, our procedure provides a sample that is close to being chosen uniformly at random. We designed a simple mitigation procedure for RLAs that accounts for any remnant non-uniformity, by adjusting the risk limit. Finally, we provided a recommendation of $k = 6$ cuts to use in practice, for sample sizes up to 1,000 ballots, based on our empirical data, with a 1% risk limit adjustment.

An earlier version of k-cut was used in pilot audits in Marion County, Indiana to increase audit efficiency. This paper provides theoretical justification for this technique, which is also scheduled to be used in Michigan in December 2018.

References

1. Baignères, T., Vaudenay, S.: The complexity of distinguishing distributions. Ph.D. thesis (2008). results also in Baigneères'
2. Banuelos, J.H., Stark, P.B.: Limiting risk by turning manifest phantoms into evil zombies (2012). https://arxiv.org/abs/1207.3413
3. Bretschneider, J., et al.: Risk-limiting post-election audits: why and how? (ver. 1.1), October 2012. http://people.csail.mit.edu/rivest/pubs.html#RLAWG12
4. Goggin, S.N., Byrne, M.D., Gilbert, J.E.: Post-election auditing effects of procedure and ballot type on manual counting accuracy, efficiency, and auditor satisfaction and confidence. Election Law J. **11**, 36–51 (2012)
5. Johnson, K.: Election verification by statistical audit of voter-verified paper ballots, 31 October 2004. http://ssrn.com/abstract=640943
6. Lindeman, M., Halvorseon, M., Smith, P., Garland, L., Addona, V., McCrea, D.: Principle and best practices for post-election audits (2008). www.electionaudits.org/files/best%20practices%20final_0.pdf
7. Lindeman, M., Stark, P.B.: A gentle introduction to risk-limiting audits. IEEE Secur. Priv. **10**, 42–49 (2012)
8. Lindeman, M., Stark, P.B., Yates, V.S.: BRAVO: ballot-polling risk-limiting audits to verify outcomes. In: Halderman, A., Pereira, O. (eds.) Proceedings 2012 EVT/WOTE Conference (2012)
9. Miller, S.J., Nigrini, M.J.: The modulo 1 Central Limit Theorem and Benford's law for products (2007). https://arxiv.org/abs/math/0607686
10. Rivest, R.L.: Reference implementation code for pseudo-random sampler (2011). http://people.csail.mit.edu/rivest/sampler.py
11. Rivest, R.L.: Bayesian tabulation audits: explained and extended, 1 January 2018. https://arxiv.org/abs/1801.00528
12. Rivest, R.L., Shen, E.: A Bayesian method for auditing elections. In: Halderman, J.A., Pereira, O. (eds.) Proceedings 2012 EVT/WOTE Conference (2012). https://www.usenix.org/system/files/conference/evtwote12/rivest_bayes_rev_073112.pdf. https://www.usenix.org/conference/evtwote12/workshop-program/presentation/rivest
13. Stark, P.B.: Papers, talks, video, legislation, software, and other documents on voting and election auditing. https://www.stat.berkeley.edu/~stark/Vote/index.htm
14. Stark, P.B.: Tools for ballot-polling risk-limiting election audits (2017). https://www.stat.berkeley.edu/~stark/Vote/ballotPollTools.htm

How to Assess the Usability Metrics of E-Voting Schemes

Karola Marky[1]([✉])[iD], Marie-Laure Zollinger[2], Markus Funk[1][iD],
Peter Y. A. Ryan[2], and Max Mühlhäuser[1][iD]

[1] Telecooperation Lab, Technische Universität Darmstadt, Darmstadt, Germany
{marky,funk,max}@tk.tu-darmstadt.de
[2] University of Luxembourg, Luxembourg City, Luxembourg
{marie-laure.zollinger,peter.ryan}@uni.lu

Abstract. Voters play an important role in end-to-end verifiable e-voting schemes because the schemes encourage them to carry out several security-critical tasks by themselves. If the voters cannot complete the tasks by themselves or experience bad usability while executing them, vote manipulations by either a faulty software or deliberate attacks cannot be detected which renders verification useless. Therefore, the scheme's usability is of crucial importance and demands an early investigation of human factors when implementing e-voting systems. In this paper, we give an overview of user study design challenges when investigating end-to-end verifiable e-voting schemes. We provide guidelines that address these challenges and support researchers in the design of user studies. The guidelines are based on the literature and the authors' experiences.

Keywords: E-voting · Usability evaluation · End-to-end verifiability

1 Introduction

Vote integrity means that an election's result must accurately reflect the voters' true intentions. *End-to-end verifiability* [12] is a measure for vote integrity and provides means for the voters to verify that their intentions are accurately represented in the election's result. Implementing end-to-end verifiable e-voting schemes constitutes a particular challenge due to competing security requirements that have to be assured simultaneously. A particular opponent of verifiability is *vote privacy* meaning that the voting system does not provide more evidence about the intention of specific voters than the election result does [38].

To maintain the vote privacy in an end-to-end verifiable e-voting scheme, the voters have to carry out several tasks by themselves. Furthermore, they have to determine the result of the verification, i.e. whether a vote is manipulated or not, by themselves. Therefore, the voters play an active role in the security of the e-voting scheme, and the scheme's usability becomes of crucial importance.

A. Bracciali et al. (Eds.): FC 2019 Workshops, LNCS 11599, pp. 257–271, 2020.
https://doi.org/10.1007/978-3-030-43725-1_18

Vote verification typically is not present in traditional paper-based voting schemes, therefore, voters are likely not familiar with the tasks that are associated with it. Furthermore, voting is no everyday activity and any election includes a share of new voters. Hence, we cannot expect that training and learning can mitigate usability issues. As a consequence, the usability of any e-voting system has to be studied thoroughly before its usage in real elections.

In this paper, we present and discuss methods for assessing the usability metrics of end-to-end verifiable e-voting systems via user studies. Hereby, we focus on the tasks of vote casting and verification. We discuss quantitative metrics, demographic data and the user study setting based on past usability studies that we carried out and a detailed literature review. We show that determining the effectiveness of a verification constitutes a particular challenge and has to be considered from early on when planning and designing the user study. We deliberately exclude expert evaluations, such as walkthroughs [35], because they do not entail voters as study participants.

2   End-to-End Verifiable E-Voting Schemes

E-voting schemes are based on cryptographic protocols to provide security properties such as vote privacy or eligibility. Voters interacting with the e-voting scheme have no means to verify, that the scheme processed their votes correctly and therefore have to trust that correct processing occurs. End-to-end verifiable e-voting schemes [12] enable individual voters to verify that their votes have been processed correctly. Hereby, no trust in the voting scheme, the voters' personal computers, election officials, or external observers is required [6]. End-to-end verifiability can be subdivided[1] into the following components:

Cast-as-intended: the cast vote corresponds to the voter's intent.
Recorded-as-cast: the recorded vote matches the cast vote.
Tallied-as-recorded: that all recorded votes are correctly included in the tally.
Eligibility: that only the votes of eligible voters are tallied.

The tallied-as-recorded, as well as the eligibility verifiability, can be executed by observers and technically-adept users for all voters, because the information that is required to perform these verification types is publicly available, and only a certain share of voters or observers is required to do this. The recorded-as-cast verifiability has to be initiated by the voters since solely the voters know about their participation in the election. Therefore, they play an active part in this component. The most challenging component from the voters' perspective is given by the cast-as-intended verifiability. Because the voters' intents are protected by vote privacy, only the voters themselves can perform verification[2]. Furthermore,

---

[1] We use the subdivision for usability investigation purposes. Note, that the components alone do not replace end-to-end verifiability [14].

[2] A scheme for delegation has been proposed [17] whereby the complexity is shifted towards vote casting indicating that even if delegation is possible, human factors are still important.

they have to determine the outcome of the verification by themselves and act properly in case they uncover an incorrect vote.

3   The Impact of Usability

E-voting systems have been investigated in several works which confirm that the usability of the e-voting scheme is crucial. Errors rooted in a poor voting client usability can propagate to the tallying result and negatively impact the election's integrity. Therefore, poor usability renders all verification useless.

The usability of vote casting on early e-voting schemes, which are paper punch cards and lever machines, has been studied in several works [10,11,18,23]. Although paper ballots are superior in terms of usability, compared to paper punch cards and lever machines and have lower error rates than punch pards, lever machines and even Direct Recording Electronics (DREs) [10]. An investigation of different DREs, which are the computers used for voting in polling stations, reveals that between 1% and 8% of cast votes do not match the voters' true intentions [13,19] which could flip the outcome of a first-past-the-post election.

Several verifiable e-voting schemes have been investigated in the literature. Not all of the investigated themes offer end-to-end verifiability, but some degree of verifiability. Participants in a user study of the Norwegian e-voting scheme [22] could not determine whether their votes were submitted [20]. The usability of the BenalohChallenge was perceived as very poor [1], only between 10% and 43% of participants were able to complete verification [1,34,48] and the BenalohChallenge was proven to be ineffective from a game-theory perspective [15]. A comparative usability evaluation of three Internet voting schemes by Kulyk et al. [28], each of which had a different level of system security, revealed that participants were willing to sacrifice 26 points on the System Usability Scale [8] when they were informed about the different degrees of system security. The first scheme was a simple click form (the least secure), the second a return code scheme, and the third used a combination of voting and return codes (being the most secure).

4   Study Design Challenges

In this section, we describe study design challenges in the scope of e-voting systems, based on our study design experiences and the literature we provide guidelines to cope with these challenges. Since not all challenges can be addressed by a generic guideline, we use the challenges in the following section to derive guidelines for specific usability metrics.

4.1   Election Setting

The election setting is the specific election scenario that is provided to the participants within the study. It encompasses the election that the participant participates in, e.g., a university council or parliament election, the number of races and all aspects that concern the election and the participants' role in it.

Elections can have various stakes; governmental elections are high-stake whereas university council elections are usually low-stake. Simple polls, e.g., asking for food preferences, have an even lower stake. The stake of the election, however, can impact the participants' behaviors and the study's ecological validity, which refers to the extent to which the results of an experiment can be applied to real-world conditions [40]. Therefore, the setting can influence attitudes towards the usage of provided e-voting system features, such as verification.

Selker *et al.* [42] recommend, based on an analysis of previous voting user studies, that the study setting should be closely related to a real-world election to strengthen the ecological validity.

4.2   Participant Vote Privacy

Any user study collects data of the participants to assess the investigated scheme's usability. While some data collection methods target very specific data types (e.g., the time stamping of actions), others such as screen recording collect a plethora of data that might also be privacy-sensitive. The voting options that the study participants mark, can be part of these data and therefore the participants' vote privacy can be compromised depending on the study design and the measurements that are taken. Vote privacy, however, is a quite delicate aspect and the disclosure of voting preferences is forbidden by the law (e.g., [46]) and should, therefore, be also preserved in user studies. Participants are not aware of the vote privacy aspect and tend to vote for the same candidate as in a real election [47]. This introduces a trade-off between maintaining the participants' vote privacy and measurements. The examiners have to decide whether they wish to either maintain vote privacy by measurements that do not compromise it or adjust the study design to take the compromising measures. We will emphasize on vote privacy when we discuss different measurement methods in Sect. 5.

4.3   Social Acceptability Bias

The *social acceptability bias* [24, 37] is the tendency of participants to give socially acceptable answers rather than answering in a way that reflects their true opinions. Therefore, participants might act differently as they would act in a real election. This introduces a challenge in designing e-voting user studies, since the social acceptability bias could impact the user study results, especially in the scope of verification. A possibility to offset the social acceptability bias is the introduction of a fictitious research goal. Budurushi *et al.* [9] used a *cover story* and told participants in the study briefing that their goal was to investigate democracy development, the general acceptability of e-voting and usability. During the debriefing, the participants were told the actual research goal.

4.4   Mental Tasks

In any usability study, the researchers require knowledge about the correct execution of required tasks in order to able to measure deviations from the correct execution. The correct execution might contain specific tasks that cannot be measured directly. Particularly challenging are tasks that the participants perform mentally. For instance, the Benaloh Challenge requires the comparison of hash values and voting options. If both match, the verified vote was cast-as-intended, therefore, a user study needs to confirm whether participants indeed perform these tasks.

4.5 Demographic Data

Demographic data is data regarding the study participants and is necessary for the determination of whether the individuals in a particular study are a representative sample of the target population for generalization purposes. Demographic data, in general, include age, gender, occupation and education level. In e-voting specific studies the general demographic data is not sufficient since opinions and previous voting experiences can impact the study outcome.

Furthermore, the participants' attitudes regarding the usage of e-voting, in general, could impact their performance and answers in the user study. Therefore, the demographics questionnaire should include questions that ask for the participants' general attitudes towards e-voting.

4.6 Motivation Interference

For the usage of any feature in any kind of system, a study participant has to be motivated to do so. The construct of usability does not encompass the motivation to attempt a task in the first place. Instead of not being able to complete a task, participants might lack the motivation to attempt it. Verification in e-voting schemes is a not anticipated extra task that is not present in most traditional paper-based voting solutions. Furthermore, there are neither media campaigns that advertise verification as "positive" nor are there other incentives for the participants to verify. The investigation of usability, however, requires that the participants at least attempt to verify. Therefore, examiners need to make sure that the participants attempt verification.

5 Usability Metrics

According to ISO 9241-11 [44] the construct *usability* is defined as the *effectiveness, efficiency* and *satisfaction* with which specified users achieve specified goals in particular environments. ISO 9241-11 is also used by the NIST [29] for investigating voting systems. In particular, the criteria are defined as:

Effectiveness The accuracy and completeness with which specified users can achieve specified goals in particular environments.
Efficiency The resources expended in relation to the accuracy and completeness of goals achieved.
Satisfaction The comfort and acceptability of the work system to its users and other people affected by its use.

5.1 Effectiveness

Effectiveness means either the accuracy and completeness with which voters cast votes or the accuracy and completeness with which voters verify votes. Based on this definition, it is crucial to determine whether participants indeed cast and/or verified a vote successfully - the *binary success* [3] - or the process that participants made - the *level of success* [3].

At first, the examiners need to determine the sequence of actions that are required to cast and/or verify a vote. The progress in this sequence has to be captured accurately to determine the effectiveness. Capturing the progress, however, constitutes a particular challenge when investigating end-to-end verifiable e-voting schemes for two reasons: (1) the participants' vote privacy might have to be preserved and (2) not each task within the action sequence can be assessed directly. Since the participants vote, process capturing might break their vote privacy. If vote privacy is important in the user study, proxy measurements that do not interfere with vote privacy are required. In the following we discuss several progress capturing methods as well as their relation to the challenges.

Observation. The examiner could *observe* the participants to determine their progress [3]. If a real election is investigated, observation is not possible since many countries demand vote privacy in the voting booth [5]. Vote privacy is also compromized in the lab setting, because the examiner could see what the participants vote for. It furthermore introduces a social acceptability bias, because the participants might alter their behavior to match the examiner's expectations. Finally, mental tasks cannot be assessed reliably by an examiner. Several studies address these problems by an unobtrusive observation [34,43] in which the examiner is present in the lab and administers the study, but cannot observe the participants interactions with the e-voting system while voting and verification. In case the study scenario does not demand a real vote, the participants can be provided with voting instructions. Several studies use intent cards to provide written voting instructions [18,28,34]. Participants in an e-voting study by De Jong *et al.* struggled in remembering their verbal voting instructions [26], therefore the instructions should be written.

Visual Recording. *Visual Recording* [3] captures the participants' screens and renders a video from it or films the participants' interactions with a camera, such that the resulting video can be analyzed after the user study. This capturing method is objective and there is no influence by the examiner's behavior. Since the entire interaction is recorded, the voting options that the participants choose, are part of the recordings which breaks the participants' vote privacy. Thus, the same aspects regarding vote privacy related to observation apply here. If the study scenario demands that the participants cast votes that match their real intents visual recordings cannot be used. Furthermore, as shown by Conrad *et al.* [13] video recording might be unreliable, since 0.5% of the contests the participants voted in were not visible on the video.

Self Reporting. Another possibility to access the progress is asking the participants directly whether they performed the required actions [3]. In doing so no recordings are required and vote privacy is maintained as long as the participants are not asked for the voting option. Self-reported answers however suffer from a few drawbacks. Since self-reporting is reactive, the participants influence the given answer. They might lie to the examiner or in the questionnaire because of the social acceptability bias [24] or because of misperceptions. For example, in a study of Helios about 25% of participants thought they successfully cast a vote although they did not [1]. 25.8% of participants in a user study by Marky et al. [34] stated in a questionnaire that they did verify their votes whereas in reality, they failed.

Thinking Aloud. In the *thinking aloud* method [7], the participants are encouraged to verbally express thoughts during the interaction with the investigated scheme. Therefore, one might assume that the participant will also comment on the tasks that they are performing. While thinking aloud can provide important insights into the participants' interactions, it is not reliable in determining the effectiveness and the fulfillment of tasks since each participant follows a different strategy while commenting. Furthermore, the thinking aloud method might impact other metrics (e.g., completion time).

Eye Tracking. Eye-tracking can be used to investigate the participants' gazes [3]. However, while looking at a certain display area, e.g., the one displaying a verification code, it can not be assured, that the user indeed executes the required mental action, e.g., comparing the code to another. Therefore, eye tracking can only be employed in settings without mental tasks. Eye-tracking has been used in completed user studies to identify eye movements and gazes [27,41].

Proxy Measurements. Often it is not possible to capture whether the participants have been successful. In the e-voting setting, this might be because maintaining vote privacy interferes with performance capturing, but also if the task is performed mentally. To be able to capture the process accurately in such a situation, *proxy measurements* [3] can be used. This refers to a measure that helps to measure the task, but requires setup adjustments.

A common proxy measurement when investigating e-voting schemes is deliberate *manipulations* [42]. In end-to-end verifiable schemes, the voters frequently have to compare data, e.g., verification codes. To capture whether the participants have indeed compared the data, the data could be manipulated. Furthermore, the voters have to be instructed on how to act if they uncover a manipulation.

Deliberate manipulations can impact other metrics in the experiment. Participants might be less satisfied if they experienced a manipulation. Therefore, other parameters of the usability study have to be adjusted to account for that:

(1) the participants could interact with the system with and without a manipulation or (2) the study is in between-subjects design, such that one group is confronted with a manipulation and the other group is not.

Error Rates. Error rates are an alternative to completion rates to assess effectiveness. In the scope of e-voting systems, this refers to the relationship between the voter's intention and the real outcome [13,32]. MacNamara *et al.* [32] investigate in the usability of the DualVote VVPAT system and measured an error rate of 11.4%. However, this was not rooted in usability issues, the reason was a technical problem of the voting machine. Voter performance might be worse in real elections since there might be pressure by other waiting voters [13].

5.2 Efficiency

According to the ISO standardization, efficiency refers to the resources expended in relation to the accuracy and completeness of goals achieved [44].

The most commonly used method in the literature to assess the efficiency is the completion time, referring to the time that a participant required in order to complete all actions that are required to cast or to verify a vote. Two types of completion times have been assessed in user studies in the literature: (1) the *ballot completion time* which refers to the time required by participants to mark a ballot and (2) the *verification completion time* which is the time participants required to successfully complete verification.

Ballot Completion Time. The ballot completion time has been investigated in several works [1,10,19,32].

The average completion time is dependent on the ballot and therefore, is similar when comparing different e-voting systems. Byrne *et al.* [10] discovered that identical ballots in different representations and voting systems require the same completion time. In particular, they investigated arrow ballots, bubble ballots, punch cards, and lever machines which all required roughly 231 seconds for completion. Everett *et al.* [19] could not find significant differences between bubble ballots, punch cards, lever machines and DREs, confirming that the completion times are ballot-dependent. Studies of Prêt á Voter implementations, which use a very specific ballot design, show that participants require more time to mark their votes [1].

Verification Completion Time. The time required for verification has been investigated in several user studies [1,34]. Marky *et al.* [34] investigated three different interfaces of the Benaloh Challenge and found significant differences in the usage of a mobile verification device and a verification website. This shows that an interface can well impact the duration of verification.

5.3   Satisfaction

Satisfaction refers to the comfort and acceptability of the system to its users and other people affected by its use [44]. It can be assessed by *standardized questionnaires* or *non-standardized* ones created by the experimenter.

System Usability Scale. The System Usability Scale (SUS) [8] has been used extensively in e-voting studies [1, 2, 10, 18, 21, 28, 31, 33, 34, 36, 49]. Therefore, it can be used to compare the subjective usability of a new e-voting scheme to a range of different existing e-voting ones.

Acemyan *et al.* [1] measured a SUS score of 20.0 when investigating the usability of the Helios implementation of the Benaloh Challenge. Marky *et al.* [34] investigated the same process, but measured 76.5. The difference results from the different scopes in both studies: While Acemyan *et al.* measured the verification task only, while Marky *et al.* accessed the SUS score of the voting client, including ballot marking and vote casting. Acemyan *et al.* also measured the SUS score of the voting client which resulted in a similar SUS score to the one obtained by Marky *et al.* Therefore, it is likely that the subjective assessments from the verification significantly differs from the satisfaction related to the voting client.

The first SUS question is *I think that I would like to use this system frequently.* When conducting the user study published in [34] we discovered that the answer to this question can correlate with the participants' general attitudes towards e-voting. In case participants express a negative attitude, their answers could not be affirmative and vice versa. This might distort the SUS measurement - and possibly others - since the question aims to investigate the usability and not the participants' attitudes. Therefore, it is important to access the attitude towards e-voting in the demographics. Since there is no possibility to correct the participants' answers, correlations should be reported as a limitation.

User Experience Questionnaire. According to ISO 9241-210 [45] *User experience* is defined as a person's perceptions and responses that result from the use or anticipated use of a product, system or service.

The User Experience Questionnaire (UEQ) [30] can be used to measure the overall experience of the participants with the e-voting system they interact with. It covers attractiveness as well as usability aspects by measuring perspicuity, efficiency, dependability, but also the hedonic aspects of stimulation and novelty. Therefore, it broadens the investigation. The UEQ has been used in many user experiments, but to our knowledge so far only in two voting experiments [16, 36]. Considering the complete user experience helps to design usable protocols that bring satisfaction and meet the voters' expectations during the voting and verification phases.

Non-standardized Questionnaires. Voter satisfaction can also be assessed by *non-standardized questionnaires* developed by the examiners depending on the study's specific purpose. Those questionnaires have been used in several e-voting studies [5,27,32,34]. It is, however, encouraged by related works [1,10,39] to use standardized questionnaires in addition to self-developed ones to have comparability to previous studies.

6   Usability Study Guidelines

In this section, we provide study design guidelines for coping with the *challenges*, *metric-based* guidelines and *general* guidelines that were derived from the literature and our own experiences.

6.1   Challenge-Based Guidelines

In this section we provide guidelines for coping with e-voting study challenges of the election setting, vote privacy, social acceptability bias, mental tasks, demographic data, and motivation interference.

G1 Provide a ballot with recognizable candidates from a past or upcoming election and use a setting that is close to a real-world election to strengthen ecological validity.

G2 The usage of a cover story can offset the social acceptability bias. But the cover story should be explained to the participants during the debrief.

G3 The collection of written post-test data instead of direct communication with the examiner can offset the social acceptability bias.

G4 Mental tasks should be identified by the examiners before the measurement methods are determined.

G5 Participants should be asked in the demographic questionnaire whether they have already participated in an election that matches the setting from the study to capture if participants have consistent voting experiences.

G6 Participants should be asked about their general attitude towards e-voting in the demographic questionnaire because it could distort user study results.

G7 Written instructions to attempt verification ensure that participants try to carry out the required tasks. The instructions should not contain detailed instructions on *how* to verify a vote and solely should instruct participants to *do* it. The instructions should be tested in a pre-study to ensure their understandability.

G8 Make sure that the motivation of participants to cast or verify their votes does not impact the usability metrics.

6.2   Metric-Based Guidelines

In the following, we provide guidelines regarding the assessment of the usability metrics. Hereby, we focus on process capturing for assessing effectiveness, error rates, efficiency, and questionnaires.

G9 The methods of observation, visual recording and think aloud break the participants' vote privacy and should not be used in studies with real votes.

G10 The methods of observation, visual recording, self-reporting, think aloud break and eye tracking should not be used for assessing the completion of mental tasks.

G11 Thinking aloud should not be used in conjunction with completion time.

G10 Self-reporting should be used if no other measurements are possible, e.g., participant opinions.

G12 Self-reporting should be used as an addition to objective measurements.

G13 Written voting instructions should be used to maintain vote secrecy when visual recording or observation is used.

G14 If the participants are videotaped, actions of them might not be visible on the video, therefore, the video positioning should be refined in a pre-study.

G15 If vote privacy is important throughout the study, examiners should be positioned in an *unobtrusive* way, such that they cannot see the participants' interactions and interfere with them.

G16 Deliberate manipulations can used as a proxy measurement to capture effectiveness.

G17 Errors can be rooted in the voting system's malfunctioning. Therefore, the malfunctioning of the e-voting system has to be ruled out.

6.3 General Guidelines

Besides the specific guidelines stated above, we derived general guidelines that concern the user study overall.

G18 The participants should be informed clearly which part of the voting scheme should be considered when answering questionnaires.

G19 A plethora of baseline data for several e-voting systems is available in the literature. The usage of the same metrics provides the opportunity to compare the investigated system to those that have already been investigated. Therefore, the SUS, ballot/verification completion time and completion rates should be measured.

G20 The assessed metrics should not be limited to usability, the bigger picture of User Experience can provide valuable insights.

7 Related Work

The usability of voting systems has been investigated in many studies and some publications focus on investigation methodologies. In the following, we describe existing guidelines and recommendations for e-voting studies that are presented in related work. Our paper aims to provide guidelines related to the challenges and usability metrics while related work provides additional guidelines for the overall protocol design.

Selker *et al.* [42] analyze three studies of polling station based voting systems and provide guidelines for future work. They compare realistic and laboratory experiments for testing voting technologies. The results reveal that real-world tests are more valuable as they add a considerable workload to the process, which uncovers additional issues related to the environment and the procedure in polling stations (distraction, confusion, the importance of poll workers assistance). However, the collected data is consistent in both test environments and the aspects of a real-world setting do not influence ballot understanding or verification results. Providing a voting card to the participants in a mock election where they know the candidates can be inefficient: participants could vote for a different candidate, which impacts error tracking. Furthermore, the authors recommend testing as close as possible to a real-world setting to strengthen ecological validity.

Olembo and Volkamer [39] conduct a literature review focusing on usability studies of e-voting systems. They review different designs and methodologies and provide a list of recommendations for user studies. They stress that expert evaluations are faster and more cost-effective and bring more data compared to user studies. They describe a methodology for future tests: at first an iteration of the tested protocol must be done with HCI experts and users must be involved in a second iteration with a pilot study. The final design must be re-tested with users and field studies can be considered.

Herrnson et al. [25] study the importance of usability by investigating six voting schemes that are already in use, with different voting procedures, with four research methodologies. In their recommendation, they do not discuss the different aspects related to the methodology in use but focus on usability findings and impacts for next studies. They notice that demography impacts the voters' needs, in particular, the need for assistance was at least 18%. Therefore, accessibility must be taken into consideration and proper assistance should be available.

Taha Ali and Murray [4] discuss the impact of usability on voting systems. In particular, they stress that the long intervals between elections confirm the importance of usability because voters have little or no voting experience. This lack of experience can be extended to poll workers and election officials, and concerns are on whether voters will be able to cast a vote successfully, but also able to go through the verification process. Therefore, the authors state that a trainee at an early stage for voters and poll workers must be done to increase usability results.

8 Conclusion

The usability of end-to-end verifiable e-voting schemes is equally important as their security and directly impacts it. Therefore, human factors should be considered early on when designing usable end-to-end verifiable e-voting systems that are intended to be put into practice. In this paper, we provide 20 guidelines for investigating vote casting and vote verification in e-voting schemes in user studies. The guidelines are derived from the literature and based on our experiences and aim to inform future user studies of e-voting schemes. In this paper, we focus on quantitative metrics as well as demographics and the study setting. It would be beneficial to see guidelines for qualitative research as a part of future work.

Acknowledgements. This work has been co-funded by the DFG as part of project "Area D.1" within the RTG 2050 "Privacy and Trust for Mobile Users" and by the Horst Görtz Foundation. We acknowledge support from the Luxembourg National Research Fund (FNR) for funding, in particular Marie-Laure Zollinger was supported by the FNR-INTER-VoteVerif project and FNR-INTER-SeVoTe project.

References

1. Acemyan, C.Z., Kortum, P., Byrne, M.D., Wallach, D.S.: Usability of voter verifiable, end-to-end voting systems: Baseline data for helios, prêt à voter, and scantegrity ii. USENIX J. Election Technol. Syst. (JETS) **2**(3), 26–56 (2014)
2. Acemyan, C.Z., Kortum, P., Byrne, M.D., Wallach, D.S.: Summative usability assessments of STAR-Vote: a cryptographically secure e2e voting system that has been empirically proven to be easy to use. Hum. factors, 1–24 (2018)
3. Albert, W., Tullis, T.: Measuring the User Experience: Collecting, Analyzing, and Presenting Usability Metrics. Newnes, Boston (2013)
4. Ali, S.T., Murray, J.: An overview of end-to-end verifiable voting systems. In: Real-World Electronic Voting: Design, Analysis and Deployment, pp. 171–218. CRC Press (2016)
5. Bederson, B.B., Lee, B., Sherman, R.M., Herrnson, P.S., Niemi, R.G.: Electronic voting system usability issues. In: SIGCHI Conference on Human Factors in Computing Systems (CHI), pp. 145–152. ACM (2003)
6. Benaloh, J., Rivest, R., Ryan, P.Y., Stark, P., Teague, V., Vora, P.: End-to-end verifiability, pp. 1–7 (2015). https://arxiv.org/pdf/1504.03778.pdf
7. Boren, T., Ramey, J.: Thinking aloud: reconciling theory and practice. IEEE Trans. Prof. Commun. **43**(3), 261–278 (2000)
8. Brooke, J.: SUS - a quick and dirty usability scale. Usability Eval. Ind. **189**(194), 4–7 (1996)
9. Budurushi, J., Renaud, K., Volkamer, M., Woide, M.: An investigation into the usability of electronic voting systems for complex elections. Ann. Telecommun. **71**(7), 309–322 (2016). https://doi.org/10.1007/s12243-016-0510-2
10. Byrne, M.D., Greene, K.K., Everett, S.P.: Usability of voting systems: baseline data for paper, punch cards, and lever machines. In: SIGCHI Conference on Human Factors in Computing Systems (CHI), pp. 171–180. ACM (2007)
11. Campbell, B.A., Byrne, M.D.: Now do voters notice review screen anomalies? A look at voting system usability. In: Conference on Electronic Voting Technology/Workshop on Trustworthy Elections (EVT/WOTE). USENIX Association (2009)
12. Chaum, D.: Secret-ballot receipts: true voter-verifiable elections. IEEE Secur. Priv. **2**(1), 38–47 (2004)
13. Conrad, F.G., et al.: Electronic voting eliminates hanging chads but introduces new usability challenges. Int. J. Hum.-Comput. Stud. **67**(1), 111–124 (2009)
14. Cortier, V., Galindo, D., Küsters, R., Mueller, J., Truderung, T.: SoK: verifiability notions for e-voting protocols. In: Symposium on Security and Privacy (S&P), pp. 779–798. IEEE (2016)

15. Culnane, C., Teague, V.: Strategies for voter-initiated election audits. In: Zhu, Q., Alpcan, T., Panaousis, E., Tambe, M., Casey, W. (eds.) GameSec 2016. LNCS, vol. 9996, pp. 235–247. Springer, Cham (2016). https://doi.org/10.1007/978-3-319-47413-7_14

16. Distler, V., Zollinger, M.L., Lallemand, C., Rønne, P.B., Ryan, P.Y., Koenig, V.: Security-visible, yet unseen? How displaying security mechanisms impacts user experience and perceived security. In: CHI Conference on Human Factors in Computing Systems, CHI 2019. ACM (2019)

17. Escala, A., Guasch, S., Herranz, J., Morillo, P.: Universal cast-as-intended verifiability. In: Clark, J., Meiklejohn, S., Ryan, P.Y.A., Wallach, D., Brenner, M., Rohloff, K. (eds.) FC 2016. LNCS, vol. 9604, pp. 233–250. Springer, Heidelberg (2016). https://doi.org/10.1007/978-3-662-53357-4_16

18. Everett, S.P., Byrne, M.D., Greene, K.K.: Measuring the usability of paper ballots: efficiency, effectiveness, and satisfaction. In: Proceedings of the Human Factors and Ergonomics Society Annual Meeting, vol. 50, no. 24, pp. 2547–2551 (2006)

19. Everett, S.P., et al.: Electronic voting machines versus traditional methods: improved preference, similar performance. In: SIGCHI Conference on Human Factors in Computing Systems (CHI), pp. 883–892. ACM (2008)

20. Fuglerud, K.S., Røssvoll, T.H.: An evaluation of web-based voting usability and accessibility. Univ. Access Inf. Soc. 11(4), 359–373 (2012). https://doi.org/10.1007/s10209-011-0253-9

21. Gibson, J.P., MacNamara, D., Oakley, K.: Just like paper and the 3-colour protocol: a voting interface requirements engineering case study. In: International Workshop on Requirements Engineering for Electronic Voting Systems, pp. 66–75. IEEE (2011)

22. Gjøsteen, K.: The Norwegian internet voting protocol. In: Kiayias, A., Lipmaa, H. (eds.) Vote-ID 2011. LNCS, vol. 7187, pp. 1–18. Springer, Heidelberg (2012). https://doi.org/10.1007/978-3-642-32747-6_1

23. Greene, K.K., Byrne, M.D., Everett, S.P.: A comparison of usability between voting methods. In: Electronic Voting Technology Workshop (EVT). USENIX Association (2006)

24. Grimm, P.: Social desirability bias. Wiley International Encyclopedia of Marketing. Wiley, Hoboken (2010)

25. Herrnson, P.S., Niemi, R.G., Hanmer, M.J., Bederson, B.B., Conrad, F.G., Traugott, M.: The importance of usability testing of voting systems. In: Electronic Voting Technology Workshop (EVT) (2006)

26. de Jong, M., van Hoof, J., Gosselt, J.: User research of a voting machine: Preliminary findings and experiences. J. Usability Stud. 2(4), 180–189 (2007)

27. Karayumak, F., Kauer, M., Olembo, M.M., Volk, T., Volkamer, M.: User study of the improved Helios voting system interfaces. In: Workshop on Socio-Technical Aspects in Security and Trust (STAST), pp. 37–44. IEEE (2011)

28. Kulyk, O., Neumann, S., Budurushi, J., Volkamer, M.: Nothing comes for free: How much usability can you sacrifice for security? IEEE Secur. Priv. 15(3), 24–29 (2017)

29. Laskowski, S.J., Autry, M., Cugini, J., Killam, W., Yen, J.: Improving the usability and accessibility of voting systems and products. NIST Spec. Publ. 500, 256 (2004)

30. Laugwitz, B., Held, T., Schrepp, M.: Construction and evaluation of a user experience questionnaire. In: Holzinger, A. (ed.) USAB 2008. LNCS, vol. 5298, pp. 63–76. Springer, Heidelberg (2008). https://doi.org/10.1007/978-3-540-89350-9_6

31. Mac Namara, D., Scully, T., Gibson, P.: Dualvote addressing usability and verifiability issues in electronic voting systems (2011). http://citeseerx.ist.psu.edu/viewdoc/summary?doi=10.1.1.399.7284
32. MacNamara, D., Carmody, F., Scully, T., Oakley, K., Quane, E., Gibson, J.P.: Dual vote: a novel user interface for e-voting systems. In: International Conference on Interfaces and Human Computer Interaction, pp. 129–138. IADIS (2010)
33. MacNamara, D., Gibson, P., Oakley, K.: A preliminary study on a dualvote and Prêt à Voter hybrid system. In: Conference for E-Democracy and Open Government, p. 77. Edition-Donau-Univ. Krems (2012)
34. Marky, K., Kulyk, O., Renaud, K., Volkamer, M.: What did I really vote for? On the usability of verifiable e-voting schemes. In: CHI Conference on Human Factors in Computing Systems (CHI), pp. 176:1–176:13. ACM (2018)
35. Marky, K., Kulyk, O., Volkamer, M.: Comparative usability evaluation of cast-as-intended verification approaches in internet voting. In: SICHERHEIT 2018, pp. 197–208. Lecture Notes in Informatics (LNI), Gesellschaft für Informatik (2018)
36. Marky, K., Schmitz, M., Lange, F., Mühlhäuser, M.: Usability of code voting modalities. In: Extended Abstracts of the 2019 CHI Conference on Human Factors in Computing Systems, CHI EA 2019, pp. LBW2221:1–LBW2221:6. ACM (2019)
37. Nancarrow, C., Brace, I.: Saying the "right thing": coping with social desirability bias in marketing research. Bristol Bus. Sch. Teach. Res. Rev. 3(11), 1–11 (2000)
38. Neumann, S.: Evaluation and improvement of internet voting schemes based on legally-founded security requirements. Ph.D. thesis, Technische Universität Darmstadt (2016)
39. Olembo, M.M., Volkamer, M.: E-voting system usability: Lessons for interface design, user studies, and usability criteria. In: Human-Centered System Design for Electronic Governance, pp. 172–201. IGI Global (2013)
40. Patrick, A.: Ecological validity in studies of security and human behaviour. In: Symposium on Usable Privacy and Security (SOUPS) (2009)
41. Realpe-Muñoz, P., Collazos, C.A., Hurtado, J., Granollers, T., Muñoz-Arteaga, J., Velasco-Medina, J.: Eye tracking-based behavioral study of users using e-voting systems. Comput. Stan. Interfaces 55, 182–195 (2017)
42. Selker, T., Rosenzweig, E., Pandolfo, A.: A methodology for testing voting systems. J. Usability Stud. 2(1), 7–21 (2006)
43. Sherman, A.T., et al.: Scantegrity mock election at Takoma Park. In: International Conference on Electronic Voting (EVOTE), pp. 45–61. LNI, Gesellschaft für Informatik (2010)
44. Standardization, I.O.F.: ISO 9241–11: Ergonomics of human system interaction - part 11: Guidance on usability (1998)
45. Standardization, I.O.F.: ISO 9241–210: Part 210: Human-centred design for interactive systems (2015)
46. Strafgesetzbuch (StGB): §107c Verletzung des Wahlgeheimnisses. https://www.gesetze-im-internet.de/stgb/__107c.html
47. Van Hoof, J.J., Gosselt, J.F., de Jong, M.D.: The reliability and usability of the NEDAP voting machine: a pilot study. University of Twente Faculty of Behavioural Sciences Department of Technical and Professional Communication (2007)
48. Weber, J.L., Hengartner, U.: Usability study of the open audit voting system Helios. http://www.jannaweber.com/wp-content/uploads/2009/09/858Helios.pdf (2009)
49. Winckler, M., et al.: Assessing the usability of open verifiable e-voting systems: a trial with the system prêt à voter. In: International Conference on Theory and Practice of Electronic Governance (ICEGOV), pp. 281–296. ACM (2009)

Improving the Performance
of Cryptographic Voting Protocols

Rolf Haenni[1(✉)], Philipp Locher[1], and Nicolas Gailly[2]

[1] Bern University of Applied Sciences, 2501 Biel, Switzerland
{rolf.haenni,philipp.locher}@bfh.ch
[2] École Polytechnique Fédérale de Lausanne, 1015 Lausanne, Switzerland
nicolas.gailly@epfl.ch

Abstract. Cryptographic voting protocols often rely on methods that require a large number of modular exponentiations. Corresponding performance bottlenecks may appear both on the server and the client side. Applying existing optimization techniques is often mentioned and recommended in the literature, but their potential has never been analyzed in depth. In this paper, we investigate existing algorithms for computing fixed-base exponentiations and product exponentiations. Both of them appear frequently in voting protocols. We also explore the potential of applying small-exponent techniques. It turns out that using these techniques in combination, the overall computation time can be reduced by two or more orders of magnitude.

1 Introduction

Parties involved in cryptographic protocols often need to calculate a large number of modular exponentiations $z = b^e \bmod p$ (modexp) with large numbers b, e, and p.[1] With regard to performance, other computational tasks are often negligible. This is why optimizing modexp computations is the most promising option for improving the overall performance of an online voting system. Often, particular attention must be given to the client side, especially if it is implemented as a web application in JavaScript, which is known for its limited performance relative to native-code applications. Clearly, computational bottlenecks on the client may lead to critical usability problems and should therefore be avoided.

1.1 Problem Description and Context

In this paper, we consider the common setup of an ElGamal encryption scheme, which is often used for encrypting votes in cryptographic voting protocols. Let p denote a safe prime and $\mathbb{Z}_p^* = \{1, \ldots, p-1\}$ the corresponding multiplicative

---

[1] Exponentiations in groups such as elliptic curves, where the potential of applying the same type of optimizations is exactly the same, are less frequently used in voting protocols. Here we focus on multiplicative groups of integers modulo p, but our theoretical results are all applicable to the general case.

© International Financial Cryptography Association 2020
A. Bracciali et al. (Eds.): FC 2019 Workshops, LNCS 11599, pp. 272–288, 2020.
https://doi.org/10.1007/978-3-030-43725-1_19

group of integers modulo p. This group has a sub-group $\mathbb{G}_q \subset \mathbb{Z}_p^*$ of prime order $q = \frac{p-1}{2}$, for which the decisional Diffie-Hellman (DDH) problem is believed to be hard. Since q is prime, all elements of $\mathbb{G}_q \setminus \{1\}$ are generators of $\mathbb{G}_q$. For such a generator $b \in \mathbb{G}_q$ and an exponent $e \in \mathbb{Z}_q$, computing the modular exponentiation $z = \mathsf{Exp}(b, e, p) = b^e \bmod p \in \mathbb{G}_q$ is the basic computational task considered in this paper. According to current recommendations [3], we have to deal with numbers of following bit lengths:

$$2048 \leq |p|, \quad 2 \leq |b| \leq |p|, \quad 112 \leq |e| \leq |p| - 1, \quad |z| = |p|.$$

In our theoretical analysis of different modexp algorithms, we will see that $\ell = |e|$ is one of the main parameters that determines the running time. If ℓ is equal or close to the above lower bound, we call e a *short exponent*.[2] Similarly, b is a *short base*, if $|b|$ is equal or close to 2. In all cases, we assume that b and e are drawn from a random uniform distribution.

The computational task considered in this paper consists of N different modexp instances for the same modulo p. Therefore, let $\boldsymbol{b} = (b_1, \ldots, b_N) \in \mathbb{G}_q^N$ and $\boldsymbol{e} = (e_1, \ldots, e_N) \in \mathbb{Z}_q^N$ denote the given vectors of values b_i and e_i. In the most general case, we need to compute values $z_i = \mathsf{Exp}(b_i, e_i, p)$ independently. The corresponding *multiple exponentiation problem* is denoted by

$$\boldsymbol{z} = \mathsf{MultiExp}(\boldsymbol{b}, \boldsymbol{e}, p) \in \mathbb{G}_q^N,$$

where $\boldsymbol{z} = (z_1, \ldots, z_N)$ is the vector of output values. We use MultiExp as reference point for judging the benefits of optimization algorithms, which can be applied to the following two special cases:

- *Product Exponentiation.* Compute the product $z = \prod_{i=1}^N z_i \bmod p$ of values $z_i = \mathsf{Exp}(b_i, e_i, p)$ for inputs $\boldsymbol{b} = (b_1, \ldots, b_N)$ and $\boldsymbol{e} = (e_1, \ldots, e_N)$:

$$z = \mathsf{ProductExp}(\boldsymbol{b}, \boldsymbol{e}, p) \in \mathbb{G}_q.$$

- *Fixed-Base Exponentiation.* Compute $\boldsymbol{z} = (z_1, \ldots, z_N)$ of values $z_i = \mathsf{Exp}(b, e_i, p)$ for inputs $\boldsymbol{b} = (b, \ldots, b)$ and $\boldsymbol{e} = (e_1, \ldots, e_N)$:

$$\boldsymbol{z} = \mathsf{FixedBaseExp}(b, \boldsymbol{e}, p) \in \mathbb{G}_q^N.$$

A similar special case arises for $\boldsymbol{e} = (e, \ldots, e)$. However, since the benefits of algorithms for solving such *fixed-exponent exponentiation* problems are rather limited (see [10, Section 14.6.2]), we do not consider them in this paper.

---

[2] There are multiple reasons for working with short exponents. In certain applications of some cryptographic schemes, a much smaller subgroup $\mathbb{G}_q \subset \mathbb{Z}_p^*$ is sufficient. To resist against the best available DL algorithms, the minimal bit length of q in such cases is 2λ, where λ denotes the security strength, for example $|q| = 224$ for $\lambda = 112$. Corresponding exponents $e \in \mathbb{Z}_q$ are then inherently restricted to $|q|$ bits. In larger groups, smaller exponents are sometimes selected on purpose, for example in the case of a challenge $c \in \mathbb{Z}_{2\lambda}$ in a zero-knowledge proof or in systems relying on the *short-exponent discrete logarithm* (DLSE) assumption, in which short exponents $e \in \mathbb{Z}_{2^{2\lambda}}$ deliver the same provable security under a slightly stronger intractability assumption. For example, using the ElGamal encryption scheme with short randomizations has been proven IND-CPA secure under the DLSE assumption [7].

1.2   Contribution and Paper Overview

The goal of this paper is to increase public awareness of the potential performance benefits that results from applying the most appropriate modexp algorithms to a particular given computational task in a cryptographic voting protocol. The state-of-the-art algorithms for solving MultiExp, FixedBaseExp, and
ProductExp most efficiently are presented in Sect. 2. We summarize the algorithmic and theoretical background of the available methods and provide an
analysis of the expected computational costs. Since all algorithms are parameterized, we give instructions for finding optimal algorithm parameters in a given
cryptographic setup. The maximal performance benefits when running the algorithms with optimal parameters are analyzed for FixedBaseExp and ProductExp.
For some of the presented algorithms, we are not aware of any references in the
literature. One of the presented algorithm turns out to be equivalent to the well-
known comb method [9], but we believe that our description is more intuitive.

A more practical perspective of this topic is given in Sect. 3. The target audience of this section are practitioners and developers of online voting systems
designed for real-world elections. We performed different performance tests for
various algorithms and measured their effective running times on different platforms. A special focus is given to the client side, in which performance bottlenecks
are more likely to appear.

2   Performance Analysis of Exponentiation Algorithms

Most programming languages or mathematical libraries providing large number arithmetic have a built-in support for modexp computations. They usually
implement general-purpose modexp algorithms from [10], for example Alg. 14.82,
Alg. 14.83, or Alg. 14.85, which we will later call HAC 14.82, HAC 14.83, and
HAC 14.85. Using such algorithms, the average time for solving MultiExp is
exactly N times the average time for solving Exp. General algorithms for Exp
are discussed in Sect. 2.2. We will use them as reference points for evaluating
the performance of several optimization algorithms. The results obtained for
ProductExp and FixedBaseExp are discussed in Sects. 2.3 and 2.4.

2.1   Measurement Methodology

In our theoretical analysis of an algorithm Alg for solving $Exp(b, e, p)$, we count
the number $M_{Alg}(\ell)$ of multiplications needed for exponents of length $\ell = |e|$.
For reasons of simplicity, we do not distinguish between squaring and multiplication operations, i.e., we assume that they are equally expensive, which may not
necessarily be true in every library. In case of ProductExp and FixedBaseExp algorithms for ℓ-bit exponents, we count the total number $M_{Alg}(\ell, N)$ of multiplications needed to solve the entire problem. To compare them with general-purpose
algorithms, we compute the *average number of multiplications per modexp*,

$$\widetilde{M}_{Alg}(\ell, N) = \frac{M_{Alg}(\ell, N)}{N},$$

and call it *relative (theoretical) running time* of Alg. Both $M_{\mathsf{Alg}}(\ell)$ and $\widetilde{M}_{\mathsf{Alg}}(\ell, N)$ may depend on algorithm parameters $\kappa_1, \ldots, \kappa_r$. We either include them explicitly in our notation as $M_{\mathsf{Alg}}^{\kappa_1, \ldots, \kappa_r}(\ell)$ and $\widetilde{M}_{\mathsf{Alg}}^{\kappa_1, \ldots, \kappa_r}(\ell, N)$, or we skip them to indicate that optimal parameters κ_i^{opt} have been chosen:

$$M_{\mathsf{Alg}}^{\mathrm{opt}}(\ell) := M_{\mathsf{Alg}}^{\kappa_1^{\mathrm{opt}}, \ldots, \kappa_r^{\mathrm{opt}}}(\ell) \quad \text{and} \quad \widetilde{M}_{\mathsf{Alg}}^{\mathrm{opt}}(\ell, N) := \widetilde{M}_{\mathsf{Alg}}^{\kappa_1^{\mathrm{opt}}, \ldots, \kappa_r^{\mathrm{opt}}}(\ell, N).$$

If we take $M_{\mathsf{Alg}^*}^{\mathrm{opt}}(\ell)$ of a general-purpose modexp algorithm Alg^* as reference point for evaluating the performance of an optimization algorithm Alg, both of them instantiated with optimal algorithm parameters, we can measure the benefit of Alg relative to Alg^* by computing the fraction

$$\mu_{\mathsf{Alg}}(\ell, N) = M_{\mathsf{Alg}^*}^{\mathrm{opt}}(\ell) / \widetilde{M}_{\mathsf{Alg}}^{\mathrm{opt}}(\ell, N).$$

This number will be called *(theoretical) impact factor* of algorithm Alg in problem instances of size N and exponents of size ℓ. To measure the benefit of combining an optimization algorithm Alg with short-exponent techniques, for example in a setting with $\ell_{\mathsf{long}} = 2047$ and $\ell_{\mathsf{short}} = 224$, we compute the fraction

$$\mu_{\mathsf{Alg}}^*(\ell_{\mathsf{long}}, \ell_{\mathsf{short}}, N) = M_{\mathsf{Alg}^*}^{\mathrm{opt}}(\ell_{\mathsf{long}}) / \widetilde{M}_{\mathsf{Alg}}^{\mathrm{opt}}(\ell_{\mathsf{short}}, N).$$

All modexp algorithms described in this section can benefit more or less equally from techniques known as *Montgomery* or *Barrett reduction* as described as Alg. 14.32 and Alg. 14.42 in [10]. We do not study their potential in this paper.

2.2 General-Purpose Exponentiation Algorithms

The most fundamental problem considered in this paper is the computation of a single value $z = \mathsf{Exp}(b, e, p)$. A widely implemented algorithm is the *window method* as described in HAC 14.82, in which the ℓ-bits exponent is written as $e = (e_{t-1} \cdots e_1 e_0)_B$ in base $B = 2^k$. The parameter k is called *window size* and $t = \lceil \frac{\ell}{k} \rceil$ denotes the number of windows $e_i \in \mathbb{Z}_{2^k}$. The algorithm processes the bits of each window en bloc by decomposing b^e using Horner's method:

$$b^e = b^{\sum_{i=0}^{t-1} e_i B^i} = b^{e_0}(b^{e_1}(b^{e_2} \cdots (b^{e_{t-2}}(b^{e_{t-1}})^B)^B \cdots)^B)^B.$$

This expression can be evaluated from inside to outside starting with the leftmost window e_{t-1}. The resulting iteration corresponds to HAC 14.82. If all values b^{e_i} have been precomputed and stored in a table, then the iteration requires $k(t-1)$ squarings and $t - 1 = \lfloor \frac{\ell-1}{k} \rfloor$ multiplications. The precomputation table may contain up to 2^k entries, which can be computed using $2^k - 2$ multiplications.

To reduce the size of this table and therefore to improve the overall computation time, consider the decomposition of each $e_i \neq 0$ into $e_i = u_i 2^{v_i}$ such that u_i is odd (e_{t-1} remains untouched). For $e_i = 0$, let $u_i = v_i = 0$. This leads to

$$b^e = (b^{u_0}((b^{u_1}(\cdots((b^{u_{t-2}}(b^{e_{t-1}})^{2^{k-v_{t-2}}})^{2^{v_{t-2}}}) \cdots)^{2^{k-v_1}})^{2^{v_1}})^{2^{k-v_0}})^{2^{v_0}},$$

from which the improved window algorithm HAC 14.83 follows. Here, the precomputation table of all possible odd values $u_i \in \mathbb{Z}_{2^k}$ contains at most 2^{k-1} entries, which can be generated using the same amount of multiplications.

To compute the running time of HAC 14.83 as precisely as possible, we have to take into account that e may contain some windows $e_i = 0$. We assume that such cases, in which one multiplication is saved, appear with probability $P_k = \frac{2^k - 1}{2^k} \in [0.5, 1)$. This leads to

$$M^k_{\text{HAC 14.83}}(\ell) = 2^{k-1} + (k + P_k) \left\lfloor \frac{\ell - 1}{k} \right\rfloor + 1 < 2^{k-1} + \ell \cdot \frac{k+1}{k},$$

which we will later use as reference point for evaluating the performance of several optimization algorithms.[3]

The remaining question regarding the window method is the selection of the optimal parameter k^{opt} that minimizes $M_{\text{HAC 14.83}}(k, \ell)$. To get the desired value for a given ℓ, we can either solve $\frac{d}{dk}[M^k_{\text{HAC 14.83}}(\ell)] = 0$ numerically, for example using Newton's method, or perform an exhaustive search over $1 \leq k \leq \ell$. The results for $80 \leq \ell \leq 15360$ are summarized in Table 1. The mapping from ℓ to k^{opt} is unique within the ranges given in Table 1, but not in the areas between these ranges, where k^{opt} jumps forth an back between two adjacent values.

Table 1. Optimal window sizes k^{opt} in HAC 14.83 for different exponent lengths ℓ.

ℓ	82–184	217–545	566–1434	1465–3759	3802–9368	>9425
k^{opt}	4	5	6	7	8	9

An even better performance offers the *sliding window method* as implemented in HAC 14.85, in which one multiplication can be saved in the average after processing $\frac{k}{2}$ windows, i.e., $\frac{2t}{k}$ multiplications can be saved in total. Since this is a non-negligible quantity, HAC 14.85 is the recommended method in [10]. Nevertheless, HAC 14.82 and HAC 14.83 (and even HAC 14.79) are implemented in some arithmetic libraries for large integers.

As a numerical example, consider the common cryptographic setting with $|p| = 2048$ and exponents of length $\ell = |e| = 2047$. In this case, we select $k^{\text{opt}} = 7$ for getting the best possible running time $M^{\text{opt}}_{\text{HAC 14.83}}(2047) = 2401$. This is about 22% faster than standard square-and-multiply, which corresponds to $M^1_{\text{HAC 14.83}}(2047) = 3071$ for windows of size $k = 1$. Using the sliding window method, the performance improves by another 3% to $M^{\text{opt}}_{\text{HAC 14.85}}(2047) = 2318$.

---

[3] The precomputation of HAC 14.82, HAC 14.83, and HAC 14.85 gets much faster for a small base. For values such as $b = 2$ or $b = 4$, multiplication during precomputation corresponds to shifting the bits a few positions to the left (modulo p), which is obviously much faster than regular multiplications. In such a case, our theoretical analysis based on counting modular multiplications gets inaccurate.

2.3   Algorithms for Product Exponentiations

Product exponentiation problems $\mathsf{ProductExp}(b, e, p)$ can be solved in a naïve way by computing the product $z = \prod_{i=1}^{N} z_i \bmod p$ of the results z_i obtained from calling an algorithm from the previous section separately for all N pairs (b_i, e_i). As we will see in this section, this is far from being an optimal solution. A special-purpose algorithm for this problem is HAC 14.88, but it only performs well for small N. The reasons for this is the size of the precomputation table, which grows exponentially with N. The total relative running time is as follows:

$$\widetilde{M}_{\mathsf{HAC\,14.88}}(\ell, N) = \frac{(2^N - N - 1) + (\ell - 1)(1 + P_N)}{N} < \frac{2^N + 2\ell}{N}.$$

If ℓ is fixed in this expression, we can derive the problem size N for which the algorithm performs best. For $\ell = 2047$, the best relative running time is $\widetilde{M}_{\mathsf{HAC\,14.88}}(2047, 9) = 510$, which we get for $N = 9$. For this particular case, the algorithm performs almost five times better than HAC 14.83, but it quickly starts to perform (much) worse when N gets larger. In the light of these considerations, applying HAC 14.88 directly for solving $\mathsf{ProductExp}$ is only possible for very small problem instances. However, it can be used as a building block for algorithms that perform well in general. The most obvious way is to split the full task into $s = \lfloor \frac{N}{m} \rfloor$ sub-tasks of size m and one sub-task of size $r = N \bmod m$.

To formalize this idea, let $I_j = \{jm + 1, \ldots, jm + m\}$ be the indices of sub-task $0 \leq j \leq s - 1$ and $I_s = \{sm + 1, \ldots, N\}$ the set of indices of sub-task s. The problem can then be decomposed into

$$z = \prod_{i=1}^{N} a_i^{e_i} \bmod p = \prod_{j=0}^{s} \prod_{i \in I_j} a_i^{e_i} \bmod p = \prod_{j=0}^{s} \mathsf{ProductExp}(b_j, e_j, p),$$

where b_j and e_j denote corresponding sub-vectors from $b = b_0 || \cdots || b_s$ and $e = e_0 || \cdots || e_s$. The relative running time of the resulting Algorithm 1 is as follows:

$$\widetilde{M}_{\mathsf{Alg.1}}^{m}(\ell, N) = \frac{sm \cdot \widetilde{M}_{\mathsf{HAC\,14.88}}(\ell, m) + r \cdot \widetilde{M}_{\mathsf{HAC\,14.88}}(\ell, r) + s}{N} \approx \widetilde{M}_{\mathsf{HAC\,14.88}}(\ell, m).$$

It follows that this algorithm performs best by selecting the parameter m according to the above discussion of the optimal value N in HAC 14.88. As an example, we select $m^{\mathsf{opt}} = 9$ for $\ell = 2047$, which leads to $\widetilde{M}_{\mathsf{Alg.1}}^{\mathsf{opt}}(2047, N) = 510$ and $\mu_{\mathsf{Alg.1}}(2047, N) = 4.7$ for large input sizes N. For a setting with $\ell_{\mathsf{long}} = 2047$ and $\ell_{\mathsf{short}} = 224$, we get $m^{\mathsf{opt}} = 7$ and $\mu_{\mathsf{Alg.1}}^{*}(2047, 224, N) = 29.99$.

The benefit of Algorithm 1 is already appealing, but it can be improved even further. For this, we need to drill a hole into HAC 14.88, by placing the squaring operation in Step 3 outside the brackets over all sub-tasks of Algorithm 1. In Algorithm 2, we assume that N is a multiple of m, which we can always achieve by filling up the inputs with $m - r$ additional values $b_i = 1$ and $e_i = 0$.

Algorithm: ProductExp$_m$(b, e, p)

Input: Bases $b = b_0 || \cdots || b_s$
  Exponents $e = e_0 || \cdots || e_s$
  Modulus p
  Sub-task size $1 \leq m \leq N$

$z \leftarrow 1$
for $j = 0, \ldots, s$ do
  $z_j \leftarrow$ HAC 14.88(b_j, e_j, p)
  $z \leftarrow z \cdot z_j \bmod p$
return z

Algorithm 1. Simple product exponentiation algorithm based on HAC 14.88.

Algorithm: ProductExp$_m$(b, e, p)

Input: Bases $b = b_0 || \cdots || b_{s-1}$
  Exponents $e = e_0 || \cdots || e_{s-1}$
  Modulus p
  Sub-task size $1 \leq m \leq N$

for $i = 0, \ldots, 2^m - 1$ do
  $(i_{m-1}, \ldots, i_0)_2 \leftarrow i$
  for $j = 0, \ldots, s - 1$ do
    $(b_0, \ldots, b_{m-1}) \leftarrow b_j$
    $B_{ij} \leftarrow \prod_{l=0}^{m-1} b_l^{i_l} \bmod p$

$z \leftarrow 1$
for $l = 0, \ldots, \ell - 1$ do
  $z \leftarrow z^2 \bmod p$
  for $j = 0, \ldots, s - 1$ do
    $i \leftarrow E_j[l]$
    $z \leftarrow z \cdot B_{ij} \bmod p$

return z

Algorithm 2. Improved product exponentiation algorithm based on HAC 14.88 and Algorithm 1.

Furthermore, let $E_j \in \{0,1\}^{m \times \ell}$ be the binary *exponent array* of e_j, whose rows are the binary representations of the exponents from e_j [10]. Let $E_j[l]$ denote the l-th column of E_j.

In the resulting Algorithm 2, which is a synthesis of Algorithm 1 and HAC 14.88, we initially perform the precomputation for all s sub-tasks. In the main loop of the algorithm, we see that the loop over the sub-tasks only performs one multiplication in each step, but no squarings. This reduces the total number of squarings from $s \cdot (\ell - 1)$ to $\ell - 1$. Therefore, the relative running time of Algorithm 2 is strictly smaller than the relative running time of Algorithm 1:

$$\widetilde{M}_{\mathsf{Alg.2}}^m(\ell, N) = \frac{s \cdot (2^m - m - 1) + (\ell - 1) + (\ell s - 1) \cdot P_m}{N} < \frac{2^m + \ell}{m} + \frac{\ell}{N}.$$

To compare this result with the numbers from above, we select $m^{\mathsf{opt}} = 9$ for $\ell = 2047$ (see Table 2), which leads to $\widetilde{M}_{Alg.2}^{\mathsf{opt}}(2047, N) = 282$ and $\mu_{Alg.2}(2047, N) = 8.51$ for large input sizes N. For $\ell_{\mathsf{long}} = 2047$ and $\ell_{\mathsf{short}} = 224$, we select $m^{\mathsf{opt}} = 6$ to get $\mu_{Alg.2}^*(2047, 224, N) = 52.15$. In both settings, Algorithm 2 is therefore approximately 45% more efficient than Algorithm 1. Note that we are not aware of any published document, in which Algorithm 2 is described and analyzed in this way.

To conclude our analysis of product exponentiation algorithms, we show in Table 2 the mapping from $80 \leq \ell \leq 15360$ to m^{opt} in a similar way as for k^{opt} in Table 1, i.e., with some fuzzy areas between the ranges of two adjacent values. It shows that for Algorithm 2 the optimal parameter m^{opt} is usually smaller than for Algorithm 1. This implies that Algorithm 2 benefits from smaller precomputation tables.

Table 2. Optimal sub-task size m^{opt} for different exponent lengths ℓ in Algorithm 1 and Algorithm 2.

Algorithm 1	ℓ	80–168	180–397	415–914	939–2068	2101–4625	4666–10270	>10321
	m^{opt}	6	7	8	9	10	11	12
Algorithm 2	ℓ	80–147	174–349	380–802	845–1839	1896–4148	4231–9284	>9285
	m^{opt}	5	6	7	8	9	10	11

2.4 Algorithms for Fixed-Base Exponentiations

Two of the most common and frequently cited fixed-base exponentiation algorithms are the *fixed-base windowing method* by Brickell et al. [2] and the *comb method* by Lim and Lee [8,9]. Brickell's method is strictly less efficient than the comb method, which itself can be seen as a generalization of the following idea. Let $z = \mathsf{FixedBaseExp}(b, e, p)$ be the problem instance to solve for given inputs b, $e = (e_1, \ldots, e_N)$, and p. Similar to the window method of Sect. 2.2, we define a bit length $1 \leq k \leq \ell$, into which the exponents are decomposed. If we consider a single exponent e, we write it as $e = (e_{t-1} \cdots e_1 e_0)_B$ in base $B = 2^k$, where $t = \lceil \frac{\ell}{k} \rceil$ denotes the resulting number of sub-exponents e_i of length k.

This decomposition of the exponent allows us to transform the computation of b^e into a product exponentiation problem of size t, which can be solved using HAC 14.88, Algorithm 1, or Algorithm 2:

$$b^e = b^{\sum_{i=0}^{t-1} e_i B^i} = \prod_{i=0}^{t-1} b^{e_i B^i} = \prod_{i=0}^{t-1} (b^{B^i})^{e_i} = \prod_{i=0}^{t-1} (b^{2^{ik}})^{e_i}$$

$$= \mathsf{ProductExp}((b_0, \ldots, b_{t-1}), (e_0, \ldots, e_{t-1}), p), \text{ for } b_i = b^{2^{ik}}.$$

The crucial point to observe here is that $b = (b_0, \ldots, b_{t-1})$, which only depends on b, will be the same for all N computations $z_i = b^{e_i}$ with base b. This implies that the precomputation of the ProductExp algorithm only needs to be conducted once for solving a full FixedBaseExp problem of size N.

To describe and analyze the algorithm resulting from this idea, let's assume that the selected ProductExp algorithm memoizes the precomputation tables from previous calls, for example by storing them in a dictionary. Therefore, whenever the same vector b is used more than once, the precomputation table is already available. Clearly, the performance of the resulting Algorithm 3 depends strongly on this assumption, because then the precomputation table can be amortized over the N modexps. In the same way, the values $\boldsymbol{b} = (b_0, \ldots, b_{t-1})$ precomputed in Algorithm 3 must stored for later use.

Algorithm: $\mathsf{FixedBaseExp}_{k,m}(b, e, p)$

Input: Base b

        Exponents $\boldsymbol{e} = (e_1, \ldots, e_N)$, $e_i = (e_{i,t-1} \cdots, e_{i,1} e_{i,0})_B$

        Modulus p

        Block size $1 \leq k \leq \ell$, $B = 2^k$

        Sub-task size $1 \leq m \leq t$

for $i = 0, \ldots, t - 1$ **do**

    $b_i \leftarrow b$

    if $i < t - 1$ **then**

        for $j = 1, \ldots, k$ **do**

            $b \leftarrow b^2 \bmod p$

$\boldsymbol{b} = (b_0, \ldots, b_{t-1})$

for $i = 1, \ldots, N$ **do**

    $z_i \leftarrow \mathsf{ProductExp}_m(\boldsymbol{b}, (e_{i,0}, \ldots, e_{i,t-1}), p)$ // using HAC 14.88, Alg.1, or Alg.2

$\boldsymbol{z} \leftarrow (z_1, \ldots, z_N)$

return $\boldsymbol{z}$

Algorithm 3. Fixed-base exponentiation algorithm based on HAC 14.88, Algorithm 1, or Algorithm 2. In case of HAC 14.88, the parameter m is irrelevant.

Let Algorithm 3.1 and Algorithm 3.2 denote the algorithms obtained from combining Algorithm 3 with HAC 14.88 and Algorithm 2, respectively. While Algorithm 3.1 is strictly inferior to Algorithm 3.2, it is the combination we found in some libraries (see Sect. 3.1). Note that we are not aware of any description of Algorithm 3.2 in this form in a published document, nor of any existing implementation. The relative running times of the algorithms, which depend on both ℓ and N, are as follows (using $E(x) = 2^x - x - 1$):

$$\widetilde{M}^k_{Alg.3.1}(\ell, N) = \frac{E(t) + (t-1)k}{N} + (k-1)(1 + P_t) < \frac{2^t + \ell}{N} + 2k,$$

$$\widetilde{M}^{k,m}_{Alg.3.2}(\ell, N) = \frac{sE(m) + (t-1)k}{N} + (k-1) + (ks-1)P_m < \frac{s \cdot 2^m + \ell}{N} + ks + k.$$

Both versions of the algorithm have the same main parameter $1 \leq k \leq \ell$. As soon as k is fixed in Algorithm 3.2 and N is sufficiently large, we can select $1 \leq m^{\mathsf{opt}} \leq t$ deterministically from Table 2. The selection of k^{opt} for a given pair (ℓ, N) is therefore the main optimization problem to solve in both algorithms. We have computed optimal parameters for $\ell = 2047$ and problem sizes $1 \leq N \leq 10^7$. Figure 1 shows the resulting impact factors $\mu_{\mathsf{Alg}}(2047, N)$ and $\mu^*_{\mathsf{Alg}}(2047, 224, N)$.

The aforementioned comb method by Lim and Lee also has two parameters $1 \leq b \leq a \leq \ell$. Here, we refer to its description in [10] as HAC 14.117. For $h = \lceil \ell/a \rceil$, $v = \lceil a/b \rceil$, its running time

$$\widetilde{M}^{a,b}_{\mathsf{HAC\,14.117}}(\ell, N) = \frac{vE(h) + (h-1)a + (v-1)b}{N} + (b-1) + (bv-1)P_h$$

is exactly the running time of $\widetilde{M}^{k,m}_{Alg.3.2}(\ell, N)$ for $a = ks$ and $b = k$ (and therefore $h = m$ and $v = s$). This implies that Algorithm 3.2 and HAC 14.117 are essentially the *same* algorithms. Note that by setting $a = b = k$ (or $v = s = 1$), they contain the strictly inferior Algorithm 3.1 as a special case.

2.5   Use Case: Cryptographic Shuffle

A particular use case for applying the algorithms presented in this paper is the shuffling of a list $E = \langle e_1, \ldots, e_n \rangle$ of ElGamal encrypted votes $e_i = (g^{r_i}, m_i pk^{r_i})$ in a verifiable re-encryption mix-net. This is one of the most time-consuming components in many voting protocols. Note that n is of the same order of magnitude as the size of the electorate, i.e., possibly several millions in a large election context. Two instances of FixedBaseExp are needed for re-encrypting the encrypted votes in a single mixing step.

The particular shuffle proof system by Wikström and Terelius [13,14] requires a total number of $8n + 5$ modexps for generating the proof and $9n + 11$ modexps for verifying the proof. In Table 3, we derived from [5] a more detailed overview of the necessary number of modexps of this particular approach. Note that some of the involved exponents play the role of a challenge in the proof protocol, i.e.,

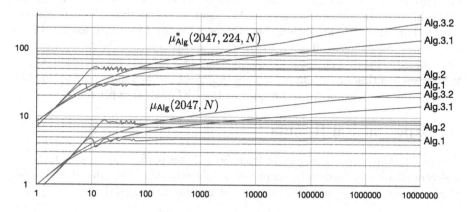

Fig. 1. Impact factors $\mu_{\mathsf{Alg}}(2047, N)$ and $\mu^*_{\mathsf{Alg}}(2047, 224, N)$ of different algorithms. The plotted curves show that ProductExp algorithms (Algorithm 1 and Algorithm 2) converge quickly to a constant speedup, whereas FixedBaseExp algorithms (Algorithm 3.1 and Algorithm 3.2) increase their speedup with increasing problem sizes. The curves also show that the benefit of short exponent-techniques multiplies the benefit of the optimization algorithms.

Table 3. Number of exponentiations for shuffling n votes in a verifiable mix-net.

		Shuffle	Generate proof	Verify proof	
		ℓ_{long}	ℓ_{long}	ℓ_{long}	ℓ_{short}
Exp		–	–	$n + 7$	n
ProductExp		–	$3n$	$3n$	$3n$
FixedBaseExp	g	n	$4n + 4$	$n + 4$	–
	h	–	n	–	–
	pk	n	1	–	–
Total		$2n$	$8n + 5$	$5n + 11$	$4n$

Table 4. Relative running times (1st column) and impact factors (2nd column) of different shuffle algorithms in a setting with $\ell_{long} = 2047$ and $\ell_{short} = 112$.

	$n = 10$		$n = 100$		$n = 1000$		$n = 10^4$		$n = 10^5$		$n = 10^6$	
Shuffle	1216	3.95	626	7.66	450	10.66	352	13.63	286	16.78	240	19.99
Generate proof	2563	7.08	1884	9.06	1623	10.44	1463	11.58	1359	12.46	1283	13.20
Verify proof	5132	2.96	3486	3.68	3306	3.81	3276	3.84	3265	3.85	3262	3.85

their lengths are restricted to the security strength λ. Therefore, we make a distinction between exponents of length $\ell_{long} = |q| = |p| - 1$ and $\ell_{short} = \lambda$.

To evaluate the usage of Algorithm 2 and Algorithm 3.2 in a verifiable mix-net, we calculated relative running times (number of modular multiplications per encrypted vote) and impact factors (benefit relative to HAC 14.83) of the shuffle algorithms for $\ell_{long} = 2047$, $\ell_{short} = 112$, and $n \in \{10, 100, \ldots, 10^6\}$. Table 4 shows that all shuffle algorithms benefit considerably from optimized modexp algorithms. Shuffling itself is up to 20 times and generating the proof up to 13 times more efficient. The smallest benefit results for the proof verification, which is between 3–4 times more efficient. These numbers can be improved even further by applying short-exponent techniques to the ElGamal encryptions.

3   Experimental Results

To confirm the theoretical results from Sect. 2, we performed various tests on different platforms. Generally, client-side performance is more critical as neither the hardware nor the runtime environment can be influenced directly.

3.1   Technologies

On both the client and the server side, we focused on testing popular open-source libraries that implement the algorithms analyzed in Sect. 2. On the server side, the choice is limited as GMP can be regarded as a de facto standard for multiple precision arithmetic. On the other hand, there are a number of potential JavaScript libraries available to be used in browser applications.

Server. The *GNU Multiple Precision Arithmetic Library* (GMP) is a C library that aims to be the fastest arbitrary-precision arithmetic library [4]. The most critical inner loops are written in optimized assembly code, specialized for different processors. There exist wrappers to many other programming language, such as C++, Java, or Python, increasing the scope of GMP remarkably. Modular exponentiation is implemented based on the sliding-window method (HAC 14.85) with Montgomery reduction. Unfortunately, GMP does not offer algorithms for fixed-base or product exponentiations. However, the *GMP Modular Exponentiation Extension* (MEE) by Douglas Wikström offers them both [16].

Client. Below we list the JavaScript libraries considered in our analysis. Their particularities relative to modular exponentiation is summarized in Table 5.

- **JSBN** is a lightweight implementation of large number arithmetic mainly developed by Tom Wu between 2009 and 2013 [18]. A few minor bugs have been fixed in recent years, but otherwise the project seems to be inactive today [12]. Modexp computations are based on the sliding-window technique in combination with Barret and Montgomery reductions.
- **Leemon** is another lightweight implementation of large number arithmetic developed by Leemon C. Baird between 2000 and 2013. Bug fixes to the code available on GitHub have been made until 2016 [1]. Modexps are computed with the square-and-multiply algorithm and Montgomery reduction.
- **VJSC** is a cryptographic library especially tailored for application in electronic voting protocols developed by Douglas Wikström [15,17]. The library is available on GitHub since February 2018. Modexp computations are performed by the improved window method. As a unique feature, VJSC offers integrated support for product and fixed-base exponentiation.
- **MiniGMP** provides a subset of the features of the GMP library [11]. Since it consists of pure C code, i.e., without any assembly optimization, it can be compiled into the WebAssembly format and used for web applications. Modexp computations are based on the square-and-multiply method.

Independently of the actual modexp performance, VJSC and MiniGMP are currently the best maintained libraries. Both of them are well tested and documented. The disadvantage of using MiniGMP in a web application is its dependency to the WebAssembly technology, which has been introduced only recently. In addition to the libraries listed above, there is also the *bn.js* JavaScript library for big numbers [6]. Its main target are elliptic curves and hence it is optimized for calculations with 256-bit numbers. For example, the window size within the modular exponentiation algorithm is hard-coded to $k = 4$.

Parallelism. A natural strategy to speed-up computations on a multi-core CPU is to execute certain tasks in parallel. On the server side, defining and executing tasks in parallel is well supported and easy to implement in many programming languages. On the client side, the situation is slightly different. Although current personal devices (notebooks, tablet computers, mobile phones) have all multi-core CPUs and hence, parallelism is possible from a hardware perspective, JavaScript

Table 5. JavaScript and C libraries for large integer arithmetic. Algorithm marked with a star (*) use Montgomery reduction.

Library	JSBN	Leemon	VJSC	MiniGMP	GMP/MEE
Language	JavaScript	JavaScript	JavaScript	C	C
Author(s)	T. Wu	L. C. Baird	D. Wikström	N. Möller	T. Granlund D. Wikström
Exp	HAC 14.85*	HAC 14.79*	HAC 14.83	HAC 14.79	HAC 14.85*
ProductExp	*unsupported*	*unsupported*	HAC 14.88	*unsupported*	Algorithm 2
FixedBaseExp	*unsupported*	*unsupported*	Algorithm 3.1	*unsupported*	Algorithm 3.1

code is intended to be executed in a single thread. Only recent advancements in the area of so-called *web workers* bring concurrency also to JavaScript by allowing web pages to run scripts in background threads. Once created, a web worker runs completely independent of the main script without any shared memory. Communication from and to the web workers goes via an asynchronous event bus. Web workers are already supported by all major web browsers, so performance benefits can be expected on all up-to-date platforms.

The remaining problem is to find a strategy that optimizes the overall benefit of using parallel computing in combination with other optimization techniques. For example, to circumvent the lack of shared memory, passing large precomputation tables for fixed-base exponentiations to different web workers might not be the best strategy. On the other hand, if multiple fixed-base exponentiations for different bases must be computed, a web worker could be created for each base. The overall computation time would then be decreased by several factors depending on the number of available cores. As the benefit of parallelism strongly relies on the underlying hardware and on the concrete computations to perform, we have excluded this aspect in the following performance analysis.

3.2 Performance Analysis

We are now going to present the results from our experiments of computing modular exponentiations with different optimizations, different libraries, and different runtime environments. All experiments were conducted on the same computer (MacBook Pro 2.9 GHz Intel Core i7) and the same web browser (Firefox v63.0.3).[4] The goal of this subsection is to present the magnitude of what can be expected in practice and to demonstrate that this magnitude corresponds to the theoretical results from Sect. 2. All results can be reproduced reliably with deviations in a range of about ±5%.

Evaluation of Libraries. We first conducted an experiment to evaluate the performance of the different libraries for large number arithmetic. We computed

---

[4] Using the same testbed, we performed further experiments on different platforms such as tablet computers and mobile phones. We obtained very similar test results on all platforms, but for reasons of brevity, we do not include them in our discussion.

with each library a series of 100 modular exponentiations. Table 6 shows the resulting average running times for a single exponentiation. On the server side, the results are somewhat surprising regarding the time difference between GMP and MiniGMP. There are two main reasons for that. First, GMP implements better algorithms than MiniGMP (see Table 5), and second, GMP provides highly optimized assembly code. In our test environment, turning off assembly optimizations makes GMP approximately three times less efficient.

Regarding the results obtained for JavaScript, we conclude that none of the JavaScript libraries can keep up with native GMP. The comparison of the different JavaScript libraries also points out the impact of selecting the best algorithm, which explains that VJSC and JSBN offer a better performance than Leeman and MiniGMP/WASM.[5] Interestingly, VJSC without Montgomery reduction performs better than JSBN with Montgomery reduction. This shows the importance of other (hidden) factors such as an optimized implementation for the given environment.

Product and Fixed-Base Exponentiation. To analyze the benefits of the optimization techniques from Sect. 2, we decided to conduct server-side experiments with GMP/MEE and client-side experiments with VJSC. It was required to adjust VJSC slightly, as VJSC selects the parameter k of Algorithm 3.1 based on $|p|$ instead of $\ell = |e_i|$, which is sub-optimal for small exponents. The experiments were conducted for problems of size $N \in \{10^2, 10^3, \ldots, 10^6\}$ and two different security strengths $\lambda = 112$ and $\lambda = 128$. The absolute running times were measured over the whole experiment and then divided by the problem size N. We also computed corresponding impact factors to demonstrate the benefit of the optimization algorithms over plain modexp computations.

Table 6. Average running times for modular exponentiations in different libraries.

	Server		Client			
ℓ	GMP	MiniGMP	VJSC	JSBN	Leeman	MiniGMP/WASM
2048	3.05 ms	19.23 ms	81.55 ms	105.68 ms	181.89 ms	133.59 ms
3072	8.97 ms	63.14 ms	248.69 ms	332.81 ms	589.74 ms	447.27 ms

Using GMP/MEE (see Table 7), short exponents yield the expected performance gain independently of the problem size N (between 7–8 for $\lambda = 112$

---

[5] We were surprised to observe that MiniGMP compiled into WASM does not provide an important advantage over pure JavaScript. We have no explanation for this, but from the tests that we conducted, we can exclude that this is due to some communication overhead between WASM and JavaScript. By passing exactly the same amount of data from JavaScript to WASM, we observed that computing n modexps in a single call is almost exactly n times more expensive than computing a single modexp.

Table 7. Relative running times in milliseconds (1st columns) and impact factors (2nd column) of different algorithms using GMP/MEE.

N	Algorithm	$\lambda = 112$				$\lambda = 128$			
		2048/2047		2048/224		3072/3071		3072/256	
100	HAC 14.85	3.049	1	0.435	7.0	8.969	1	0.902	9.9
	Algorithm 2	0.637	4.8	0.113	27.0	1.708	5.25	0.196	45.8
	Algorithm 3.1	0.799	3.8	0.104	29.3	1.999	4.5	0.213	42.0
1,000	HAC 14.85	2.980	1	0.360	8.0	8.852	1	0.797	11.1
	Algorithm 2	0.610	4.9	0.108	27.6	1.508	5.8	0.207	42.8
	Algorithm 3.1	0.588	5.1	0.079	37.7	1.556	5.7	0.170	52.1
10,000	HAC 14.85	3.008	1	0.367	8.2	8.831	1	0.816	10.8
	Algorithm 2	0.636	4.7	0.100	30.1	1.518	5.8	0.204	43.3
	Algorithm 3.1	0.495	6.1	0.066	45.6	1.288	6.9	0.137	64.5
100,000	Algorithm 3.1	0.422	7.1	0.050	60.2	1.122	7.9	0.111	79.6
1,000,000	Algorithm 3.1	0.389	7.7	0.044	68.4	0.983	9.0	0.089	99.2

and 10–11 for $\lambda = 128$). Also independent of N is the benefit of Algorithm 2 for product exponentiations, which is between 5–6 times faster than computing plain modexps. For Algorithm 3.1, the amortization of the precomputation can be observed by looking at the increasing benefit when N gets larger. The measurements also demonstrate that the benefit of short exponents multiples the benefit of the optimization algorithm. For $\lambda = 128$ and $N = 10^6$, for example, fixed-base exponentiations with short exponents results in an impact factor of $99.2 \approx 9.0 * 10.8$.

Using VJSC in a web browser (see Table 8), the resulting impact factors are similar to GMP/MEE. However, some of the values are slightly misleading because of the less optimized plain modexp implementation in VJSC. This explains that Algorithm 1 for product exponentiation in VJSC has only a slightly lower impact factor in comparison with Algorithm 2 in GMP/MEE, although theory predicts a difference of approximately 37%.

Overall, the conducted performance analysis shows that in practice the observed benefits of the optimizations are slightly lower than what could be expected from theory. Possible reasons are manifold. In the theoretical analysis, some simplifications have been made, like for example the counting of squarings and multiplications in the same way. On the other hand, specific optimizations on an implementation level are manifested to varying degrees depending on the computation. The plain modexp in GMP is strongly optimized including Montgomery reduction, straining the theoretical results based on counting multiplications. Nevertheless, the presented optimization techniques accelerate the computation of multiple modexps also in practice by orders of magnitude.

Table 8. Relative running times in milliseconds (1st columns) and impact factors (2nd column) of different algorithms using VJSC.

		$\lambda = 112$				$\lambda = 128$			
N	Algorithm	2048/2047		2048/224		3072/3071		3072/256	
100	HAC 14.83	81.55	1	11.73	7.0	248.69	1	25.10	9.9
	Algorithm 1	18.69	4.4	3.22	25.3	58.44	4.3	7.52	33.1
	Algorithm 3.1	15.16	5.4	2.89	28.2	47.41	5.2	6.14	40.5
1,000	HAC 14.83	81.83	1	11.79	7.0	254.80	1	25.25	10.1
	Algorithm 1	17.85	4.6	3.11	26.3	55.49	4.6	7.21	35.3
	Algorithm 3.1	10.81	7.6	1.67	49.0	32.71	7.8	3.72	68.5

4   Conclusion

Our analysis of modular exponentiation algorithms in this paper demonstrates the potential of the available optimized methods for different types of exponentiation problems. While product exponentiation problems can be solved 5–10 times more efficiently, we can solve large fixed-based exponentiation problems up to two orders of magnitude more efficiently than with conventional methods. Using short-exponent techniques, the impact of these methods can be strengthened by another order of magnitude. The resulting overall benefit is very promising for making cryptographic protocols more efficient, particularly for web applications on the client side. On the server side, we also obtain a considerable speedup, for example for shuffling a list of encryptions in a verifiable mix-net. We expect similar benefits for other cryptographic tasks.

Regarding the available libraries implementing the algorithms presented in this paper, we believe that there is some room for future work. For the best available algorithms for fixed-base exponentiation, Algorithm 3.2 or HAC 14.117, we were surprised not to find an implementation in any of the libraries we looked at. By looking at the source code of these libraries, we also realized that they do not always select optimal algorithm parameters. Improving and completing these libraries is an open task, for which this paper provides a solid starting point.

References

1. Baird, L.C.: Big Integer Library by Leemon. https://github.com/Evgenus/BigInt
2. Brickell, E.F., Gordon, D.M., McCurley, K.S., Wilson, D.B.: Fast exponentiation with precomputation. In: Rueppel, R.A. (ed.) EUROCRYPT 1992. LNCS, vol. 658, pp. 200–207. Springer, Heidelberg (1993). https://doi.org/10.1007/3-540-47555-9_18
3. Giry, D.: Cryptographic Key Length Recommendation. https://www.keylength.com

4. Granlund, T.: The GNU Multiple Precision Arithmetic Library - Edition 6.1.2 (2016). https://gmplib.org
5. Haenni, R., Locher, P., Koenig, R., Dubuis, E.: Pseudo-code algorithms for verifiable re-encryption mix-nets. In: Brenner, M., et al. (eds.) FC 2017. LNCS, vol. 10323, pp. 370–384. Springer, Cham (2017). https://doi.org/10.1007/978-3-319-70278-0_23
6. Indutny, F.: BigNum in Pure Javascript. https://github.com/indutny/bn.js
7. Koshiba, T., Kurosawa, K.: Short exponent Diffie-Hellman problems. In: Bao, F., Deng, R., Zhou, J. (eds.) PKC 2004. LNCS, vol. 2947, pp. 173–186. Springer, Heidelberg (2004). https://doi.org/10.1007/978-3-540-24632-9_13
8. Lee, P.J., Lim, C.H.: Method for exponentiation in a public-key cryptosystem. United States Patent No. 5999627, December 1999
9. Lim, C.H., Lee, P.J.: More flexible exponentiation with precomputation. In: Desmedt, Y.G. (ed.) CRYPTO 1994. LNCS, vol. 839, pp. 95–107. Springer, Heidelberg (1994). https://doi.org/10.1007/3-540-48658-5_11
10. Menezes, A.J., van Oorschot, P.C., Vanstone, S.A.: Handbook of Applied Cryptography. CRC Press, Boca Raton (1996)
11. Möller, N.: Mini-GMP - A Minimalistic Implementation of a GNU GMP Subset. https://godoc.org/modernc.org/minigmp
12. Perlitch, A.: JSBN - Javascript Big Number. https://github.com/andyperlitch/jsbn
13. Terelius, B., Wikström, D.: Proofs of restricted shuffles. In: Bernstein, D.J., Lange, T. (eds.) AFRICACRYPT 2010. LNCS, vol. 6055, pp. 100–113. Springer, Heidelberg (2010). https://doi.org/10.1007/978-3-642-12678-9_7
14. Wikström, D.: A commitment-consistent proof of a shuffle. In: Boyd, C., González Nieto, J. (eds.) ACISP 2009. LNCS, vol. 5594, pp. 407–421. Springer, Heidelberg (2009). https://doi.org/10.1007/978-3-642-02620-1_28
15. Wikström, D.: User Manual for the Verificatum Mix-Net - VMN Version 3.0.3. Verificatum AB, Stockholm, Sweden (2018)
16. Wikström, D.: GMP Modular Exponentiation Extension. https://github.com/verificatum/verificatum-gmpmee
17. Wikström, D.: Verificatum JavaScript Cryptography Library. https://github.com/verificatum/verificatum-vjsc
18. Wu, T.: RSA and ECC in JavaScript. http://www-cs-students.stanford.edu/~tjw/jsbn

Short Paper: Coercion-Resistant Voting in Linear Time via Fully Homomorphic Encryption
Towards a Quantum-Safe Scheme

Peter B. Rønne[1]([✉]), Arash Atashpendar[1], Kristian Gjøsteen[2], and Peter Y. A. Ryan[1]

[1] SnT, University of Luxembourg, Luxembourg City, Luxembourg
{peter.roenne,arash.atashpendar,peter.ryan}@uni.lu
[2] Norwegian University of Science and Technology, NTNU, Trondheim, Norway
kristian.gjosteen@ntnu.no

Abstract. We present an approach for performing the tallying work in the coercion-resistant JCJ voting protocol, introduced by Juels, Catalano, and Jakobsson, in linear time using fully homomorphic encryption (FHE). The suggested enhancement also paves the path towards making JCJ quantum-resistant, while leaving the underlying structure of JCJ intact. The pairwise comparison-based approach of JCJ using plaintext equivalence tests leads to a quadratic blow-up in the number of votes, which makes the tallying process rather impractical in realistic settings with a large number of voters. We show how the removal of invalid votes can be done in linear time via a solution based on recent advances in various FHE primitives such as hashing, zero-knowledge proofs of correct decryption, verifiable shuffles and threshold FHE. We conclude by discussing some of the advantages and challenges resulting from our proposal, followed by an outline of future work and possible lines of attack.

1 Introduction

Over the past few decades, we have witnessed significant advances in cryptographic voting protocols. Yet, despite all the progress, see e.g., [1], secure e-voting is still faced with a plethora of challenges and open questions, which largely arise as a result of the interplay between intricate properties such as vote privacy, individual and universal verifiability, receipt-freeness, and a notoriously difficult requirement, namely that of coercion-resistance. Coercion-resistance can be viewed as a stronger form of privacy that should hold even against an adversary who may instruct honest parties to carry out certain computations while potentially requiring that they reveal secrets in order to verify their behavior and ensure compliance. This property is typically enforced by providing honest parties with a mechanism that allows them to either deceive the coercer or to deny having performed a particular action. Due to limited space, we do not

© International Financial Cryptography Association 2020
A. Bracciali et al. (Eds.): FC 2019 Workshops, LNCS 11599, pp. 289–298, 2020.
https://doi.org/10.1007/978-3-030-43725-1_20

elaborate on the long series of works in this area and instead refer the reader to [11,12,21,22] and references therein for more details.

Since the breakthrough work of Gentry [15] on fully homomorphic encryption (FHE), there has been a surge of interest in this line of research that remains very active to this day, with a series of recent advances including, but not limited to, a homomorphic evaluation of AES [16]. Although the use of additively or multiplicatively homomorphic cryptosystems is common place in the e-voting literature, the relevance of FHE for potentially quantum-safe secure e-voting, with better voter verifiability, was only recently discussed by Gjøsteen and Strand [17]. In our work, instead of designing an FHE-based protocol from scratch, we apply the machinery of FHE to a well-known, classical voting scheme, in order to improve its time complexity and to replace its reliance on the hardness assumption of solving the discrete logarithm problem with a quantum-resistant solution, namely lattice-based cryptography. So far, no efficient quantum algorithms capable of breaking lattice-based FHE schemes have been discovered.

Although constructions with varying degrees of coercion-resistance do exist, the voting protocol introduced by Juels, Catalano, and Jakobsson [21], often referred to as the *JCJ protocol*, is among the most well-known solutions in the context of coercion-resistant voting schemes. JCJ provides a reasonable level of coercion-resistance using a voter credential faking mechanism, and it was arguably the first proposal with a formal definition of coercion-resistance. However, JCJ suffers from a complexity problem due to the weeding steps in its tallying phase, which are required for eliminating invalid votes and duplicates. The exhaustive, pairwise comparison-based approach of JCJ using plaintext equivalence tests (PET) [19] leads to a quadratic blow-up in the number of votes, which makes the tallying process rather impractical in realistic settings with a large number of voters or in the face of ballot-box stuffing. For instance, in the Civitas voting system [10] based on JCJ, voters are grouped into blocks or virtual precincts to reduce the tallying time.

Here we propose an enhancement of the JCJ protocol aimed at performing its tallying work in linear time, based on an approach that incorporates primitives from the realm of fully homomorphic encryption (FHE), which also paves the path towards making JCJ quantum-safe.

In Sect. 2, we describe the JCJ protocol and cover some related work. Next, in Sect. 3, we show how the weeding of "bad" votes can be done in linear time, with minimal change to JCJ, via an approach based on recent advances in various FHE primitives such as hashing, zero-knowledge (ZK) proofs of correct decryption, verifiable shuffles and threshold FHE. We also touch upon some of the advantages and challenges resulting from such an approach in Sect. 3.2 and in Sect. 4, we conclude with an outline of future work and possible lines of attack.

2   The JCJ Model and Voting Protocol in a Nutshell

Cryptographic Building Blocks. JCJ relies on a modified version of ElGamal, a threshold public-key cryptosystem with re-encryption, secure under the hardness assumption of the Decisional Diffie-Hellman (DDH) problem in a multiplicative cyclic group $\mathcal{G}$ of order q. A ciphertext on message $m \in \mathcal{G}$ has the form $(\alpha, \beta, \gamma) = (mh^r, g_1^r, g_2^r)$ for $r \in_U \mathbb{Z}_q$, with (g_1, g_2, h) being the public key where $g_1, g_2, h \in \mathcal{G}$, and the secret key consisting of $x_1, x_2 \in \mathbb{Z}_q$ such that $h = g_1^{x_1} g_2^{x_2}$. The construction allows easy sharing of the secret key in a threshold way. The weeding steps make use of a plaintext equivalence test (PET), which is carried out by the secret key holders and takes as input two ciphertexts and outputs 1 if the underlying plaintexts are equal, and 0 otherwise. The PET produces publicly verifiable evidence with negligible information leakage about plaintexts. Finally, JCJ uses non-interactive zero-knowledge (NIZK) proofs and mix-nets, which are aimed at randomly and secretly permuting and re-encrypting input ciphertexts such that output ciphertexts cannot be traced back to their corresponding ciphertexts. Throughout, it is assumed that the computations of the talliers and registrars are done in a joint, distributed threshold manner. We use $\in_U$ to denote an element that is sampled uniformly at random.

Agents. JCJ mainly consists of three sets of agents, described as follows.

1. **Registrars**: A set $\mathcal{R} = \{R_1, R_2, \ldots, R_{n_R}\}$ of n_R entities in charge of jointly generating and distributing credentials to voters.
2. **Talliers**: A set $\mathcal{T} = \{T_1, T_2, \ldots, T_{n_T}\}$ of *authorities* in charge of processing ballots, jointly counting the votes and publishing the final tally.
3. **Voters**: A set of n_V voters, $\mathcal{V} = \{V_1, V_2, \ldots, V_{n_V}\}$, participating in an election, where each voter V_i is publicly identified by an index i.

Bulletin Board and Candidate Slate. A *bulletin board*, denoted by $\mathcal{BB}$, is an abstraction representing a publicly accessible, append-only, but otherwise immutable board, meaning that participants can only add entries to $\mathcal{BB}$ without overwriting or erasing existing items. A *candidate slate*, C, is an ordered set of n_C distinct identifiers $\{c_1, c_2, \ldots, c_{n_C}\}$ capturing voter choices. A *tally* is defined under slate C, as a vector $X = \{x_1, x_2, \ldots, x_{n_C}\}$ of n_C positive integers, where each x_j indicates the number of votes cast for choice c_j.

Main Security Assumptions. The adversary may corrupt only a minority of agents in $\mathcal{T}$, as otherwise privacy would be lost. In the registration phase, it is assumed that the distribution of voter credentials is done over an untappable channel and that no registration transcripts can be obtained, assuming that secure erasure is possible. Cast votes are transmitted via anonymous channels, which is a basic requirement for ruling out forced-abstention attacks.

2.1   The JCJ Protocol

Setup and Registration. The key pairs $(sk_{\mathcal{R}}, pk_{\mathcal{R}})$ and $(sk_{\mathcal{T}}, pk_{\mathcal{T}})$ are generated in a trustworthy manner, and the public keys, i.e., $pk_{\mathcal{T}}$ and $pk_{\mathcal{R}}$, are published with other public system parameters. The registrars $\mathcal{R}$ generate and transmit to eligible voter V_i a random string $\sigma_i \in_U \mathcal{G}$ that serves as the credential of the voter. $\mathcal{R}$ adds an encryption of σ_i, $S_i = E_{pk_{\mathcal{T}}}(\sigma_i)$, to the voter roll L, which is maintained on the bulletin board $\mathcal{BB}$ and digitally signed by $\mathcal{R}$.

Voting. An integrity-protected candidate slate C containing the names and unique identifiers in $\mathcal{G}$ for n_C candidates, along with a unique, random election identifier ϵ are published by the authorities. Voter V_i generates a ballot in the form of a variant of ElGamal ciphertexts (E_1, E_2), for candidate choice c_j and voter credential σ_i, respectively, e.g., for $a_1, a_2 \in_U \mathbb{Z}_q$, we have $E_1 = (g_1^{a_1}, g_2^{a_1}, c_j h^{a_1})$ and $E_2 = (g_1^{a_2}, g_2^{a_2}, \sigma_i h^{a_2})$. V_i computes NIZK proofs of knowledge and correctness of σ_i and $c_j \in C$, collectively denoted by P_f. These ensure non-malleability of ballots, also across elections by including ϵ in the hash of the Fiat-Shamir heuristic. V_i posts $B_i = (E_1, E_2, P_f)$ to $\mathfrak{BB}$ via an anonymous channel.

Tallying. In order to compute the tally, duplicate votes and those with invalid credentials will have to be removed. The complexity problem crops up in steps 2 and 4 such that given n votes, the tallying work has a time complexity of $\mathcal{O}(n^2)$. To tally the ballots posted to $\mathfrak{BB}$, the authority $\mathcal{T}$ performs the following steps:

1. $\mathcal{T}$ verifies all proofs on $\mathfrak{BB}$ and discards any ballots with invalid proofs. Let $\boldsymbol{A_1}$ and $\boldsymbol{B_1}$ denote the list of remaining E_1 candidate choice ciphertexts, and E_2 credential ciphertexts, respectively.
2. $\mathcal{T}$ performs pairwise PETs on all ciphertexts in $\boldsymbol{B_1}$ and removes duplicates according to some fixed criterion such as the order of postings to $\mathfrak{BB}$. For every element removed from $\boldsymbol{B_1}$, the corresponding element with the same index is also removed from $\boldsymbol{A_1}$, resulting in the "weeded" vectors $\boldsymbol{B_1'}$ and $\boldsymbol{A_1'}$.
3. $\mathcal{T}$ applies a mix-net to $\boldsymbol{A_1'}$ and $\boldsymbol{B_1'}$ using the same, secret permutation, resulting in the lists of ciphertexts $\boldsymbol{A_2}$ and $\boldsymbol{B_2}$.
4. $\mathcal{T}$ applies a mix-net to the encrypted list $\boldsymbol{L}$ of credentials from the voter roll and then compares each ciphertext of $\boldsymbol{B_2}$ to the ciphertexts of $\boldsymbol{L}$ using a PET. $\mathcal{T}$ keeps a vector $\boldsymbol{A_3}$ of all ciphertexts of $\boldsymbol{A_2}$ for which the corresponding elements of $\boldsymbol{B_2}$ match an element of $\boldsymbol{L}$, thus achieving the weeding of ballots with invalid voter credentials.
5. $\mathcal{T}$ decrypts all ciphertexts in $\boldsymbol{A_3}$ and tallies the final result.

2.2   Properties

Vote **privacy** is maintained as long as neither a threshold set of talliers nor all the mixing servers are corrupted. A colluding majority of talliers can obviously decrypt everything and colluding mixing authorities could trace votes back to $\boldsymbol{L}$.

Regarding **correctness**, voters can refer to $\mathfrak{BB}$ to verify that their vote has been recorded as intended and that the tally is computed correctly. Similar attacks become possible in case of collusion by a majority of authorities. As for **verifiability**, anyone can refer to $\mathfrak{BB}$, P_f and $\boldsymbol{L}$ to verify the correctness of the tally produced by $\mathcal{T}$.

The **coercion-resistance** provided by JCJ is essentially achieved by keeping voter credentials hidden throughout the election. A coerced voter can then choose a random fake credential σ' to cast a fake vote and present it as their real vote.

Any vote cast with the fake credential will not be counted, and the voter can anonymously cast their real vote using their real credential.

2.3   Related Work

We focus on the most closely-related works on improving the efficiency problem of the tallying work in JCJ. Smith [25] and Weber et al. [29,30] follow a similar approach in that they do away with comparisons using PETs, and instead, they raise the credentials to a jointly T-shared secret value and store these blinded terms in a hash table such that collisions can be found in linear time. The use of a single exponent means that a coercer can test if the voter has provided them with a fake or a real credential by submitting a ballot with the given credential and another with the credential raised to a known random value.

In [4,5], Araujo et al. move away from comparing entries in L with terms in the cast ballots to a setting in which duplicates are publicly identifiable and a majority of talliers use their private keys to identify legitimate votes, and in [3] the authors use algebraic MACs. Spycher et al. [26] use the same solution proposed by Smith and Weber to remove duplicates and apply targeted PETs only to terms in L and A, identified via additional information provided by voters linking their vote to the right entry in L. In [18], publicly auditable conditional blind signatures are used to achieve coercion-resistance in linear time using a FOO-like [14] architecture, the downsides being the need for extra authorization requests for participation privacy and a double use of anonymous channels.

3   JCJ in Linear Time via Fully Homomorphic Encryption

Our proposal revolves around replacing the original cryptosystem of JCJ with a fully homomorphic one, thus allowing us to preserve the original design of JCJ. The main idea is to homomorphically evaluate hashes of the underlying plaintext of the FHE-encrypted voter credentials, perform FHE-decryption and post the hash values of the credentials to the bulletin board $\mathfrak{BB}$. Now the elimination of invalid and duplicate entries can be done in linear time by using a hash table.

FHE Primitives. Constrained by limited space, we only enumerate the cryptographic primitives that will be required for the enhancement suggested below and refer the reader to the cited sources for further details. Let $\mathcal{E}_{pk}(m)$ denote an FHE-encryption of a message $m \in \{0,1\}^n$ under the public key pk. At its core, for $b_0, b_1 \in \{0,1\}$, given $\mathcal{E}_{pk}(b_0)$ and $\mathcal{E}_{pk}(b_1)$, FHE allows us to compute $\mathcal{E}_{pk}(b_0 \oplus b_1)$ and $\mathcal{E}_{pk}(b_0 \cdot b_1)$ by working over ciphertexts alone, without having access to the secret key, thus enabling the homomorphic evaluation of any boolean circuit, i.e., computing $\mathcal{E}_{pk}(f(m))$ from $\mathcal{E}_{pk}(m)$ for any computable function f. We make use of FHE [7,15], fully homomorphic hashing [13], zero-knowledge proofs of correct decryption for FHE ciphertexts [8], verifiable shuffles [27] and threshold FHE [6], see Sect. 3.2 for more details on open questions and the state-of-the-art.

3.1   Enhancing JCJ with FHE and Weeding in Linear Time

We now describe how FHE primitives can be incorporated into JCJ while inducing minimal change in the original protocol. We assume threshold FHE throughout.

Setup and Registration. The setup and registration phases remain unchanged w.r.t. JCJ, except that $\mathcal{R}$ now adds an FHE-encryption of σ_i, $S_i = \mathcal{E}_{pk_{\mathcal{T}}}(\sigma_i)$, to the voter roll L. We adopt the same assumptions mentioned earlier in Sect. 2.

Voting. Instead of using ElGamal encryption, the credentials posted on the $\mathfrak{BB}$ are encrypted under some FHE scheme, say BGV [7], with a key pair (pk, sk). Each voter V_i adds $\mathcal{E}_{pk_{\mathcal{T}}}(\sigma_i)$, along with the required NIZK proofs, to $\mathfrak{BB}$.

Tallying. The tallying phase remains largely the same except that for removing duplicates and invalid votes, we leverage our use of FHE to carry out simple equality tests between hash digests of credentials. Since the concealed credentials are now stored in FHE ciphertexts, we can process them using an FHE hashing circuit. More precisely, for a jointly created $\mathcal{T}$-shared key k, published under encryption $\mathcal{E}_{pk}(k)$, the credentials σ_i contained in the FHE-encrypted terms $\mathcal{E}_{pk}(\sigma_i)$ are homomorphically hashed (see [13] by Fiore, Gennaro and Pastro and [9] by Catalano et al.), under key k resulting in $\mathcal{E}_{pk}(h_k(\sigma_i))$, such that upon decryption we obtain $h_k(\sigma_i)$. A ZK proof of correct decryption is also posted to $\mathfrak{BB}$ for verifiability, see [8] by Carr et al. for an approach to this.

Once the hash values of the credentials are posted on the $\mathfrak{BB}$, the weeding of duplicates can be done in $\mathcal{O}(n)$ using a simple hash table look-up, i.e., iterate, hash and check for collision in constant time, thus an overall linear-time complexity in the number of votes. Next, the registered credentials and the submitted vote/credential pairs are mixed [27] and the homomorphic hashing procedure is carried out again using a new secret key on all credential ciphertexts. Comparing the hashed registered credentials with those from the cast ballots allows us to remove invalid votes in $\mathcal{O}(n)$. Finally, the remaining valid votes are verifiably decrypted.

3.2   Advantages, Potential Pitfalls and Open Questions

Apart from the linear-time weeding algorithm, as already pointed out by Gjøsteen and Strand in [17], in addition to being a novel application of FHE to secure e-voting, obtaining better voter verifiability and a scheme believed to be quantum-resistant are among the noteworthy benefits of such an approach.

The quantum safety property is conjectured based on the fact that efficient quantum algorithms for solving certain problems used in lattice-based cryptography remain to be discovered. While our solution offers a step towards making JCJ potentially quantum secure, a thorough analysis aimed at determining if its various security properties are secure against quantum adversaries is needed.

Clearly, in terms of real world FHE implementations, the state-of-the-art still suffers from efficiency issues. However, some significant progress has already been made in this area, e.g., the homomorphic evaluation of AES [16] or block ciphers designed for homomorphic evaluation [2]. Moreover, it should be pointed out that some of the needed primitives, e.g., turning ZK proofs of correct decryption for FHE [8,23] into NIZK proofs, are still not satisfactory and remain the subject of ongoing research and future improvements.

Finally, another study that we leave as future work would focus on the overhead induced by specific choices of FHE implementations and analyzing whether or not the resulting solution, despite having linear time complexity, might become less efficient than the original JCJ scheme beyond a certain point.

4   Future Work and Further Security Remarks

A security analysis aimed at providing proofs of security for various properties such as correctness, verifiability and coercion-resistance will remain future work. One possibility would be to investigate whether the required security properties in our modified variant of JCJ hold against classical adversaries, under the same oracle access assumptions for mixing, PETs, threshold decryption and hashing. The post-quantum security aspect will have to be analyzed in an appropriate framework, e.g., by incorporating the quantum random oracle model.

Eligibility Verifiability. Assuming a majority of colluding authorities, apart from a compromise of vote privacy, another, perhaps more damaging problem with JCJ and its improved variants is that of *eligibility verifiability*. A colluding majority would be able to retrieve voter credentials and submit valid votes for non-participating voters, i.e., perform ballot stuffing.

A solution in [24] suggests performing the registration phase in such a way that only the voter would know the discrete logarithm of their credential. Votes are then cast with an anonymous signature in the form of a ZK proof of knowledge of the discrete logarithm of the encrypted credential, thus preventing ballot stuffing. A similar approach could be used here, with the potential downside of having inefficient proofs and a discrete logarithm hardness assumption, thus not being quantum secure.

Post-Quantum Considerations. For a relaxation of the trustworthiness assumption of $\mathcal{R}$, without assuming secure erasure, quantum-resistant designated verifier proofs [20,28] could replace the classical ones suggested in the original JCJ [21]. To obtain post-quantum security for eligibility verifiability, future research will investigate the use of a quantum-resistant signature scheme that can be evaluated under FHE to preserve ballot anonymity.

As a naive, but illustrative example that is one-time only and non-distributive, consider that the voter creates their credential as $\sigma_i = h(x)$, and that only the voter knows the preimage x. The voter now submits both $\mathcal{E}_{pk}(x)$ and $\mathcal{E}_{pk}(\sigma_i)$ to $\mathfrak{BB}$. Before weeding, the hash is homomorphically evaluated on the ciphertext of the preimage, i.e., $\mathcal{E}_{pk}(h(x))$, followed by an equality test against the ciphertext of the credential $\mathcal{E}_{pk}(\sigma_i)$. A malicious authority can now cast only a valid ballot with a registered credential after the corresponding voter has cast a ballot, and an attempt to vote on their behalf is detectable in the weeding phase.

Acknowledgments. The authors acknowledge support from the Luxembourg National Research Fund (FNR) and the Research Council of Norway for the joint project SURCVS. The project was also supported by the FNR INTER-VoteVerif, the FNR CORE project Q-CoDe, and the European Union's Horizon 2020 research and innovation programme under grant agreement No. 779391 (FutureTPM).

References

1. Adida, B.: Helios: web-based open-audit voting. In: USENIX Security Symposium, vol. 17, pp. 335–348 (2008)
2. Albrecht, M.R., Rechberger, C., Schneider, T., Tiessen, T., Zohner, M.: Ciphers for MPC and FHE. In: Oswald, E., Fischlin, M. (eds.) EUROCRYPT 2015. LNCS, vol. 9056, pp. 430–454. Springer, Heidelberg (2015). https://doi.org/10.1007/978-3-662-46800-5_17
3. Araújo, R., Barki, A., Brunet, S., Traoré, J.: Remote electronic voting can be efficient, verifiable and coercion-resistant. In: Clark, J., Meiklejohn, S., Ryan, P.Y.A., Wallach, D., Brenner, M., Rohloff, K. (eds.) FC 2016. LNCS, vol. 9604, pp. 224–232. Springer, Heidelberg (2016). https://doi.org/10.1007/978-3-662-53357-4_15
4. Araújo, R., Foulle, S., Traoré, J.: A practical and secure coercion-resistant scheme for remote elections. In: Dagstuhl Seminar Proceedings. Schloss Dagstuhl-Leibniz-Zentrum für Informatik (2008)
5. Araújo, R., Ben Rajeb, N., Robbana, R., Traoré, J., Youssfi, S.: Towards practical and secure coercion-resistant electronic elections. In: Heng, S.-H., Wright, R.N., Goi, B.-M. (eds.) CANS 2010. LNCS, vol. 6467, pp. 278–297. Springer, Heidelberg (2010). https://doi.org/10.1007/978-3-642-17619-7_20
6. Boneh, D., et al.: Threshold cryptosystems from threshold fully homomorphic encryption. In: Shacham, H., Boldyreva, A. (eds.) CRYPTO 2018. LNCS, vol. 10991, pp. 565–596. Springer, Cham (2018). https://doi.org/10.1007/978-3-319-96884-1_19
7. Brakerski, Z., Gentry, C., Vaikuntanathan, V.: (Leveled) fully homomorphic encryption without bootstrapping. ACM Trans. Comput. Theory **6**(3), 13 (2014)
8. Carr, C., Costache, A., Davies, G.T., Gjøsteen, K., Strand, M.: Zero-knowledge proof of decryption for FHE ciphertexts. IACR Cryptology ePrint Archive 2018, p. 26 (2018). http://eprint.iacr.org/2018/026
9. Catalano, D., Marcedone, A., Puglisi, O.: Authenticating computation on groups: new homomorphic primitives and applications. In: Sarkar, P., Iwata, T. (eds.) ASIACRYPT 2014. LNCS, vol. 8874, pp. 193–212. Springer, Heidelberg (2014). https://doi.org/10.1007/978-3-662-45608-8_11
10. Clarkson, M.R., Chong, S., Myers, A.C.: Civitas: Toward a secure voting system. In: IEEE Symposium on Security and Privacy, pp. 354–368. IEEE (2008)

11. Cortier, V., Galindo, D., Küsters, R., Mueller, J., Truderung, T.: SoK: verifiability notions for e-voting protocols. In: 2016 IEEE Symposium on Security and Privacy (SP), pp. 779–798. IEEE (2016)
12. Delaune, S., Kremer, S., Ryan, M.: Coercion-resistance and receipt-freeness in electronic voting. In: 19th IEEE Computer Security Foundations Workshop, p. 12. IEEE (2006)
13. Fiore, D., Gennaro, R., Pastro, V.: Efficiently verifiable computation on encrypted data. In: Proceedings of the 2014 ACM SIGSAC Conference on Computer and Communications Security, pp. 844–855. ACM (2014)
14. Fujioka, A., Okamoto, T., Ohta, K.: A practical secret voting scheme for large scale elections. In: Seberry, J., Zheng, Y. (eds.) AUSCRYPT 1992. LNCS, vol. 718, pp. 244–251. Springer, Heidelberg (1993). https://doi.org/10.1007/3-540-57220-1_66
15. Gentry, C.: Fully homomorphic encryption using ideal lattices. In: Proceedings of the 41st Annual ACM Symposium on Symposium on theory of Computing-STOC\2009, pp. 169–169. ACM Press (2009)
16. Gentry, C., Halevi, S., Smart, N.P.: Homomorphic evaluation of the AES circuit. In: Safavi-Naini, R., Canetti, R. (eds.) CRYPTO 2012. LNCS, vol. 7417, pp. 850–867. Springer, Heidelberg (2012). https://doi.org/10.1007/978-3-642-32009-5_49
17. Gjøsteen, K., Strand, M.: A roadmap to fully homomorphic elections: stronger security, better verifiability. In: Brenner, M., et al. (eds.) FC 2017. LNCS, vol. 10323, pp. 404–418. Springer, Cham (2017). https://doi.org/10.1007/978-3-319-70278-0_25
18. Grontas, P., Pagourtzis, A., Zacharakis, A., Zhang, B.: Towards everlasting privacy and efficient coercion resistance in remote electronic voting. IACR Cryptology ePrint Archive 2018, p. 215 (2018)
19. Jakobsson, M., Juels, A.: Mix and match: secure function evaluation via ciphertexts. In: Okamoto, T. (ed.) ASIACRYPT 2000. LNCS, vol. 1976, pp. 162–177. Springer, Heidelberg (2000). https://doi.org/10.1007/3-540-44448-3_13
20. Jao, D., Soukharev, V.: Isogeny-based quantum-resistant undeniable signatures. In: Mosca, M. (ed.) PQCrypto 2014. LNCS, vol. 8772, pp. 160–179. Springer, Cham (2014). https://doi.org/10.1007/978-3-319-11659-4_10
21. Juels, A., Catalano, D., Jakobsson, M.: Coercion-resistant electronic elections. In: Proceedings of the 2005 ACM Workshop on Privacy in the Electronic Society, pp. 61–70. ACM (2005)
22. Küsters, R., Truderung, T., Vogt, A.: A game-based definition of coercion resistance and its applications 1. J. Comput. Secur. 20(6), 709–764 (2012)
23. Luo, F., Wang, K.: Verifiable decryption for fully homomorphic encryption. In: Chen, L., Manulis, M., Schneider, S. (eds.) ISC 2018. LNCS, vol. 11060, pp. 347–365. Springer, Cham (2018). https://doi.org/10.1007/978-3-319-99136-8_19
24. Roenne, P.B.: JCJ with improved verifiability guarantees. In: The International Conference on Electronic Voting E-Vote-ID 2016 (2016)
25. Smith, D.: New cryptographic voting schemes with best-known theoretical properties. In: Workshop on Frontiers in Electronic Elections (2005)
26. Spycher, O., Koenig, R., Haenni, R., Schläpfer, M.: A new approach towards coercion-resistant remote e-voting in linear time. In: Danezis, G. (ed.) FC 2011. LNCS, vol. 7035, pp. 182–189. Springer, Heidelberg (2012). https://doi.org/10.1007/978-3-642-27576-0_15
27. Strand, M.: A verifiable shuffle for the GSW cryptosystem. IACR Cryptology ePrint Archive 2018, p. 27 (2018). http://eprint.iacr.org/2018/027

28. Sun, X., Tian, H., Wang, Y.: Toward quantum-resistant strong designated verifier signature from isogenies. In: 2012 4th International Conference on Intelligent Networking and Collaborative Systems (INCoS), pp. 292–296. IEEE (2012)
29. Weber, S.G.: Coercion-Resistant Cryptographic Voting: Implementing Free and Secret Electronic Elections. VDM Publishing, Saarbrücken (2008)
30. Weber, S.G., Araujo, R., Buchmann, J.: On coercion-resistant electronic elections with linear work. In: The Second International Conference on Availability, Reliability and Security, ARES 2007, pp. 908–916. IEEE (2007)

PrivApollo – Secret Ballot E2E-V Internet Voting

Hua Wu[1](✉), Poorvi L. Vora[1], and Filip Zagórski[2]

[1] Department of Computer Science, The George Washington University,
Washington, D.C., USA
huawu@gwu.edu
[2] Department of Computer Science, Wroclaw University of Science and Technology,
Wroclaw, Poland

Abstract. The Apollo voting protocol improves on the integrity properties of Helios by enabling voters to communicate to the public the failure of the cast-as-intended check, in the event that the voting terminal changes the vote on receiving the credential. It also enables the voter to detect a dishonest registrar and to prove misbehaviour. It provides an explicit description of the role of one or more computational *voting assistants* which help the voter perform the checks without obtaining information on the vote. Unfortunately, neither Helios nor Apollo provides ballot secrecy, because the voting terminal knows the vote. We present PrivApollo, a protocol that improves Apollo by providing ballot secrecy from the voting terminal.

1 Introduction

Since the first cryptographic protocol for secure voting, the area has grown considerably and has led to a number of protocols that have been used in real elections. We focus on Internet voting approaches—such as Helios [1] and Apollo [7]—whose privacy properties are conditional on the security of the cryptographic techniques used. In proposals of this kind, ballot secrecy is typically protected through the encryption of the vote by the voting terminal. A malicious entity on the terminal could leak the vote, which could lead to ballot selling, coercion or selective denial of service. We propose a voting system, PrivApollo, which ensures that the vote is private from the voting terminal.

PrivApollo is an extension of Apollo. In Apollo, the voter relies on a number of voting assistants—computational devices whose role is to assist the voter in checking the actions of the voting system and the voting terminal. The voting

H. Wu and P. L. Vora—This material is based upon work supported in part by the Maryland Procurement Office under contract H98230-14-C-0127 and NSF Award CNS 1421373.

F. Zagórski—Author was partially supported by Polish National Science Centre contract number DEC-2013/09/D/ST6/03927 and by Wroclaw University of Science and Technology [0401/0052/18].

A. Bracciali et al. (Eds.): FC 2019 Workshops, LNCS 11599, pp. 299–313, 2020.
https://doi.org/10.1007/978-3-030-43725-1_21

assistants do not obtain any information on the vote, while the voting terminal knows the vote. PrivApollo also relies on voting assistants. Additionally, in PrivApollo, one specific voting assistant is denoted the *active voting assistant*, and enables the stronger privacy properties of PrivApollo. It is expected that software for the voting assistants will be written by citizen interest groups, in much the same way that tally-verification software is written independently of the voting system.

The ballot secrecy property of PrivApollo is based on indirection: the active voting assistant generates one half of the indirection map, and the voting terminal the other half. The actions of the voting terminal and the active voting assistant can be checked for correctness using a version of what is known as the Benaloh Challenge, instantiated as Helios. The vote is secret from the voting terminal and the active voting assistant if at least one of the two is honest. Even if both are dishonest and collude, the privacy is no worse than that of Helios or Apollo (in which the voting terminal knows the vote). Integrity in PrivApollo holds if at least one voting assistant (not necessarily the active voting assistant) is honest.

Coded voting systems such as Surevote [3], Scantegrity II [4], DEMOS [6] and Remotegrity [13], as well the voting system Punchscan [10], also use indirection to provide privacy from the voting terminal. In these other proposals, however, the indirection map is generated ahead of time by the voting system. Pre-generated indirection maps need to be delivered to the voter before voting begins and after the candidate lists are finalized; this is generally a small time window. Delivery on paper through the postal system can be a challenge, especially for voters who are abroad or in remote locations. If the indirection map is not delivered on paper, the electronic entity performing the delivery knows the map, and the vote is not private from this entity.

In PrivApollo, the indirection map is generated in real time, jointly by the voting terminal and the active voting assistant. PrivApollo's splitting of the indirection map into two components is similar to Punchscan's approach of splitting it into two ballot halves. With Punchscan too, however, the information on both ballot halves is pre-generated by a single entity, the voting system. The Du-Vote protocol [8] also generates the indirection map in real time and splits it into two halves. However, both privacy and integrity properties of Du-Vote require that the two entities not collude. In PrivApollo, integrity properties hold even if the two entities do collude.

In spite of the benefit of ballot secrecy with respect to the voting terminal, the use of indirection is known to pose usability challenges. We do not study usability in this paper, and more usability research and improvements are required before PrivApollo may be deployed in real elections.

This paper is organized as follows. Section 2 presents related work, and Sect. 3 the trust model. Section 4 describes the protocol, Sect. 5 provides a brief description of security and usability properties and Sect. 6 concludes.

2   Related Work

Helios [1] is perhaps the earliest practical proposal for end-to-end-verifiable voting without the use of paper. Several elections have been held using it, including those for the IACR and ACM. In the Helios protocol the voter enters her vote into the voting terminal, which provides her with an encryption of the vote. The Apollo protocol improves the verifiability of Helios with a two-step vote-casting process; voters enter a second credential after the encrypted vote is posted on the bulletin board, thus confirming it is correct. In both systems, the terminal encrypts the vote and hence knows it.

Riva and Ta-Shma [11] propose a precinct-based protocol where the voter prepares two ballots at home, each consisting of a list of encrypted votes indexed by candidate. The terminal in the voting booth re-encrypts all encrypted votes. The voter challenges one encryption for each candidate and then casts the unchallenged one for her choice. Voter privacy is protected if the voting terminal at the precinct and the voter's home computer do not collude.

Code-voting systems, such as Surevote [3], provide voters with a code for each choice, and the voter casts the code in order to vote. The use of codes provides ballot secrecy and prevents the voting terminal from replacing the vote with another valid one. Remotegrity [13] is an extension of code-voting, enabling remote voting through the use of two credentials: one for casting the vote, and the other for confirming it.

Paper-based precinct voting system Punchscan [10] splits its indirection map onto two sheets, which when overlaid form the ballot and reveal the vote. Each sheet bears a mark, but the mark simply denotes the choice on one half of the indirection map, and each sheet by itself reveals no information about the vote. We use a similar idea to construct our electronic ballots; however, our ballots are constructed at the time of voting without secure communication with the voting system. While all voting systems, including PrivApollo, require secure communication with the voter for credential delivery, this may be done many months or weeks before the candidate lists are finalized, and does not pose the same challenge as that of delivering indirection maps in the small time window between finalization of candidates lists and the election.

Our use of indirection is similar to that of Chaum et al. [5]. An important distinction is that the voting assistant communicates with the voting system only through the voting terminal in [5]. In PrivApollo *Codes* the voting assistant directly posts information on the bulletin board.

In addition to the voting systems described above, there are other proposals that address the privacy problem, but do so requiring participants or hardware to be trusted for integrity properties.

The Du-Vote [8] proposal has a voter experience similar to that of PrivApollo, but differs because it assumes a dedicated hardware token, and verifiability requires that the token and the voting terminal do not collude.

Backes et al. [2] propose that voters encrypt the vote using a one-time pad, communicated through a trusted mobile phone using a secure channel.

The Pretty Good Democracy (PGD) voting system [12] has a vote casting phase that is identical to that of a generic code voting system. Its contribution is in the addition of a back-end: the return code that confirms vote receipt to the voter is sent only after a group of trustees verify that the corresponding vote is posted on the bulletin board. Thus the integrity property of PGD relies on the honesty of the group of trustees.

3   Model

We first introduce PrivApollo participants and then the assumptions.

3.1   Participants

Registrar: A registrar, R, generates, issues and checks credentials, which are delivered to the voter.

Election Authority: The election authority, EA, includes servers and election officials, and any software deployed on their behalf.

Voting Terminal: The voting terminal, VB, is the terminal and voting software used by the voter to cast her vote.

Voter: The human voter, V can read and compare strings, generate a cast or audit challenge and choose a candidate.

Voting Assistants: V has access to a number of voting assistants after the voting phase of the protocol is completed. The assistants help check that the voter's ballot was cast-as-intended and recorded-as-cast but do not participate in the protocol. The n additional devices are denoted $VA_1, VA_2, ..., VA_n$.

Active Voting Assistant: In PrivApollo, one of the voting assistants is an active voting assistant, AVA, which helps the voter generate ballots and check on VB and EA. AVA is a participant introduced in PrivApollo to protect privacy from the voting terminal.

3.2   Assumptions, Including Trust Assumptions

First, we begin with the standard assumptions made by all internet voting systems, also shared by Apollo and PrivApollo.

Bulletin Board: A secure bulletin board, BB—with append-only-authenticated-write and public-read access—is available to all participants.

Channel Between Registrar and Voter: Credentials cannot be accessed by anyone and cannot be altered while in the channel.

Additionally, the following trust assumptions are standard regarding participants.

Registrar: The registrar is assumed honest[1].

---

[1] Apollo relaxes this requirement by using irrepudiable credentials (such as credentials under scratch-off as in Remotegrity) to thwart a registrar who attempts to use the voter's credentials to cast a vote. PrivApollo does not make any changes to Apollo's registrar and credentials.

Election Authority: The *EA* is not assumed honest for integrity properties, but is assumed honest for privacy properties. To achieve privacy in this context, a threshold-encryption scheme may be used.

For other participants, we first describe the standard assumptions, then any modifications due to Apollo, and, lastly, further modifications due to PrivApollo. **Voting Terminal**: In the standard model, the voting terminal and any software on it (denoted *VB*, as in Apollo), like the *EA*, is not assumed honest for integrity properties, but is assumed honest for privacy properties. In particular, this assumption is made by Helios and Apollo. In PrivApollo, the voting terminal is not assumed honest for integrity *or* privacy properties.

Voter: The standard model assumes a human voter, *V*, who can read and compare strings, generate a cast or audit challenge and choose a candidate. *V* is not assumed honest, and among other things, may make false complaints against other participants.

In order to avoid clash attacks, Apollo additionally assumes *V* can generate low entropy strings to help create distinct ballots; this approach may be used in PrivApollo as well. This assumption is not easily satisfied by all voters, and a random number generator in the form of a token may be used instead, but the token would need to be trusted not to collude with the voting system or the voting terminal.

PrivApollo further assumes that *V* can read, remember and compare short strings for the purpose of indirection, which is also challenging. Large scale attacks may be thwarted by a few voters who are capable of checking low entropy strings and detecting the attack.

Voting Assistants: The standard model assumes that at least one of the assistants does not collude with the voting terminal for integrity properties. The assistants are not trusted for privacy properties.

Active Voting Assistant: As in Apollo, integrity requires that at least one voting assistant is honest. (For this purpose, an *AVA* is like any other voting assistant.) The privacy properties require that at least one of *VB* and the *AVA* is honest and does not collude with the other to determine the vote.

4   The PrivApollo Protocol

In this section we present the PrivApollo protocol. In the steps outlined below, all steps except the pre-voting phase and the ballot generation step are exactly as in Apollo. The pre-voting phase differs slightly, as noted below. Ballot generation is completely different from Apollo and forms the main contribution of this paper. It is described in detail in Sects. 4.1 and 4.2.

Credentials: *V* receives her credentials from *R*: a set of k *casting codes* and a *lock-in code*. k is the number of times a voter may correct an incorrect vote posted on *BB* against one of her casting codes. This would happen if the voting terminal changed the encrypted vote after receiving the casting code. In such a case, the voter would change the terminal and try again. $k - 1$ is thus the maximum number of dishonest terminals (who change the vote, not simply those who deny service by not posting the vote) the voter may encounter before successfully casting her vote. There could be another process to request more casting codes.

Pre-voting Phase: Before the voting session begins, V chooses n voting assistants $VA_1, VA_2, ...VA_n$. Larger values of n improve the robustness of the integrity properties. New to PrivApollo, she chooses one AVA to be used for the ballot generation procedure.

Role of Voting Assistants: After each protocol step, VB, every VA and the AVA each checks BB and provides feedback to V. If V is satisfied with the outcome of the check, she moves to the next step. If she determines that there is a problem, she should try to vote again on another terminal. She should always reuse an old credential unless she hears from the EA that it has been used (which would imply it had been used to post a vote on BB). This is because the number of casting codes is limited, and if they were all used up, the voter would have to make an effort to contact the EA to obtain more.

Initialization: V opens the voting application on VB and provides a short string for the session title. VB displays the (voting) session ID and a QR-code, and sends session ID to BB, which displays it. V scans the QR-code into an AVA and any VAs, and checks that they display the session ID (and) Title. That is, that they are able to see these on BB. The QR code contains, in addition to the session-ID, a symmetric key k_{rand} shared by VB and VAs, including AVA. k_{rand} can be used to decrypt posted messages related to encryption audits, so that the voter may choose who sees them. The QR code, and hence k_{rand}, are not posted on BB.

Ballot Generation: Here our protocol differs considerably from Apollo. We have two approaches to ballot generation: *PrivApollo Colors* and *PrivApollo Codes*, which we describe in Sects. 4.1 and 4.2 respectively.

Lock-in Phase: Once the ballot has been generated and the voter casts it using her Apollo casting credential, the VAs check the BB and inform the voter what has been posted for her session. If the voter is satisfied that the string posted is the one originally represented to her as her encrypted vote, she may return at any time to lock-in her vote. She may do so from any computer by identifying her session ID and adding her lock-in code, a second Apollo credential used to communicate that the encrypted vote has been posted correctly. Finally, she may check that the lock-in code has been posted, again, from any (other) computer. If it is not, she may try to lock-in the vote again, from any other computer.

4.1 *PrivApollo Colors*

In this section we present the simpler protocol for ballot generation, *PrivApollo Colors*. Note that colors may be replaced with shapes, for example, or audio words for audio (as opposed to visual) presentation of the ballot.

1. **Candidate-Color Correspondence Display:** VB generates a pseudoran-dom permutation π of the colors, leading to a candidate-color correspondence.

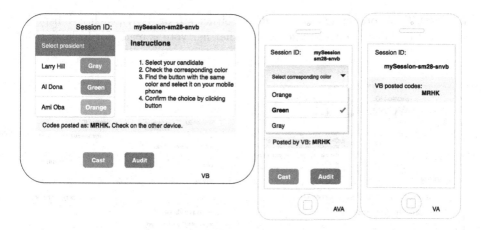

Fig. 1. Ballot Generation: *PrivApollo Colors*. *VB* permutes the colors and displays the candidate-color pairs. *VB* posts encryptions (here, the identifier of the encryption is *MRHK*). *AVA* displays that the encryptions were posted. The voter observes that the color for her candidate, Al Dona, is *Green*, selects *Green* on the *AVA* and confirms this choice. (Color figure online)

    VB publishes, on *BB*, public-key encryptions of each candidate-color correspondence using the public key of the *EA* and symmetric-key encryption of the set of colors used with k_{rand}. *VB displays candidate-color pairs.*

2. **Color Display**: *AVA* obtains all the encrypted information from the *BB*, informs the voter that it is available, decrypts the list of colors with k_{rand}, generates a pseudo-random permutation γ and *displays the corresponding permuted list of colors*, see Fig. 1.

3. **Color Choice**: *V* sees the correspondence between candidates and colors displayed on *VB*, selects her candidate, observes the corresponding color on *VB*, selects the same color on *AVA* and confirms it.

4. **Color Encryption**: *AVA* encrypts the chosen color and posts the encryption on *BB*. *V* checks on *VB* that, indeed, an encryption has been posted by *AVA* (see Fig. 2).

5. **Encryption Challenge**: *V* makes a choice: whether to audit or cast the generated (encrypted) ballot.

    cast *V* enters an unused *casting code* (Apollo casting credential).

    audit *V* checks if her encrypted ballot represents the candidate she chose.

6. (audit) If the voter chooses to audit, *VB* and *AVA* each reveal, on *BB*, the randomness required to check the encryption. Each *VA* checks the encryption by trial and error over all possibilities, and communicates the result of the check:

   - The correspondence between candidates and assigned colors as generated by *VB*.
   - Which color was encrypted (and submitted by *AVA* to the BB).

   The voter may repeat the audit step as many times as she wishes. Each time, a fresh candidate-color correspondence is generated (goto step: 3).

7. (cast) If the voter enters a cast code (on either VB or AVA), each VA displays the code she entered and informs her that her vote is ready for locking.

Fig. 2. Encryption Challenge: *PrivApollo Colors*. *VB* informs the voter that a string purporting to be the encrypted choice (of selected color *Green*) was published on *BB* by the *AVA* (in this case, the identifier of the encryption is *NJQA*). The voter may initiate an audit on either device: *VB* or *AVA*. (Color figure online)

4.2   *PrivApollo Codes*

In this version of the ballot-generation procedure, *VB* presents to the voter, as in the *PrivApollo Colors* procedure, a list of candidate-color pairs, where the correspondence is pseudorandomly generated (see Fig. 3). The *AVA* does more work than in the *PrivApollo Colors* procedure, generating a list of short codes, a distinct one for each color, and presenting a correspondence between color and code.

The two correspondences taken together result in a correspondence between candidate and code, and neither *VB* nor *AVA* can determine any information on this correspondence without collusion with the other. The voter identifies the color for her candidate on *VB*, then the code for the color on the *AVA*, and enters the code into *VB*, see Fig. 3.

4.3   Tallying

Each of N cast ballots consists of several encryptions.

PrivApollo Colors. Protocol 1.1.
- Encryption of the ballot layout (sent by *VB* to *BB* in Step 1(c))
- List of encrypted inner codes (sent by *VB* to *BB* in step 1c)
- Encryption of inner code (color) selected by the voter (inner code sent by *V* to *AVA* in step 4, encryption sent by *AVA* to *BB* in step 5).

PrivApollo: *Colors*

1. *VB* generates an encoded ballot with:
   (a) a canonical list of voting options $\langle o_1, o_2, \ldots, o_k \rangle$,
   (b) a random permutation π,
   (c) the permuted list of colors $\langle c_{\pi(1)}, c_{\pi(2)}, \ldots, c_{\pi(k)} \rangle$ (see Figure 1).
   VB submits to the bulletin board the following encrypted values:

   $$ballotLayout \leftarrow \begin{aligned}[\langle \mathsf{Enc}_{EA}(o_1, r_{o_1}), \mathsf{Enc}_{EA}(c_{\pi(1)}, r_{c_1}) \rangle, \ldots \\ \ldots, \langle \mathsf{Enc}_{EA}(o_k, r_{o_k}), \mathsf{Enc}_{EA}(c_{\pi(k)}, r_{c_k}) \rangle]\end{aligned}$$

   $$innerCodes \leftarrow \mathsf{Enc}_{k_{rand}}(\langle c_1, \ldots, c_k \rangle).$$

   VB displays the ballot to *V*:
o_1	$c_{\pi(1)}$
o_2	$c_{\pi(2)}$
...	
o_k	$c_{\pi(k)}$

2. Each *VA* performs the following steps:
   (a) downloads encrypted *ballotLayout* from *BB* and informs *V* that encryptions were posted by *VB*.
   (b) decrypts *innerCodes* with k_{rand} to obtain $\langle c_1, \ldots, c_k \rangle$.

3. Each *VA* displays the color options:
$c_{(1)}$
$c_{(2)}$
...
$c_{(k)}$

4. *V* finds her candidate o_i and a corresponding color $c_{\pi(i)}$ on *VB*. Then it picks the same color on *AVA* – position j such that $c_{\pi(i)} = c_{(j)} = x$.

5. *AVA* does the following:
   (a) computes the encryption of the ballot: $c \leftarrow \mathsf{Enc}_{EA}(x, r)$, where r is the randomness used during encryption,
   (b) sends the encrypted vote to *BB*: $AVA \xrightarrow{c} BB$

6. *VB* and *VAs* inform the voter that c is posted on *BB* in the transcript of her *sessionID*

7. *V* makes a decision about cast/audit:
   Audit is selected: Protocol 1.3 is carried out.
   Cast is selected:
   (a) *V* is asked to enter: *Login* and *CastCode* (these can be combined into a single long string)
   (b) *VAs* display the *Login/CastCode* pair; *V* checks if they are as expected.

Protocol 1.1. The vote-casting procedure of PrivApollo *Colors* (simple; see Figs. 1 and 2).

PrivApollo: Codes

1. *VB* generates an encoded ballot with:
   (a) a canonical list of voting options $\langle o_1, o_2, \ldots, o_k \rangle$,
   (b) a randomly selected list of inner-codes $\langle c_1, c_2, \ldots, c_k \rangle$ (see Figure 3 where the c_is are colors).
   (c) a permutation π.
   VB submits to the bulletin board the following encrypted values:

$$ballotLayout \leftarrow \begin{array}{l} [\langle \mathsf{Enc}_{EA}(o_1, r_{o_1}), \mathsf{Enc}_{EA}(c_1, r_{c_1}) \rangle, \ldots \\ \ldots, \langle \mathsf{Enc}_{EA}(o_k, r_{o_k}), \mathsf{Enc}_{EA}(c_k, r_{c_k}) \rangle], \end{array}$$

$$innerCodes \leftarrow \mathsf{Enc}_{k_{rand}}(\langle c_{\pi(1)}, \ldots, c_{\pi(k)} \rangle).$$

   VB displays the ballot to *V*:
   $$\begin{array}{ll} o_1 & c_1 \\ o_2 & c_2 \\ \ldots \\ o_k & c_k \end{array}$$

2. Each *VA* performs the following steps:
   (a) downloads *ballotLayout, innerCodes* from *BB* and informs *V* that encryptions were posted by *VB*.
   (b) decrypts *innerCodes* with k_{rand} to obtain $\langle c_{\pi(1)}, \ldots, c_{\pi(k)} \rangle$.
   (c) displays list of decrypted *innerCodes*.

3. *AVA*
   (a) generates randomly selected list of vote-codes $\langle v_1, v_2, \ldots, v_k \rangle$.
   (b) submits to *BB* an encryption of the correspondence between inner-codes and vote-codes:

$$voteCodes \leftarrow \begin{array}{l} [\langle \mathsf{Enc}_{EA}(c_{\pi(1)}, r_{\pi_1}), \mathsf{Enc}_{EA}(v_1, r_{v_1}) \rangle, \ldots \\ \ldots, \langle \mathsf{Enc}_{EA}(c_{\pi(k)}, r_{\pi_k}), \mathsf{Enc}_{EA}(v_k, r_{v_k}) \rangle]. \end{array}$$

   (c) displays the code-sheet:
   $$\begin{array}{ll} c_{\pi(1)} & v_1 \\ c_{\pi(2)} & v_2 \\ \ldots \\ c_{\pi(k)} & v_k \end{array}$$

4. *V* who wants to cast a ballot for candidate o_i:
   (a) finds the corresponding inner code c_i ($o_i \leftrightarrow c_i$) displayed on *VB*,
   (b) finds the corresponding vote code $x = v_{\pi^{-1}(i)}$

   sends vote choice to *VB*: $V \xrightarrow{x} VB$

5. *VB* sends to the bulletin board $VB \xrightarrow{c} BB$ the encryption of the vote code $c \leftarrow \mathsf{Enc}_{EA}(x, r)$, where r is the randomness used for encryption

6. *VAs* inform the voter that x is posted on *BB* in the transcript of her *sessionID*. Moreover *AVA* highlights color c_i corresponding to x.

7. *V* makes a decision about cast/audit:
   Audit is selected then Protocol 1.3 is performed.
   Cast is selected:
   (a) *V* is asked to enter: *Login* and *CastCode* (these can be combined to be a single long string)
   (b) *VAs* display the *Login/CastCode* pair; *V* checks if they are as expected.

Protocol 1.2. The vote-casting procedure of *PrivApollo Codes* (see Fig. 3).

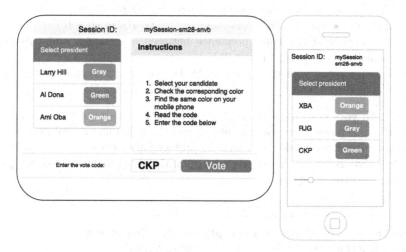

Fig. 3. Ballot Generation: *PrivApollo Codes*. The voter observes that the color corresponding to her candidate *Al Dona*, as displayed by *VB*, is *Green*. The corresponding code for *Green* displayed on *AVA* is *CKP*. The voter enters *CKP* in *VB*. (Color figure online)

Audit (*PrivApollo Colors* and *PrivApollo Codes*)

1. *VB* sends to *BB* the randomness used to generate the ballot and encrypt the vote:
$$c_{\mathrm{VB}} = \mathsf{Enc}_{k_{rand}}(r, \langle r_{o_1}, \ldots, r_{o_k} \rangle, \langle r_{c_1}, \ldots, r_{c_k} \rangle)$$

2. *AVA* sends to *BB* the randomness:
$$c_{\mathrm{AVA}} = \mathsf{Enc}_{k_{rand}}(r), \quad \text{in color version}$$
$$c_{\mathrm{AVA}} = \mathsf{Enc}_{k_{rand}}(r, \langle r_{\pi_1}, \ldots, r_{\pi_k} \rangle, \langle r_{v_1}, \ldots, r_v \rangle), \quad \text{in code version.}$$

3. The *VA*s decrypt c_{VB} and c_{AVA} and present the vote x' to V (with the randomness, *VA*s can recover the plaintext by brute force).

4. V accepts or not based on what the other *VA*s say the vote decrypted to:
   $x = x'$ Prepares new encryption; goto step (1) of the Protocols 1.1 1.2
   $x \neq x'$ Begins again with new *VB* and, if necessary, new *VA*s

---

Protocol 1.3. The audit procedure PrivApollo– both versions.

PrivApollo Codes. Protocol 1.2.
- Encryption of the ballot layout (sent by *VB* to *BB* in Step 1(c))
- List of encrypted inner codes (sent by *VB* to *BB* in step 1c)
- Encryption of the correspondence between inner codes and vote codes (sent by *AVA* to *BB* in step 3b)
- An encrypted vote code selected by the voter (inner code sent by *V* to *VB* in step 4, encryption sent by *VB* to *BB* in step 5).

For both vote casting methods, the tally phase consists of two phases. The role of the first phase is to select a valid row of the ballot layout that corresponds to the submitted vote code (or color). To protect ballot privacy, the corresponding row – that is (re)encrypted selected option, goes through the second phase of mixing and re-encryption.

PrivApollo: VoteCodes ReEncryption – Tallying Phase 1a

Input: $\langle ballotLayout_i, voteCodes_i, c_i \rangle_{i=1}^{N} = \langle bL_i, vC_i, c_i \rangle_{i=1}^{N}$

1. pick at random σ a permutation of N elements.
2. for each $i = 1 \dots N$ do:
   (a) select k-element permutations $\pi_{i,1}, \pi_{i,2}$
   (b) on input:
   $bL_i = [\langle \alpha_1, \beta_1 \rangle, \dots, \langle \alpha_k, \beta_k \rangle];$
   $vC_i = [\langle \gamma_1, \delta_1 \rangle, \dots, \langle \gamma_k, \delta_k \rangle];$
   $c_i.$
   (c) output (for $j = 1 \dots k$):
   $bL_{\sigma(i)}[j] := \langle \mathsf{ReEnc}(\alpha_{\pi_{i,1}(j)}), \mathsf{ReEnc}(\beta_{\pi_{i,1}(j)}) \rangle;$
   $vC_{\sigma(i)}[j] := \langle \mathsf{ReEnc}(\gamma_{\pi_{i,2}(j)}), \mathsf{ReEnc}(\delta_{\pi_{i,2}(j)}) \rangle;$
   $c_{\sigma(i)} := \mathsf{ReEnc}(c_i).$

Protocol 1.4. Tallying phase 1a for *PrivApollo Codes*. A code for a mix-server. ReEnc() denotes (ElGamal) re-encryption.

After the end of phase 1 (1a and 1b), the last element (c_i) of each 3-tuple of vote i gets decrypted: revealing the vote code that was entered by the voter. Since $c = \mathsf{Enc}_{EA}(x, r)$ and $x = v_{\pi^{-1}(i)}$, the value $v_{\pi^{-1}(i)}$ becomes public.

Also each of $\delta_{i,j}$ is decrypted ($\delta_{i,j} = \mathsf{Enc}_{EA}(c_{\pi(j)})$). For each ballot i, exactly one decrypted $\delta_{i,j}$ will match decrypted c_i. The mix-server deletes all unmatched rows of $\langle \gamma_{i,j}, \delta_{i,j} \rangle$.

PrivApollo: VoteCodes Decryption – Tallying Phase 1b
Input: $\langle ballotLayout_i, voteCodes_i, c_i \rangle_{i=1}^N = \langle bL_i, vC_i, c_i \rangle_{i=1}^N$
Shared key: $\mathcal{K}_m$

1. pick at random σ a permutation of N elements.
2. for each $i = 1 \ldots N$ do:
   (a) select k-element permutations $\pi_{i,1}, \pi_{i,2}$
   (b) on input:
       $bL_i = [\langle \alpha_1, \beta_1 \rangle, \ldots, \langle \alpha_k, \beta_k \rangle]$;
       $vC_i = [\langle \gamma_1, \delta_1 \rangle, \ldots, \langle \gamma_k, \delta_k \rangle]$;
       c_i.
   (c) output (for $j = 1 \ldots k$):
       $bL_{\sigma(i)}[j] := \langle \mathsf{ReEnc}(\alpha_{\pi_{i,1}(j)}), \mathsf{ReEnc}(\beta_{\pi_{i,1}(j)}) \rangle$;
       $vC_{\sigma(i)}[j] := \langle \mathsf{ReEnc}(\gamma_{\pi_{i,2}(j)}), \mathsf{Dec}_{\mathcal{K}_m}(\delta_{\pi_{i,2}(j)}) \rangle$;
       $c_{\sigma(i)} := \mathsf{Dec}_{\mathcal{K}_m}(c_i)$.

Protocol 1.5. Tallying phase 1b (*PrivApollo Codes*). A code for a mix-server. $\mathsf{Dec}_{\mathcal{K}_m}(\cdot)$ denotes shared key of threshold encryption which was used to generate *EA*'s public key.

After the Phase 1 the following cryptograms remain:

$$\langle ballotLayout_i, \gamma_{i,j_i} \rangle_{i=1}^N = \langle bL_i, c_i \rangle_{i=1}^N.$$

In Phase 2 Protocols 1.4 and 1.5 are run sequentially (with bL playing the role of vC). After Phase 2 is completed, one can decode the only matching α which encodes the voting option selected by the voter, o_x.

5 Security and Usability Discussion

In the *PrivApollo Colors* procedure, the *AVA* could easily replace the vote with another valid one (change the color to another valid color), though it would not know which candidate the color corresponded to (the randomization attack). On the other hand, while the *PrivApollo Codes* procedure requires the voter to deal with two indirections and is hence more complex, it is hard for *VB* to change the vote to another valid vote. This is because it does not know other valid codes without colluding with *AVA*, or maliciously attempting to determine a valid code by, for example, photographing the *AVA* screen. While the *PrivApollo Codes* procedure makes the randomization attack harder, it does allow the adversary to easily invalidate the vote. As in Apollo, each attack would be detected by the alert voter. The randomization attack and vote validation can be successfully carried out on Apollo and Helios as well.

Note that, while the integrity properties of the protocol are resilient to collusion between the *BB* and the *AVA*, we do rely on the assumption that neither party knows all the valid credentials (casting codes and lock-in codes). That is, for example, *AVA* is not able to photograph the credential sheet that the voter may have received in the post.

If either *AVA* or *VB* wishes to learn the ballot contents, it needs to cooperate with the other in order to learn the indirection. Such cooperation includes the surreptitious access to data by one of the parties.

The tallying process is divided into two phases; the information revealed at the end of each phase helps neither *VB* nor *AVA* get more knowledge about the cast ballot.

As in Apollo, the use of the *Benaloh challenge* enables voters to detect attempts to manipulate the vote. This approach hence has all the strengths and weaknesses of a cast-and-challenge approach, including the fact that voters may believe they had already verified when they had not [9]. The use of lock-in codes allows her to communicate that a problem occurred, and allows her to attempt to vote again. The inclusion of an active voting assistant does not change these properties, because the actions of the voting assistant are included in the audit. The integrity properties of Apollo are unchanged. The use of the active voting assistant may be viewed as a splitting of the voting terminal into two entities, reducing the reliance on a single entity to protect ballot secrecy, and improving on the privacy properties of PrivApollo.

We do assume independent devices, but, even if the devices are not independent, or malware is transmitted from *VB* to all the *VA*s through the QR code, the verifiability properties hold if the voter performs all the checks using a different *VA* into which the voter herself keys in the session ID, or if the voter goes through the verification steps as in an end-to-end-verifiable protocol that does not explicitly incorporate a voting assistant. The voter, may, in fact, use a number of out-of-band voting assistants, in which case the interaction with the voting assistant will be no less usable than in, say, Helios, though privacy with respect to the voting terminal will be greater. If the voter uses a single *AVA* and no other *VA*s, one of the *VB* or the *AVA* need to be honest for the integrity property, which is the same requirement as Apollo used with a single *VA*.

The scheme seems to be well suited for elections with few candidates. When the number of candidates is large, it would not be possible to find a large enough number of colors that are sufficiently easily distinguished by voters. Beyond a couple of candidates, it is likely that the error rate of the indirection would increase. Similar problems would arise if one used shapes instead of colors. In such a case, the use of a short alphanumeric code would be a better choice. Even so, voters might make errors while comparing alphanumeric strings. Finally, the encryption audit check requires the *VA* to check every possibility with the randomness revealed, and hence this would be very inefficient for a large number of candidates or for more complex elections (other than plurality elections).

We are not aware of any protocols that offer similar security properties given a similar trust model. We acknowledge that this has been with a loss in usability; however, that presents interesting future work.

6   Conclusions

We have presented a fully electronic scheme that is end-to-end voter verifiable and also provides ballot secrecy from the devices used to cast a ballot. The privacy property holds if the Voting Booth does not collude with the Active Voting Assistant. Integrity is achieved as long as at least one Voting Assistant used by the Voter is honest.

References

1. Adida, B.: Helios: web-based open-audit voting. In: USENIX Security Symposium, pp. 335–348 (2008)
2. Backes, M., Gagné, M., Skoruppa, M.: Using mobile device communication to strengthen e-voting protocols. In: Proceedings of the 12th ACM Workshop on Privacy in the Electronic Society, pp. 237–242. ACM (2013)
3. Chaum, D.: Surevote. International Patent WO 01/55940 A1. Technical report (2001)
4. Chaum, D., et al.: Scantegrity: end-to-end voter verifiable optical-scan voting. IEEE Secur. Priv. **6**(3), 40–46 (2008)
5. Chaum, D., et al.: Paperless independently-verifiable voting. In: Kiayias, A., Lipmaa, H. (eds.) Vote-ID 2011. LNCS, vol. 7187, pp. 140–157. Springer, Heidelberg (2012). https://doi.org/10.1007/978-3-642-32747-6_9
6. Chondros, N., et al.: D-DEMOS: a distributed, end-to-end verifiable, internet voting system. In: 36th IEEE International Conference on Distributed Computing Systems, ICDCS 2016, Nara, Japan, 27–30 June 2016, pp. 711–720 (2016)
7. Gaweł, D., Kosarzecki, M., Vora, P.L., Wu, H., Zagórski, F.: Apollo – end-to-end verifiable internet voting with recovery from vote manipulation. In: Krimmer, R., et al. (eds.) E-Vote-ID 2016. LNCS, vol. 10141, pp. 125–143. Springer, Cham (2017). https://doi.org/10.1007/978-3-319-52240-1_8
8. Grewal, G.S., Ryan, M.D., Chen, L., Clarkson, M.R.: Du-Vote: remote electronic voting with untrusted computers. In: 2015 IEEE 28th Computer Security Foundations Symposium (CSF), pp. 155–169. IEEE (2015)
9. Marky, K., Kulyk, O., Renaud, K., Volkamer, M.: What did I really vote for? On the usability of verifiable e-voting schemes. In: Proceedings of the 2018 CHI Conference on Human Factors in Computing Systems, United States, April 2018. Association for Computing Machinery (ACM) (2008)
10. Popoveniuc, S., Hosp, B.: An introduction to Punchscan. In: WOTE (2006)
11. Riva, B., Ta-Shma, A.: Bare-handed electronic voting with pre-processing. In: EVT (2007)
12. Ryan, P.Y.A., Teague, V.: Pretty good democracy. In: Christianson, B., Malcolm, J.A., Matyáš, V., Roe, M. (eds.) Security Protocols 2009. LNCS, vol. 7028, pp. 111–130. Springer, Heidelberg (2013). https://doi.org/10.1007/978-3-642-36213-2_15
13. Zagórski, F., Carback, R.T., Chaum, D., Clark, J., Essex, A., Vora, P.L.: Remotegrity: design and use of an end-to-end verifiable remote voting system. In: Jacobson, M., Locasto, M., Mohassel, P., Safavi-Naini, R. (eds.) ACNS 2013. LNCS, vol. 7954, pp. 441–457. Springer, Heidelberg (2013). https://doi.org/10.1007/978-3-642-38980-1_28

End-to-End Verifiable Quadratic Voting with Everlasting Privacy

Olivier Pereira[1] and Peter B. Rønne[2(✉)]

[1] Université catholique de Louvain, B-1348 Louvain-la-Neuve, Belgium
olivier.pereira@uclouvain.be
[2] SnT, University of Luxembourg, Luxembourg, Luxembourg
peter.roenne@uni.lu

Abstract. Quadratic voting is an intriguing new method for public choice suggested by Lalley and Weyl, which they showed to be utilitarian efficient. Voters are given a budget of credits and can assign each of the candidates a (perhaps negative) value, where the price paid for their voting choice is the sum of the squared values. From a security viewpoint, we generally request elections to be private and have integrity, and even further (end-to-end) verifiability which entails public bulletin boards. Such public data might be troublesome when considering future adversaries capable of breaking current cryptographic primitives, either due to computational power advances, broken primitives or scientific breakthroughs. This calls for election schemes with everlasting privacy and perfectly private audit trails. In the case of quadratic voting this is even more crucial since budget balances have to be linked between elections in a verifiable way, and revealing old budget values partially break privacy in later elections. In this paper, we suggest an efficient construction of electronic quadratic voting with end-to-end verifiability and a perfectly private audit trail inspired by the methods of Cuvelier, Pereira and Peters, but adapted to include the quadratic relations and keeping budget balances everlasting private.

1 Introduction

Finding good public choice methods is a notoriously hard problem. Recently a novel intriguing approach has appeared: quadratic voting [16]. The quadratic voting method works by providing the voter with a budget b of credits for buying votes, however, the voting credit does not have to be connected to a real financial currency. The peculiarity is that a voter casting v votes for a candidate has to pay a quadratic amount v^2 of credits for this choice. That is, the voter assigns vote values $v_1, \ldots, v_c$ to the c candidates, or choices, and has to pay the sum of squared values which have to be within budget

$$v_1^2 + \cdots + v_c^2 \leq b \ .$$

© International Financial Cryptography Association 2020
A. Bracciali et al. (Eds.): FC 2019 Workshops, LNCS 11599, pp. 314–329, 2020.
https://doi.org/10.1007/978-3-030-43725-1_22

The advantage of quadratic voting is that it theoretically satisfies utilitarian efficiency at least in the asymptotic case [16], and in the finite case the inefficiency is suppressed by the number of voters, see also [8]. To put it differently, the quadratic pricing gives incentive for the voter to buy a number of votes corresponding to her internal value.

An enlightening example demonstrating the effect of quadratic voting on real users can be found in [19]. Here voting was not directly considered but rather closely related surveys. In a combined between-groups and within-subjects study, participants were asked about their opinion on 10 proposals. One group of participants gave answers on a Likert 7-choice scale ranging from "Very strongly against" over "Neutral" to "Very strongly in favor" whereas another group gave responses using quadratic voting with a total budget of 100 credits for all answers i.e. being able to vote in the range $\{-10, \ldots, 0, \ldots, 10\}$. As is intuitive the quadratic voting resulted in much less extreme answer but, further, the answers were also much closer to being normal distributed. The quasi-normal distribution could be an indication that the answers were closer to expressing the true internal value.

Once the vote is complete, the collected payments are redistributed among the voters. The method suggested by Lalley and Weyl [16] is to split the revenue of the election evenly among the voters. However, other solutions have been proposed, including lotteries [17]. The actual choice is not essential for the utilitarian efficiency. For simplicity we will focus on the even split of revenue in this paper.

Quadratic voting is also an interesting challenge from a security viewpoint, as we have to cryptographically deal with squared values and checks of budget balances. A first solution for running end-to-end verifiable elections with quadratic voting is described by Park and Rivest [17]. Here security properties of voting schemes are discussed, and the importance of budget privacy is stressed, especially if revealing individual votes due to Italian attacks. Our scheme uses homomorphic tallying, partially sidestepping the Italian attacks. Still, budget balances should be kept private by the voters, as they could result in vote privacy leaks. Note that a very small leak in privacy is unavoidable since we reveal the total revenue by refunding it to the voters. Park and Rivest also analyze strategic voting and refunding rules for quadratic voting, and further suggest schemes for in-person and electronic voting, with cryptography based on the BGN encryption scheme [6], which allows to calculate squares of encrypted values, and to further homomorphically add those squares. Regarding the handling of the payments, it is also mentioned as a possible option to use an anonymous cryptocurrency such as Zerocash [20].

We create a different solution, which offers several additional benefits:

- Our protocol offers a perfectly private audit trail (PPAT), that is, all the data needed for public verifiability perfectly hide all the votes and budgets. The previous solution requires publishing ciphertexts that would eventually leak vote content.

- Our protocol is compatible with traditional threshold key generation protocols in the discrete log setting [15,18], even in the malicious setting. The BGN scheme requires the use of an RSA modulus with unknown factorisation, which is considerably more challenging to obtain (see discussion in [6] for instance).
- Our solution is quite efficient: voter computation takes place in prime order groups on elliptic curves (e.g., BN curves [2]), and only requires to compute one pairing per election. The BGN based solution requires to compute on curves with a modulus that has the size of an RSA modulus, and requires the evaluation of pairings for each vote.

We believe that everlasting privacy of the audit data is an important improvement for any secure election scheme: we want these data to be widely available to the public, but then need to take care that votes do not leak in the future. An adversary may benefit from the ever-increasing efficiency improvements in computing, the breaking of believed-secure cryptographic assumptions or technical breakthroughs such as quantum computers. However, in quadratic voting such future-proofing is even more essential, since the budget can be carried over from election to election. Thus breaking the privacy of earlier elections might (partially) leak the later budget in the present of the future adversary.

We also conjecture that handling the payments inside the voting system (compared to relying on an externally managed cryptocurrency) is an interesting feature: this avoids mixing the systems of incentive that come with cryptocurrencies with those in the election process, and it also makes it easier to control that all voters start from an equal budget.

The outline of the paper is as follows. In Sect. 2 we present the necessary cryptographic tools, that will be used in the cryptographic protocol presented in Sect. 3. In Sect. 4 we discuss the security properties of the protocol. We end with a conclusion and discussion of future research directions.

2   Background and Cryptographic Tools

2.1   Commitment Consistent Encryption

The first component of our quadratic voting protocol is commitment consistent encryption (CCE) [12], a cryptographic tool that was proposed to facilitate the design of universally verifiable voting schemes with a perfectly private audit trail.

A CCE scheme is a traditional public key encryption scheme offering an extra feature: from any ciphertext, it is possible to derive a perfectly hiding commitment, as well as an opening of that commitment to the value that is encrypted. The commitment derivation operation, DCom, only requires using the public key, while the computation of the opening, Open requires the secret key.

It is convenient to have, associated to a CCE scheme, the possibility to use efficient proof systems, which can serve several purposes, and which we will need in our application:

- A proof of validity of a ciphertext, that guarantees election organisers that the Open operation would succeed without performing it. Quite often, ciphertexts are never decrypted but rather homomorphically combined, e.g., in order to add votes. A single invalid ciphertext would then suffice to make it impossible to open the election result.
- A proof of knowledge of the plaintext. This can be used to make ciphertexts non-malleable [5,22], and avoid attacks on privacy.
- A proof of validity of a plaintext, which guarantees that the plaintext that is encrypted encodes a valid vote.

These will be discussed in the next subsection.

We use the PPATS encryption scheme of Cuvelier et al. [12], which is described in Fig. 1. This scheme works in an asymmetric bilinear group setting, which can be obtained using BN curves [2] for instance. In the group $\mathbb{G}_1$, two random generators (g_1, h_1) are given in order to produce Pedersen-like commitments and, in the group $\mathbb{G}_2$, an ElGamal key (g_2, h_2) is produced. The main twist of the scheme is to open a commitment $g_1^v h_1^r$ using g_2^r and to verify it using the pairing operator, instead of using r directly as with Pedersen commitments: the pairing makes it possible to verify, after removal of the g_1^v term, whether $e(h_1^r, g_2) = e(h_1, g_2^r)$. Using this alternate way of opening the commitment offers two benefits: (i) the opening is now a group element, which can be conveniently encrypted using the ElGamal key (ii) all the secret values are in exponents, which eases compatibility with traditional, efficient, Σ-protocols.

PPATS encryption

Setup(1^λ) Return, as a public parameter pp, type-3 pairing-friendly groups $\mathbb{G}_1, \mathbb{G}_2, \mathbb{G}_T$ of prime order q s.t. $|q| = \lambda$, together with random generators g_1, h_1 of $\mathbb{G}_1$ and g_2 of $\mathbb{G}_2$. We assume that pp is available to all other algorithms.

Gen(1^n) Generate an ElGamal public encryption key $\mathsf{pk} = h_2 = g_2^x$. The secret key is the uniformly random $\mathsf{sk} = x \in \mathbb{Z}_q$.

Enc$_{\mathsf{pk}}(v)$ Encrypt vote v as $(d, c_1, c_2) = (g_1^v h_1^r, g_2^s, g_2^r h_2^s)$, using uniformly random $(r, s) \leftarrow \mathbb{Z}_q^2$.

Dec$_{\mathsf{sk}}(d, c_1, c_2)$ Return the discrete logarithm of $e(h_1, c_1^x/c_2)e(d, g_2)$ in basis $e(g_1, g_2)$.

DCom$_{\mathsf{pp}}(d, c_1, c_2)$ Derive and return the perfectly hiding commitment d.

Open$_{\mathsf{sk}}(d, c_1, c_2)$ The commitment opening is computed as $a = c_2/c_1^x$.

Vrfy$_{\mathsf{pk}}(d, v, a)$ (v, a) is an opening of d iff $e(h_1, a) = e(d/g_1^v, g_2)$.

Fig. 1. The PPATS encryption scheme

2.2 Sigma Protocols

A Sigma protocol [13], or Σ-protocol, for a relation R enables a prover P to convince a verifier V that he knows a witness w for a statement x such that $(w, x) \in R$.

Sigma-protocols are structured as follows: based on a joint input x, P sends a commitment a to V, who answers with a uniformly random challenge e and, finally, P sends a response f. Based on this response, V accepts or rejects the proof.

Σ-protocols exhibit the following properties:

Completeness. If P and V follow the protocol honestly and if P actually knows a witness w for the statement x, then V accepts the proof.

Special Honest Verifier Zero-Knowledge. There is a simulator S that, from any valid statement x and challenge e from the set of possible challenges, is able to produce a full valid protocol transcript (a, e, f). If e is uniformly distributed, then this transcript is distributed exactly like a real protocol execution. (Note that no valid witness w for x is given to S.)

Special Soundness. From any two valid proof transcripts (a, e_1, f_1) and (a, e_2, f_2) for a statement x, with a single commitment a and two distinct challenges $e_1 \neq e_2$, it is possible to extract a witness w s.t. $(w, x) \in R$.

Σ-protocols come with two interesting features: (i) They can be efficiently turned into non-interactive zero-knowledge in the random oracle model thanks to the Fiat-Shamir heuristic [5,14]; (ii) their perfect ZK property makes them suitable to be published as part of a perfectly private audit trail.

We need to use several standard Σ-protocols, which we list below.

Opening of a Commitment. We use a protocol $\pi_{op}^b(c)$ to prove knowledge of an opening of a commitment c to a value b s.t. $c = g^b h^r$. This can be achieved using Schnorr's protocol [21], which takes a single exponentiation.

CCE Ciphertext Validity. We use a protocol $\pi_{va}(c)$ that proves the validity of a PPATS ciphertext c, by demonstrating the knowledge of the vote v and randomness (r, s) used to produce c. This protocol guarantees to the talliers that they will be able to run the tallying protocol successfully, as explained above. Such a protocol has been constructed for PPATS by Cuvelier et al. [12] and requires 2 exponentiations in $\mathbb{G}_1$ and 3 exponentiations in $\mathbb{G}_2$.

Range Proof. We use a protocol $\pi_r^n(c)$ that proves the ability to open a commitment $c = g^v h^r$ on a vote v that is included in the range $[0, 2^n]$, with $n < \log q - 1$. Note that the notion of "positive" has a slightly unusual meaning here, as the values we are committing to lie in $\mathbb{Z}_q$; this is the reason of our upper bound on n, which guarantees that values do not "overflow" to negative values, interpreted as those above $(q - 1)/2$.

This protocol will be used by the voters to prove that they are not over-spending, that is, that their budget after each vote remains positive.

Many such proofs have been proposed, with their efficiency differing depending on the value of the range upper bound 2^n (among other factors). As we work in prime order groups and our range upper bound is a power of 2, we simply rely on the protocol by Bellare and Goldwasser [3]. This protocol makes a sequence of

n commitments $c_0, \ldots, c_n$ on the individual bits $v_0, \ldots, v_i$ of the binary decomposition of v, proves that each commitments actually commit to bits, and then show that $c/\prod c_i^{2^i} = h^s$ for a known s.

If the $0/1$ proofs are made using the disjunctive proofs of Cramer et al. [10], which takes 3 exponentiations in the group in which the commitment lies, then the total cost of such a proof is (i) n exponentiations for the bit commitments, (ii) $3n$ exponentiations for the proofs that they can be opened on bits, (iii) 1 exponentiation for the final proof on s. The total is then $4n+1$ exponentiations.

2.3 Proof of Square

Finally, a key ingredient of our quadratic voting protocol is a proof π_{sq} that one can open two perfectly hiding commitments on values such that one is the square of the other. This will be used by the voters to show that they commit on an accurate payment based on their vote.

Such a proof can be achieved using the usual technique systematically described by Camenisch [7]. We propose here a slightly more efficient method, which we detail.

Suppose that P publishes two commitments c_1 and c_2 and wishes to demonstrate that he knows pairs (v_1, r_1) and (v_2, r_2) such that $c_1 = g^{v_1} h^{r_1}$, $c_2 = g^{v_2} h^{r_2}$ and $v_2 = v_1^2 \bmod q$. He can then follow the Square protocol depicted in Fig. 2.

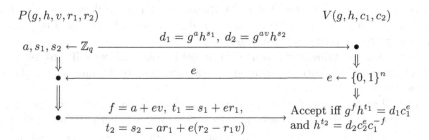

Fig. 2. Square: a Σ-protocol for commitments on values in quadratic relation.

Theorem 1. *The protocol $\pi_{sq}(c_1, c_2)$ described in Fig. 2 is a Σ-protocol for the relation $\{v, r_1, r_2 | c_1 = g^v h^{r_1}, c_2 = g^{v^2} h^{r_2}\}$.*

Proof. We show the completeness, the special soundness and the perfect honest verifier ZK of the protocol.

Completeness: The perfect completeness of the protocol follows from the inspection of the verification equations. In particular, we see that $d_2 c_2^e c_1^{-f}$ is a commitment on $av + ev^2 - v(a + ev) = 0$.

Special Soundness: Let us imagine that we have two valid transcripts for the same c_1, c_2, d_1, d_2, that is, we have (e, f, t_1, t_2) and (e', f', t_1', t_2') that are both consistent with the verification equations. Dividing the two versions of the verification equations gives: $g^{f-f'}h^{t_1-t_1'} = c_1^{e-e'}$ and $h^{t_2-t_2'} = c_2^{e-e'}c_1^{f'-f}$.

The first of these equations shows that $v = \frac{f-f'}{e-e'}$ and $r_1 = \frac{t_1-t_1'}{e-e'}$ are a valid opening of c_1. Inserting the extracted v in the second equation gives $c_2^{e-e'} = c_1^{v(e-e')}h^{t_2-t_2'}$. Isolating c_2, we can open it on the pair $(v^2, r_1 v + \frac{t_2-t_2'}{e-e'})$, and observe that the second element of that pair equals r_2.

Special HVZK: Given any e, we can select f, t_1, t_2 uniformly at random in $\mathbb{Z}_q$, then compute d_1 and d_2 from the verification equations. If e is uniformly random, then it is distributed as in the real protocol. The uniform selection of a, s_1, s_2 in a real execution guarantees that f, t_1, t_2 are random in the absence of d_1 and d_2, and those two commitments only enforce the verification equations. Hence, the simulated view is distributed exactly as a real one.   □

The cost of this protocol is 3 exponentiations (considering that v is small), which is slightly better than the 4 exponentiations that would be obtained using the more common approach [7]. This may make this protocol of independent interest.

3   Verifiable Quadratic Voting

We now describe the steps of our quadratic voting protocol in detail. The main participants are the Election Authority with a set of Tally Tellers jointly holding the election secret key, the Voters and a Public Bulletin Board used to publish and verify the outcome of the election.

Our election setting and adversarial model is standard (we will discuss security in the next section) and similar to the one used by Cramer et al. [11] or Helios 2.0 [1].

The Election Authority orchestrates the election, publishing the questions and election public parameters (keys) on the public bulletin board, which is assumed to behave as a trustworthy broadcast channel. The Election Authority also handles the voter lists, and offers authentication services to the voters if needed.

We aim for an end-to-end verifiable protocol: the election result should be verifiable without requiring to trust any particular entity or entities.

Regarding privacy, we want that votes remain computationally secret in front of the Tally Tellers: Tally Tellers would only be able to break privacy if a computational assumption is broken, or if enough of them are malicious (the threshold can be arbitrarily chosen). Furthermore, we want that all the data published on the Bulletin Board guarantee the perfect privacy of the votes: someone who can only access the Bulletin Board should never be able to learn the votes, independently of the falsification of any computational assumption.

3.1   Election Setup

Parameter Generation. Given a security parameter n, generate public parameters $\mathsf{pp} = (\mathbb{G}_1, \mathbb{G}_2, \mathbb{G}_t, q, g_1, h_1, g_2)$ and a key pair $(\mathsf{pk}, \mathsf{sk}) = (h_2, x)$ for the

PPATS encryption scheme. The key pair may be generated in a distributed or threshold fashion by the Tally Tellers. We define the commitment key as $\mathsf{cpk} = (g_1, h_1)$, taken from pp.

Initialization. Before the voting starts, a public bulletin board is initialized, the public parameters and keys $(\mathsf{pp}, \mathsf{pk}, \mathsf{cpk})$ are published there, together with the initial budget of every voter b and the first election question.

We assume that b is a reasonably small value, e.g., $b < 2^{20}$, so that it will be possible to run the PPATS decryption of sum of the payments made by all voters in an election. If we have less than a million voters, then the total payment will be less than 2^{40}. A discrete logarithm of this size can be extracted in less than a second, e.g., using a baby-step giant-step algorithm. We define the bound for our range proofs $n = \lceil \log b \rceil$, that is, 20 in our example above.

Each voter publishes a commitment $c_b = \mathsf{Com}_{\mathsf{cpk}}(b; r_b) = g_1^b h_1^{r_b}$ on his budget b together with a proof of validity of this commitment $\pi_{op}^b(c_b)$, and saves the opening r_b.

3.2 Voting

Ballot Preparation. A voter who wishes to submit a vote of value v computes two ciphertexts $c = (d, c_1, c_2) \leftarrow \mathsf{Enc}_{\mathsf{pk}}(v)$ and $\hat{c} = (\hat{d}, \hat{c}_1, \hat{c}_2) \leftarrow \mathsf{Enc}_{\mathsf{pk}}(v^2)$ and proofs π_{va} and $\hat{\pi}_{va}$ of the validity of these ciphertexts.

The commitments d and $\hat{d}$ derived from these ciphertexts and a proof $\pi_{sq}(d, \hat{d})$ is computed in order to prove that the right payment is committed to. Eventually, we need to make sure that v lies in a proper range, that is, in $[-2^{n/2}, 2^{n/2}]$. This can be done by computing a proof $\pi_r^{n/2+1}(dg^{n/2})$. Note that if only positive votes are allowed the factor $g^{n/2}$ is simply left out.

In the case of several vote questions we need to repeat this process for each question.

Budget Update. The voter then updates his budget as $c_b := c_b/\hat{d}$, and also records the updated opening $r_b := r_b - \hat{r}_d$, where $\hat{r}_d$ is the random exponent that was used to compute $\hat{d} = g_1^{v^2} h_1^{\hat{r}_d}$.

He then produces a proof that this budget is still positive, which can be done by computing a range proof $\hat{\pi}_r^n(c_b)$. For several vote questions we only need to do this once after having updated the budget with the vote payments for each question.

We may wonder why both proofs π_r and $\hat{\pi}_r$ are needed: the π_{op}^b and $\hat{\pi}_r$ proofs show that the initial budget is less than 2^n and that the payment v^2 that is made is less than b. However, the proof π_{sq} only proves that v^2 is a square of v in Z_q. As a result, v^2 could actually be any quadratic residue modulo q, which opens to many undesirable values thanks to modulo reduction. Showing in π_r that v is actually with the $[-2^{n/2}, 2^{n/2}]$ range makes sure that no reduction happens during the squaring.

Still, the square proof π_{sq} conveniently handles the case of negative votes: both roots of v^2 are valid witnesses.

Ballot Preparation Audit. The ballot preparation system of the voters is expected to provide a verification mechanism for this process. A traditional solution is to use a so-called Benaloh challenge [4]: the ballot preparation system commits to the voter on the value of these ciphertexts and proofs, e.g., by displaying a hash of all these values. The voter can then decide to challenge the ballot preparation system who then needs to release all the randomness that it used to prepare the ballot, which allows verifying the commitment on an independent device.

Ballot Submission. When the voter finished to challenge his ballot preparation device, he sends his vote $(c, \hat{c}, \pi_{va}, \hat{\pi}_{va}, \pi_{sq}, \pi_r, \hat{\pi}_r)$ to the Election Authority.

The Election Authority verifies π_{va} and $\hat{\pi}_{va}$, then publishes the vote audit data $(\mathsf{DCom}(c), \mathsf{DCom}(\hat{c}), \pi_{sq}, \pi_r, \hat{\pi}_r)$ next to the name of the voter on the public bulletin board. (Publishing the names makes it possible to verify who voted, e.g., by interrogating the voters, and removes the need to trust an Election Authority, or any other entity, for voter authentication – even if such authentication can remain useful to protect from ballot flooding).

The publication of $\mathsf{DCom}(\hat{c})$ is accompanied by an update of the commitment c_b on the budget available for the voter, which is publicly recomputed as $c_b := c_b/\mathsf{DCom}(\hat{c})$ and posted on the bulletin board.

3.3   Election Tally

Computing the Election Results. The PPATs ciphertexts are homomorphically additive. So, multiplying the first series of PPATS cipehertexts, i.e., the c's together and decrypting the result yields the sum of the votes.

This decryption process can be made publicly verifiable without any additional proof: the authorities just need to publish the opening on the product of the d commitments of all voters: correctness follows from the binding property of the commitment scheme.

Budget Updates. The same homomorphic addition can be performed on the second series of ciphertexts, i.e., the $\hat{c}$, which, after decryption, reveals the total amount spent during the election. This amount is posted on the bulletin board, together with an opening of the product of the $\hat{d}$ commitments of the voters.

That amount can now be equally split among the voters as a sum b_u per voter, and all the budget commitments on the board are then updated as $c_b := c_b g_2^{b_u}$. Voters can verify their updated budget, and keep making new proofs based on it, as the update process does not change the randomness of c_b, which the voter knows.

3.4   Election Audit

The various steps of the protocol can be verified in the natural way.

Parameter Generation and Initialization. The auditor verifies that pp have been produced according to the expected security parameter, and possibly verify the process of the generation of h_1 (in order to avoid the risks of a trapdoor).

The auditor also verifies that the right budget has been announced, and that the budget commitments c_b posted by the voters come with valid proofs π_{op}^b.

Vote Validity. The auditor then verifies the validity of the π_{sq} and π_r proofs associated to each vote, and their uniqueness on the board. He verifies that each vote is associated to a legitimate voter, and questions voters (whether they are reported to have voted or not) to check that they agree with what is posted on the bulletin board on their behalf.

Tally Validity. The auditor then computes the product of the d and $\hat{d}$ commitments in all the valid votes, and verifies that the Tally Tellers published a result and total election payments that is an opening of these commitment products.

Budget Verification. The auditor recomputes the value of budget redistribution b_u and that all individual voter budgets have been updated accordingly.

3.5   Protocol Efficiency

Most of the computational cost of our protocol lies in two steps: ballot preparation, and election tally. The setup cost (key generation, initial budget commitment) is essentially negligible (unless a large number of Tally Tellers is chosen, but we expect it to be more in the range of 3–5).

We make a rough estimate of these costs, focusing on the cost of the exponentiations in $\mathbb{G}_1$ and $\mathbb{G}_2$, and on the cost of multiplications when they come in a potentially large number compared to the exponentiations, that is, during the tally. We neglect the cost of computing hashes and of the arithmetic in $\mathbb{Z}_q$ in the NIZK proofs, which is expected to be smaller by a level of magnitude compared to the cost of the exponentiations that these proofs contain.

Our estimate gives an idea of the order of magnitude of the timings and of the practicality of our protocol. The exact performance will strongly depend on the actual arithmetic and cryptographic libraries that are used, and on the computing platform that is chosen.

Our timings are based on the benchmark of the PandA library of Chuengsatiansup et al. [9], and on the execution of the protocol on a single core of a 2012 Intel i5-3210M processor running at 2.5 GHz. Their numbers are given in number of CPU cycles, which we convert into time based on the processor clock frequency.

Cost of Ballot Preparation. We consider a budget upper bound of $2^n = 2^{20}$ and a single choice question (which is the typical application case of quadratic voting). The operation count for the preparation of a ballot is available in Table 2. The resulting timing, based on the performance in Table 1, is then less than 8.4 ms.

Table 1. Cost of the main group operations

	G_1	G_2	G_T
Fixed base exponentiation	51 µs	135 µs	244 µs
Single multiplication	2.4 µs	6.4 µs	3 µs

Table 2. Count of exponentiations for ballot preparation.

	G_1	G_2
c	1	3
$\hat{c}$	1	3
π_{va}	2	3
$\hat{\pi}_{va}$	2	3
π_{sq}	3	0
π_r	$2n+1$	0
$\hat{\pi}_r$	$4n+1$	0
π_{op}	1	0
Total:	$6n+12$	12

Cost of the Election Tally. The bulk of the cost of the election tally will come from the verification of the validity of the individual ballots, which will be essentially the same as the cost of producing all the NIZK proofs. The marginal cost per ballot coming from the homomorphic addition of the votes and costs is indeed negligible: 1 multiplication in G_1 and 2 multiplications in G_2, that is, around $15\mu s$. The decryption operation has a cost that is constant and independent of the number of voters and will then be negligible as soon as we have a few thousand voters. The cost of the final discrete logarithm operation, needed to obtain the actual number of votes and election budget, will be around $\sqrt{m2^n}$ multiplications in G_T using the baby-step giant-step algorithm in an election with m ballots. If $m = 2^{20}$, we obtain a timing around 3 s.

4   Protocol Analysis

We briefly discuss the security properties of the quadratic voting protocol presented in last section, their main assumptions and give arguments why the properties are satisfied.

4.1   Protocol Correctness

The correctness of the protocol essentially follows from the additive homomorphic property of the PPATS encryption scheme and of Pedersen commitments.

As in traditional schemes based on homomorphic encryption, votes are encrypted, but now with their value that can be any integer (provided that the corresponding payment can be made). Tally tellers homomorphically add these votes and decrypt the election result.

The same happens with the encrypted quadratic payments. The balance of each voter is then adjusted twice: once after submission of the vote, then after redistribution of the election spending.

4.2 Ballot Privacy

The protocol offers computational privacy against the Election Authorities, provided that sufficiently many of them are honest (as defined by the threshold key generation protocol). These authorities receive ballots that are encrypted with a CPA secure encryption scheme, accompanied with various Σ-protocols that prove, among other things, the knowledge of the vote content.

This combination of encryption and proof of knowledge has been shown to lead to an NM-CPA non-malleable encryption scheme. This combination is known to be sufficient to offer ballot privacy when duplicate ballots are rejected [5].

Note that the amount of information revealed on the bulletin board is also very minimal, that is, we only reveal the total votes for each candidate/question and the total budget amount spent in the election.

4.3 Perfectly Private Audit Trail

The protocol offers a perfectly private audit trail, or everlasting privacy in front of adversaries who can only access the election bulletin board. This follows from the fact that the only information posted by voters on the board is perfectly hiding commitments and perfect zero-knowledge proofs, and that the result of the election is posted as a simple opening of a perfectly hiding commitment on that result.

So, provided that the voters have access to good sources of randomness when they prepare their vote, the content of the board is simply statistically independent of each vote content.

Note that for usability, it might be better for the voters to hold only a single long-term key that can generate openings to their budgets via a pseudorandom generator, instead of having to update the key in each election. However, this would endanger the everlasting privacy.

4.4 Verifiability

Cast-as-Intended Verifiability. The Benaloh challenge allows the voter to verify that the ballot preparation system prepares ciphertexts that match the voter intent.

Recorded-as-Cast Verifiability. The bulletin board, assumed honest, displays the perfectly hiding part of the submitted ballot, which the voter can control to be correct. If it is correct, then the voter is guaranteed that his vote cannot be interpreted in an unexpected way, provided that the commitment scheme's binding property is not broken.

The Election Authorities are prevented from claiming that the vote is actually invalid due to an issue in the non-published part, because they are required to verify that validity (thanks to the corresponding π_{va} proofs) before publishing a ballot on the board. (Of course, authorities could also reject a valid ballot and not publish it, arguing that the voter transmitted it incorrectly. But this is the case of any verifiable remote voting scheme: the voter can only know that his vote will be taken into account after his vote is included on the bulletin board.)

Eligibility Verifiability. The bulletin board includes the name of every voter next to the ballot that it submitted. This is enough for an auditor to interrogate the voters, ask them whether they submitted a ballot or not and, if they did, ask them if it is accurately displayed on the bulletin board.

This mechanism protects form malicious authentication authorities who would submit votes on behalf of potential voters who would not pay attention to the election. The use of an authentication mechanism of course remains important in order to avoid that voters submit arbitrary ballots on behalf of arbitrary voters, which would simply result in declaring the election invalid as soon as it is observed.

Actually the eligibility verifiability is also strengthened by the extra budget structure compared to ordinary PPAT voting schemes. In order to vote, and pay for your vote, you need to hold an opening to your budget commitment. If a voter has already voted in an earlier election, this prevents ballot stuffing on their behalf. As an example, if the adversary somehow knows a voter will not be paying attention to the bulletin board e.g. being without internet connection for some time, then the adversary cannot abuse this and vote on his behalf. For first time voters we can, however, not give such guarantees.

Budget Verifiability. The c_b commitments and π_{op}^b proofs make it possible for anyone to observe that every voter received his correct initial budget.

The update of the voter budget is publicly performed, using the spending amount $\mathsf{DCom}(\hat{c})$ committed to as part of the ballot. The proof $\hat{\pi}_r$ makes it possible to verify that the spending is within the correct range, and the proof π_r ensures that the actually paid amount is the square value of the vote, seen as integers, as mentioned in last section.

Tallied-as-Recorded Verifiability. After verification of the ballots that need to be included in the tally, any auditor can multiply the vote commitments $\mathsf{DCom}(c)$ together and obtain a commitment on the election result. The Tally Tellers are able to open that commitment thanks to the openings that they received for each individual vote. The finding of any different opening would break the computational binding property of the commitment scheme, which relies on the DDH assumption.

Budget Update Verifiability. The opening of the total spending in an election can be verified just as the vote tally. From this, the voter refund can be recomputed, and the updated commitments of every voter budget c_b can also be recomputed.

5   Conclusion and Outlook

In this paper we have presented an efficient protocol for electronic quadratic voting with everlasting privacy and end-to-end verifiability. The protocol uses perfectly hiding commitments for both vote choices and budgets to create a perfectly private audit trail. The constructions also facilitates easy threshold sharing of the secret election. In total, we have improved many aspects of the earlier protocol suggested in [17].

As it stands we don't allow transfer between different voters' budgets. This could easily be changed, but we think that both the everlasting privacy, universal verifiability and non-coupling to real currencies is an advantage over solutions using anonymous cryptocurrencies such as Zerocash. Note that allowing budget transfers also opens up to strategic voting since it would be more favorable to have equal-sized budgets when voting [17].

An improvement of the scheme would be to achieve receipt-freeness. In the present scheme, the commitments and corresponding openings could be used directly to prove to a vote-buyer that you voted according to his instructions. It is an important piece of future work to improve on this situation. If we allow budget transfers, it would maybe also impede strategic voting since you cannot get proof that the budget you give away will be used according to your preference. Note that whereas the receipt-freeness of the vote choice can follow similar ideas in other e-voting schemes, the budget is less straight-forward since in our construction we hold a key to unlock the budget. Especially to prevent forced-abstention attacks, it will be necessary to hide the budget from the coercer.

Acknowledgements. The authors acknowledge support from the Luxembourg National Research Fund (FNR) and Belgium Fonds de la Recherche Scientifique for the joint FNR/F.R.S.-FNRS project SeVoTe. PBR also acknowledges the FNR INTER project VoteVerif. This work has also been funded in part by the European Union (EU) and the Walloon Region through the FEDER project USERMedia (convention number 501907-379156).

References

1. Adida, B., De Marneffe, O., Pereira, O., Quisquater, J.-J.: Electing a university president using open-audit voting: analysis of real-world use of Helios. In: Proceedings of the 2009 Conference on Electronic Voting Technology/Workshop on Trustworthy Elections, EVT/WOTE 2009, Berkeley, CA, USA, p. 10. USENIX Association (2009)
2. Barreto, P.S.L.M., Naehrig, M.: Pairing-friendly elliptic curves of prime order. In: Preneel, B., Tavares, S. (eds.) SAC 2005. LNCS, vol. 3897, pp. 319–331. Springer, Heidelberg (2006). https://doi.org/10.1007/11693383_22

3. Bellare, M., Goldwasser, S.: Verifiable partial key escrow. In: Proceedings of the 4th ACM Conference on Computer and Communications Security, pp. 78–91. ACM (1997)

4. Benaloh, J.: Ballot casting assurance via voter-initiated poll station auditing. In: USENIX/ACCURATE Electronic Voting Technology Workshop, EVT 2007. USENIX Association (2007)

5. Bernhard, D., Pereira, O., Warinschi, B.: How not to prove yourself: pitfalls of the fiat-shamir heuristic and applications to Helios. In: Wang, X., Sako, K. (eds.) ASIACRYPT 2012. LNCS, vol. 7658, pp. 626–643. Springer, Heidelberg (2012). https://doi.org/10.1007/978-3-642-34961-4_38

6. Boneh, D., Goh, E.-J., Nissim, K.: Evaluating 2-DNF formulas on ciphertexts. In: Kilian, J. (ed.) TCC 2005. LNCS, vol. 3378, pp. 325–341. Springer, Heidelberg (2005). https://doi.org/10.1007/978-3-540-30576-7_18

7. Camenisch, J.: Group signature schemes and payment systems based on the discrete logarithm problem. PhD thesis, ETH Zurich (1998)

8. Chandar, B., Weyl, E.G.: Quadratic voting in finite populations (2017)

9. Chuengsatiansup, C., Naehrig, M., Ribarski, P., Schwabe, P.: PandA: pairings and arithmetic. In: Cao, Z., Zhang, F. (eds.) Pairing 2013. LNCS, vol. 8365, pp. 229–250. Springer, Cham (2014). https://doi.org/10.1007/978-3-319-04873-4_14

10. Cramer, R., Damgård, I., Schoenmakers, B.: Proofs of partial knowledge and simplified design of witness hiding protocols. In: Desmedt, Y.G. (ed.) CRYPTO 1994. LNCS, vol. 839, pp. 174–187. Springer, Heidelberg (1994). https://doi.org/10.1007/3-540-48658-5_19

11. Cramer, R., Gennaro, R., Schoenmakers, B.: A secure and optimally efficient multi-authority election scheme. In: Fumy, W. (ed.) EUROCRYPT 1997. LNCS, vol. 1233, pp. 103–118. Springer, Heidelberg (1997). https://doi.org/10.1007/3-540-69053-0_9

12. Cuvelier, É., Pereira, O., Peters, T.: Election verifiability or ballot privacy: do we need to choose? In: Crampton, J., Jajodia, S., Mayes, K. (eds.) ESORICS 2013. LNCS, vol. 8134, pp. 481–498. Springer, Heidelberg (2013). https://doi.org/10.1007/978-3-642-40203-6_27

13. Damgård, I.: On sigma protocols (2010). http://www.daimi.au.dk/~ivan/Sigma.pdf

14. Fiat, A., Shamir, A.: How to prove yourself: practical solutions to identification and signature problems. In: Odlyzko, A.M. (ed.) CRYPTO 1986. LNCS, vol. 263, pp. 186–194. Springer, Heidelberg (1987). https://doi.org/10.1007/3-540-47721-7_12

15. Gennaro, R., Jarecki, S., Krawczyk, H., Rabin, T.: Secure distributed key generation for discrete-log based cryptosystems. J. Cryptol. 20(1), 51–83 (2007)

16. Lalley, S.P., Weyl, E.G.: Nash equilibria for a quadratic voting game. CoRR, abs/1409.0264 (2014)

17. Park, S., Rivest, R.L.: Towards secure quadratic voting. Public Choice 172(1–2), 151–175 (2017). https://eprint.iacr.org/2016/400

18. Pedersen, T.P.: A threshold cryptosystem without a trusted party. In: Davies, D.W. (ed.) EUROCRYPT 1991. LNCS, vol. 547, pp. 522–526. Springer, Heidelberg (1991). https://doi.org/10.1007/3-540-46416-6_47

19. Quarfoot, D., von Kohorn, D., Slavin, K., Sutherland, R., Goldstein, D., Konar, E.: Quadratic voting in the wild: real people, real votes. Public Choice 172(1), 283–303 (2017). https://doi.org/10.1007/s11127-017-0416-1

20. Sasson, E.B., et al.: Decentralized anonymous payments from Bitcoin. In: Proceedings of the 2014 IEEE Symposium on Security and Privacy, SP 2014, Washington, DC, USA, pp. 459–474. IEEE Computer Society (2014)

21. Schnorr, C.P.: Efficient identification and signatures for smart cards. In: Brassard, G. (ed.) CRYPTO 1989. LNCS, vol. 435, pp. 239–252. Springer, New York (1990). https://doi.org/10.1007/0-387-34805-0_22

22. Wikström, D.: Simplified submission of inputs to protocols. In: Ostrovsky, R., De Prisco, R., Visconti, I. (eds.) SCN 2008. LNCS, vol. 5229, pp. 293–308. Springer, Heidelberg (2008). https://doi.org/10.1007/978-3-540-85855-3_20

Lattice-Based Proof of a Shuffle

Nuria Costa[1], Ramiro Martínez[2(✉)], and Paz Morillo[2]

[1] Scytl Secure Electronic Voting, Barcelona, Spain
nuria.costa@scytl.com
[2] Universitat Politècnica de Catalunya, Barcelona, Spain
{ramiro.martinez,paz.morillo}@upc.edu

Abstract. In this paper we present the first fully post-quantum proof of a shuffle for RLWE encryption schemes. Shuffles are commonly used to construct mixing networks (mix-nets), a key element to ensure anonymity in many applications such as electronic voting systems. They should preserve anonymity even against an attack using quantum computers in order to guarantee long-term privacy. The proof presented in this paper is built over RLWE commitments which are perfectly binding and computationally hiding under the RLWE assumption, thus achieving security in a post-quantum scenario. Furthermore we provide a new definition for a secure mixing node (mix-node) and prove that our construction satisfies this definition.

Keywords: Mix-nets · E-voting · Post-quantum · RLWE encryption · RLWE commitment · Proof of a shuffle

1 Introduction

In the last years, several countries have been introducing electronic voting systems to improve their democratic processes, in particular, they provide voters with the chance to cast their votes from anywhere. Anonymity and verifiability are two fundamental requirements for internet voting systems that seem to be contradictory. Anonymity requires that the link between the vote and the voter who has cast it must remain secret during the whole process, while verifiability requires that all the steps of the electoral process - vote casting, vote storage and vote counting - can be checked by the voters, the auditors or external observers. One of the resources used by the actual internet voting systems to achieve anonymity are mixing networks (mix-nets). Informally we can define a mix-net as a multiparty protocol that, given a number of encrypted messages at the input, performs a permutation over them followed by a cryptographic transformation using a re-encryption and/or a decryption algorithm. This operation is called a shuffle [9] and it is done in such a way that the correlation between the input and the output of the process is hidden, and it is not possible to trace it back. The proof of the shuffle guarantees that the ciphertexts at the output of the mix-net are those at its input permuted and re-encrypted/decrypted, without revealing any secret information. One way to construct a mix-net is to define

© International Financial Cryptography Association 2020
A. Bracciali et al. (Eds.): FC 2019 Workshops, LNCS 11599, pp. 330–346, 2020.
https://doi.org/10.1007/978-3-030-43725-1_23

several mixing nodes (mix-nodes) each one performing in turns this operation. It is clear that if at least one of the nodes is honest, unlinkability is preserved.

On the other hand, in order to build verifiable systems one key instrument is the Bulletin Board: a public place where all the audit information of the election (encrypted votes, election configuration, proof of a shuffle, ...) is published by authorized parties and can be verified by anyone: voters, auditors or third parties. However, once published in the Bulletin Board anyone can save a copy, and long-term privacy may not be ensured by encryption algorithms used nowadays, for example due to the efficient quantum algorithm given by Shor [29] that breaks computational problems such as the discrete logarithm (DL) or the integer factorization problems. Learning how a person voted some years ago may have political, as well as personal implications.

Some cryptosystems have appeared in the last years that are believed to be secure against quantum attacks: hash-based, code-based, lattice-based or multivariate-quadratic-equations. Lattice-based cryptography is a great promise to get cryptosystems that will remain secure in the post-quantum era [23]. These ones enjoy strong security guarantees from worst-case hardness, meaning that breaking their security implies finding an efficient algorithm for solving any instance of the underlying lattice problem, e.g., the Shortest Vector Problem (SVP) or the Closest Vector Problem (CVP). Furthermore, these constructions mainly involve linear operations such as matrix and vector sum or multiplication modulo relatively small integers, which make them highly parallelizable and consequently faster in certain contexts. Given the interest aroused by this type of cryptography, several lattice-based protocols have been proposed like public key encryption schemes, digital signatures schemes, hash functions, identity-based encryption schemes or Zero-Knowledge Proofs of Knowledge (ZKPoK). Our contribution increases the literature of the latter, providing a fully lattice-based proof of a shuffle that will remain secure in a post-quantum scenario.

To the best of our knowledge there are two proposed e-voting schemes [10,15] that are constructed using lattices. They both follow an alternative approach without shuffling, making use of the homomorphic property of their encryption schemes to compute the tally. However mix-net based schemes are more flexible and provide a better support for complex electoral processes.

On the other hand [11] and [31] give proofs of a shuffle for lattice-based cryptography. The first requires Pedersen commitments (based on the DL problem). The latter requires a Fully Homomorphic Encryption scheme, and works with any homomorphic commitment scheme, that is, using the lattice-based commitment scheme presented in [4] their proof is fully post-quantum.

We propose a proof of a shuffle that is fully constructed over lattice-based cryptography and the first for RLWE encryption schemes, which makes it secure in a post-quantum scenario. The proof uses a commitment scheme which is perfectly binding and computationally hiding under the Learning With Errors over Rings (RLWE) assumption. This lattice computational problem has been shown to be as hard as certain worst-case problems in ideal lattices (such as SVP and CVP in ideal lattices) and thus resistant to quantum attacks. We also provide a formal definition for security of a mix-node and prove security of our proposal using the sequence of games approach.

1.1 Previous Work

After the introduction of the idea of a shuffle by Chaum in 1981 [9], several schemes have been proposed. The first universally verifiable mix-net is presented in [28] and gives a proof to check the correctness of the shuffle. Later, several solutions for an efficient universally verifiable mix-net are proposed [1–3,22] and in [17] Furukawa and Sako suggest a paradigm based on permutation matrices in the common reference string model (CRS) for proving the correctness of a shuffle, that was improved in [16,20]. The latest proposal for a CRS based proof of a shuffle is [8] by Bünz *et al.* Wikström also uses this idea of the permutation matrix and presents in [36] a proof of a shuffle that can be split in an offline and online phase in order to reduce the computational complexity in the online part.

On the other hand, Neff [24] proposes another paradigm based on polynomials being identical under permutation of their roots, obtaining Honest Verifier Zero-Knowledge (HVZK) proof and improved later in [18,25] with the drawback that these constructions are 7-move proofs. Unlike previous proposals, Groth and Ishai [19] and Bayer and Groth [6] give a practical shuffle argument with sub-linear communication complexity.

The proof of a shuffle presented in this paper requires lattice-based ZKPoK to prove that some hidden elements have small norm and also that several committed elements satisfy a polynomial relation. As these proofs are generally costly we are going to use amortized protocols to reduce the communication cost. The first amortized protocol is presented in [12] by Cramer *et al.*, it is improved first by del Pino and Lyubashevsky [14] and later by Baum and Lyubashevsky in [5].

Recently, Costa *et al.* [11] have presented a proof of a shuffle based on lattices but it cannot be considered fully post-quantum since they use Pedersen commitments, whose binding property relies on the DL problem. Moreover in [11] there is no formal definition of security, necessary to precisely know how it can be embedded in a larger construction. Strand [31] presents a verifiable shuffle for the GSW cryptosystem using homomorphic commitment schemes. Using the lattice-based commitment scheme [4] makes the proof fully post-quantum. Additionally, there have been some proposals for a lattice-based universal re-encryption for mix-nets [30] but none of them give a proof of a shuffle.

In [35] Wikström provides a definition of security for a single re-encryption mix-node. It is important to note that as Wikström remarks this is not enough to completely ensure privacy since a definition of security of a complete mix-net must involve several other aspects, regarding validity of the input messages or decryption proofs.

1.2 Our Contribution

We propose a proof of a shuffle fully constructed over lattices. It is based on the technique introduced by Bayer and Groth in [6] to construct a shuffle argument;

nevertheless it is not a direct adaptation of it since working with lattices requires different techniques to be applied.

The first step of the proof, that is also the first difference with [6], consists on committing the re-encryption parameters in order to demonstrate that they meet certain constraints. This is done using the commitment scheme and the ZKPoK proposed by Benhamouda et al. [7] which are perfectly binding and computationally hiding under the RLWE assumption and satisfy special soundness and special HVZK. The next step consists on proving knowledge of the permutation. The general idea here is to prove that two sets contain the same elements. This is done by computing two polynomials, each of them having as roots the elements of each set, and proving that both polynomials are equal.

The last step will prove knowledge of the re-encryption parameters, and this introduces another difference between Bayer and Groth's protocol and ours. While they demonstrate that there exists a linear combination of the parameters such that an equality holds, we have to use a different technique, since the re-encryption parameters in a RLWE re-encryption scheme are taken from an error distribution and a linear combination of them would imply the error grows uncontrollably, causing decryption errors.

Finally, we give a definition of security, based on the one proposed by Wikström in [35], and we provide a proof of security for our mix-node. His proposal implies that no adversary can properly compute two indices for the input and the output respectively such that the messages encrypted in the corresponding ciphertexts are the same, except with a probability negligibly close to the probability given by a random guess. In his definition the adversary might have some knowledge of correlations between the input messages. We provide a definition of security allowing the adversary to have full control over the input of the mix-node, and we prove that our construction meets this definition.

Organization of the Paper. In Sect. 2 we introduce some notation and give some cryptographic background necessary to understand the proof presented in Sect. 4. In Sect. 3 we describe the computational problem on which the security of our scheme is based and we also give a description of a RLWE-based commitment scheme. Finally in Sect. 4 we present our fully post-quantum proof of a shuffle and the results about the security of the mix-node. We briefly conclude in Sect. 5.

2   Preliminaries

We denote column vectors by boldface lower-case roman letters, v or w. Matrices are represented by boldface upper-case roman letters, M or A. Given two vectors $v, w \in \mathbb{Z}_q^N$, we define the standard inner product in $\mathbb{Z}_q^N$ as $\langle v, w \rangle = \sum_{i=1}^{N} v_i w_i$, the l_∞ norm as $\|v\|_\infty = \max_{1 \leq i \leq N} |v_i|$ and the general norm l_p as $\|v\|_p = (\sum_{i=1}^{N} |v_i|^p)^{1/p}$ for $p \geq 1$.

We let $\lfloor x \rfloor$ denote the largest integer not greater than x, and $\lfloor x \rceil := \lfloor x + 1/2 \rfloor$ denote the integer closest to x, with ties broken upward.

We write $a \xleftarrow{\$} A$ when a is sampled uniformly at random from a set A, and $a \xleftarrow{\$} D$ if it is drawn according to the distribution D.

Finally, in order to avoid confusions we are going to identify the ciphertexts' elements with the subscript E, and those corresponding to the commitments with subscript C. When working with lattices we are going to follow the notation proposed in [21].

The ZKPoK between a prover $\mathcal{P}$ and a verifier $\mathcal{V}$ constructed in this paper satisfies the properties of *completeness*, *special soundness* and *special HVZK* as they are defined in [13]. We will use them to prove knowledge of valid openings of commitments that satisfy several polynomial relations.

2.1 Generalized Schwartz–Zippel Lemma

The proof of a shuffle presented in this paper uses a generalized version of the Schwartz-Zippel lemma to prove polynomial equalities. This lemma works in general commutative rings that are not necessarily integral domains. Unlike Bayer and Groth we need the generalized version since we work with polynomials whose coefficients belong to another ring of polynomials.

Lemma 1. *Let $p \in R[x_1, x_2, \ldots, x_n]$ be a non-zero polynomial of total degree $d \geq 0$ over a commutative ring R. Let S be a finite subset of R such that none of the differences between two elements of S is a divisor of 0 and let $r_1, r_2, \ldots, r_n$ be selected at random independently and uniformly from S. Then:*
$\Pr[p(r_1, r_2, \ldots, r_n) = 0] \leq \frac{d}{|S|}$.

We will use this lemma to prove that two polynomials, p_1 and p_2, are equal with overwhelming probability if $p_1(r_1, r_2, \ldots, r_n) - p_2(r_1, r_2, \ldots, r_n) = 0$ for $r_1, r_2, \ldots, r_n \xleftarrow{\$} S$. The proof of this generalization directly follows from the original proof of the lemma. We have included it in a full version of this paper for the reader interested on it.

3   Ideal Lattices

A lattice is a set of points in an n-dimensional space with a periodic structure. We are going to work with *ideal* lattices that have some extra algebraic structure and introduce some redundancy allowing a more compact representation and thus reducing significantly the storage space. We refer the interested reader to [26] for a survey on lattices.

Let $R_q = \mathbb{Z}_q[x]/\langle f(x)\rangle$ be the ring of polynomials modulo $f(x) = x^n + 1$ for n a power of 2, which makes the polynomial irreducible over the rationals. The ideal lattice $\mathcal{L}(a)$ generated by $a(x) = a_1 + a_2 x + \ldots + a_n x^{n-1} \in R_q$ is the set of polynomials $v(x)$ obtained as $v(x) = a(x) \cdot p(x) \mod x^n + 1$, where $p(x) \in R_q$.

There is currently no known way to take a significant advantage of this extra structure introduced in this class of ideal lattices, and the running time required to solve lattice problems on such lattices is comparable to that for general lattices.

3.1 RLWE Problem

The security of lattice-based cryptosystems relies on the hardness of solving some computational problems on lattices, such as the Learning With Errors (LWE).

Lyubashevsky *et al.* [21] introduced in 2010 the ideal lattice based variant of LWE, called Ring Learning With Errors (RLWE). This was motivated by the necessity of constructing efficient LWE-based cryptosystems.

Definition 1 (RLWE Distribution). *For a secret* $s \in R_q$, *the RLWE distribution* $\mathcal{A}_{s,\chi}$ *over* $R_q \times R_q$ *is sampled choosing* $a \in R_q$ *uniformly at random,* $e \xleftarrow{\$} \chi^n$ *(that is,* $e \in R_q$ *with its coefficients drawn from* χ*), and outputting samples of the form* $(a, b = a \cdot s + e \mod q) \in R_q \times R_q$.

Analogously to LWE [27], the goal will be either to distinguish random linear equations, perturbed by a small amount of noise, from truly uniform pairs, or recover the secret $s \in R_q$ from arbitrarily many noisy products. Usually the error distribution χ is a *discrete Gaussian distribution* on $\mathbb{Z}$, that is $\chi = D_\sigma$, where σ is the standard deviation.

Hardness of RLWE . Certain instantiations of RLWE are supported by worst-case hardness theorems [21], related to the Shortest Vector Problem (SVP). For the error distribution χ where $\sigma \geq \omega(\sqrt{\log n})$, and for any ring, there exist a quantum reduction from the $\gamma(n)$-SVP problem to the RLWE problem to within $\gamma(n) = \mathcal{O}(\sqrt{n} \cdot q/\sigma)$. Additionally, RLWE becomes no easier to solve even if the secret s is chosen from the error distribution, rather than uniformly [21].

3.2 RLWE Encryption Scheme

The additive homomorphic RLWE encryption scheme proposed in [21] consists of three algorithms (KeyGen$_E$, Encrypt, Decrypt) defined below. We denote the security parameter as κ.

- KeyGen$_E(1^\kappa)$: Given a uniformly random $a_E \in R_q$ and two *small* elements $s, e \in R_q$ drawn from the error distribution χ^n, the public key is an RLWE sample $(a_E, b_E) = (a_E, a_E \cdot s + e) \in R_q \times R_q$ and the secret key is s.
- Encrypt$((a_E, b_E), r_E, e_{E,u}, e_{E,v}, z)$: Given three random small elements $r_E, e_{E,u}, e_{E,v} \in R_q$ drawn from the error distribution χ^n, the encryption of an n-bit message $z \in \{0, 1\}^n$ (identified as a polynomial of degree $n-1$ with coefficients 0 or 1) is $(u, v) = (a_E \cdot r_E + e_{E,u}, b_E \cdot r_E + e_{E,v} + \lfloor \frac{q}{2} \rfloor z) \in R_q \times R_q$.
- Decrypt$(s, (u, v))$: Given the secret key and the ciphertext this algorithm computes: $v - u \cdot s = (r_E \cdot e - s \cdot e_{E,u} + e_{E,v}) + \lfloor \frac{q}{2} \rfloor z \mod q$. Then recovers each bit of z by rounding each coefficient to 0 or $\lfloor \frac{q}{2} \rceil$.

Correctness. Notice that in case of lack of error the decryption would always be correct since the algorithm will return directly 0 or $\lfloor \frac{q}{2} \rceil$ depending on the encrypted bit. Given that, a decryption error will occur if the coefficients of $(r_E \cdot e - s \cdot e_{E,u} + e_{E,v})$ have magnitude greater than $q/4$.

As the messages encrypted using this scheme will pass through a mixing process we will need to also re-encrypt them. Due to the homomorphic property of the scheme we can compute the re-encryption just adding to the original ciphertext the encryption of the element 0.

- Re-encrypt$((u, v), (a_E, b_E), r'_E, e'_{E,u}, e'_{E,v})$: Given the small elements $r'_E, e'_{E,u}, e'_{E,v}$ drawn from the error distribution χ^n, the re-encryption of a ciphertext (u, v) is $(u', v') = (u, v) + \mathsf{Encrypt}((a_E, b_E), r'_E, e'_{E,u}, e'_{E,v}, 0) \in R_q \times R_q$.

Security. RLWE encryption scheme and consequently the RLWE re-encryption scheme are semantically secure based on the RLWE assumption. It is demonstrated that if there exists a polynomial-time algorithm that distinguishes between two encryptions then there exists another algorithm able to distinguish between $\mathcal{A}_{s,\chi}$ and a uniformly random distribution over R_q for a non-negligible fraction of all possible s. Notice that, even though these schemes do not achieve circuit privacy, the secrecy of the shuffle is not affected since the randomness used during the encryption and re-encryption procedures is never revealed. In order to demonstrate that the random values are of the right form, that is, that they are small enough, we use zero-knowledge proofs.

3.3 Commitments from RLWE

The commitment scheme used to build our proof of a shuffle is that described by Benhamouda *et al.* in [7] and consists of the following three algorithms:

- KeyGen$_C(1^\kappa)$: given as input the security parameter κ (we omit the details about κ here and we refer the reader to [7]) this algorithm generates the public commitment key $pk_C = (a_C, b_C)$ where $a_C, b_C \overset{\$}{\leftarrow} (R_q)^k$, $q \equiv 3 \mod 8$ is prime and n is a power of 2.
- Com: in order to commit to a message $m \in R_q$, the algorithm chooses $r_C \overset{\$}{\leftarrow} R_q$ and $e_C \overset{\$}{\leftarrow} D_{\sigma_e}^k$ conditioned on $\|e_C\|_\infty \leq n$ and computes:

$$c = \mathsf{Com}_{a_C, b_C}(m; r_C, e_C) = a_C m + b_C r_C + e_C$$

The opening of the commitments is defined as $(m, r_C, e_C, 1)$.
- Ver: given (c, m', r'_C, e'_C, f') the verification algorithm accepts if and only if:

$$a_C m' + b_C r'_C + f'^{-1} e'_C = c \wedge \|e'_C\|_\infty \leq \left\lfloor \frac{n^{4/3}}{2} \right\rfloor \wedge \|f'\|_\infty \leq 1 \wedge \deg f' \leq \frac{n}{2}$$

This commitment scheme satisfies the security requirements of correctness, perfectly binding and computational hiding as they are explained in [7].

The main reason for us to choose this commitment scheme is that [7] gives efficient ZKPoK to prove knowledge of an opening of a given commitment or to prove that the messages inside some commitments satisfy any polynomial relation.

4   Proof of a Shuffle for RLWE Encryptions

The existing published proposal for a universally verifiable proof of a shuffle for RLWE encryptions [11] based on [32], uses Generalized Pedersen commitments to hide the secret re-randomization elements. This would not be sound in a post-quantum scenario, as it is based on DL assumptions.

Naively replacing the commitment scheme with the one proposed by Benhamouda *et al.* yields several difficulties since it is useful when committing to polynomials, but is quite inefficient if we only want to commit to a bit, as is the case with the entries of a permutation matrix. The fact that $\mathbb{Z}_q[x]/\langle x^n + 1\rangle$ is not an integral domain also has some implications for the characterization of a permutation matrix proposed in [32], that cannot be proven directly and would require additional statements different from the ones discussed in [11].

In this section we construct a post-quantum verifiable mix-node following the paradigm given by Bayer and Groth in [6]. Once again, replacing Pedersen commitments with the ones proposed by Benhamouda *et al.* is not immediate.

We first show an overview of the shuffling protocol, then we present our proof of a shuffle and give details regarding the ZKPoK involved in the construction of the main proof and finally we prove that our mix-node is secure based on a new formal definition of security, stronger than that given in [35].

Proofs of a shuffle commonly require universal verifiability, meaning that a proof must be generated and also published, so it can be verified by any observer. Classically, this kind of interactive protocols can be transformed into non-interactive protocols by means of the Fiat-Shamir heuristics, replacing the random responses from the verifier with a hash of the previous elements in the conversation, achieving a protocol secure in the Random Oracle Model (ROM).

However, as it is exposed in [34], this method is not secure anymore in the Quantum Random Oracle Model (QROM). As far as we know the only quantum secure general transformation from an interactive protocol to a non-interactive version is the one described by [33]. Therefore, a universally verifiable version of our protocol requires further considerations.

4.1   Protocol Overview

Given a permutation π and a set of re-encryption parameters $\left\{ r_{\mathsf{E}}^{\prime(i)}, e_{\mathsf{E},u}^{\prime(i)}, e_{\mathsf{E},v}^{\prime(i)} \right\}$ for each one of the messages, the shuffling of N RLWE encryptions is defined as $\left(u^{\prime(i)}, v^{\prime(i)} \right) = \mathsf{Re\text{-}encrypt}\left(\left(u^{\pi(i)}, v^{\pi(i)} \right), r_{\mathsf{E}}^{\prime(i)}, e_{\mathsf{E},u}^{\prime(i)}, e_{\mathsf{E},v}^{\prime(i)} \right)$.

A mix-node will perform the shuffling over the input ciphertexts and will generate a proof of a shuffle, see (1), to demonstrate that it knows the permutation π and the random elements $r_{\mathsf{E}}^{\prime(i)}, e_{\mathsf{E},u}^{\prime(i)}, e_{\mathsf{E},v}^{\prime(i)}$, without revealing any information about them.

This proof will be published so everybody is convinced that the ciphertexts have been permuted and re-encrypted without modifying the encrypted plaintexts (even if some of the nodes are dishonest and leak the permutation).

The first step of the protocol will be to commit to the encryptions of 0 used to compute the RLWE re-encryptions and a ZKPoK of the resulting commitments containing valid encryptions of 0. Additionally, it will also be demonstrated that the small polynomials $r'_E, e'_{E,u}, e'_{E,v}$ used to compute the re-encryptions have an infinity norm that is bounded by some parameter $\delta \ll q/4$.

$$
\text{ZKPoK} \left[\left\{ r'^{(i)}_E, e'^{(i)}_{E,u}, e'^{(i)}_{E,v} \right\}_{i=1}^{N} \; \middle| \; \text{Re-encrypt} \left(\left(u^{\pi(i)}, v^{\pi(i)} \right), r'^{(i)}_E, e'^{(i)}_{E,u}, e'^{(i)}_{E,v} \right) \atop \left\| r'^{(i)}_E \right\|_\infty, \left\| e'^{(i)}_{E,u} \right\|_\infty, \left\| e'^{(i)}_{E,v} \right\|_\infty \le \delta \right]
\tag{1}
$$

As it is explained in [7] for a suitable δ even if this additional restriction on the re-encryption parameters norm is applied, the re-encryptions remain pseudorandom, as the two probability distributions are statistically close. The last part of the protocol consists on proving that two sets contain the same elements:

$$
\left\{ \left(u'^{(i)}, v'^{(i)} \right) - \left(a_E r'^{(i)}_E + e'^{(i)}_{E,u}, b_E r'^{(i)}_E + e'^{(i)}_{E,v} \right) \right\}_{i=1}^{N} = \left\{ \left(u^{(i)}, v^{(i)} \right) \right\}_{i=1}^{N}
$$

This is done following the strategy proposed by Bayer and Groth in [6], that consists on building two polynomials, each of them having as roots the elements of each of the sets and then prove that both polynomials are equal. To convince a verifier that two polynomials are equal the prover evaluates them in a random point chosen by the verifier and uses the generalized version of Schwartz-Zippel lemma (Lemma 1). Our polynomials will be evaluated and have coefficients in R_q, that is, we will work in $R_q[A]$ and the variable A takes values on R_q.

We define the mixing protocol using the following algorithms:

- Setup(1^κ): generate parameters (n, q, σ) and run the following algorithms:
  - KeyGen$_E(1^\kappa)$ to obtain the public and the private key of the RLWE encryption scheme: $(a_E, b_E) \in R_q \times R_q$ and $s \in R_q$.
  - KeyGen$_C(1^\kappa)$ to generate the public commitment key: $a_C, b_C \xleftarrow{\$} (R_q)^k$.
  Output $\{\{(a_E, b_E), s\}, (a_C, b_C)\}$
- MixVotes($pk_E, pk_C, \{(u^{(i)}, v^{(i)})\}_{i=1}^{N}$): taking as input a list of N encrypted messages $\{(u^{(i)}, v^{(i)})\}_{i=1}^{N}$ compute the shuffling of these RLWE encryptions. Generate commitments and ZKPoK (we denote by ZK$_i$ its corresponding protocols and by Σ_i the proofs they output) as it is explained in Sect. 4.2 in order to demonstrate the correctness of the process. We can explicitly state the permutation and/or random elements to be used writing MixVotes(pk_E, pk_C, $\{(u^{(i)}, v^{(i)})\}_{i=1}^{N}; \pi, \{r'^{(i)}_E, e'^{(i)}_{E,u}, e'^{(i)}_{E,v}\}_{i=1}^{N}$).

Output $\left(\{(u'^{(i)}, v'^{(i)})\}_{i=1}^{N}, \{(c_{u_0^{(i)}}, c_{v_0^{(i)}}, c_{\pi(i)}, c_{\alpha^{\pi(i)}})\}_{i=1}^{N}, \Sigma_1, \Sigma_2, \Sigma_3, \Sigma_4 \right)$.

We denote $\Sigma_0 = \{c_{u_0^{(i)}}, c_{v_0^{(i)}}, c_{\pi(i)}, c_{\alpha^{\pi(i)}}\}_{i=1}^{N}$ to unify the notation of the output of MixVotes.

– VerifyMix($pk_E, pk_C, \{(u^{(i)}, v^{(i)})\}_{i=1}^N, \{(u'^{(i)}, v'^{(i)})\}_{i=1}^N, \{\Sigma_l\}_{l=0}^4$): given an input and an output of the mixing process and the ZKPoK generated, this algorithm outputs 1 if the proofs are valid and 0 otherwise.

4.2   Proof of a Shuffle

In this subsection we present the proposed proof (see Protocol 1.1) and explain in detail how it can be used as a proof of a shuffle.

Notice that each mix-node runs the algorithm MixVotes and acts as a prover. He first commits to N encryptions of zero. Each commitment $(c_{u_0^{(i)}}, c_{v_0^{(i)}})$ is:

$$\left(a_C \left(a_E r_E'^{(i)} + e_{E,u}'^{(i)}\right) + b_C r_{C,u}^{(i)} + e_{C,u}^{(i)}, a_C \left(b_E r_E'^{(i)} + e_{E,v}'^{(i)}\right) + b_C r_{C,v}^{(i)} + e_{C,v}^{(i)}\right)$$

That is, the commitment is a linear combination of the polynomials, with the additional condition of $r_E'^{(i)}, e_{E,u}'^{(i)}, e_{E,v}'^{(i)}, e_{C,u}^{(i)}, e_{C,v}^{(i)}$ having small norm.

Then, $\mathcal{P}$ sends the commitments to the verifier and proves using the amortized proof of knowledge of secret small elements [14] that the public commitments are indeed commitments to encryptions of zero.

As the relation is always the same we will use the amortized proposal by del Pino and Lyubashevsky [14], which is a direct improvement of the proposal by Cramer et al. [12]. For a linear function f, a small vector x and its image $y = f(x)$ we can prove knowledge of a small vector x' such that $f(x') = y$. As it is usual in this kind of proofs there is a gap τ between the upper bound of the norm we use for witness x and the upper bound we get for the extracted x'. This has to be taken into account when determining specific parameters so that this possible error multiplied by the number of mix-nodes does not exceed the bounds allowed for a correct decryption. We refer the reader to [14] for details, as we directly use their protocol as a building block for the ZKPoK of linear relations in ZK$_1$ (Protocol 1.1).

In order to commit to a permutation, $\mathcal{P}$ starts committing to $\pi(1), \ldots, \pi(N)$ in $c_{\pi(i)}$ and receives a polynomial α chosen uniformly at random from the subset:

$$S = \{p(x) \in R_q \mid \deg p(x) < n/2\}$$

Observe that the subset S meets the required conditions for Lemma 1, as all differences of two different elements in S are invertible. This is true as the condition $q \equiv 3 \mod 8$ required for the Benhamouda et al. commitment scheme implies that $x^n + 1$ splits into two irreducible polynomials of size exactly $n/2$. Then all polynomials of degree smaller that $n/2$ have an inverse that can be computed using the Chinese Remainder Theorem.

$\mathcal{P}$ commits to each power $\alpha^{\pi(i)}$ in commitments $c_{\alpha^{\pi(i)}}$ and publishes them. $\mathcal{P}$ receives two more random polynomials $\beta, \gamma \xleftarrow{\$} S$. Using the Σ-protocols from [7] that allow him to prove polynomial relations between committed messages, $\mathcal{P}$ proves that he knows openings $m_i, \widehat{m}_i$ to commitments $c_{\pi(i)}, c_{\alpha^{\pi(i)}}$ that satisfy the following relation (ZK$_2$ in Protocol 1.1).

$$\prod_{i=1}^N \left(\beta i + \alpha^i - \gamma\right) = \prod_{i=1}^N \left(\beta m_i + \widehat{m}_i - \gamma\right) \tag{2}$$

Protocol 1.1. Proof of a shuffle

$$\mathcal{P}\left(u^{(i)}, v^{(i)}, u'^{(i)}, v'^{(i)}; \pi, r'^{(i)}_{\mathsf{E}}, e'^{(i)}_{\mathsf{E},u}, e'^{(i)}_{\mathsf{E},v}\right) \qquad\qquad \mathcal{V}\left(u^{(i)}, v^{(i)}, u'^{(i)}, v'^{(i)}\right)$$

$\forall i \in [1, \dots, N]$

$c_{u_0^{(i)}} = \mathsf{Com}\left(a_{\mathsf{E}} r'^{(i)}_{\mathsf{E}} + e'^{(i)}_{\mathsf{E},u}\right)$

$c_{v_0^{(i)}} = \mathsf{Com}\left(b_{\mathsf{E}} r'^{(i)}_{\mathsf{E}} + e'^{(i)}_{\mathsf{E},v}\right)$

$$\xrightarrow{\quad c_{u_0^{(i)}}, c_{v_0^{(i)}} \quad}$$

$$\mathsf{ZKPoK}\left[\begin{array}{c} r'^{(i)}_{\mathsf{E}}, e'^{(i)}_{\mathsf{E},u}, e'^{(i)}_{\mathsf{E},v} \\ r^{(i)}_{\mathsf{C},u}, e^{(i)}_{\mathsf{C},u}, r^{(i)}_{\mathsf{C},v}, e^{(i)}_{\mathsf{C},v} \end{array} \;\middle|\; \begin{array}{l} c_{u_0^{(i)}} = a_{\mathsf{C}}\left(a_{\mathsf{E}} r'^{(i)}_{\mathsf{E}} + e'^{(i)}_{\mathsf{E},u}\right) + b_{\mathsf{C}} r^{(i)}_{\mathsf{C},u} + e^{(i)}_{\mathsf{C},u} \\ c_{v_0^{(i)}} = a_{\mathsf{C}}\left(b_{\mathsf{E}} r'^{(i)}_{\mathsf{E}} + e'^{(i)}_{\mathsf{E},v}\right) + b_{\mathsf{C}} r^{(i)}_{\mathsf{C},v} + e^{(i)}_{\mathsf{C},v} \\ \left\|r'^{(i)}_{\mathsf{E}}\right\|_{\infty}, \left\|e'^{(i)}_{\mathsf{E},*}\right\|_{\infty} \le \tau\delta, \quad \left\|e^{(i)}_{\mathsf{C},*}\right\|_{\infty} \le \tau\delta' \end{array}\right] \text{(ZK}_1)$$

$\forall i \in [1, \dots, N]$

$c_{\pi(i)} = \mathsf{Com}(\pi(i))$

$$\xrightarrow{\quad c_{\pi(i)} \quad}$$

$$\alpha \xleftarrow{\$} S$$

$$\xleftarrow{\quad \alpha \quad}$$

$\forall i \in [1, \dots, N]$

$c_{\alpha^{\pi(i)}} = \mathsf{Com}\left(\alpha^{\pi(i)}\right)$

$$\xrightarrow{\quad c_{\alpha^{\pi(i)}} \quad}$$

$$\beta, \gamma \xleftarrow{\$} S$$

$$\xleftarrow{\quad \beta, \gamma \quad}$$

$$\mathsf{ZKPoK}\left[\begin{array}{c} m_i, r_i, e_{\mathsf{C},i}, f_i \\ \widehat{m}_i, \widehat{r}_i, \widehat{e}_{\mathsf{C},i}, \widehat{f}_i \end{array} \;\middle|\; \begin{array}{l} \left(\prod_{i=1}^{N}\left(\beta i + \alpha^i - \gamma\right) = \prod_{i=1}^{N}\left(\beta m_i + \widehat{m}_i - \gamma\right)\right), \\ \bigwedge_{i=1}^{N}\left(\mathsf{Ver}(c_{\pi(i)}; m_i, r_i, e_{\mathsf{C},i}, f_i) = \mathsf{accept}\right), \\ \bigwedge_{i=1}^{N}\left(\mathsf{Ver}(c_{\alpha^{\pi(i)}}; \widehat{m}_i, \widehat{r}_i, \widehat{e}_{\mathsf{C},i}, \widehat{f}_i) = \mathsf{accept}\right) \end{array}\right] \text{(ZK}_2)$$

$$\mathsf{ZKPoK}\left[\begin{array}{c} y \in \left\{\begin{array}{c} \alpha^{\pi(i)} \\ u_0^{(i)} \end{array}\right\}_i \\ r_y \\ e_{\mathsf{C},y} \\ f_y \end{array} \;\middle|\; \begin{array}{l} \sum_{i=1}^{N} \alpha^i u^{(i)} = \sum_{i=1}^{N} m_{\alpha^{\pi(i)}}\left(u'^{(i)} - m_{u_0^{(i)}}\right) \\ \bigwedge_y \left(\mathsf{Ver}(c_y; m_y, r_y, e_{\mathsf{C},y}, f_y) = \mathsf{accept}\right) \end{array}\right] \text{(ZK}_3)$$

$$\mathsf{ZKPoK}\left[\begin{array}{c} y \in \left\{\begin{array}{c} \alpha^{\pi(i)} \\ v_0^{(i)} \end{array}\right\}_{i,j,l} \\ r_y \\ e_{\mathsf{C},y} \\ f_y \end{array} \;\middle|\; \begin{array}{l} \sum_{i=1}^{N} \alpha^i v^{(i)} = \sum_{i=1}^{N} m_{\alpha^{\pi(i)}}\left(v'^{(i)} - m_{v_0^{(i)}}\right) \\ \bigwedge_y \left(\mathsf{Ver}(c_y; m_y, r_y, e_{\mathsf{C},y}, f_y) = \mathsf{accept}\right) \end{array}\right] \text{(ZK}_4)$$

outputs accept if all
ZKPoK are correct

Notice that the prover claims that each $c_{\pi(i)}$ is a commitment to $\pi(i)$ with a fixed permutation π. But until it proves that it has indeed committed to a permutation we will refer to the opening of the commitment $c_{\pi(i)}$ as m_i and for the same reason we will call $\widehat{m}_i$ to the opening of the commitment $c_{\alpha^{\pi(i)}}$.

We can consider the two expressions as polynomials in a variable that we can call Γ evaluated in a specific $\gamma \in R_q$ with coefficients in $\mathbb{Z}_q[x] / \langle x^n + 1 \rangle$. The prover has shown that they are equal when evaluated in this specific γ chosen by the verifier, but we would like them to be equal as polynomials in $R_q[\Gamma]$. The left hand side of the equation has been determined by the choices of the verifier, and in the right hand side, by the binding property of the commitment scheme, we know that $m_i, \widehat{m}_i$ were determined before the choice for γ was made.

We have already checked that subset S satisfies the conditions of the Generalized Schwartz-Zippel lemma (Lemma 1). Then the verifier is convinced that with overwhelming probability the two polynomials defined by (2) are equal in $R_q[\Gamma]$ and have the same roots. These roots may be in different order, defined by a permutation $\tilde{\pi}$. For all $i \in [1, \ldots, N]$ we have:

$$\beta m_i + \widehat{m}_i = \beta \tilde{\pi}(i) + \alpha^{\tilde{\pi}(i)}, \quad \text{then} \quad \beta(m_i - \tilde{\pi}(i)) = \alpha^{\tilde{\pi}(i)} - \widehat{m}_i.$$

The polynomials m_i and $\widehat{m}_i$ were fixed before β was chosen. But the permutation $\tilde{\pi}$ was not predetermined. However looking at one i and fixed m_i and $\widehat{m}_i$ we can consider all possible j and study $\beta(m_i - j) = \alpha^j - \widehat{m}_i$. If $(m_i - j) \neq 0$ then there exists at most one $\beta_j \in S$ that fulfills the equation with this particular j (this was trivial in Bayer and Groth's proof, but in our case is again given by the condition of set S). The probability of choosing β equal to one of these (at most N) β_j is negligible. This implies that for each i there exists a j such that $m_i = j$ and $\widehat{m}_i = \alpha^j$. With this reasoning for each i and the previous equations we finally get that, with overwhelming probability $m_i = \tilde{\pi}(i)$ and $\widehat{m}_i = \alpha^{\tilde{\pi}(i)}$.

This means that $c_{\alpha^{\pi(i)}}$ are indeed commitments to α with exponents from 1 to N permuted in an order that was fixed by $c_{\pi(i)}$ before α was chosen.

Then we again need to prove polynomial relations between committed messages using the Σ-protocols from [7]. We get that the input and output of the mix-node hold the following relation (ZK$_3$ and ZK$_4$ in Protocol 1.1).

$$\sum_{i=1}^{N} \alpha^i u^{(i)} = \sum_{i=1}^{N} m_{\alpha^{\pi(i)}} \left(u'^{(i)} - a_{\mathsf{E}} r'^{(i)}_{\mathsf{E}} - e'^{(i)}_{\mathsf{E},u} \right)$$

We already know that $m_{\alpha^{\pi(i)}} = \alpha^{\pi(i)}$ for a secret π and that the claimed small elements used for the re-encryption are in fact small.

$$\sum_{i=1}^{N} \alpha^i u^{(i)} = \sum_{i=1}^{N} \alpha^{\pi(i)} \left(u'^{(i)} - a_{\mathsf{E}} r'^{(i)}_{\mathsf{E}} - e'^{(i)}_{\mathsf{E},u} \right)$$

Once again we can see them as polynomials in $R_q[A]$ with coefficients in R_q that are equal when evaluated in α.

Both polynomials were determined before α was picked up, so we can apply Lemma 1 and conclude that with overwhelming probability they are equal as polynomials, and so:

$$u'^{(i)} = u^{\pi(i)} + a_{\mathsf{E}} r'^{(i)}_{\mathsf{E}} + e'^{(i)}_{\mathsf{E},u} \qquad\qquad v'^{(i)} = v^{\pi(i)} + b_{\mathsf{E}} r'^{(i)}_{\mathsf{E}} + e'^{(i)}_{\mathsf{E},v}$$

The verifier $\mathcal{V}$ can conclude that the mix-net has behaved properly and the output is a permuted re-encryption of the input. Completeness, zero-knowledge and soundness follow from this reasoning and are discussed in a full version of this paper.

4.3 Security

Finally we propose a security definition and provide a proof of security for our proposed mix-node. Informally, a mix-node should ensure that it is not possible to link an input ciphertext with its corresponding output. However, there might be more than one ciphertext encrypting the same message (this is particularly the case in an election with many voters and only a few voting options), and we have to precisely say that it is not possible to link an input of the mix-node to an output encrypting the same message.

Some security definitions assume that the original messages are independently and uniformly distributed over the message space, but it was pointed out by Wikström in [35] that there might be known correlations between some of the input plaintexts that cannot be ignored.

We base our secure mix-node definition in the one presented by Wikström in [35], but we notice that he assumes that the inputs of the mix-node are correctly computed encryptions of the messages. However the input of each mix-node comes from the (possibly malicious) previous node, and while the proofs of a shuffle ensure that the input is a set of valid encryptions we do not know if the re-encryption parameters have been drawn randomly from the adequate distributions or specifically chosen by the possibly malicious previous nodes. Therefore we present a stronger definition where we even allow an adversary $\mathcal{A}$ to choose the messages and compute something of the form of an encryption, that is, a pair of polynomials in R_q, allowing him to completely determine the input of the mix-node. Even though, he should not be able to identify an input and output index corresponding to the same message with a probability significantly greater than a random guess. Let MixVotes be an algorithm that performs a shuffle and outputs a zero-knowledge proof Σ. Then we can define:

$\mathbf{Exp}_{\mathcal{A}}^{sec}(\kappa)$

- $(pk, sk) \leftarrow \mathsf{Setup}(1^\kappa)$
- $(z^{(1)}, \ldots, z^{(N)}, aux) \xleftarrow{\$} \mathcal{A}(pk)$
- **for** $k \in \{1, \ldots, N\}$
  $(u^{(k)}, v^{(k)}) \xleftarrow{\$} \mathcal{A}(pk, z^{(k)}, aux)$
  end for
- $\pi \xleftarrow{\$} \mathfrak{S}_N$
- $(\{(u'^{(k)}, v'^{(k)})\}_{k=1}^N, \Sigma) \leftarrow \mathsf{MixVotes}(pk, \{(u^{(k)}, v^{(k)})\}_{k=1}^N; \pi)$
- $(i_\mathcal{A}, j_\mathcal{A}) \xleftarrow{\$} \mathcal{A}(\{(u^{(k)}, v^{(k)})\}_{k=1}^N, \{(u'^{(k)}, v'^{(k)})\}_{k=1}^N, \Sigma, aux)$
- **if** $z^{(i_\mathcal{A})} = z^{\pi(j_\mathcal{A})}$ **then** Return 1 **else** Return 0

Now we can formalize our security definition saying that no adversary can have a significant advantage over a random guess.

Definition 2 (Secure Mix-Node). *Let J be a uniform random variable taking values in $[1, \ldots, N]$. We say that a mix-node defined by an algorithm MixVotes is secure if the advantage of any PPT adversary $\mathcal{A}$ over a random guess is negligible in the security parameter. That is, for all c there exists a κ_0 such that if $\kappa \geq \kappa_0$:*

$$Adv_{\mathcal{A}}^{sec}(\kappa) = \left| \Pr\left[z^{(i_A)} = z^{\pi(j_A)} \right] - \Pr\left[z^{(i_A)} = z^{\pi(J)} \right] \right|$$

$$= \left| \Pr\left[Exp_{\mathcal{A}}^{sec}(\kappa) = 1 \right] - \Pr\left[z^{(i_A)} = z^{\pi(J)} \right] \right| < \frac{1}{\kappa^c}$$

We allow the adversary to corrupt all mix-nodes except one, and the non-corrupted one is that considered in the experiment $Exp_{\mathcal{A}}^{sec}$. In order to take into account any possible control of the adversary over those other corrupted nodes and possibly a subset of the voters we even allow him to fully control all the input of the mix-node. Even though, if at least one of the mix-nodes is honest, the link between the ciphertexts at the output and those at the input of the mix-net remains completely hidden.

Observe that this security definition has to be complemented with additional security proofs when this mix-node is used as a building block in a larger scheme. For instance Wikström in [35] shows how a malleable cryptosystem can be used to break anonymity. Therefore additional validity proofs are required to enforce non-malleability, as well as strict decryption policies to prevent any leakage of information during the decryption phase.

Theorem 1. *The proposed mix-node given by our MixVotes algorithm is a secure mix-node according to Definition 2, under the RLWE hardness assumption.*

The proof of Theorem 1 is given in a full version of this paper.

5   Conclusions

We present a shuffle that consists of a permutation and re-encryption of a set of RLWE ciphertexts. The lattice-based encryption scheme used is that proposed by Lyubashevsky *et al.* and we provide a proof of correctness of the shuffle using a lattice-based commitment scheme proposed by Benhamouda *et al.* Furthermore we give a security definition and we prove that our shuffle satisfies it.

As future work it would be worthy to have an implementation with concrete parameters in order to accurately test efficiency in a real setting. We also remark that this shuffle has to be combined with additional security requirements regarding how the input is generated as well as how the output is decrypted, in order to guarantee privacy for the overall scheme that uses this shuffle as a building block, and these requirements will depend on the specific application.

Acknowledgements. We would like to thank Kristian Gjøsteen for his helpful comments that greatly improved the proposal.

This work is partially supported by the European Union PROMETHEUS project (Horizon 2020 Research and Innovation Program, grant 780701) and the Spanish Ministry of Economy and Competitiveness, under Project MTM2016-77213-R.

References

1. Abe, M.: Universally verifiable mix-net with verification work independent of the number of mix-servers. In: Nyberg, K. (ed.) EUROCRYPT 1998. LNCS, vol. 1403, pp. 437–447. Springer, Heidelberg (1998). https://doi.org/10.1007/BFb0054144
2. Abe, M.: Mix-networks on permutation networks. In: Lam, K.-Y., Okamoto, E., Xing, C. (eds.) ASIACRYPT 1999. LNCS, vol. 1716, pp. 258–273. Springer, Heidelberg (1999). https://doi.org/10.1007/978-3-540-48000-6_21
3. Abe, M., Hoshino, F.: Remarks on mix-network based on permutation networks. In: Kim, K. (ed.) PKC 2001. LNCS, vol. 1992, pp. 317–324. Springer, Heidelberg (2001). https://doi.org/10.1007/3-540-44586-2_23
4. Baum, C., Damgård, I., Lyubashevsky, V., Oechsner, S., Peikert, C.: More efficient commitments from structured lattice assumptions. In: Catalano, D., De Prisco, R. (eds.) SCN 2018. LNCS, vol. 11035, pp. 368–385. Springer, Cham (2018). https://doi.org/10.1007/978-3-319-98113-0_20
5. Baum, C., Lyubashevsky, V.: Simple amortized proofs of shortness for linear relations over polynomial rings. Cryptology ePrint Archive, Report 2017/759 (2017). http://eprint.iacr.org/2017/759
6. Bayer, S., Groth, J.: Zero-knowledge argument for polynomial evaluation with application to blacklists. In: Johansson, T., Nguyen, P.Q. (eds.) EUROCRYPT 2013. LNCS, vol. 7881, pp. 646–663. Springer, Heidelberg (2013). https://doi.org/10.1007/978-3-642-38348-9_38
7. Benhamouda, F., Krenn, S., Lyubashevsky, V., Pietrzak, K.: Efficient zero-knowledge proofs for commitments from learning with errors over rings. In: Pernul, G., Ryan, P.Y.A., Weippl, E. (eds.) ESORICS 2015, Part I. LNCS, vol. 9326, pp. 305–325. Springer, Cham (2015). https://doi.org/10.1007/978-3-319-24174-6_16
8. Bünz, B., Bootle, J., Boneh, D., Poelstra, A., Wuille, P., Maxwell, G.: Bulletproofs: short proofs for confidential transactions and more. In: 2018 IEEE Symposium on Security and Privacy, pp. 315–334. IEEE Computer Society Press, San Francisco (2018). https://doi.org/10.1109/SP.2018.00020
9. Chaum, D.L.: Untraceable electronic mail, return addresses, and digital pseudonyms. Commun. ACM **24**(2), 84–90 (1981). https://doi.org/10.1145/358549.358563
10. Chillotti, I., Gama, N., Georgieva, M., Izabachène, M.: A homomorphic LWE based E-voting scheme. In: Takagi, T. (ed.) PQCrypto 2016. LNCS, vol. 9606, pp. 245–265. Springer, Cham (2016). https://doi.org/10.1007/978-3-319-29360-8_16
11. Costa, N., Martínez, R., Morillo, P.: Proof of a shuffle for lattice-based cryptography. In: Lipmaa, H., Mitrokotsa, A., Matulevičius, R. (eds.) NordSec 2017. LNCS, vol. 10674, pp. 280–296. Springer, Cham (2017). https://doi.org/10.1007/978-3-319-70290-2_17
12. Cramer, R., Damgård, I., Xing, C., Yuan, C.: Amortized complexity of zero-knowledge proofs revisited: achieving linear soundness slack. In: Coron, J.-S., Nielsen, J.B. (eds.) EUROCRYPT 2017, Part I. LNCS, vol. 10210, pp. 479–500. Springer, Cham (2017). https://doi.org/10.1007/978-3-319-56620-7_17
13. Damgard, I.: On σ-protocols. Lecture on Cryptologic Protocol Theory. Faculty of Science, University of Aarhus (2010)

14. del Pino, R., Lyubashevsky, V.: Amortization with fewer equations for proving knowledge of small secrets. In: Katz, J., Shacham, H. (eds.) CRYPTO 2017, Part III. LNCS, vol. 10403, pp. 365–394. Springer, Cham (2017). https://doi.org/10.1007/978-3-319-63697-9_13

15. del Pino, R., Lyubashevsky, V., Neven, G., Seiler, G.: Practical quantum-safe voting from lattices. In: Thuraisingham, B.M., Evans, D., Malkin, T., Xu, D. (eds.) ACM CCS 2017, pp. 1565–1581. ACM Press, Dallas (2017). https://doi.org/10.1145/3133956.3134101

16. Furukawa, J.: Efficient and verifiable shuffling and shuffle-decryption. IEICE Trans. **88-A**, 172–188 (2005)

17. Furukawa, J., Sako, K.: An efficient scheme for proving a shuffle. In: Kilian, J. (ed.) CRYPTO 2001. LNCS, vol. 2139, pp. 368–387. Springer, Heidelberg (2001). https://doi.org/10.1007/3-540-44647-8_22

18. Groth, J.: A verifiable secret shuffe of homomorphic encryptions. In: Desmedt, Y.G. (ed.) PKC 2003. LNCS, vol. 2567, pp. 145–160. Springer, Heidelberg (2003). https://doi.org/10.1007/3-540-36288-6_11

19. Groth, J., Ishai, Y.: Sub-linear zero-knowledge argument for correctness of a shuffle. In: Smart, N. (ed.) EUROCRYPT 2008. LNCS, vol. 4965, pp. 379–396. Springer, Heidelberg (2008). https://doi.org/10.1007/978-3-540-78967-3_22

20. Groth, J., Lu, S.: Verifiable shuffle of large size ciphertexts. In: Okamoto, T., Wang, X. (eds.) PKC 2007. LNCS, vol. 4450, pp. 377–392. Springer, Heidelberg (2007). https://doi.org/10.1007/978-3-540-71677-8_25

21. Lyubashevsky, V., Peikert, C., Regev, O.: On ideal lattices and learning with errors over rings. In: Gilbert, H. (ed.) EUROCRYPT 2010. LNCS, vol. 6110, pp. 1–23. Springer, Heidelberg (2010). https://doi.org/10.1007/978-3-642-13190-5_1

22. Markus, J., Ari, J.: Millimix: mixing in small batches. Technical report, Center for Discrete Mathematics, Theoretical Computer Science (1999)

23. Micciancio, D., Regev, O.: Lattice-based cryptography. In: Bernstein, D.J., Buchmann, J., Dahmen, E. (eds.) Post-Quantum Cryptography, pp. 147–191. Springer, Heidelberg (2009). https://doi.org/10.1007/978-3-540-88702-7

24. Neff, C.A.: A verifiable secret shuffle and its application to e-voting. In: Reiter, M.K., Samarati, P. (eds.) ACM CCS 2001, pp. 116–125. ACM Press, Philadelphia (2001). https://doi.org/10.1145/501983.502000

25. Neff, C.A.: Verifiable mixing (shuffling) of ElGamal pairs. VoteHere, Inc. (2003)

26. Peikert, C.: A decade of lattice cryptography. Cryptology ePrint Archive, Report 2015/939 (2015). http://eprint.iacr.org/2015/939

27. Regev, O.: On lattices, learning with errors, random linear codes, and cryptography. In: Gabow, H.N., Fagin, R. (eds.) 37th ACM STOC, pp. 84–93. ACM Press, Baltimore (2005). https://doi.org/10.1145/1060590.1060603

28. Sako, K., Kilian, J.: Receipt-free mix-type voting scheme - a practical solution to the implementation of a voting booth. In: Guillou, L.C., Quisquater, J.-J. (eds.) EUROCRYPT 1995. LNCS, vol. 921, pp. 393–403. Springer, Heidelberg (1995). https://doi.org/10.1007/3-540-49264-X_32

29. Shor, P.W.: Polynomial-time algorithms for prime factorization and discrete logarithms on a quantum computer. SIAM J. Comput. **26**(5), 1484–1509 (1997). https://doi.org/10.1137/S0097539795293172

30. Singh, K., Pandu Rangan, C., Banerjee, A.K.: Lattice based mix network for location privacy in mobile system. Mob. Inf. Syst. **2015**, 1–9 (2015). https://doi.org/10.1155/2015/963628

31. Strand, M.: A verifiable shuffle for the GSW cryptosystem. In: Zohar, A., et al. (eds.) FC 2018. LNCS, vol. 10958, pp. 165–180. Springer, Heidelberg (2019). https://doi.org/10.1007/978-3-662-58820-8_12

32. Terelius, B., Wikström, D.: Proofs of restricted shuffles. In: Bernstein, D.J., Lange, T. (eds.) AFRICACRYPT 2010. LNCS, vol. 6055, pp. 100–113. Springer, Heidelberg (2010). https://doi.org/10.1007/978-3-642-12678-9_7

33. Unruh, D.: Non-interactive zero-knowledge proofs in the quantum random oracle model. In: Oswald, E., Fischlin, M. (eds.) EUROCRYPT 2015, Part II. LNCS, vol. 9057, pp. 755–784. Springer, Heidelberg (2015). https://doi.org/10.1007/978-3-662-46803-6_25

34. Unruh, D.: Post-quantum security of Fiat-Shamir. In: Takagi, T., Peyrin, T. (eds.) ASIACRYPT 2017, Part I. LNCS, vol. 10624, pp. 65–95. Springer, Cham (2017). https://doi.org/10.1007/978-3-319-70694-8_3

35. Wikström, D.: The security of a mix-center based on a semantically secure cryptosystem. In: Menezes, A., Sarkar, P. (eds.) INDOCRYPT 2002. LNCS, vol. 2551, pp. 368–381. Springer, Heidelberg (2002). https://doi.org/10.1007/3-540-36231-2_29

36. Wikström, D.: A commitment-consistent proof of a shuffle. In: Boyd, C., González Nieto, J. (eds.) ACISP 2009. LNCS, vol. 5594, pp. 407–421. Springer, Heidelberg (2009). https://doi.org/10.1007/978-3-642-02620-1_28

Author Index